THE DEMOCRATIC CENTURY

THE JULIAN J. ROTHBAUM DISTINGUISHED LECTURE SERIES

Also by Seymour Martin Lipset

Agrarian Socialism (Berkeley, 1950)

Political Man: The Social Bases of Politics (Garden City, N.Y., 1960; Baltimore, 1981)

The First New Nation: The United States in Historical and Comparative Perspective (New York, 1963; New Brunswick, N.J., 2003)

Revolution and Counterrevolution: Change and Persistence in Social Structures (New York, 1968)

(with Earl Raab) *The Politics of Unreason: Right Wing Extremism in America, 1790–1997* (New York, 1970)

American Exceptionalism: A Double-Edged Sword (New York, 1996)

THE
DEMOCRATIC
CENTURY

SEYMOUR MARTIN LIPSET
and
JASON M. LAKIN

UNIVERSITY OF OKLAHOMA PRESS : NORMAN

To Sydnee and Claudia
From us
Survivors all

Library of Congress Cataloging-in-Publication Date

Lipset, Seymour Martin.
    The democratic century / by Seymour Martin Lipset and Jason M. Lakin.
        p. cm. — (The Julian J. Rothbaum distinguished lecture series; v. 9)
    Includes bibliographical references and index.
    ISBN 0-8061-3618-9 (alk. paper)
    1. Democracy—History—20th century. 2. Democracy—United States—History—20th century. 3. Democracy—Latin America—History—20th century. I. Lakin, Jason M., 1976–.
II. Title. III. Series.

JC421.L57 2004
321.8'09'04—dc22

                                                    2004041231

The Democratic Century is Volume 9 in the Julian J. Rothbaum Distinguished Lecture Series.

The paper in this book meets the guidelines for permanence and durability of the Committee on Production Guidelines for Book Longevity of the Council on Library Resources, Inc.∞

1 2 3 4 5 6 7 8 9 10

CONTENTS

List of Figures and Tables   vii
Foreword, by Carl Albert   ix
Preface   xi
Acknowledgments   xvi
Introduction: Pessoptimism   3

Part I   Democracies: What They Are,
How They (Should) Work

1 Democracy Defined   19
2 Executive Systems   38
3 Parties   50
4 Civil Society   92

Part II   Making Democracy Happen (and Endure)

5 Socioeconomics   139
6 Traditions, Norms, and Expectations   169
7 Culture: Religion and Region   184
8 Reflections on Legitimacy   209
9 Conclusion   227

Part III   Hemispheric Divide:
The United States and Latin America

10 The Argument and Cases   241

11 The Colonial Legacy   281
12 Economics: Underdevelopment and Overregulation   312
13 Institutions   347

Conclusion   408
Notes   417
Index   464

FIGURES AND TABLES

FIGURES

3.1	The Cleavage Divide	72
4.1	Impact of Associations on Mass Opinion Concerning Elite Policy and Information	125
13.1	Comparison of U.S. Urbanization Measures, Late Eighteenth Century to 1920	386

TABLES

I.1	Comparing Waves of Democratization	5
4.1	Correlation Matrix for Interpersonal Trust and Trust-in-Government Variables	110
4.2	Mean Trust in Local Government by Race	114
4.3	Mean Trust in National Government by Race	114
4.4	Regression: Trust Scale, TRSTREG	134
4.5	Regression: Single Question, TRSTLOG	135
5.1	Poor Democracies, 1990 and 2001	147
10.1	Durations of Democratic and Authoritarian Rule in Latin America	279
12.1	GDP per Capita in Latin America and Selected Organization for Economic Cooperation and Development (OECD) Countries, 1999 and 2000	315

12.2   Family Farm Index: North America, Latin America,
        and Selected OECD Countries, 1850–1979   325
12.3   Proportion of Labor Force in Agriculture,
        Latin America and the United States, 1950–2000   326
12.4   Gini Coefficient of Land Distribution by Decade,
        1940–1990   328
12.5   Level of "Capitalism" in Latin America and the
        United States, 1970–1997   337
12.6   Level of "Capitalism" in Some Statist European
        Countries, 1970–1997   340
12.7   Estimated Size of the Working Class in Latin
        America, the United States, and Selected OECD
        Countries, 1920s   342
12.8   Income Inequality, 1990s   343
12.9   Measures of Poverty and Well-Being, Late
        Twentieth Century   345
13.1   Participation in Organizations in Selected Latin
        American Countries, the United States, and
        Sweden, 1995   380
13.2   Urbanization in Latin America and the United
        States, Late Eighteenth Century to 1920   385
13.3   Percent of Total Population in Towns over 20,000
        Persons, 1850–1970   388
C.1   Participation in Organizations, Latin America
        and the United States, 2000   415

FOREWORD

AMONG THE MANY GOOD THINGS that have happened to me in my life, there is none in which I take more pride than the establishment of the Carl Albert Congressional Research and Studies Center at the University of Oklahoma, and none in which I take more satisfaction than the Center's presentation of the Julian J. Rothbaum Distinguished Lecture Series. The series is a perpetually endowed program of the University of Oklahoma, created in honor of Julian J. Rothbaum by his wife, Irene, and son, Joel Jankowsky.

Julian J. Rothbaum, my close friend since our childhood days in southeastern Oklahoma, has long been a leader in Oklahoma

civic affairs. He has served as a Regent of the University of Oklahoma for two terms and as a State Regent for Higher Education.
In 1974 he was awarded the University's highest honor, the Distinguished Service Citation, and in 1986 he was inducted into the
Oklahoma Hall of Fame.

The Rothbaum Lecture Series is devoted to the themes of representative government, democracy and education, and citizen
participation in public affairs, values to which Julian J. Rothbaum
has been committed throughout his life. His life-long dedication
to the University of Oklahoma, the state, and his country is a
tribute to the ideals to which the Rothbaum Lecture Series is
dedicated. The books in the series make an enduring contribution to an understanding of American democracy.

CARL B. ALBERT

Forty-sixth Speaker
of the
United States House of Representatives

PREFACE

THIS BOOK IS BASED ON THREE presentations that Seymour Martin
Lipset gave at the University of Oklahoma in 1996 as part of the
Julian J. Rothbaum Distinguished Lecture Series; additional sections and research have expanded the lectures' initial length by
approximately six times. Professor Lipset's three lectures were
loosely titled "The Conditions for Democracy," "Democracy in
Latin America," and "The Role of George Washington." When I
began work as Marty's research assistant at George Mason University in the fall of 1999, very little had been done to transform
the original lectures into book form except that Bruce Robinson
had rewritten the lecture on Latin America (this redraft, further
reworked, now makes up a little less than a third of part II, on
Latin America).

Every academic year for almost a decade before my work with
Marty began, he hired a recent graduate to work with him on
various projects. Marty preferred to hire recent graduates over
graduate students, because he demanded full-time service and,
as he put it, a jack-of-all-trades. He thought graduate students
should spend their time studying. The assistants who worked with
Marty before me would all agree, I think, that this was a fantastic
opportunity. Each of us got to work closely with one of the most
eminent scholars of the twentieth century—a man of generous
character who, in the twilight of his career, enjoyed passing the

time sharing his enormous storehouse of knowledge with eager audiences and with aspiring political scientists and sociologists. To my knowledge, most of Marty's research assistants spent nine months or so with him and then went on to pursue graduate studies. Many of them (myself excluded, of course) undoubtedly will join the ranks of eminent former students of Marty's, among them James Coleman, Juan Linz, and Larry Diamond.

To avoid imposing my own experience on the memories of others, I asked a few of his former assistants to share their thoughts about working with Marty. Steve Wuhs, who went on to earn his Ph.D. at the University of North Carolina (UNC), Chapel Hill, and take a fellowship at the Center for U.S.-Mexican Studies at the University of California, San Diego, emphasized Marty's "willingness to help his assistants both figure out their goals and then help them achieve them. He understands the importance of getting to a place where people are supportive, and definitely in my case took care to make sure that I could be in a place like that [UNC]." Steve also pointed out that he discovered only when he got to graduate school the "prolific and wide-ranging scholarship [Marty] put out over his many years of research." Given that Marty published over five hundred articles, I suspect that nearly all of us former assistants have run upon one of them on a subject we never knew Marty researched.

Marcella Ridlen Ray, who came to the George Mason University Ph.D. program late in life and whose dissertation, *The Changing and Unchanging Face of U.S. Civil Society*, has recently been published by Transaction Publishers, recalls,

> I met Marty after I came in "from the field," after accumulating thirty years of work and professional experience. I came with decades' worth of observations and experiences of which to make sense, but knew not exactly where to begin. Working within Marty's intellectually rich orbit, as his graduate research assistant, I found the time and opportunity necessary to sort things out intellectually and to frame my questions. Marty pointed me toward relevant authors and literatures I might wish

to explore. One memorable day, just as Marty was heading out of his office, I mentioned a question that was preoccupying me, saying that it seemed to be important. He stopped in midstride, turned to me, and said, "That *is* the question!" This question, of course, was the precursor to my dissertation research.

For Marcella, Marty was an ideal adviser and teacher. "Marty generously made his own lifetime accrual of knowledge available to me. What a rich resource! Fortunately, he was generous with his criticism as well, consistently modeling his own high standards of scholarship. His is a nondirective and supportive style of research supervision that is teaching in the truest sense. It is the finest of gifts and the highest of honors to have been Marty's student."

I had the special privilege—largely a result of fortune—to work with Marty for over two years. When our nine months were up, I had not applied to graduate school and had no definite plans. Marty was happy with the direction the book was taking and did not want to bother with finding a new research assistant he would have to retrain. So he asked me to stay on. He promised me a raise and a chance at coauthorship, and he delivered on both promises.

I write this now because in May of 2001 Marty Lipset suffered a debilitating stroke as a result of an otherwise successful operation on his heart. Unfortunately, although we had made substantial progress before this tragedy occurred, we had not yet finished the manuscript. A difficult decision thus fell to me. Because it was unclear at the time whether Marty would recover to the point that he could resume work, everything was suddenly up in the air. Should I continue working or wait until Marty was better? What would happen to the manuscript if I put it aside now but Marty did not make a full recovery? I knew Marty felt we were close enough that he wanted to see this book published. He felt that in many ways, it was his opportunity to come full circle, to reinject the important work he did in *Agrarian Socialism, Political Man,* and *Union Democracy* into current debates.

Ultimately, Marty would not return to this book, though he has recovered somewhat and is now at home with his wife, Sydnee. I had to pull the manuscript together and do my best to accurately represent what I believe Marty wanted to say. I undoubtedly have failed in many respects. But in others, I believe I have succeeded. (One of the manuscript's anonymous readers referred to part I as "pure Lipset." A higher honor I cannot conceive of.) Fortunately, although Marty has never read the finished product, he reviewed most of the content in draft form before his stroke. I feel confident therefore that, in the broad strokes, I have represented his vision. Marty and I do not agree on everything, and this is in part a result of his having studied the subject for over half a century whereas I have studied it for less than half a decade. But there are also differences of approach and style. Marty is far more of a culturalist than I claim to be, for example. The one section that Marty did not have much of an opportunity to review is the one on institutions in Latin America, and it probably departs more than Marty would have liked from cultural explanations. Nevertheless, I have done my best to subordinate my own vision to that of Marty's, because this is, first and foremost, his book. I will, I hope, have other opportunities to develop my own line of thinking. Unfortunately Marty will not.

I write these words from Santiago de Chile, where I have completed the revisions to the manuscript. They are not easy words to write. Marty was in many ways my intellectual father. Everything I know about political science, I learned from him and through this work. I was not ready for him to leave this project entirely to me. I was still brimming with unanswered questions, pining for our rambling discussions on the car ride from Arlington to Fairfax, looking forward to further revision sessions punctuated by endless lunches, many cooked by or shared with Sydnee (a phenomenal cook and entertainer par excellence), even craving the stories that I had heard so many times—the one about Juan Linz and the buzzard that crashed into their car when they were driving cross-country, or the one about how Marty's father met Stalin when the latter was still just an organizer in Russia, or the one about how James Coleman was so dedicated that even when "the boys" at Harvard broke for poker, he would have his wife continue typing manuscripts upstairs while he played a round.

After Marty's stroke, I felt utterly alone. Marty and I had always worked together, and there had been nobody else. I had lost the person who had guided me intellectually through the morass of academic political science. Yet this book project gave me the opportunity to comply with Marty's wishes, to try to live up to his grand vision, to pull together the myriad pieces of wisdom he had shared with me into a whole. In this way, I hope, not only Marty's work but also his spirit—his intellectual combativeness, his wide-ranging humanistic impulses, and his eclectic interests—may continue to animate new generations of social scientists, not just those of us who have been blessed with the opportunity to work closely with him.

If I have the unfortunate honor of having been the last Boy Scout in this troop, I hope that it has not been in vain. On that note, I'll close with Marty's favorite cheer: "We are the boys of the institute; we are not rough, we are not tough, but boy, are we determined." Onwards and Upwards.

JASON M. LAKIN
Santiago de Chile, 2002

ACKNOWLEDGMENTS

THE PEOPLE WHO MADE THIS book possible are too many to count. Here we wish to acknowledge those who contributed in small ways and large. They have made this book as good as it is; the flaws are ours alone.

Bruce Robinson ably researched, edited, and drafted part of the chapter on Latin America. Jose Loyola Trujillo provided valuable research and insight. Larry Diamond gave us considerable advice and moral support. Cynthia McClintock thoughtfully and thoroughly critiqued our manuscript on behalf of the publisher, a service for which we are extremely grateful. She was joined by an anonymous reader, whose comments were also invaluable. Miguel Centeno and Marc Plattner provided helpful commentary on the Latin America chapter. Karlyn Bowman (American Enterprise Institute) and Marta Lagos (Latinobarómetro) provided polling data and advice. Steven Baker lent his phenomenal copy-editing skills to this enterprise, and it is a far better book for his having held it in his able hands. And we are most indebted to Don Kash, whose gift for gab and easygoing manner make it seem sunny all the time and who made sure this book actually got published the way it was supposed to be.

We wish to thank the following people who have made valuable contributions to this work over the many years of its gestation: Charles Blitzer, Lee Hamilton, the Rothbaums, the late Carl

Albert, Sean "McQuitty" McQuitty for computer support, Jessica Cogen, Torcuato diTella, Gabriel Lenz, Ivan Katchanovski, Denise Hanchulak, Juan Linz, Terry Karl, and Carl Gershman.

The following people provided indispensable moral support in trying times, and without them we would never have finished this book: Sydnee Lipset, Claudia Canepa, Shmuel Eisenstadt, Earl Raab, Karlyn Bowman, Team Lipset, Thelma Marshall, Loren Goldkorn, Kathy Schwartz, Sharon DiMarco, Ayele and Anastazi, and the rest of the staff at Hopkins Bayview Geriatric Center.

Marty also wishes to thank the following people who have had a particular impact on his thinking and career over the years: Robert Lynd, Robert Merton, the late Paul Lazarsfeld, Irving Kristol, and Irving Horowitz. Marty's friend and erstwhile colleague Earl Raab, who has contributed to every work he has written, deserves special acknowledgement here, as does Professor Shmuel Eisenstadt of the Hebrew University in Jerusalem.

Jason would like to thank the following people who, through their insights, conversations, and/or emotional support, helped him to complete this project: Jennifer Dowdell, Justine Kwiatkowski, Justin Stokes, Fabian Victora, Katie Lagoni-Masters, Andrew Selee, Joe Tulchin, Javier Corrales, Michael Coppedge, Tatu Vanhannen, Katie Rusnak, and Jordan, Judah, and Jonah Lakin.

We would both like to thank our parents, Max Lipset and Lena Lippman, and Milton and Susan Lakin, for their enduring support and love and for setting us on our current paths.

Several institutions have provided vital support to this project over the past several years. They include the Earhart Foundation, the Woodrow Wilson International Center for Scholars, the patient staff of the Carl Albert Center and of the University of Oklahoma Press, and the sympathetic staff at the School of Public Policy at George Mason University.

This list is not exhaustive; to anyone we have missed: thank you for making our work a little better.

SEYMOUR MARTIN LIPSET
JASON M. LAKIN
Washington, D.C.

THE DEMOCRATIC CENTURY

INTRODUCTION

Pessoptimism

In the summer of 1997, I was asked by a leading Japanese newspaper what I thought was the most important thing that had happened in the twentieth century. I found this to be an unusually thought-provoking question, since so many things have happened over the last hundred years. . . . Nevertheless, among the great variety of developments that have occurred in the twentieth century, I did not, ultimately, have any difficulty in choosing one as the preeminent development of the period: the rise of democracy.

—Amartya Sen (1998 Nobel Laureate in Economic Sciences), *Journal of Democracy* (July 1999)

IN THE PAST THREE DECADES, democracy has spread throughout the world, faster and more extensively than at any time in human history. According to Freedom House, a democracy think tank that produces annual rankings of civil and political liberties, there are currently 120 democracies in the world, which is equivalent to approximately 63 percent of the world's countries. Nearly 40 percent of the world's population lives in societies that Freedom House deems to be "free"—states where a broad list of political and civil liberties are secure. This is the highest level of experimentation with democracy in world history.[1] North America, Latin America, Europe, and South Asia are dominated by free and partly free societies. Only the Middle East, Africa, and Southeast Asia are still predominantly "unfree."

This latest "wave of democratization," a term popularized by Samuel Huntington, marks the third dramatic shift in the balance of democracies versus nondemocracies in the modern world. In *The Third Wave,* Huntington argues that the first shift stretched from the first quarter of the nineteenth century to the first quarter of the twentieth, during which period the United States and several West European nations became democratic. There was considerable movement toward democracy in Southern and Eastern Europe as well. In the period between World Wars I and II, democratization lost steam, and Southern and Eastern Europe reverted to outright authoritarianism. But Huntington identifies a second wave of democratization in the wake of World War II, stretching into the early 1960s. This time, much of Latin America and Southern Europe and some parts of Asia moved toward democratization, though in many of these states, authoritarian governments returned in the mid- to late 1960s and early 1970s. Finally, in the mid-1970s, beginning with the democratization of Portugal and spreading to Greece and Spain and then on to Latin America, Eastern Europe, and Africa, the globe entered the third and perhaps most dramatic period of democratization.[2] Statistics Huntington provides imply that the third wave is exceptional. From the first to the second wave of democratization, the proportion of the world's states that were democratic rose by about 13 percentage points. From the second to the third wave, the percentage rose by about 20 percentage points *through* 1990. If we extend the analysis to 2000, the increase is certainly even higher—over 35 percentage points (about 60 percent of total states, as compared to 25 percent at the beginning of the third wave). The third wave has been far more extensive than the second. The first wave saw a significant increase, as well; there were basically no democracies at its inception, and the percentage of democratic to total states was about 45 percent at its peak.

TABLE I.1
Comparing Waves of Democratization

Wave	Percentage-point increase in the number of democratic states	Approximate duration (Years)
First	45	100
Second	13	20
Third	35	25

Source: Modified from Samuel Huntington, *The Third Wave: Democratization in the Late Twentieth Century* (Norman: University of Oklahoma Press, 1991), 26

Yet, as Table I.1 demonstrates, the first wave lasted about four times as long as the third wave. In its intensity over a relatively brief period, the third wave has been truly remarkable.[3]

One reason for this intensive change is the confluence of many global political shifts since the 1970s. The explosion of the infectiously radical generation of 1968 in the United States and Europe, the astonishing liberalization of the Catholic Church, the rapid decolonization of Africa and Asia and shattering of the European empires, and then, when radicalism seemed to have dried up in the 1980s, the unimaginable end of the Cold War and the fall of communism—each of these dramas was worldwide in its reach and influence. Each portended a new kind of politics in core and periphery alike, on Main Street and in far-flung places. And they all happened at the rapid-fire pace we are now becoming accustomed to. Over the past three decades, liberalism has, in fits and starts, been on the march.

The shifting dynamics of the Cold War merit special attention. While we believe that democracy's success in a particular country is primarily determined by endogenous factors, the dictates of the Cold War undeniably influenced the relative failure of democracies in between the second and third waves. American realpolitik concerning the balance of power between communism and capitalism led the United States to encourage and support militarized right-wing movements throughout Latin America, and thinly veiled thugs in other regions, rather than risk the assumption of power by potentially radical, left-wing movements. Likewise, the imperial aspirations and security concerns of the Soviet Union suppressed liberal political aspirations throughout Eastern Europe and aided hard-line anti-democratic forces far and wide. Regardless of one's assessment of the moral virtues of either side in the Cold War, it is clear that both sides helped to prevent democratization and democratic stability in countries that figured in their strategic plans. Nevertheless, even before the Cold War ended, the United States began to play a much more activist role in encouraging democracies around the globe, particularly in Latin America. Both the Carter and Reagan administrations began a push to support—through financial, military, and diplomatic means—the spread of democracy. To cite just one example of the kinds of dramatic shifts entailed in these new policies, the United States, which had supported the overthrow of Chilean president Salvador Allende by Augusto Pinochet in 1973, provided financial support to ensure a fair vote on the Pinochet referendum that ended authoritarian rule in Chile in 1988–89.[4] Meanwhile, the Soviets began to take a more hands-off approach in Eastern Europe, allowing and in some cases encouraging hard-line Communist regimes to fail.

By the late 1990s, then, because of worldwide shifts in attitudes and in the balance of power, the world was a far more hospitable place for democracy than it had been only a couple of decades before.

For democratic activists, the turn of the century was an exhilarating time in many respects. Power changed hands peacefully in Chile, where Ricardo Lagos, the first socialist candidate to occupy the presidency since Salvador Allende, won in spite of a strong challenge from the right. A truly historic vote in Mexico

on July 2, 2000, marked the first time—in seven decades of hegemonic rule—that the once dictatorial Institutional Party of the
Revolution (PRI) was turned out of power. A number of African
countries are in the preliminary stages of transition from authoritarian to more liberal regimes. Senegal is a recent success story.
Nigeria's president, Olusegun Obasanjo, appears dedicated to
staying the democratic course; the Human Rights Violations
Investigation Commission, modeled on South Africa's Truth and
Reconciliation Commission, should provide some accountability
to a system that has been rife with abuses of power.[5] Even in
Zimbabwe, where the June 24–25, 2000, parliamentary elections
were marred by state-sponsored violence, the opposition front
seized fifty-seven parliamentary seats, to the ruling Zimbabwe
African National Union–Patriotic Front (ZANU-PF) party's
sixty-two. Prior to these elections, ZANU controlled all but three
parliamentary seats.[6] The February 18, 2000, elections in Iran, in
which nearly two-thirds of the parliamentary seats went to
modernizing reformist elements—and over two-thirds of the
population voted—are cause for enthusiasm, as well.[7] In Peru the
decision by Alberto Fujimori to step down after his election to a
constitutionally murky, third term should be recognized as a triumph for democracy, as should the subsequent free and fair elections that brought Alejandro Toledo to power. In October 2000
Slobodan Milosevic agreed to hand over power, after his electoral
defeat, to Vojislav Kostunica in Serbia, marking a historic political
shift in one of the world's most troubled regions. A few weeks
later, the people of Ivory Coast took to the streets to dispense with
military dictator Robert Guei after he attempted to steal the
October 22, 2000, presidential elections.[8]

Yet, as the winning side at a high school football game often
does when the other team starts cheering, we must shout "Score-
board!" and direct our attention to the many strikes *against* democracy since the 1990s. There was, of course, the military coup in
Pakistan on October 12, 1999. In Venezuela Hugo Chavez has been

consolidating power in a seemingly dangerous manner, empowering the country's military and consorting with such disciples of authoritarianism as Saddam Hussein. A popular military coup in Ecuador suggests, though the government was quickly returned to the civilian vice president, that democracy remains weak there. In Uganda Yoweri Museveni's postponement of democracy has come to look more like cancellation. The assassination of the head of the Congo, Laurent Kabila, who had deferred democracy, and his replacement by his son, Joseph Kabila, portend hints of only mild reform. The 2000 election in Sri Lanka, which has lead to government paralysis on the pressing issue of constitutional reform, suggests that the conflict there is far from resolution. Northern Ireland is still struggling with its peace process. Relatively high voter turnout in Belarus and in Kyrgystan does not make their elections any less rigged nor their dictatorships any less arbitrary and oppressive.[9] Elections were held in Tajikistan and Uzbekistan in 2000 but were subject to fraud, manipulation, and government intervention.[10] Russia's semidemocracy founders, with attacks on the media as common as efforts to deal with the nation's most serious substantive problems. Democracy in Colombia is conducted at gunpoint by a potent mix of official troops, paramilitaries, and the Revolutionary Armed Forces of Colombia (FARC);[11] the U.S.-sponsored Plan Colombia, funded in 2000, is hardly likely to lead to peaceful democratic play any time soon. The Muslim world is decidedly not democratic, and violence has been rife in the Middle East.

It is difficult to generalize about democracy when so many countries have experienced so many, vastly different evolutionary paths. Yet perhaps the best way to gauge the current pulse of global democracy is to return to the imperfect democratic triumphs of 2000. All of these are mitigated by the persistence of anti-democratic forces, rampant corruption, weak parties, and oppositions that are at best tolerated and at worst intimidated. What at first looks exhilarating appears, upon closer inspection, increasingly muddled. Zimbabwe's 2000 election was a step in the right direction, but there is little chance that ruler Robert Mugabe will abstain from further violence, or further damage to his own (now abandoned) policy of racial reconciliation. In Iran president Muhammad Khatami mostly watched quietly while one of the leading reformers of his first administration, Ayatollah Mohajerani, came under increasing fire from religious conservatives. [12] His second cabinet, after a resounding victory in his bid for a second term, is less ostentatiously radical. Reformers may have been elected in Iran, but in a country that is still subject to a clerical veto, voting for reform is hardly the same as reforming. In Nigeria even the most competent ruler faces an uphill battle against rampant corruption that will yield results only slowly and by no means surely. [13] In Peru military unrest increased as Fujimori triangulated between public opinion and various factions of the Peruvian brass over the firing of, and subsequent manhunt for, his top security adviser, Vladimiro Montesinos. [14] Fujimori's resignation on November 20, 2000, marked the start of an at best uncertain future for Peru, with institutional power seriously eroded at the center. In Ivory Coast the brief display of popular power manifested general rejection of authoritarianism, but Laurent Gbagbo, the socialist who seized power in that country, has few democratic bona fides. Serbians rejected their former strongman ruler, but it is not clear what they were trying to *support*. Kostunica cannot still be definitively labeled a democrat. Recent events notwithstanding, victory for democracy is far from assured. Even those triumphs that seem conclusive—such as that of Vicente Fox and the Partido Acción Nacional (PAN) in Mexico—at best spell only the beginning of a long transition that will be rough and nonlinear. After transition euphoria, citizens must buckle down and do the hard work.

What then is the state of democracy today? Perhaps we can borrow from journalist Leon Wieseltier's comment on October 23, 2001, concerning the Kostunica victory in Serbia:

Something smaller than exhilaration is needed, something more stoical, an engaged joylessness, a skepticism about historical action that does not rule it out. The Palestinian writer Emile Habibi nicely described this state of mind as "pessoptimism." Disillusionment, after all, is usually a mark of intelligence. Those are not history's winds at our backs, those are history's fumes.[15]

Wieseltier was urging on the press that was covering the Serbian transition a degree of detachment. Comparisons to Vaclav Havel (former president of the Czech Republic) and the fall of the Iron Curtain—which were frequent—were unwarranted. The new leaders of Serbia, after all, are rabid nationalists with strong dislike of the West. Havel, in contrast, is a liberal democrat, committed not only to freedom from communism for his people but freedom for them through democracy. There are no grounds for thinking that the earth has moved very much with the defeat of Milosevic. Leaders' names may change, but the countries they govern do not become liberal, democratic, or capitalist overnight, even when—as is *not* the case in Serbia—that is the new leaders' expressed desire.

What we can say about democracy currently is precisely this: there have been victories, and no small ones, but the road ahead is long and paved with dangers, and triumph is not assured. Nothing is assured but that we continue to move—sometimes forward, sometimes back—and never stay quite the same. Predictions about the future remain as perilous as ever. We should remember that in 1984 Samuel Huntington predicted that there would be few more transitions to democracy; he was particularly pessimistic about Africa and Eastern Europe.[16] As we now know, the third wave has in fact extended from 1974 to the present, with dictator after dictator falling to the forces of popular self-determination. And indeed, in the late 1980s and early 1990s, liberalization spread from Eastern Europe to several parts of Africa.

Democracy is of course a political concept. And it is with good reason that we have opened this work with a catalog of political events that describe the general state of democracy in the world. But while *democracy* does refer to a political system—strictly speaking, a system for designating leadership—its success or failure depends on much more than simply the acceptance of political rules. A number of economic, social, and institutional factors make it much more or less likely that democracy will survive the many plagues that afflict it. For this reason, a catalog of events can tell us only so much about democracy's prospects. Our "pessoptimism" is rooted in our understanding not only of the political but of the economic and sociological as well.

The argument has even been made that democracy's success in a country can be predicted almost entirely from the country's economic status. According to Adam Przeworski, once a country becomes reasonably affluent, democracy becomes a rational equilibrium in the sense that attempts to overthrow democracy are risky and expensive. At high levels of wealth, the expected utility of the alternatives is lower than democracy for most actors in society. For this reason, democracy always survives in wealthy countries. By this logic, Przeworski argues that constitutions are irrelevant and that elections are much less important than they are often taken to be.[17] While Przeworski uses sophisticated statistics to reiterate a relationship that Lipset identified long ago[18]—that there is a robust positive correlation between level of economic development and democracy—we think Przeworski overstates the case. Democracy also depends on political factors and on that vital but elusive ingredient, "leadership." Nevertheless, the point is well taken: democracy is supported by a variety of nonpolitical factors, including, and preeminent among them, economic well-being.

The study of democratization is, quite simply, an exercise in multivariate thinking, which in social science analysis translates into a study of structural correlates, particularly those related to economic productivity and stratification, as well as cultural variables. Attempts to discriminate among and explicate political regime types dates back to the Greeks. Aristotle differentiated between democracy (popular rule), oligarchy (domination by traditional elites), and tyranny (authoritarianism that is mass based), hypothesizing that the latter two forms are more likely to occur amidst poorer, highly stratified polities, while the first is facilitated by a large middle class. Subsequent political thinkers—Montesquieu, Locke, and Hobbes, followed by the American founders and Karl Marx—owe a debt to Aristotle for the now common discussions of the effects of wealth, class, and income distribution on regime type.[19] Modern research has expanded far beyond economic correlates, but twentieth- and twenty-first-century social scientists, consciously or not, have rooted their research in Aristotle's analysis of class differences.

Lipset has dealt with correlates of democratic governance since his first quantitative work on the subject in the 1950s, which he elaborated over the next four decades.[20] In expanding on his Rothbaum lectures, originally delivered at the University of Oklahoma, we have tried to pull together and reflect on the past forty years of research on democracy. Rather than provide only a survey of what has been learned since *Political Man* was published (1960)—though this book certainly does that—we have tried to focus on the most complex and contentious issues under discussion, particularly questions of culture.[21] At the heart of both the successes and failures of social science in explaining democracy lies the problem of culture. Social science hopes to be able, through the rigors of the scientific method and mathematical modeling, to quantify the seemingly nonquantifiable. The measurement of democracy, a political condition, has become ever more sophisticated since Lipset originally undertook its study in the 1950s. Yet many factors elude easy quantification, and the most potent of these is culture. Time will tell, of course, whether we can successfully dissect cultures into distinct variables—or whether the question becomes obsolete. But for now, the question of how culture—or values, attitudes, traditions, or even institutions (proxies for culture abound)—influences politics remains obscure.

The book is divided into three parts. In the first part, we lay out and defend a definition of democracy. We are principally concerned with explaining what democracy *is*. Theoretical and operational notions of democracy are followed by an in-depth examination of the institutions that actually constitute democracy, primarily legislatures and executives, political parties, and civil society. We examine the institutional underpinnings of democratic praxis and explore how these institutions should function ideally. Here we look at how democracy *works*. Having established what democracies are and what they actually look like institutionally, the book moves in part II to identify the socioeconomic and cultural origins of democracy and democratic stability. We lay the groundwork for a multivariate but primarily endogenous analysis of how democracy *comes to be* and why it *endures*. In short, the book first asks what democracies are, then how they should be organized, and finally what factors help bring them into existence and make them last.

At this point, we should make our own biases explicit here and also clarify the scope of this work. We believe that regime type is primarily the result of endogenous factors. International pressure can play a significant role in democratization, and in recent times, Cold War dynamics were particularly important. However, the scope of this work has been generally limited to internal factors. Where international factors are of paramount importance, we note as much.

We are mindful that critics may argue that we have not adequately accounted for the international impact of the Cold War. While this is certainly a fair criticism, we would point out that international factors—wars, interstate competition, imperialism—have been important in all eras, not simply the most recent. We ignore these factors consistently. Overemphasizing recent international factors would unduly suggest that they have become more important over time. It would also suggest that international factors were more relevant in newly democratizing states than in old democracies, whereas it is far from clear that this is true. Many scholars have argued that the dictates of international wars contributed mightily to the mobilization of citizens that ultimately led to democratization in older states. Theda Skocpol has assessed the impact of interstate competition on evolving nation-states in the nineteenth century:

> Especially as England underwent commercialization and the first national industrialization, competition within the European states system spurred modernizing developments throughout Europe. Recurrent warfare within the system of states prompted European monarchs and statesmen to centralize, regiment, and technologically upgrade armies and fiscal administrations. And, from the French Revolution on, such conflicts caused them to mobilize citizen masses with patriotic appeals. Political developments, in turn, reacted to modify patterns of economic development, first through bureaucratic attempts to guide or administer industrialization from above, and ultimately also through the harnessing of mass involvement by revolutionary regimes, as in Soviet Russia.[22]

From Skocpol's analysis we may deduce three points of relevance to our current discussion. First, international factors interact in complex ways with domestic politics and require detailed analysis. Second, international factors played a significant role in citizen mobilization and almost certainly affected democratization in Europe. Third, even so, it is not possible to conclude that this mobilization tended ultimately toward democratization, as it obviously did not do so in the Soviet Union. A great deal of additional analysis, beyond what will be attempted here, would be necessary to explain the Soviet exception. We have more or less systematically excluded international factors from our analysis not just for theoretical reasons but also because we are aware of our own limitations. International factors do play a role in democratization and in bringing about political outcomes generally; we believe their analysis would best be left to other scholars.

In the third and final part, we attempt to use our analytic structure to explain the variation in democratic success between the United States and Latin America. This analysis is a considerably expanded version of Lipset's second Rothbaum lecture. Our argument is that by referring to social structure, economics, political institutions, and especially the cultural heritage of Latin America, we can explain why Latin American nations have systematically performed poorly on democratic indicators from independence until today. The broad scope of our analysis in part III inevitably gives short shrift to individual cases—an unfortunate but necessary by-product of large-scale comparative analysis. However, we believe that there is much to be gained from this type of project, and we hope that it stimulates discussion and further research.

We have tried throughout this book to raise questions that may help illuminate directions for future research. Even as the problem of democracy is attacked with statistical analyses, we must also deal with it as a theoretical issue, striving to understand, aside from the math, how variables really interact to produce observed political results. Regressions only hint at this. Theoretical formulations—ultimately, one hopes, backed by numbers—help to explain our world. And that is the point of social science inquiry.

There is much research to be done by the next generation of social scientists. We hope that this volume will serve as a guide to the issues that have been resolved, as well as the many that will be in the century ahead. It is not unreasonable, though it is certainly optimistic, to hope that, as the last century was the American Century, culminating with the United States at the apex of global power, so this will be the Democratic Century. Amartya Sen, quoted at the beginning of this introduction, has written that the greatest event of the twentieth century was the acceptance on a global level of the value of democracy.[23] It is our hope that the greatest development of the twenty-first will be the consolidation of democracy in every corner of the globe.

PART I

DEMOCRACIES

What They Are, How They (Should) Work

CHAPTER 1

DEMOCRACY DEFINED

THERE ARE ALMOST AS MANY theoretical definitions of democracy as there are scholars who study democratic politics. Yet there is a basic divide between those who present a maximalist definition and those who prefer a minimalist one. We side with the minimalists, along with such theorists of democracy as Joseph Schumpeter. The difference between a maximalist and a minimalist definition of democracy stems, as do all quibbles over semantics, from the putative purpose of the definition. It is also for this reason that theoretical and operational definitions of democracy may diverge. We agree with Adam Przeworski, however, that the degree to which democracies, minimally defined, translate into guarantees for certain political or civil rights is an empirical question that we should investigate rather than define away.[1]

The minimal definition of democracy we prefer is

> An institutional arrangement in which all adult individuals have the power to vote, through free and fair competitive elections, for their chief executive and national legislature.

Thus democracy is a system of political rights that specifies how leadership should be designated at the highest national level in a polity. This definition is a modified version of Joseph Schumpeter's classic elitist conception of democracy as professed in *Capitalism, Socialism and Democracy*.[2] It has been attacked for not being specific enough about the civil and political liberties

beyond the right to vote that it ignores. For example, this definition makes no mention of freedom of speech or freedom of association. The definition has also been criticized for limiting democracy to the sphere of the political, rather than tackling social or
economic "democracy"—both of which may be understood as
conceptual attempts to equate democracy with equality or other
nonpolitical objectives. Yet we question whether these are really
flaws in the definition.

Considering our definition and what it implies, the meat of
the concept is that everyone is included—"all adult individuals"—and that elections must be contested, "competitive," to be
fair. One may extrapolate many things from this definition, but
none of them is given a priori. That is the beauty of such a definition. For example, how do we know whether an election is
competitive? Presumably, there must be choices, but how many?
It depends. The choices should probably appeal to a broad section of the population, but not necessarily everyone. The election
need not represent the views, for example, of the anti-democratic
citizen who wants the system destroyed. But how do we know
what representing a broad section of the population means?
Nowadays, it could mean the expression of public opinion
through polling. Most will likely agree that it means some level
of free speech and expression but not necessarily on how much.
How do we decide what degree of free speech is necessary for
a democracy? We decide, as we should, by reference to our definition, specifically to its twin principles—inclusiveness and
contestation.

We have presented these principles as our own but must credit
them to Robert Dahl, who formulated a concept of "polyarchy,"
or imperfect democracy, and mapped it on a Cartesian plane,
with inclusion lying along the x-axis and competitiveness along
the y-axis. Democracy is thus the most rightward and highest
point on that grid.[3]

Dahl himself takes a maximalist approach to defining democracy by enumerating various essential rights and liberties associated with it. But we do not see this as a necessary next step. Since it is always a matter for debate whether certain liberties are inherently part of democracy and to what degree they must be protected by democratic institutions, we gain little by including these in our definition.[4] Furthermore, the inclusion of various institutions—political parties, an independent judiciary, or a free press—in a definition of democracy is confounding because many nondemocratic regimes also have these institutions. Yes, political parties are important for democracy, but they are nearly ubiquitous in modern states, regardless of regime type. Some nondemocratic regimes have a relatively free press or even relatively free speech. These institutions may exist, but they will have lifeblood only in a democratic context defined by inclusive, competitive elections.

To exclude freedom of speech as a defining aspect of democracy may seem reactionary, but consider the following (not very) hypothetical situation. To increase public awareness of which policies candidates will support if elected and to inhibit the development of personalistic smear campaigns, the government of country X passes a new law. The law bans private advertising for candidates and guarantees all candidates equal time and money for public advertising. It also creates a public regulatory body to insure that all statements made by candidate advertisements relate to their policy proposals and make no negative references to other candidates, but only to policies they support. Such a law would seriously infringe on freedom of speech. It would prohibit private groups from making statements for or against candidates and likewise prohibit candidates from attacking their opponents on personal grounds.[5]

Would such a law be anti-democratic? If freedom of speech is included in the definition of democracy, most likely so. But if democracy is defined simply in terms of contestation and inclusion at the national level, this law might have two pro-democratic features. First of all, it might increase contestation by forcing candidates to focus on the issues that divide them, thus increasing voter choice. Secondly, by publicly funding candidates, it might allow a wider variety of candidates to participate, increasing both contestation and inclusion. These very issues have to some extent been at stake in the campaign finance reform bills discussed in U.S. policy circles since the mid-1990s. First Amendment defenders line up against "pro-democracy" rebels in a showdown over the meaning and importance of freedom of speech, ignoring the issue of whether the reform affects contestation and inclusion. In debating whether a bill like the one hypothesized above is democratic or not, we should focus on the degree to which it affects contestation and inclusion, not freedom of speech.[6] Freedom of speech is a value in its own right and may be worth protecting at any cost. But that is a debate about freedom of speech, not democracy. The two are not the same and should not be confused.

Ted Gurr's definition of democracy is more expansive than ours, but he too distinguishes between the end of democracy and the means of achieving it. As he puts it, "Other aspects of plural democracy, such as the rule of law, systems of checks and balances, freedom of the press, and so on are means to, or specific manifestations of, these general principles."[7] We think this an important distinction, because the achievement of particular ends can almost always be accomplished with various means. To evaluate the relative merits of the various means, we must know what the ends are. In this case, the ends should be clearly laid out in our definition of democracy, as they are.

Thus we believe that a minimal definition of democracy allows us to hone in on what matters about democracy—potentially universal participation and choice among candidates—and to avoid getting bogged down in debates about other values that may be important but are subject to disagreement on the basis of distinct values and opinions. Also consistent with this perspective is our rejection of the equivalence between democracy and economic equality that some leftist ideologists propose. *Democracy and equality are not the same.* Nor is democracy a system designed for the purpose of imposing on a society an ideological vision of (limited) economic stratification. If the voters choose redistribution, so be it. If they vote against redistribution, that does not make the system any less a political democracy. The whole point of democracy is to leave outcomes—particularly those related to vital issues like redistribution—to the electoral process, thus rendering them uncertain.[8] Any system that predetermines these outcomes is not democratic. This vision of democracy militates against any presumptions about redistribution, supporting neither redistribution nor the status quo. It simply endorses a vote to decide whether to redistribute.

It may be said that democracy per se is therefore worthless, since it does not inherently eliminate oppression through, for example, reducing income inequality or poverty. But this view is naive. It ignores the whole course of human history, which has been a perennially bloody battle for power in which, for the most part, the powerful have imposed their rules, regulations, and economic priorities on everyone else. Against this backdrop the evolution and acceptance of a system that reshuffles the deck so that the powerful are not guaranteed victory, so that they win only sometimes and must be constantly vigilant to insure such victories, and so that the less powerful receive an unparalleled degree of voice in public policy is nothing less than extraordinary.

It must be recognized that this is not an endorsement of the status quo. But it is a moderate position, lying between two recognizable poles. At one extreme, which may be termed "reactionary," lie the older oligarchic systems, wherein power is allied to wealth and that power and wealth are guaranteed by political systems that allow no dissent. The powerful cannot guarantee the subservience of the less powerful, but as Karl Marx and

Antonio Gramsci emphasized, the basic opinion- and value-forming institutions foster that subservience. At the other extreme, which may be called "radical," lie the prospects for revolutionary dissent, which urge that the powerful be stripped of their power by the underprivileged and that wealth be ultimately redistributed by the fists of the masses. In our view, regimes animated by such prospects led to the worst disasters of the twentieth century—Stalin's Russia, Pol Pot's Cambodia, and so forth. Democracy, of course, lies between these poles. It is a system that by definition guarantees no redistribution of wealth, but it does separate wealth and power, by giving votes (political power) to those who do not have wealth, as Tocqueville emphasized.[9] Primarily, it is different from either extreme case in its lack of predictability and in its flexibility.[10] It is not a panacea. But as we close the chapter on the ravaged century, we believe that this is precisely one of democracy's virtues.

THE MORAL VALUE OF DEMOCRACY AND VALUE-FREE SOCIAL SCIENCE

The preceding treatment of democracy invokes both normative and positive aspects of democratic systems. Yet as social scientists study the nature and origins of democracy and democratic stability, they must be careful not to confuse moral considerations with scientific inquiry. The moral value of democracy is an issue altogether different from the study of its existence. Social scientists may, and probably should, be motivated by moral concerns, but their task is not to moralize but to identify and analyze. Once the data have been compiled and the facts made available, people may begin to use that information to moral ends. For data to be useful, however, their compilers must first present them clearly and concisely and avoid confounding moral with positive concepts.

In particular, we believe that democracy is often confused with "the good society." Most social scientists believe that democracy is a good thing. They study democracy because they believe that the world would be a better place and that individual welfare would improve if everyone lived under some form of democracy. But while democracy itself may constitute some part of what it means to live in a good society, it is unwise for scientists to ascribe any moral value to democracy that enlarges the concept beyond its meaning as a political system. We are dealing with democracy, not freedom nor equality, not social policy nor free markets. That democracy is related to (e.g., correlated with) these other concepts is beyond question, but it is hardly the same as these concepts.

Moves toward democracy need not be equated, as they commonly are, with moves toward a better society. On Dahl's graph a move toward higher contestation and higher inclusion represents democratization. Suppose that a polity moves toward the use of frequent referenda to settle complex social problems. This widens the sphere of inclusion by allowing more individuals to exercise their vote on a broad range of issues. Yet is this necessarily "good" in the moral sense? Many have argued that the spate of state propositions in the United States is not a good thing; the more famous propositions have been reactionary—for example, denying rights and benefits to immigrants.[11] Likewise in Switzerland, cantonal voting in 2000 on the naturalization of immigrants has limited citizenship.[12] Referenda may be democratic, in Dahl's terms, but they are quite possibly regrettable.

Another example of ways in which democratization may be viewed negatively relates to the debate over parliamentary versus presidential systems. Gurr's operational democracy variable (DEMOC) allocates a higher democracy score to nations that have presidential systems, because these have weaker executives than parliamentary regimes and therefore both encourage contestation (between executive and legislature) and enhance inclusion (stronger legislature, which puts more power in the hands of particularist representatives).[13] Yet there are good reasons to question, as Juan Linz does, the preference for presidential over parliamentary systems. In fact, Przeworski has shown in his analysis of regime life expectancy that parliamentary systems are more than three times as likely to survive as democracies than presidential ones. If stability and longevity are good, then more "democratic," presidential systems are worse than less "democratic," parliamentary ones.[14] This suggests that democratization cannot always be evaluated in terms of a "better" or more "moral" society. Some, but not all, of these problems are eliminated by using a minimal definition of the term.

Finally, it is now commonplace to hear about the "democratization" of different aspects of society—the economy or the university, for example. Although this phraseology does touch upon important changes in society that may increase contestation or inclusion in other spheres of life, it has a tendency to vulgarize the term *democracy*, unless it refers specifically to institutionalized contestation. It is true that democracy grants the demos a greater degree of input into political outcomes than do other regime types. But the manner in which this input is given is circumscribed by institutional rules. Inclusion and contestation apply specifically to the political system that designates leadership; not every system that allows for popular input is necessarily a democracy. A democracy grants citizens access, in the form of a vote, to the state or organization for the sole purpose of filling leadership positions through open and contested elections.

Returning to the referendum, according to our definition, referenda may not technically be "democratic." While reserving judgment on whether referenda are beneficial to society, we maintain that they are ambiguously democratic, because, rather than designating the leadership of polities, they may subvert the power of democratic institutions.[15] If democratic institutions are those that force elected, contending interests to confront one another and produce compromise solutions, referenda tend to avoid bargaining and compromise in favor of unilateral positions. A yes or no vote on a complex issue potentially undermines the basis for negotiated settlement, in which a yes on one issue is often tied to a no on another issue. This is not to say that referenda are by definition undemocratic: they do often widen participation on issues that would otherwise be decided by a small group of elites. Nevertheless, referenda subvert the logic of democratic legislatures by selectively removing issues from the normal give-and-take of parliamentary debate and policy making. In so doing, they pit a version of direct popular rule against representative democracy. But representative democracy is what we mean by institutionalized democracy: the electorate must have choices regarding its representatives to elected bodies, not directly regarding every issue that arises in a polity.

The broader point we want to make is that increasing citizen input and improving democratic institutions are not always synonymous or complementary processes. Another example of this distinction is the balance between the state and civil society. A vigorous civil society in which many interests are represented is in general a bulwark to democracy, but not if it undermines support for political parties or other vital political institutions. We mean not to imply that citizen input and democratic institutions are opposed to one another but rather to point out that the two concepts are distinct and that our focus is on the latter.

THE OPERATIONAL DEFINITION

Defining democracy in theoretical terms helps us to measure it empirically, but the task is still awesome. As with most concepts, operationalizing democracy is not easy. It is simple enough to determine whether a country or trade union holds elections. The real trouble is determining whether they are competitive. Generally, there must be a realistic chance that the party in power will lose, that at least two different candidates or parties have a chance of winning. Even this rule of thumb presents us with ambiguous cases—such as Japan before 1993 or Botswana up to now—in which, in spite of seeming competition, a dominant party always wins.[16] Is the chance of loss "realistic" in such cases? The best we can do is guess whether a dominant party that lost an election would freely give up power. We are liable to err in assessing dominant-party regimes no matter which way we guess. One could argue that multiparty systems are inherently more competitive than dominant party systems because dominant parties tend to control more political resources than their smaller counterparts, but such comparison takes us into murky waters. After all, incumbents, whether from dominant parties or not, always have political resource advantages, such as greater media coverage and international visibility. Operationally, the level of competitiveness is still best measured in terms of the likelihood of alternation in power.

Yet this conception of competitiveness seems somewhat shallow. If two parties that are virtually identical ideologically, alternate in power, as in Ireland, is the political arena really competitive? There is no easy answer to this question, but it returns us to a prior question: why measure competitiveness at all?

Our preference for democracy, though only imperfectly realized, is that competition yields some degree of candidate responsiveness to the electorate. In contrast to some other scholars, we have not made responsiveness a definitional characteristic of democracy.[17] We assume rather that the competitive elections feature of our definition means that democratic polities are likely to be more responsive to their electorates than nondemocratic ones. In principle, candidates who must compete for votes will be more responsive to the electorate than those who are assured of election. Competition is presumed to yield a degree of differentiation among candidates, thereby creating a degree of choice for the electorate. These assumptions, we believe, are not heroic; we do not assume high levels of responsiveness, only relatively greater responsiveness than under dictatorship.[18]

To return, then, to our central question, How do we measure competitiveness and the likelihood of alternation in power? Adam Przeworski and his colleagues have argued that competitive systems must have more than one political party. There are no modern thriving democracies that do not have multiple political parties.[19] The existence of more than one party does not in itself imply that more than one party has a realistic chance of gaining office. Thus Przeworski adds another condition: elections must be predicated on the real possibility of incumbent loss. In order to estimate this possibility, he investigates a polity's history to see if incumbents have lost power in the past or if they have been able to hold on to power for more than two terms. This rule is intended to eliminate those polities from being considered democracies whose leaders hold elections only because there is no realistic chance of their losing.[20]

Przeworski's operationalization is useful, but the question still remains as to whether a polity like Japan before 1993 should be considered a democracy. Clearly, a definite answer is not possible. But other measures of competitiveness could serve as useful guides. For example, one could look at survey data to determine voters' awareness of other parties and their positions and the degree to which voters' choice of party at the polls reflect their preferences on different issues. That is, elections' competitiveness could be measured according to how clear and distinct the options are to voters. This standard for competitiveness is admittedly rougher, more continuous, and subject to more problems of comparability than Przeworski's simpler metric. However, we believe that there are good reasons to distinguish between countries like Japan and Botswana and that a more subtle grading can be achieved by combining Przeworski's operationalization, taken as a lower bound, with a more rigorous measurement of competitiveness based on public opinion data and field research.

Another case that blurs boundaries is Colombia. In the 1980s and 1990s, competition returned to the political arena in Colombia after many years of consociational/coalition government. Colombia has more than one party, but before 1980 these parties formed a cartel that excluded the political left. In those years, Colombia was not a democracy, because there was no real party competition for the executive. Since 1980 these parties have begun to compete, but systematic violence has reduced the sphere of competition by eliminating the left. Does Colombia meet our definition of democracy? Although this is a difficult case, we do not believe it does. Neither the lack of choice nor the prevalence of violence alone is enough to throw Colombia into the nondemocratic category. A system with free and competitive elections that has high levels of random criminal violence is not undemocratic, it is just unsafe. Rather, we label Colombia nondemocratic because the violence is directed specifically and systematically at eliminating competition and choice in the electoral system. If parties competing for power were to systematically use violence to defeat one another, we would consider the polity nondemocratic because choice was constrained and elections were not truly competitive or free and fair. The violence in Colombia is being prosecuted not by the competing parties but by praetorian militias. Yet in a democracy, the state must have enough coercive power over its territory to permit competitive elections without the specter of constant violence. Whether the state or a particular party actually utilizes violence is irrelevant: if it cannot prevent the violence, the result is the same. Colombia is not a democracy because the state cannot guarantee the conditions necessary for competitive and free elections to occur.

The minimalist nature of our and others' operational definitions of democracy has become the norm across the field. As Michael Coppedge and Wolfgang Reinicke write of their own measurements, "because polyarchy is concerned with imperfect approximations rather than ideals, the standard for most democratic regimes is rather low, . . . limited to the most basic institutional requirements for democracy, specifically those that had been met in most Western European countries by the end of the First World War . . . polyarchy does not take into account varying degrees of democracy at different levels of the polity: it is concerned with national regime only."[21] While democracy is often thought of in loftier terms, social science research is primarily concerned with the lower limits of democracy.

DO DEFINITIONS MATTER?

Clearly there is considerable debate over both theoretical and operational definitions of democracy. Although there is convergence toward minimalist definitions, these vary considerably in how they measure democraticness. Given the controversy over definition in the political science literature, one might expect conceptual variations to yield distinct and inconsistent results in research. Yet this is not in fact the case.

Surprising as it may be, there is a consistently high correlation between different measurements of democracy. Przeworski found that the Coppedge-Reinicke, Bollen, Gurr, and Gastil scales all predicted his own democracy classifications over 85 percent of the time—91 percent when Bollen was excluded.[22] In an independent assessment, Gurr found that among eight different measurements of democracy, the lowest correlation coefficient between any one measurement and another was 0.72. Amongst the most widely used indicators that he considered (Gurr, Bollen, and Gastil), the lowest correlation was 0.87.[23]

For all of the methodological fury, then, most measurements of democracy appear to be nearly parallel tests. This suggests that many facets or indicators of democracy reinforce one another. It may also reflect similar biases among researchers. Whatever the cause, any of the major democracy indices we select is bound to give us fairly similar results. This does not rule out the possibility of particular studies producing results biased by their choice of democracy index—particularly in the cases of borderline regimes.[24] It does mean, however, that methodological critiques based on the assumption that different definitions yield different results—that one is more correct than others—exaggerate the problem.

We can thus answer the question, reservedly. Do operational definitions of democracy matter? A bit, but apparently not that much.

DEFENDING DEMOCRACY

It remains to be seen whether there is anything to recommend democracy, minimally defined. That is, if democracy does not a priori involve a basket of political and civil liberties—if we strip it of all the things associated with it—is there anything particularly important that inheres in the minimal social science definition? Once we have thus emasculated the term, should we care if a country is democratic or not?

We should.

Robert Dahl, who includes a variety of liberties in his definition of polyarchy, gives pride of place among justifications for democracy to these very same liberties. While we do not define democracy as including these freedoms, it is nevertheless clear that a society that functions on the basis of contested elections will be more likely to sustain such liberties. There is an extremely high correlation between civil and political liberties,[25] and it is generally true that polyarchies have many of these liberties.

But even if this were not the case, institutionalized conflict has its own rewards. A contested system, as Dahl points out, brings a wider range of interests and people into the polity. It affects the structure and style of leadership and gives people more control over their own lives.[26] This does not necessarily translate into better policies, but nothing we have said about democracy implies that it is inherently better from a policy perspective. Yet the moral case can be made, and has been countless times, that, whatever mistakes people may commit in pursuit of their own interests, some degree of self-determination is more likely to result in policies that benefit a large proportion of the population than is dictation by self-interested autocrats or organized minorities.

This argument has been elaborated by some institutional economists and political scientists in recent years, among them Mancur Olson and Bruce Bueno de Mesquita. These scholars argue that democracy does mean better policy in the limited sense that the institutional incentives provided by democratic regimes promote the provision of more and better public goods. According to Olson, majority governments will tend to have lower levels of rent-seeking taxation than those sought by autocrats. Since majorities themselves play a greater role in producing national income than autocrats, they lose much more, and more quickly, from high taxation than autocrats, whose sole source of income is taxation. Since lower taxes generally lead to higher productive investment, it follows that democracies will tend to have higher levels of economic growth.[27]

In a related argument, Bueno de Mesquita and his colleagues James D. Morrow, Randolph Siverson, and Alastair Smith have noted that conditions associated with democracy promote the provision of public goods in place of private ones. Why? Democracies are systems in which there are large selectorates and winning coalitions. A selectorate is the portion of the society that chooses leaders and from which leaders may come; in a system with universal suffrage, the selectorate is potentially everyone of voting age. A winning coalition comprises the voters, groups, and supporters upon whom a government depends. In a democracy this is again a very large group of people, generally equivalent in number to the voting support of the second-place candidate plus one. Bueno de Mesquita et al. cite the case of the 1992 U.S. election in which George Bush lost with 38 percent of the vote. Ignoring the role of the electoral college, Clinton's winning coalition would have had to be 38 percent of the votes plus one, the number needed to elect him. Since democracies depend on large selectorates and large winning coalitions, it is inefficient for leaders to provide private goods to all of their supporters in exchange for their votes.[28] Leaders are more apt to dole out public goods, which benefit citizens outside their winning coalition but are relatively easy to provide. Only in systems with small winning coalitions will leaders be able, through corruption and nepotism, to provide selective benefits to their supporters that are substantial enough to keep them from defecting. Thus Bueno de Mesquita and colleagues' argument follows Olson's in that both assume that the wider the support needed to maintain power in a polity, the more public minded the regime's policies will be.[29]

Finally, Dahl and R. J. Rummel point out that democracies tend to be less violent, both internally and against other democracies.[30] If lack of violence is not the first thing that comes to mind when one thinks of the merits of democracy, a quick survey of the mind-boggling number and size of state-supported massacres of citizens in Communist China and Russia should remind us that domestic peace is not to be sneezed at. What explains democracies' lower levels of violence?

Przeworski makes a strong case for the minimalist definition of democracy based on the lower levels of domestic violence that accompany democratic systems. He argues that the mechanism of voting serves as a public proxy for violence. By allowing both winners and losers in political scraps to see the limits of their support in the distribution of votes, both are pressed to accept the results of nonviolent elections, and losers are discouraged from engaging in rebellion against winners. Elections document the lack of unanimity in society. The most popular parties or leaders rarely garner more than about 65 percent of the vote, meaning that at least one in three people rejects their leadership. Most victors receive much less support. Awareness of substantial opposition should lead to a certain degree of restraint—not simply in policy or in rhetoric but also in the use of coercion and violence—since everyone can see from the way citizens vote that coercion would lead to costly violence. Exercising control through force is costly. As Przeworski puts it, "Dictatorships do not generate this information; they need secret police to find out."[31]

Lipset has observed that opposition and government in new systems tend to accept and institutionalize democracy when both realize that they cannot eliminate the other without destroying the fabric of society or of their organizations.[32] The elimination of strong political opponents—even of weak ones—exacts a heavy cost in terms of domestic security, infrastructure, and conditions for economic growth. Even self-interested rent seekers find they can more profitably pursue their own interests in a growing economy than in a destroyed one.

Democracy promotes the institutionalization of nonviolent forms of social conflict and the substitution of nonviolent for violent struggle. While its inception may be the result of rational choice rather than any deep moral commitment, the institutionalization of nonviolent conflict through repeated practice eventually cultivates abiding moral support. Likewise, out-groups that have to fight for entrance into the political game often develop democratic ideologies that suit their purposes, but upon seizing power, they find that the democratic ideal has rooted itself in society, that many adherents genuinely believe in it. Thus what began as instrumental support becomes culturally entrenched.[33]

In sum, even a minimalist definition of democracy has much to recommend it. We can now turn to the more complicated task of determining how democracies actually function and then how to achieve and sustain them.

THE CORRELATES OF DEMOCRACY

The political arrangements that constitute democracy emerge from and must be bolstered by economic, cultural, and institutional factors that cannot be created overnight. But they can emerge

over time. Indeed, our pessoptimism may be best thought of as
pessimism about the short run combined with optimism about
the long-run conditions of democracy. We now address correlates of democracy. It is important to keep in mind that correlates
are not iron-clad causal mechanisms—they represent, at best,
probabilistic statements about what is likely. Democracy is more
likely to persist in wealthy countries; this does not mean that it
cannot survive in poorer countries, as the cases of contemporary
India, Costa Rica, and Botswana demonstrate. When all of the correlates of democracy are considered in tandem, a potent mix is
obtained. A country that lacks most of these factors is unlikely to
sustain democracy, while one that possesses them all is very likely
to do so. Most countries fall in between. Therefore, what they lack
in one area—for example, wealth—they may compensate for in
another—say, a vigorous, socially egalitarian civil society (e.g., the
early United States) or multiple, cross-cutting cleavages (e.g.,
India). It is therefore both unwise and improper to label democracy "unlikely" simply because a country lacks some particular
elements. Underlying democracy, as with all social phenomena, is
a multivariate causal pattern. We must attempt to look at the independent effects of the various subphenomena that constitute the
phenomenon of democracy. There is no magic bullet for democracy, only complex, layered patterns of interrelated factors, to
which we turn in the next several chapters.

Having answered the question, What is a democracy? we now
turn to the actual organization of democracies. The question that
animates chapters 2 through 4 is How do democracies work?
Democracies, understood as regimes centered on national elections, consist of various institutions that organize political competition—legislatures, executives, political parties, bureaucracies,
civil society, and so on. As paper definitions move off the page
and into real societies, multiple questions arise about how concepts, such as national representative bodies, should be realized.
This section of the book explores institutional variations in

democracies and what differences they make. In part II of the book, we turn to economic and cultural factors underlying democratization and democratic stability. We ask, What factors cause democratization and what makes democracies last? Part III, Hemispheric Divide, is an extended case study examining the United States and Latin America in comparative perspective, asking why democracy has been so much more successful in the United States than in a large sample of Latin American nations. This part of the book returns to some ideas developed earlier by Lipset concerning values and elites in Latin America and develops them into a much broader and deeper analysis of the history of democracy. It also serves as a compliment to *Continental Divide*, Lipset's book comparing Canada and the United States.

CHAPTER 2

EXECUTIVE SYSTEMS

DEMOCRATIC SYSTEMS ARE NOT JUST hodgepodge affairs, a residual category of states where people generally get along and there are occasional elections for national offices. Democracies are built, constructed out of institutions that, with luck, have been carefully designed but that more often are the result of happenstance or political negotiation. It follows not only that all institutions are not created equal but that as a burgeoning literature on "varieties of capitalism" argues, not all *combinations* of institutions are created equal.[1] As we will argue below, any particular electoral system may be a reasonable one in and of itself. Combine that electoral system with a particular executive-legislative system, however, and it may or may not perform as well as others.

In the remainder of part I, we focus on the institutions at the heart of any democracy, the actual bricks and mortar of democratic states. The purpose of chapters 2 to 4 is to analyze the concrete ways in which democracies function in order to understand better how the institutions that constitute democracy interact to produce outcomes. We suggest that institutions—like economics and culture, which we discuss later—matter, though they explain only part of the variance.

Recent discussions about the role of institutions have exaggerated their importance for democracy. What matters more than institutions per se are the ways that *formal* institutions interact with *informal* structures to produce democratic outcomes. The late Daniel J. Elazar, who dedicated many years to the study of federalism, distinguished between "federal processes," the informal ways in which federalism works, and "federal structures," the formal institutions of federalism. Federalist structures, in and of themselves, he argued, may have little effect—as has been the case in much of Latin America—whereas federalist processes are vital. These processes include partnership, cooperation, negotiation, openness.[2] Obviously, these processes are very similar to those associated with democracy and democratic culture. Elazar believed not that institutions were irrelevant but rather that they demand, for effective functioning, a culture of give-and-take, which can be encouraged by institutional arrangements but not entirely created by them.

Even if it is assumed that all institutional arrangements are embedded in social and economic contexts that may help or hinder them, attributing causal consequences to any single institution—a presidential system, for example—is a dangerous exercise. After all, institutions interact not just with their socioeconomic contexts but also with the other institutional systems that define a particular regime. In this regard, a presidential regime combined with a particular electoral system—say, plurality single-member districts—may have very different results than one combined with proportional representation (PR). And institutions that go by the same name may be highly divergent in practice. Compare, for example, the president of the United States with that of Mexico or Argentina. The U.S. president is a constitutionally weak executive (relative to the country's internal balance of power, not in the domain of foreign affairs). He proposes but Congress disposes. Much of the job consists of campaigning to pressure Congress into approving his proposals. Presidencies throughout Latin America, in contrast, are generally much stronger; their parliaments or congresses have been much weaker than the U.S. legislature. To lump all presidential executive systems under one heading can be seriously misleading.

It seems foolish, therefore, to enumerate the most useful, pro-democratic institutions, since so much depends upon the *mix*. Often, only some institutions can be modified. We might say that a particular executive system is "better" than another, but this would only be true given a particular electoral system or range of conditions that might not hold. Thus giving advice about institutions is perilous as, often, only some institutions can be modified. Dominant parties may undermine democracy but are likely to resist changes to the electoral system that promote competition. Deep affective ties for the presidential office may prevent the transformation from a presidential to a parliamentary regime. Some reforms are easier to make than others. If a parliamentary system suffers from excessive party fragmentation, changes in the electoral law are likely to be easier (and more efficacious) than switching to a presidential system. If a presidential system suffers from undue concentration of power in the executive, perhaps the power of the legislature should be increased, rather than shifting to a parliamentary system. Clearly, analyses must be done on a case-by-case basis.

In this spirit, a number of different institutions, and their importance for democracy, will be briefly discussed in this and the next two chapters. Identifying the functional significance of particular tried-and-true institutions is important to replicating at least those functions, if not the institutions themselves. Below, we discuss executive systems, political parties, and civil society. Many other sets of institutions are important to democracy— such as the judiciary, federalism, consociationalism, electoral systems—but we deal here only with what we deem to be the most ubiquitous and important institutional structures.

Executive systems define the relationship between the executive office and the legislature in democracies. The executive system not only determines the balance of power between the head of state and the legislature but also affects the attitudes, experiences, and personal histories of the leaders of these branches of government and how these leaders interact. A prime minister, for example, tends to rise up through her party in the parliament, while a president may not even be involved in national politics prior to his presidential term. The relationship between a prime minister and her fellow parliamentarians can thus vary greatly from that between a president and the legislature.

Debates about executive systems normally center on the relative merits of parliamentarism versus presidentialism. Juan Linz has consistently advocated parliamentary systems, arguing that they are more flexible than presidential systems and more likely to lead to positive-sum outcomes. Arend Lijphart has also advocated parliamentary systems because, he claims, they are less majoritarian (and thus more consensual) than presidential systems. He argues that parliamentarism is better suited to divided societies, particularly those in which the basic cleavages are along ethnolinguistic or religious lines.[3] Recently Adam Przeworski has produced empirical work that ostensibly demonstrates that parliamentary regimes outlive presidential regimes. According to his analysis, the average life expectancy of parliamentary systems is more than three times that of presidential regimes.[4]

Although the weight of the political science profession falls on the side of parliamentary regimes, several criticisms can be leveled against the conclusions reached by pro-parliamentarism scholars. Linz has argued that presidentialism suffers from, among others, two irreconcilable flaws: it is winner-take-all, and it leads to gridlock.[5] It is winner-take-all in the sense that there is only one president and the loser of the presidential election plays no role in government after the election. It encourages gridlock—an impasse in legislative enactment—because when the president is from a different party than the legislature, the two branches will presumably disagree frequently, and it will be difficult to enact legislation.

But these claims are incompatible. If presidentialism is viewed as winner-take-all in the sense that the winner of the presidential contest wins everything, then how can this system also lead to gridlock? It is only because the presidency is a weaker office than that of the prime minister that gridlock can ensue under presidentialism. Gridlock is in fact a sign that a system is not winner-take-all, that the opposition can play an important role in the legislative branch.[6] This is not to say, of course, that gridlock is to be admired. Whether presidentialism leads to a winner-take-all situation or to gridlock within a system depends on the balance of power between the executive and the legislature. In the United States, gridlock is much more likely because the president is weak in relation to the legislature. In Latin America, the reverse has been true because presidents have often resorted to decree powers that allow them to circumvent the legislature.

The version of presidentialism that is most likely to foster democratic outcomes is one in which the president is relatively weak (as in the U.S. case) and has few if any decree powers, which can produce authoritarian outcomes. In advocating this version of presidentialism, we are also choosing between the faults that Linz has identified, avoiding the problems of winner-take-all elections while accepting those stemming from gridlock. But one may ask an empirical question: to what extent does gridlock occur under presidential regimes? Gridlock should occur, of course, only when a president of one party faces a legislature dominated by another party or when her own party has a plurality but not a majority.

Surprisingly, empirical evidence suggests that gridlock is not so big a problem as critics of presidentialism claim. Few presidencies are as weak vis-à-vis their congresses as that of the United States.[7] One case of a relatively weak non-U.S. presidency, at least until Hugo Chavez, has been Venezuela. Though Michael Coppedge argues that gridlock has occurred under the Venezuelan system, he provides sparse evidence. The yearly average number of legislative enactments passed by unified governments versus divided governments from 1959 to 1982 came to 27.3 versus 23.9.[8] Though this difference is in the direction one would expect, the lower number for divided government does not really constitute deadlock. Using sophisticated regression analysis, David Mayhew's study of the United States also concludes that the effect of divided government on quantity of major legislation is slim to none. Many of the major pieces of legislation that passed under divided rule in the post–World War II era were enacted by veto-proof majorities. There are a number of possible reasons for this, including the relatively constant need for new legislation and the spur to legislate caused by the need to campaign in frequent elections. Under divided rule, opposition leaders may be more likely to seek legislative accords, knowing they can take credit for bills passed. Because a majority legislative leader under an executive of his own party has to defer to the president and cannot claim as much credit for the passage of legislation on his watch, he is likely to be less pliant. Furthermore, the specter of public opinion induces both parties to reach accord on legislation that is particularly popular, regardless of whether the government is unified or divided.[9] Whatever the precise reasons, the notion that divided presidential government produces deadlock has little empirical support. Meanwhile, divided parliaments without effective majorities, such as those in Israel and Italy in the 1990s, have produced serious deadlocks.

If presidentialism does not lead to substantial gridlock, why does it appear to be so much less successful in Przeworski's analysis? Although Przeworski's regression analysis controls for a wide range of factors, it does not control for two omitted variables—presidential power or the electoral system—both of which could skew the results. It should be noted that any comparison of parliamentary with presidential regimes tends to pit Latin America against Europe, because Europe is entirely parliamentary while the vast majority of presidential regimes are in Latin America. Nearly all of the presidential systems in Latin America have two characteristics in common: they have strong presidencies and weak congresses, and they employ PR electoral systems. Why does this matter?

With strong presidencies the winner-take-all problem can become a serious issue. Gridlock is not a major concern, but overuse of decree powers is. As Latin American presidents have often abused their decree powers, presidentialism appears to be a winner-take-all system. Crises such as those in Chile under Salvador Allende were precipitated by the use of decree powers to impose a program supported by a slim plurality (minority) of Chileans. (At the same time, it is worth remembering that Westminster-style plurality parliamentary systems are also winner-take-all and they can be more majoritarian than presidential regimes.[10] Although overly strong presidents are a problem, we should be cautious in preferring any type of parliamentary system.)

How does proportional representation affect presidentialism? PR systems are more likely than plurality systems to sustain greater party fragmentation, thus hindering the formation of legislative majorities. A president is thus likely to find it more difficult to get legislation passed. Agreements are harder to reach in a fissiparous congress, and there are fewer incentives to maintain coalitions under presidentialism. Faced with these obstacles, a president is more likely to use decree powers to circumvent the legislature. Plurality systems are less susceptible to these outcomes. Although plurality systems for electing legislatures "manufacture" majorities, they also tend to force parties into larger, more aggregative blocs than are found under PR.[11] Thus, as in the United States, both major parties are usually centrist coalitions. A manufactured majority is not necessarily a problem if parties are forced to be moderate in order to maintain that majority. Furthermore, as Fred Riggs has argued, plurality constituency elections lead to weak party discipline, which is a boon to presidential democracy because it allows for legislative flexibility and eschews gridlock. Strong party discipline, encouraged by PR, would be much more likely to lead to legislative impasse if there were no majority.[12]

The important point here is that the apparently more impressive performance of parliamentary regimes depends on a number of unwarranted assumptions about presidential systems. There is some reason to think that presidentialism works best when it is modeled on the U.S. system—weak presidency, plurality congressional electoral system—and that Latin American efforts to imitate the United States have not worked in part because of PR.[13] Neither logic nor the empirical evidence sustains the conclusion that parliamentary systems in and of themselves outperform presidential regimes.

Another important objection to presidentialism is the fixed terms of legislatures and presidents—two or four years, for example. In parliamentary systems new elections may be called whenever a cabinet chooses or when it loses its majority in the legislature. As Juan Linz notes, fixed terms mean that every governmental crisis—a loss of public support because something goes wrong—threatens to precipitate a regime crisis as well, because there is no legitimate way to get rid of a president who becomes unpopular or is viewed as incompetent. Parliamentarism, in contrast, has an institutional mechanism—the vote of no confidence—that allows for governmental change without a regime crisis. New democratic systems, which tend to be inherently unstable and low in legitimacy, may particularly benefit from such flexibility.

In enduring regimes, however, fixed terms have advantages. They can encourage a president to implement policy that may be desirable but that will be unpopular in the short term, since they give the executive time to recoup her popularity before the next election. Conversely, the ability to call frequent elections in parliamentary systems may encourage an unstable government to use demagogic appeals to enact temporarily popular policies. The case of the rise to power of the Nazis suggests that frequent elections—four between 1930 and 1933—can work to the advantage of anti-system parties by reducing the time for sober reflection from election to election. In Germany frequent elections were called as a result of the absence of stable majorities. In these elections the anti-system parties—Nazis and Communists—gained progressively more votes until they swamped the democratic parties. France during the same years also had a parliamentary system but with fixed terms. Although support for anti-system parties grew in the early 1930s in France as well, there were no elections, and ministers were simply shuffled around. In this case, fixed terms provided a bulwark against anti-system parties. Although the French system was a rare case of fixed terms under parliamentarism, almost all systems with fixed terms are presidential. On this evidence, presidentialism has an advantage rather than a disadvantage. Flexible terms under parliamentarism may lead to a snowballing effect—less likely with fixed terms—for ill-conceived policies with a high anti-democratic potential.

Finally, Linz notes that parliamentary systems lead to more experienced cabinet ministers because members of Parliament (MPs) have to work their way up through the party hierarchy to the top positions. As Alfred Stepan and Cindy Skach have shown empirically,[14] this greater experience of cabinet ministers is due in large part to the coincidence of strong party systems with parliamentary systems. Under proportional representation, as in most parliamentary systems, parties control who is at the top of their lists, and members of parliament generally owe their position to the party. Hence, MPs tow the party line.

But this behavior is not entirely a result of parliamentarism per se. The degree to which parliamentarism encourages strongly disciplined parties depends not only on the government's need to prevent a vote of no confidence but also on the electoral system. The party has somewhat more control with closed-list voting than with constituency voting, open-list, or single transferable vote (STV) systems, in all of which the parliamentary party may be somewhat weaker and more dependent on its members.[15]

Clearly, governments have much more power in strong party systems than in systems with weak parties, which are more common with constituency elections. As some critics of PR list systems have argued, voters in such systems opt for parties, which in turn form the government. The separation between voters and the government under PR systems is less evident where voters directly elect their representatives, as under a plurality district system,[16] which allows the electorate a slightly greater say in what their government looks like. But since PR systems tend to encourage an increased number of parties, they enhance choice and representativeness.

In sum, parliamentarism has both advantages and disadvantages when compared to presidentialism, but these are limited, relative, and generally exaggerated in the literature. Given the role of institutions such as elections and parties operating within parliamentary or presidential systems and of the relative strength of the executive and legislative branches, the parliamentary advantage is probably smaller than most political scientists believe.

It may ultimately be more useful to conceptualize regimes less in terms of executive-legislative systems and to begin using alternative constructs from game theory such as the concept of "veto players." George Tsebelis, a purveyor of this approach, defines a veto player as any "individual or collective actor whose agreement . . . is required for a change of the status quo."[17] Tsebelis argues that, from a policy perspective at least, the number and type of veto players is much more determinative of governmental outcomes than the alternative categories of presidential and parliamentary. "In particular," he points out, "presidential systems (with multiple institutional veto players) present characteristics of policy-making stability similar to coalition governments in parliamentary systems (with multiple partisan veto players). These common characteristics of presidential and multiparty parliamentary systems contrast with two-party systems, dominant parties and minority governments in parliamentary democracies (which have single veto players)."[18]

Tsebelis argues that the contending factions within a parliamentary multiparty coalition may be just as likely to inhibit the passage of legislation as is division between an executive and legislature. Whether parliamentary deadlock occurs depends on, among other things, the configuration of parties in the legislature, but the same could be said for the presidential versus parliamentary models—the comparison rests on assumptions about the party and electoral systems. Tsebelis attempts to partially account for these additional variables by reference to interparty "congruence" and intraparty "coherence," the ideological distance between the players, and the ideological space within the party itself. Congruence makes policy compromise more likely: obviously, the closer the parties are to one another ideologically, the more likely they are to find common ground. Coherence, Tsebelis argues, has the opposite effect: the less coherent a party is, the more likely some of the party members will be willing to compromise. The more coherent the party is, the more likely it is to stand its ground as a unified force.

Sarah Binder has provided some empirical evidence from research on the United States that supports Tsebelis's model.

In Binder's analysis, policy distance between parties (congruence) and number of ideologically centrist legislators (lack of coherence) have a greater effect on policy change than unified versus divided government, though the latter also had a statistically significant impact.[19] A study of the Italian legislative process also supports Tsebelis's theory of veto players. Amie Kreppel finds a negative relationship between the number of veto players in a government coalition and the number of policies approved by the parliament.[20] She argues, however, that coherence in the Italian system may have a positive effect on policy output. The members of the government are systematically more moderate than their parties since they are generally elected by some majoritarian principle. Hence, a coherent party in the legislature is likely to accept compromises agreed to by the party in government.[21]

This last argument suggests that the impact of coherence may vary with institutional type. While coherence may have a beneficial impact under multiparty coalition government, it may be dysfunctional under two-party presidential government (e.g., the United States'), as Binder's evidence suggests. Coherence may not be particularly important at all in a two-party parliamentary regime, such as the United Kingdom's. Therefore, while Tsebelis's model deepens our understanding of the workings of political regimes, it does not entirely supplant the important distinctions that a presidential-parliamentary conceptual framework draws attention to.

CHAPTER 3

PARTIES

TO SHOW THAT EXECUTIVE SYSTEMS determine the interactions between head of state and legislature and that electoral systems determine balances of power between different parties is to describe wars without interests. We have up to now surveyed the artillery and the battlefield but not met the opposing forces or learned what goals animate their struggle. It remains to be seen who populates these political institutions and how these people are recruited. The crux of any system of government, not only democracy, is the process by which social interests are converted into legislation or, at the least, legislative activity. Even in dictatorships, there is a process by which certain social interests, usually those in whose name the dictator rules, make their legislative preferences known. In democracies, the representation of social interests, and the filling of executives and legislatures, is accomplished by the joint work of political parties and civil society. In this and the following chapter, we explore the crucial roles these institutions play in democracies and how they interact with each other. We have studied how government power is organized. Now we look at how a vast panorama of interests in the wider society are compressed into the much smaller institutions of democratic governance we have been discussing.

In his early work Lipset examined the social conditions that correlated with democracy in a variety of arenas, including nation-states (*Political Man*), organizations (*Union Democracy*), and the local and regional level of polities (*Agrarian Socialism*). Certain common denominators emerged from this work about the underlying conditions that facilitated democracy in all settings. In particular, all of Lipset's early work was permeated by a Tocquevillian emphasis on mediating/voluntary associations. In this chapter we revisit this work as an introduction to the importance of mediating institutions in democracy, situating our discussion of political parties and civil society within the context of both economic and cultural variables.

Agrarian Socialism was a study of democracy in Saskatchewan, Canada, focusing on the socialist Cooperative Commonwealth Federation (CCF) party. In explaining the extraordinarily high level of political participation in Saskatchewan, Lipset assessed the expansive civil society with which it was entangled. He found that, due to the extreme weather and highly unpredictable market conditions, farmers in Saskatchewan relied heavily on cooperative organizations. For a population of 125,000 farmers, there were between forty thousand and sixty thousand elective posts. Although this did not translate into one in every three farmers holding a post (many farmers occupied more than one), it did translate into a very high level of civil activity among the general population.[1] This in turn led to higher levels of political knowledge and acumen, which in turn led to more political activism. Other "natural" environmental factors—such as the egalitarian distribution of wealth within the farmer population—also contributed to democratic activism. Lipset summarized his findings:

> Widespread community participation and political interest have developed in Saskatchewan in response to the environmental and economic problems involved in creating a stable community. No one factor—the small units of government, the vulnerable one-crop economy, the "one-class" society, the sparse settlement of the area, the continual economic and climatic hazards—developed

because of an interest in maintaining an active grass-roots democracy. The combination of all of these factors, however, has made for a healthy and active democracy. Unplanned structural conditions have facilitated rapid popular response to economic and social challenges and the acceptance of new methods and ideas.[2]

Lipset found that, at least for regional democracy, conditions that facilitated an egalitarian distribution of wealth, small variations in status, and high levels of civil society activism were positively associated with democracy. These themes and others would be expanded upon in Lipset's later work, particularly *Union Democracy*.

In 1956 Lipset, Martin Trow, and James Coleman conducted a study of democracy inside the union of American printers, the International Typographical Union (ITU).[3] At the time, the ITU was unique among labor unions in the degree and longevity of its democracy. Although democracy within organizations is distinct from that within polities, there are nevertheless many analogues between the two.[4] In fact, *Union Democracy* generated many important hypotheses—most of which have stood the test of time—about the nature of democracy in macropolities. In particular, Lipset, Trow, and Coleman posited a structural similarity between political parties, civil society, and federalism that may be referred to as the "Tocquevillian triad" and that we believe to be a formulation as useful when applied to national polities as when applied to the ITU. In the next section, we cull some of these hypotheses from *Union Democracy* and reflect on their potential for assessing democracy in polities.[5]

One of *Union Democracy*'s most important lessons was that the formation of successful political parties is rooted in structural cleavages that predate the organization of those parties.[6] The political system of the ITU, defined by institutionalized competition between two intraunion parties, was grounded in cleavages based outside the union that in turn created an ideological split.

"It is this underlying ideological difference between the liberal and conservative printers," the authors wrote, "which ultimately provides the foundation for a *continuing* opposition."[7] Underlying social factors such as religion, education, age, and immigration status, existing more or less independently of the subsequent politics of the ITU, contributed to the evolution of these ideological distinctions.

Although these cleavages evolved independently of the union polity, within the ITU, they formed the basis of two political parties. Lipset, Trow, and Coleman argued that understanding how cleavages are transformed into parties required studying the historical record. In doing so, they found that union parties had been born of fundamental ideological differences concerning the union's role. In one particularly salient split, radicals and conservatives were divided over the issue of industrialism versus mutual assistance. Radicals believed the union's primary purpose was to extract better working conditions from employers, by strike when necessary; conservatives believed the union should constitute a benevolent society that helped its own members and dealt only infrequently with management.

Lipset, Trow, and Coleman argued that it was issues like this one that made the democratic system possible, because they reflected splits over *ideology* or values rather than *self-interest*.

> As a general proposition, it may be asserted that one of the necessary conditions for a sustained democratic political system in an occupational group is that it be so homogeneous that only ideology and not the more potent spur of self-interest divides its members. It is an important property of the ITU's political system that in those "foreign policy" areas where the most important questions are raised, the self-interest of the members is rarely involved, and relatively altruistic ideological commitments dominate political conflict.[8]

That such a situation existed among printers was a reflection of the homogeneity of income and status within the occupation as a whole and of the generally high level of both that these workers enjoyed in comparison to other manual laborers.[9]

This homogeneity has its parallel at the national polity level in the existence of a strong middle class and a relatively well-to-do lower class whose political outlook has been moderated by its wealth and that is not driven by an urgent need for immediate redistribution of wealth. Rather, these social strata follow a gradualist approach and are more inclined to centrism than radicalism. The relative wealth of the society reduces heterogeneity (inequality) of status and lifestyle, homogenizing consumption patterns and reducing the strength of interest cleavages (though by no means eliminating them). Of course, at the polity level, self-interested class-based cleavages have proven to be quite compatible with democracy, as long as the cleavages have been moderate. Extreme cleavages on this dimension, like those in many parts of Latin America, have racked democratic systems with perpetual instability.

Lipset, Trow, and Coleman emphasized that the homogeneity of status and the ideological, as opposed to interest-based, splits among printers contributed to the long-enduring two party system, the well-established *legitimacy* that printers accorded their political system, and particularly, the rights of institutionalized political opposition within that system. Furthermore, the authors argued, "the evidence from the ITU and other trade unions suggests that *an internal opposition gains legitimacy only when it rests on independent and enduring bases of support and power which cannot be destroyed or repressed without seriously weakening the union itself.*"[10]

It is legitimacy that allows political parties in a democracy—whether a private organization or a polity—to form an enduring organized opposition. But organized political parties, by their behavior and success, also help to maintain that democracy's legitimacy and effectiveness. Legitimacy is a two-way street for the opposition in a democracy. How does legitimacy help the opposition in a democracy to survive? According to Lipset, Trow, and Coleman, "legitimacy greatly eases the problem of survival in a number of ways: first, and foremost, by sharply limiting the kinds of weapons that can be directed against it; second, by providing it with additional channels of access to the membership; and third, by making it easier for an opposition to recruit members and active partisans."[11]

Legitimacy permitted an organized opposition in the ITU to promote its position vocally at union meetings, through circulars and bulletins, and in political campaigns—even though this threatened the power of incumbents.[12] And what made these lines of communication possible, effective, and permanent was the organization of the opposition into a party. An organized opposition can scuttle the hegemonic grip of the central authority; a disorganized opposition is unlikely to be so successful. Organization is therefore critical to democracy.

But this raises an important question: what made the organization of political parties possible? Lipset, Trow, and Coleman made the neo-Tocquevillian argument in the mid-1950s that the organization of political parties in the ITU was facilitated by the existence of independent, voluntary organizations within the union, combined with a strong "federalist" system. The absence of such "secondary organizations, or a mass society," the authors argued,

> helps maintain a conservative oligarchy, such as is found in South American dictatorships, in Europe before the nineteenth century, or the average stable American trade union. . . . Existence of secondary organizations controlled by the government helps maintain revolutionary totalitarianism, intent on making changes within the society which it governs, as in Nazi Germany or Soviet Russia. . . . [Existence of secondary organizations] independent of the government helps maintain democracy, such as is found within the ITU or in the United States or most European democracies."[13]

Following Tocqueville, the authors saw that the independent bases of power in the ITU—from recreational club memberships (voluntary associations) to large, independent shop chairmen ("federalism")—helped to create a potential network of support for those opposed to the activities of the central administration at any given time. Independent sources of power and prestige in the union translated into independent sources of information. As Lipset, Trow, and Coleman demonstrated, when people (members) have access only to information supplied by incumbents, they tend to support incumbents. The conclusion is obvious: without alternative sources of information, a one-party system becomes much more likely.[14]

Lipset, Trow, and Coleman's analysis brought together several important concepts that have since been viewed as more distinct: civil society, political parties, and federalism. Though each is worthy of its own treatment, the critical Tocquevillian link among them should not be ignored. All three are significant in part because *they create a network of suballiances that are independent of the central, national state or of the administration of private organizations.* They promote the interests and perceptions of groups within society other than the ones in power, and they often compete with the state for attention, funding, and employees.

In the ITU, three important institutions represented independent bases of power and encouraged the party system. First, there were a multitude of apolitical, recreational groups. Though explicitly nonpartisan, these groups nevertheless served as independent bases of support, arenas of politicization, and avenues to recognition and eventual political power for many.[15] They were secondary civil society associations in the Tocquevillian sense, in which members learned the habits of associating and human and social capital were generated.[16]

Within the printing industry itself, the institution of the chapel (shop) chairmen was consequential. These were elected leaders of each shop who not only had real power in their dealings with management but also were important within the union. "In contrast to the [union] steward in large-scale industry," the authors found, "the chapel chairman deals with the employer and with his direct representative in the shop, rather than with a supervisor who is so low in a long management structure that he has no effective power or authority."[17] Since these leaders had effective power, printers usually went to them rather than higher-ups in the union leadership structure. This served to ratify and enlarge their power, giving them independent authority within the union, in a version of union "federalism."

Along the same federalist lines, the independent status of large locals—such as the Big Six in New York, which Lipset and his collaborators studied in detail—contributed heavily to the continuing bases of opposition within the international (United States and Canada) union. Since local leaders were elected and operated relatively free of international officialdom, they had every incentive to break with the international incumbents if their membership did not agree with international policy. This autonomy was moderated somewhat because locals depended in part on the international—particularly in strike situations— yet because the international leadership needed the votes of the large locals, the latter had room to maneuver vis-à-vis the administration.[18] In this way, large locals, like states in federal polities, both supported and manipulated the central governing structure.

These organizational conditions helped maintain the union's then unique two-party system and supported the tenacity and continuity of opposition. But that system also interacted with those conditions to perpetuate them. As Lipset, Trow, and Coleman noted, "If the chapel chairmen [shop stewards] in the ITU are not as vulnerable to such controls from above, it is not simply because the printing industry is relatively decentralized and unconcentrated, but is at least as much a consequence of the operation of the union's two-party system . . . the political independence of the chapel, which could only exist in a democratic union, contributes to the maintenance of democracy in the union. And the value system which defines administrative control of the chapel as illegitimate is a product of the union's intense internal political life."[19]

In other words, the political system and the social organization of the union reinforced one another, as well as the legitimacy of two-party democracy. It remains difficult to disentangle cause and effect, but without doubt, all of these systems supported one another in the union, as comparable institutions do in larger democratic polities.[20]

The triad of federalism, civil society, and party systems is remarkable not only because these institutions compete with and weaken the power of the central state, or of the summits of private organizations, but also because they simultaneously contribute to the legitimacy and effectiveness of the same. Lower-order governments, voluntary associations, and political parties all act as training grounds, supplying political and organizational skills to a cadre of individuals. They can be critical sources of backing for potential leaders of the central state or organization. Because they send their leaders on to serve in the state or administration and because they may support the opposition, they serve to legitimize the political system. They help the populace or membership distinguish between the polity and the parties. They defend the state or administration and hope to control it, even as they attack the incumbents.[21]

The existence of a subset of independent institutions also contributes to democracy by providing an outlet for status desires. Where the status that accompanies leadership of the state is much greater than can be achieved in the private sector or in other areas of leadership, individuals who gain power are inclined to keep it even at the cost of undermining the democratic system. "The insecurity of leadership status endemic in democracy, the pressure on leaders to retain their achieved high status, and the fact that by their control over the organizational structure and the use of their special skills they can often maintain their office, all help in the creation of dictatorial oligarchies," the authors wrote.[22]

Democracy is more successful where status and income differentials between leaders and led are slight, because leaders do not have as much incentive to hold on to power. A dense web of private sector leadership positions and opportunities that provide status, prestige, and high income allows central-state leaders to leave their jobs without a significant loss of prestige. As noted earlier, the myriad private sector opportunities for former civil officials in the United States suggests that, for many, income, if not status per se, increases considerably upon leaving state office. An interesting historical footnote highlights this point. In the early days of the American republic, few officials wanted to stay on in Washington, which was a small, dirty, and uninteresting town. Hence, many did not run for reelection. The average term of service for House members was three years, or a term and a half. The lure of holding power was real, but the benefits were not sufficient to keep representatives coming back for more year after year.

Union Democracy has been criticized recently in an evaluation of the political organization of the United Automobile Workers (UAW) union.[23] Judith Stepan-Norris finds that, although the occupational community (offering opportunities for association) within the union was not independent of the union and although status differentials were high (though income differentials were not) between unit leaders and workers, union democracy prevailed in the UAW Local 600 from the 1950s to the 1980s. She claims that the reason for this effect was the organizing energies of outside groups such as the Communists and the Association of Catholic Trade Unionists (ACTU), as well as the importance of ideological factionalism in dividing the population and inspiring continued dedication to politics.

Stepan-Norris credits the Communists with playing the greatest role in preserving democracy in the union and argues that this role stemmed from the Communists' ideological appeal to workers, as well as their theoretical support for democracy. There is no question that the Communists have contributed to democracy within some unions. But they did so not because they were pro-democratic but because the party's drive for power and its effective use of the "organizational weapon" helped sustain prolonged struggles between strong local Communist blocs and an international union leadership that was strongly anti-Communist or simply sought to retain office.[24] Further, powerful Communist factions or officeholders have often motivated strong anti-Communist opposition groups. In UAW Local 600 the opposing forces of the Progressive Caucus and Right Wing Caucus were irreconcilable, and prolonged competitive politics led to the creation of democratic norms, much as in the ITU.[25] What supported democracy was not so much the intrinsic character of the Communists as the insoluble conflict between Communists and "conservatives." We put more emphasis than Stepan-Norris does on the first part of her own observation that *"in the context of an anti-Communist international union*, units with left-wing leaders, including those influenced by the Communist Party, provided support for union democracy."[26]

Apropos of the Tocquevillian triad, the implications of Stepan-Norris's study are that, where an independent occupational community (analogous to a civil society) is *lacking*, "foreign" or external pressures may create a sphere of independent political contestation, independent information channels, and additional spaces for organization and leadership; in other words, it is possible that external pressure substitutes for an independent civil society by stimulating competitive politics.[27] This process is bolstered by organizational "federalism," which was present in both the ITU and the UAW. In a polity, external pressure may take the form of support for one or more domestic factions, international public opinion, loan conditionality, globalized media sources, or in nations that possess weak domestic civil societies (such as Bangladesh), the presence of international nongovernmental organizations. Indeed, the quote by Amartya Sen that opens this book

intimates that the global climate of opinion affects local information and contestation. Of course, external pressure operates only
where it feeds into local factionalism; it cannot create a viable
opposition, but it can help sustain one, as outside donors did for
Solidarity in Poland.

The more general point is that forces that increase factionalism
weaken the potential for hegemonic centralized control of organizations or polities. Whether faction-inducing forces are democratic or authoritarian is irrelevant to their role in the overall
polity or organization. What matters is that they bolster distinct
centers of power that contribute to democracy in the larger organization or polity.

Stepan-Norris's criticism points to the fact that no general
approach to democracy is inviolable. While the UAW sustained
local democracy with only two of the three elements of the triad
firmly in place—parties and federalism—external pressure
enhanced that democracy even without a fully independent
"civil society." Nor can federalism be considered a structure
essential to democracy, since democracy exists in unitary as well
as federal states. However, while federalism per se is nonessen-
tial, decentralization may be very important. Tocqueville himself
was skeptical of federalism but laudatory of decentralization. He
believed that whereas federalism promoted disintegrative tensions within states, decentralization promoted unity of purpose
while still encouraging the development of human capital and
independent bases of power at the local level: "If the municipal
bodies were made powerful and independent, it is feared that
they would become too strong and expose the state to anarchy.
Yet without power and independence a town may contain good
subjects, but it can have no active citizens."[28]

Tocqueville also believed that decentralization would—like
federalism, political parties, and a strong civil society—create an
outlet for status desires and help contain those ambitious persons
who would otherwise be tempted to engage in all-or-nothing

struggles for control of central authority. "The Federal government confers power and honor on the men who conduct it," he argued,

> but these individuals can never be very numerous. The high station of the Presidency can only be reached at an advanced period of life; and the other Federal functionaries of a high class are generally men who have been favored by good luck or have been distinguished in some other career. Such cannot be the permanent aim of the ambitious. But the township, at the center of the ordinary relations of life, serves as a field for the desire of public esteem, the want of exciting interest, and the taste for authority and popularity.[29]

The Tocquevillian triad implies that democracy requires a broad array of faction-inducing mediating institutions that are independent of the central state. Many institutions can play a mediating role in a polity, so it cannot be assumed that all states must have the same mix of strong parties, civil society, and federalism to sustain democracy. The empirical evidence suggests, however, that political parties are necessary, that some degree of civil society is important, and that federalism can be a strong supporting institution but is not critical.

If the UAW is a good example of how the ends of the Tocquevillian triad may be accomplished without slavish adherence to any standard formula at the organization level, then Spain is a good parallel case at the polity level. Spain's political history since the 1970s seems to demonstrate that a weak civil society is not necessarily an unresolvable problem for a democracy, particularly where already many forces—ethnic regionalism (encouraged by European Union incentives), pseudofederalism, and sharp ideological cleavages—are conspiring to weaken the central state and promote distinct centers of power.[30] Protracted struggle between central state and regions over the nature of decentralization helped not only to consolidate central authority in Spain but also to limit it and strengthen subnational bargaining power.[31] Given the sharp cleavages in Spain, there was greater reason to fear state disintegration than an overwhelming central state. Thus tendencies that strengthened central authority—such as corporatism, statewide founding elections and political parties, and a generally weak civil society—were balanced by the potentially explosive regional, ideological, and religious divisions in Spanish society and by the decentralization process.[32] This balance has proved amenable to democratization.

Another institutional arrangement can be viewed through the lens of the Tocquevillian triad—consociationalism. Arend Lijphart has elaborated on consociational arrangements at great length, so we will not do so here. Consociational arrangements guarantee to vulnerable minorities both representation in national bodies and vetoes over certain types of legislation.[33] Suffice it to say that consociationalism is a device for empowering factions that might, in the absence of institutional supports, be too weak to form a counterweight to other, large or well-organized factions. In particular, the purpose of the minority veto is to empower a faction in a polity that would otherwise be overwhelmed by a majority, thus creating conditions for more balanced factional struggle. Generally a temporary solution to problems of heightened ethnic strife in heterogeneous states, over time, consociationalism often evolves into federalism or decentralization.

Having established what we believe to be a vital, functional link between political parties, civil society, and federalism, we now turn to a more detailed examination of political parties and civil society. While all three components serve a Tocquevillian purpose as defined here, we believe that political parties and civil society approach the status of necessary (though not sufficient) institutions for the success of democracy.[34] We now move from organizational analogues to a more substantive and direct investigation of these institutions and their importance for national democratic systems.

POLITICAL PARTIES

Why are parties important to democracy? Giovanni Sartori has argued persuasively that political parties arose as a response to the state's need to communicate with mass publics in complex societies. The political party, even in a one-party state, is a necessary vehicle for organizing and channeling information and authority because "a modern state cannot be left unchanneled."[35] The first function of the political party, therefore, is to channel communication *from the state to the public*.

But political parties in a democracy do more. According to Sartori, the critical distinction between parties in a pluralistic system and the party in a one-party state is that parties under pluralism serve an *expressive function*.[36] That is, they not only transmit or organize information from above but express political preferences from below.[37] The second function of the party, therefore, is to channel communication *from the public to the state*.

Finally, parties also form part of the web of civil society. In this sense, their function is to mediate not only between the atomized individual and the state but also between different groups within civil society. The Republican party in the United States counts the Democratic party as a critical part of its environment. It is made aware of and responds to the interests of those members of society who identify as Democrats by the actions of the Democratic party.[38] Thus the third function of the party is to channel communication *among different groups* in a civil society.

The information that is communicated among groups and between state and society through parties includes, inter alia, perspectives on the role of the state, citizen preferences, inadequacies of current policy, criticism of the incumbent administration, and formulation of alternative policies. One might rightly ask whether social movements or other voluntary associations could not also fill the expressive and communicative roles filled by the political party as we have defined it. Movements formed around particular social concerns—nuclear nonproliferation, civil rights, "smart growth"—serve an expressive and communicative function that is difficult for the state to ignore. Theoretically, the state can also channel communication through these groups to the public as it does with political parties.

Indeed, it is impossible to articulate a principle that distinguishes fully between political parties and other associations of civil society. However, there are general differences between the two. These distinctions derive from the political party's unique purpose: to win government power. In a democracy, political parties seek votes because votes translate into seats in the national legislature and a degree of state power. Other associations do not seek votes. The constraints they face and their resultant political calculus are very different from those of political parties. How so?

First, parties do seek votes, but they do not always seek to maximize votes. Consider a Catholic party in a society with large confessional divisions—Protestant, Catholic, secular, Jewish. A Catholic party that fashioned a broad appeal to religious persons, regardless of denomination, could probably win more votes than if it just appealed to Catholics. But often it will target its appeal to Catholics in order to rally its base, rather than diluting its message and reaching out to more voters. Why?

A party's behavior is largely determined by the country's party and electoral systems, as well as the country's social cleavages and the party's own ideological niche. In a relatively homogeneous society with a two-party plurality system that encourages broad coalitions, a hard-line Catholic party is unlikely to do well.[39] Rallying the Catholic base will ensure some votes but not enough to guarantee significant representation. A broader appeal will more likely yield a modicum of state power. In a divided society with a multiparty proportional representation system, however, a Catholic party, by rallying its base, may be able to maximize its parliamentary representation and even play an important role in a governing coalition. Thus the party's strategy will likely be very different under the two scenarios. On one hand, in a significantly divided society—in which, say, 40 percent of voters are Greeks, 25 percent are Turks, and 35 percent are Albanians—no single faction can get a majority, and thus, in a parliamentary system, a coalition will be virtually assured. On the other hand, the calculus is different in a country like Zimbabwe, where 80 percent of the citizens belong to one ethnic group (Shona) and about 20 percent to another (Ndebele). An ethnic appeal by the Shona party will pay off; one by the Ndebele may not.

An interesting example of how the institutional arrangements in a society affect the translation of social cleavages into a party system comes from the Netherlands. Into the 1960s, the Dutch had a multiparty proportional representation system in a religiously divided society. Five major parties dominated the electoral scene—two "class" parties, liberal and social democratic; two Protestant parties; and a Catholic party. Material prosperity and secularization in the 1960s led to a weakening of the ties between traditional parties and voters. Because the Dutch system is highly permeable—a party need receive only two-thirds of 1 percent of the vote to achieve representation in the parliament—these social changes led to a rapid transformation of the party system. The total vote share of the dominant five parties fell from a high of around 95 percent to around 75 percent in less than twenty years. In response to pressure from new parties, the older parties decentralized, merged, consolidated, and polarized. They refashioned old appeals and moved swiftly toward the left or right. In the late 1980s, the reformed and revitalized dominant parties together secured over 90 percent of the vote. Only one of the new parties that had emerged in the 1960s, Democrats 66, was able to compete successfully with the older parties. Dems 66 was largely responsible, however, for pushing the old parties to metamorphose. Although the socioeconomic trends in the Netherlands—growth in the middle class, deconfessionalization—were similar to trends elsewhere in the West, the shake-up in the Dutch party system was more profound because of the particular constellation of party and electoral systems and the low barriers to entry for new parties.[40] While both parties and associations react to social change, only parties react specifically to the incentives of the party and electoral system that regulates access to state power.

The quest for state power influences not only a party's behavior and organization but also its platform. Political parties perform another role that is not assumed by other organizations in civil society and that enhances parties' unique intermediary status between state and society: the *syncretic function*. By *syncretic function*, we mean the aggregation of a wide array of issues and their translation into the practice of governance. Although movements and nongovernmental organizations may rally around a specific cause and thus operate as highly successful expressive units, their success derives from their avoidance of the syncretic function. Parties bring together under one tent the diverse policy problems facing a state, not just one set of interests. A successful Green party, for example, cannot restrict its governing agenda to environment-related issues; it must incorporate an agenda and positions that reach beyond its core concerns, as the Green party platform in the 2000 U.S. election did.[41] The Prohibition party of the late nineteenth and early twentieth centuries included positions on many issues unrelated to alcohol consumption. Confessional parties in Europe have necessarily been concerned with issues of governance beyond the role of religion in society; even in Turkey, Islamic "fundamentalist" groups like Refah have included strong social democratic planks in their platforms that were not directly related to their religious agendas.[42]

In general, the demands of governance require that parties, unlike associations, take the multifaceted responsibilities of state power seriously and develop plans for government that extend beyond a single interest issue. The party is an interest group, a faction, that wishes to take control of the whole, of the state. The party is responsible for crafting a platform that both speaks to the main issues or concerns that it claims as its own and presents them in the context of governance as a whole. The party, and ultimately no other association, is responsible for translating interest issues into the exercise of state power, with all the attendant compromises and pragmatic choices this entails. Only the party simultaneously legitimates both the power of the coercive state—by acknowledging that state power is a worthy end to strive for—and the influence of the voluntary interest association—by its existence as a voluntary organization in opposition; and only the party takes responsibility for merging the public and the private. In a democracy the success or failure of parties in meeting these responsibilities is judged by the voters.

Of course, some small parties may be elected and serve in coalition governments on a narrow issue platform. From this vantage point, they may exercise undue influence with a small vote share. They may be able to eschew compromise on certain matters without jeopardizing their grip on office, as with the religious parties in Israel. In some cases, small political parties can treat syncretism as an externality, shifting responsibility for syncretic behavior to the coalition government so that they can remain true to their principles. Governance can never be reduced to a single issue, however. The problem of national defense does not disappear simply because a party's core interest is protecting the environment or supporting religious schools. Nor can a far-right party hope to steer the national economy toward high productivity simply by ending immigration. Even if a party succeeds in gaining office on a single-issue platform, it can retain support—and continue to function as a party—only if it, or the coalition it is part of, demonstrates knowledge of, or competence on, a broad range of issues.

The syncretic function, then, is not simply a rhetorical device, nor does it apply only to issues that excite the public. It is far broader than either. In performing the syncretic function, a party (or system of parties), whatever its base, must take a position on all, or at least most, of the affairs of state. Through this distinctive function, the party becomes more entangled in the web of the state, and less free to press its original concerns, than other types of associations.

Finally, parties represent the only organized opposition that is prepared not only to challenge the power of the state but to actually assume office. Civil associations do not represent the same kind of threat to the central authorities as an organized political opposition, because civil society is generally organized not to displace the current regime but only to influence it. Organized parties, in contrast, expressly intend to displace society's present rulers, and they seek to convince the public that they are capable of carrying out the functions of state, that they are not parochial in their interests.

Party Promotion: Institutional and Organizational Incentives

If parties are vital to democracy, how does one encourage their development in new democracies? The majority of successful, established parties in the older democracies have been organized around social cleavages.[43] As Stein Rokkan and Lipset reported over three decades ago, the major cleavages that prevailed in European party systems were class, culture, religion, and geography.[44] Although all four types of cleavages have been important, none has been more ubiquitous than class. This was recognized long ago by James Madison, who wrote in *The Federalist* no. 10 under the name Publius that "the most common and durable source of factions has been the various and unequal distribution of property. Those who hold and those who are without property have ever formed distinct interests in society."[45] Following this reasoning, Lipset referred to elections as the "democratic class struggle."[46] Party builders in new democracies need to identify salient cleavages and develop political parties around them. Class is a reliable first guess as a cleavage likely to become salient, but class parties, like all parties, are not simply manifestations of objective existing divisions but rather represent consciously created subjective identities. People have to learn to think in terms of class, so party builders (elites) must not only find cleavages but in some sense construct them as well. In other words, cleavages both percolate from below—manifesting objective conditions—and are instigated and molded from above—representing subjective interests and articulation of those interests.

So how does one apply the Lipset-Rokkan paradigm to the contemporary world? Herbert Kitschelt's study of party systems in East Central Europe represents a good start. Kitschelt tries to predict the constellation of voter alignments and party alternatives given structural conditions in post-Soviet East Central Europe. He superimposes several dichotomies on expected party formation. First, he sees a status quo dichotomy at the start of the post-Communist period—those who benefit from the status quo and those who do not. This is hitched to two ideological dichotomies—that between market allocation and political (state) allocation of resources and that between authoritarian and libertarian political values.

The internal logic of these cleavages can be used in conjunction with existing political and economic conditions to predict voter alignments. According to Kitschelt, those who benefit from the existing economic order, regardless of its type, will align themselves with political authoritarianism, fearing that a shift toward political libertarianism will threaten the owners of economic resources. These defenders of the status quo prefer stability and certainty to the "institutionalized uncertainty" of greater democracy and the threat of state-led redistribution of resources.[47] Therefore, if on one hand the status quo is a nonmarket system, then its defenders will align themselves with authoritarianism, and the opposition to the status quo will consist of libertarians, in *both* a political and economic sense (classic liberals). If on the other hand the status quo is a market system, then its defenders will align themselves with authoritarianism, and their competitors will be politically libertarian but economically leftist (political allocationist). (See Figure 3.1.) This should approximate the situation in some Latin American countries in the postauthoritarian period, since many of Latin America's military dictatorships supported market-friendly policies, though widespread elite support in the region for neoliberalism may confound this.

Kitschelt then proposes a schema for predicting how individual, rational citizens will vote:

> My guiding hypothesis is that those individuals and groups who are confident that they will succeed in converting their assets into valuable resources in a capitalist market society will support parties with libertarian pro-market outlooks. In contrast, those groups and individuals whose resources prove inconvertible will resist the marketization of economic relations and resort to authoritarian-nonmarket politics. [48]

There is, then, a continuum along which those who have convertible skills and those who do not fall. In the post-Communist states, according to Kitschelt, one might expect a pro-reform/anti-reform divide separating those who support economic and political reforms from those who do not. This schema has some support in evidence from East Central Europe but does not seem to hold in Russia. [49]

Mapping social cleavages in this way is an important step in which party-building elites think meaningfully about how to utilize these cleavages to construct a viable, democratic party system. [50] Beyond this, however, democratic activists also must consider whether, how, and to what extent existing institutions can be changed to improve the salience of parties.

Of course, a major institutional constraint in developing strong party systems in new democracies is that many of these new states have inherited at least one strong party from predemocratic times. The effect of this older controlling party on the evolving party system can be substantial. The post-Communist states have

FIGURE 3.1
The Cleavage Divide

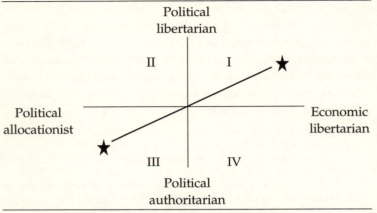

NOTE: Stars represent likely location of citizens with respect to major cleavages. Quadrants II and IV are relatively empty, while most citizens are located in Quadrants I and III.

inherited the Communist party—in some sense reformed, rebaptized, and often reinvigorated. The holdover Communist parties complicate the task of establishing a left and a right in some new democracies because, as former ruling parties, the (former) Communists represent a conservative, status quo force composed of the nomenklatura while also claiming the mantle, as the Communists always did, of the party of the workers and the peasants. These parties confound traditional class distinctions of left and right.[51]

This complication is probably more serious in those countries where the Communists were able to retain power throughout and after the transition than in those where they immediately lost power. In Hungary and Poland, where the Communist parties lost the first postregime elections but then regained office, they transformed themselves into recognizably center-left social democratic–style parties. In the other post-Communist states, where Communists oversaw the regime transition, the break with the past was compromised in both political and economic terms, and the resulting party systems exhibit ambiguous ideological positions and cleavages.

The same evaluation applies to the Partido Revolucionario Institucional (PRI) in Mexico, which was defeated at the national level only in 2000, after holding power for over seventy years. Indeed, the PRI's very name, "Institutional Revolutionary Party," is eponymous, suggesting the contradictions that inhere in an organization that has been both a ruling hegemon and an ostensible force for justice for labor and the poor. Like the Communists, the PRI is fundamentally for the status quo, but rhetorically it remains leftist and still incorporates trade unions and poor rural voters. It will take time to create in systems like these a standard left-right continuum running from social-democratic parties to free market–oriented groups.

In other cases, democratic or anti-colonial movements emerge from authoritarian or totalitarian regimes. These movements, as in Italy (Party of Action), East Germany (New Forum), Poland (Solidarity), Czechoslovakia (Civic Forum), and India (Congress), have often collapsed after the first election. Initially, they unite all democrats; anti-fascists, anti-Communists, or anti-imperialists; conservatives; and leftists. But once the dictatorship or foreign ruler is gone, they lose support or break up. Solidarity and Lech Walesa rather quickly lost much of their support. In India, Congress managed to buck this trend, remaining in control until the 1990s, but now it is but one of a number of parties. These heterogeneous coalitions have a hard time holding together in the era of electoral politics.

There is some evidence that, despite the confusion that follows the end of authoritarianism, party systems can respond positively to institutional change with reasonable rapidity. Arthur Miller and his colleagues found surprisingly high and consistent levels of voter identification with parties, and fairly high ideological coherence within them, in the context of a limited degree of underlying social cleavages in a study of Russia, Ukraine, and Lithuania in the late 1990s. [52] Education, income, rural-versus-urban residence, and age had some effects on voter identification, though in Russia the effects of age have been insignificant. Occupation has a crude effect on voting in Russia and Ukraine, though not in Lithuania. Blue-collar workers are more likely to vote Communist and anti-reform in both. There was a limited association between rural, low-income, low-education voters and anti-reform parties, an optimistic if weak harbinger of cleavage development.

In Brazil, notorious for its fragmented and chaotic party system, party discipline improved dramatically in the 1990s. Argelina Cheibub Figueiredo and Fernando Limongi, discussing the Brazilian legislature, note that "if one assumes perfect discipline, that is, that the members of all parties in the chamber follow the vote announced by their leaders, and computes the expected result, one can correctly predict the approval or rejection of 95 percent of the roll call votes. The decision-making process is thus far from random." [53]

Party discipline is only one measure of the maturity of a party system, but it contributes to the system's general stability. Mature parties offer voters a fairly predictable set of choices that do not change radically in the short run. The party line, if party members tow it at least most of the time, can guide voters trying to distinguish between parties on the basis of policy.

These are just a handful of cases, but what both the Brazilian and post-Soviet examples suggest is that institutions matter. Within a relatively short time—less than a decade in both cases—weak and chaotic party systems have been disciplined, primarily through institutional reform (Brazil) and democratic practice (post-Soviet countries). In Brazil changes to the constitution coupled with legislative practices requiring discipline have increased the hands of the executive and party leaders and limited the ability of individual legislators to grandstand.[54] In the post-Communist cases, experience with the practice of democracy has altered party behavior, even more so in the states outside the former Soviet Union (FSU) than those inside.

Scott Mainwaring, a student of Latin America, emphasizes the role of institutional changes in strengthening democracies with weakly institutionalized party systems. Certain arrangements—among them parliamentary systems, closed-list voting, unitary states, weak presidencies, and proportional representation with higher thresholds[55]—seem to help institutionalize parties. It is important, however, to recognize the limitations of institutions, and the importance of organizational efforts as a complement to institutional change (discussed in the following section). Ideally, the two work in tandem. As Stefano Bartolini and Peter Mair argue, "Socio-organisational bonds and institutional incentives appear as the two most powerful 'structural' determinants of the extent of electoral availability [susceptibility of electoral preferences to suasion], with high levels of the former clearly depressing mobility."[56] We now turn to the other half of Bartolini and Mair's equation, organizational ties. We have looked at what parties do, what role they play in the context of other institutions, why they are important. We now must look at how they are formed, the historical basis for party membership, and whether or how this basis has changed.

The Importance of Being Organized

Whereas political scientists tend to focus on the impact of changes in the rules of the game, political sociologists remind us that only certain groups and constituencies can take advantage of these rules. The remarkable stability of West European party systems over the twentieth century owes as much to the innovative efforts of political leaders to organize constituents as it does to institutional rules. Party organization deserves considerable attention in attempts to consolidate democratic contestation.

Lipset and Rokkan, in their 1967 article, "Cleavage Structures, Party Systems and Voter Alignments," attempted to explain the origins and consistency in European party systems by emphasizing the initial organization. A brief review of that article's thesis provides a foundation for our remarks about organization.

Lipset and Rokkan argued that the particular formation of Western European parties depended on the sequence and fallout of three major historical cleavage-forming "dichotomies"—the Protestant Reformation, the "Democratic Revolution," and the Industrial Revolution. In the first two cases, the struggle was mainly between secular and church authority. In the Protestant Reformation the classic conflict between church and state arose, wherein some states subjugated the church while others remained attached to the Vatican. Subsequently, tempers flared over the control of mass education, and again church and state squared off. Where the Catholic church had been subjugated, a Protestant state church was dominant or struggled against strong Catholic minorities. Where the state was still allied with the Vatican, the battle was between the secular left and the Catholics. Finally, the Industrial Revolution split landed from urban interests. The accumulation of these cleavages led to the formation of eight different party types in Western Europe. [57]

In all eight types, a further cleavage between workers and employers became salient. Lipset and Rokkan argued that although "in sheer statistical terms the fourth cleavage [worker-employer] will in at least half of all cases under consideration explain much more of the variance in the distributions of full-suffrage votes than any one of the others," the other three cleavage lines explained most of the variance *between* party systems. [58] That is, the fourth cleavage did not substantially alter the cross-national typology. However, they specified an owner-worker divide that predated, but was modified by, the Russian Revolution, and they identified this—the class cleavage—as the most salient cleavage of all *within* most countries.

Two important ideas can be extrapolated from the original Lipset-Rokkan typology. First, parties may organize around non-class-related issues and may be very successful at doing so. Americans tend to be queasy about organizing parties around religious or cultural divides, but in Europe such divisions have proved viable.[59] Second, although parties can organize around noneconomic divisions, every European party system has been at least partially organized around an economic cleavage. Without a doubt, class is the most common and most viable source of cleavage in party systems.[60]

Lipset and Rokkan enunciated what has become a famous proposition, now known as the "freezing hypothesis": *"The party systems of the 1960's reflect, with few but significant exceptions, the cleavage structures of the 1920's. . . . [T]he party alternatives, and in remarkably many cases the party organizations, are older than the majorities of the national electorates."*[61] What explained this remarkable stability? According to Lipset and Rokkan, the source of frozen alignments was socio-organizational: "The narrowing of the 'support market' brought about through the growth of mass parties during this final thrust toward full-suffrage democracy left very few openings for new movements."[62] Implicit in this formulation is the notion that once voters become attached to parties through socialization or organizational drives, they tend to stick with them, even across generations, unless a catastrophic event upsets these attachments. Lipset and Rokkan also assumed that parties which appealed to deep-rooted cleavages would tend to endure because the basis for voter attachment to the parties—such as religion or social class—would tend to change slowly, if at all.

Organizational bonds limit the ability of party elites to radically alter party platforms or behavior. The fear of alienating a large base of supporters constrains elite actors, who would otherwise prefer to manipulate the "free" electorate with a loose, personalistic party incapable of placing demands on its leaders.

Likewise, competitive, organized parties that are unable to destroy one another ultimately may have to compromise. This is the original source of democratic legitimacy, of acceptance of opposition rights; strategic actors realize that they cannot eliminate their opposition without tearing the fabric of polity or society. Large contending blocs have worked out democratic compromises— whereby they grant legitimacy to the opposition—as the best way to hold society together. Organized political parties are necessary to ensure the viability of these compromises, the enduring commitment of the compromising parties to the democratic accord. This was as true during the original struggles leading to democracy in Europe as it has been in the past three decades during third-wave democratic transitions.

Scholars studying political "pacts" as a device for moving from authoritarian to democratic governance have emphasized the importance of parties as guarantors of democratic accords. The potential for successful pacted transitions of the type completed in Venezuela in the late 1950s and Spain in the 1970s is increased by the existence of organized parties that have the muscle to both enter into and carry out the pacts. Political pacts require strategic actors to moderate their own agendas in the interests of stability and therefore require disciplined organizations. As Guillermo O'Donnell and Philippe C. Schmitter note, parties entering pacts must typically "(1) limit the agenda of policy choice, (2) share proportionately in the distribution of benefits, and (3) restrict the participation of outsiders in decision making. In exchange, they agree to forgo appeals to military intervention and efforts at mass mobilization."[63] Although a primary determinant of pact success is whether elite actors trust one another, this trust is made easier when organized parties exist to back up the promises made and threaten effective sanctions. As Terry Lynn Karl has put it, "Pacts depend upon the organizational resources that key actors bring to the bargaining table at a particular moment, their perception of those resources, their understanding of their opposition's strengths and weaknesses, and their ability to control their constituencies."[64]

Strong organization and popular commitment have been powerful antidotes to the weak and overly flexible parties that have cropped up in many new democracies. Stable, organized parties do not crumble at the first crisis that confronts them. An organized opposition is also an important counterweight to the former hegemon in post-Communist countries and in Mexico, where the former single party retains a powerful, organized base in the new era of democratic politics. In sum, organized parties perform a variety of important functions in democracies and democratic transitions.

Yet party organization in the modern world faces significant challenges. In the past, parties offered a vital source of entertainment, access to information, and a place for community interaction where members' worldview could be sharpened and validated. In particular, both left-wing and conservative church-related parties actively provided a panoply of services and opportunities to their followers, organized along partisan lines. Both sets of parties, according to Lipset and Rokkan, "tended to isolate their supporters from outside influence through the development of a wide variety of parallel organizations and agencies: they not only built up schools and youth movements of their own, but also developed confessionally distinct trade unions, sports clubs, leisure associations, publishing houses, magazines, newspapers, in one or two cases even radio and television stations."[65] In his own exploration of how parties organize, Jack Veugelers has argued, citing Lipset and Rokkan, that these subcultures, "segmenting society along partisan lines, . . . helped to maintain cleavage structures by ensuring the reproduction of political loyalties among party supporters, their offspring and the new recruits made available by social mobility, change in the occupational structure and migration (both rural-urban and international). These subcultures also stabilized party systems by insulating supporters from cross-cutting communications and pressures."[66]

Party penetration of civil society was present not only in Europe but also in Chile and Venezuela, where parties actively participated in the organizational life of civil society.[67] As Michael Coppedge notes of Venezuela,

> By cooptation, infiltration, or direct party sponsorship, virtually all organizations in civil society besides the church, the military, and business associations were subordinated to party control. . . . Party penetration of organizations played an important role in the establishment and consolidation of democracy in Venezuela. Control of organizations gave party leaders the ability to mobilize thousands of supporters on short notice to overthrow dictators in 1945 and 1958. It also gave them the ability to *restrain* supporters when democracy required restraint.[68]

Nor is the integration of civil society merely a tactic of the past. Veugelers, researching modern European party systems, explains that encapsulation of civil society continues to be profitable tactically for some new far-right parties. He notes, for example, that the French Front National (headed by Jean Marie Le Pen) "sponsors a multitude of parallel organizations that target a wide and somewhat bewildering variety of social categories."[69]

Yet while past party organizational tactics may not be defunct, modern political parties in new and old democracies face unique organizing challenges in the modern era. Many of the old, targeted nonpolitical incentives for joining a party have dissolved. Access to politically relevant information, once the province of the party newspaper and meetings, has been rendered widely available through mass communications, multimedia, and slowly but not insignificantly, the Internet. As a result, "cross-cutting communications and pressures" that challenge partisan beliefs are nearly impossible to prevent. The entertainment industry has exploded with inexpensive ways to fill leisure time that bypass party functions.

The raison d'etre of new parties is also less easily perceived by potential members than that of the parties of yore. While the successful parties of the past with extensive branch organization,[70] such as the socialists and Catholics, were organized at a time when the working-class and peasantry were excluded from politics,[71] most new democracies begin with full suffrage. The working classes are not, and do not feel, excluded from the political process to the same degree as their predecessors were during the original struggle for democracy in Europe in the nineteenth and early twentieth centuries. The modern process of democratization in many new democracies is decidedly different from that earlier struggle. Whereas European parties pushed for inclusion in a reasonably well functioning, contested system—a fairly clear, concrete goal—new parties in emerging democracies are included from the start in a system that may function poorly and be undercontested. Today's parties must offer something other than simply "the vote" in order to recruit supporters and members. Thus the goals of modern parties have become more complicated, dedicated more frequently to technical changes in public policy than broad, organization-friendly themes like inclusion.

In other cases the problem is that full suffrage has been established but the rights of citizens are constrained through subtler state manipulation, weak respect for the rule of law, or slavish media that permit repression and abuses to go unreported. Thus a state that is democratic on paper does not accept democratic competition. As Lipset and Rokkan noted in 1967, the evolution of party systems in Europe was determined by the interaction of important political "thresholds" with social cleavages. The threshold of incorporation was the granting of full citizenship rights to those in opposition; the threshold of legitimation, the acceptance of opposition as legitimate within a polity.[72] In Europe the threshold of legitimation was often crossed early within an oligarchic framework, while the threshold of incorporation formed the centerpiece of the struggle for democracy. In many new democracies, however, the reverse is true: everyone has been incorporated, but the idea of an opposition still has limited legitimacy. It becomes difficult to organize around smaller, more complex issues. The abstract concept of legitimacy is not as satisfying a rallying cry as "the vote."

Given that the old purposes of parties to provide diversion and information have been undermined and that organizing around the critical issues is more difficult in many young democracies today, should mass-membership party organization still be considered a viable option for new democracies? Does organization still work?

INTERLUDE: THE DEATH OF ORGANIZATION?

In the advanced industrial democracies, technology, education, and the increasing flexibility of modern life (particularly the high number of service sector employees and the diversification of entertainment outlets) are gradually obviating the mass membership organization. Katz and Mair have argued that the political party has come increasingly to rely on the state in lieu of civil society—replacing, to a certain degree, membership with state funding, and organizational capacity with reliance on state communication channels. [73] If citizens no longer rely on parties for information, entertainment, or their worldview, then the costs of joining or staying in an organization (time spent, principles compromised) become more significant relative to the benefits. We may ask two immediate questions of this argument: First, is it valid? Second, if it is, is there a parallel effect in developing democracies as well, or does the generally weaker level of technological penetration in poor countries mean that they are insulated from these effects?

To begin with the latter question, while its effects depend on the degree of penetration, technology is having a similar impact in the new democracies as in the older ones. There is evidence from Venezuela, for example, that technology and new forms of organization like social movements and NGOs are having the same effect on parties there as in the industrialized countries. Venezuela has traditionally had very strong, organized parties, somewhat like those in the European polities.[74] Yet a burgeoning civil society has begun to capitalize on new forms of technology to circumvent the party system.[75] Do we await a new type of party organization that can somehow integrate the new social movements into a politically feasible party? Or is decline and weakened organization to be the fate of parties? The increasing decentralization proffered by technology suggests that national governments may indeed be inevitably subject to this fate, where the government is run by a legion of technocrats who adapt to the changing environment of pressure groups, rather than parties that serve an aggregative function.

Giovanni Sartori gives these themes further treatment in his customarily deft piece, "Video-Power," which deals with the impact of television on politics and apathy.[76] Although Sartori is concerned primarily with the matter of local versus global concerns, or more accurately, private versus public horizons, his argument necessarily indicts "video-power" for its alleged contributions to the public's inability to get itself together. What does the quality of news media production have to do with politics? Sartori sees it as essentially a force for dumbing down, manipulating, and creating opinion that is then used to justify action or nonaction, in an ironic but vicious cycle. It seems to us that the reduction in attention spans, the limited horizons, the scattered facts and instantaneous polls on seemingly simple issues—these must be part and parcel of the ever increasing flexibility of modern life, the continuous progress in freeing every individual from responsibility to, or comprehension of, any kind of whole or any entity worth sacrificing for. "Video-power" does seem conducive to apathy born of ignorance. In a TV-saturated environment, the likelihood of forging strong organizational bonds is limited.

Juan Linz has argued, expanding Sartori's argument, that the weakening of organization is a product not just of "video-power" but also of important structural changes, such as a more differentiated workforce, reduction of class rigidity, higher literacy and education levels, and the ever increasing mobility of modern life that allows more people to spend time alone and away from their neighbors. These forces are at work, to varying degrees, in both old and new democracies, old and new industrializing states.[77]

In the past, access to information and a holistic worldview were two of the benefits of joining a politically active organization. The socialist party or the church provided access to information within a relatively segmented environment in which political elites and the masses were able to reduce the likelihood that evidence contrary to their worldview would undermine commitment and activism. Organizations enabled citizens to become part of a working unit providing them with inspiration, a vision, and political skills and resources—a point that goes back to Tocqueville.

Today, information is accessible to everyone without the costs of membership. And the fragmented, disconnected nature of "video-power" helps to prevent holistic worldviews from emerging. The awareness of contradictions that is inherent in the torrent of information and opinion reduces the possibility of unified collective action. The spawning of the Internet may augment this phenomenon by multiplying the number of media outlets not directly controlled by any one establishment or environment and thus increasing the likelihood of contradictions. The mounting contradictions serve to debilitate us, leading to apathy.

The irony is that although organizational membership helps to reduce exposure to contradictions and dispel apathy, we are prevented from joining by our preexisting sense of hopelessness amidst so many contradictions. As a result, citizens turn away from syncretic organizations toward "social movements." These loose and flexible organizations—if they can be called that—do not commit their members to more than a single vector of purpose nor do they demand the kind of intensive interactions with diverse people that older party organizations required.

Here is manifest the impact of increased organizational flexibility, and reasons to fear the spread of hyperflexibility. Syncretic organizations, membership bodies with multiple responsibilities, press us, as part of the act of belonging, to make commitments that involve compromise. We vote for the mass party that seems closest to our views, given that, for most of us, the major parties are not a perfect match. In the process of attracting our votes, parties and their supporters are forced into the position of prioritizing: Is the right to choose more important than lower taxes? Do school vouchers outweigh tighter handgun controls? Is the environment more important than free trade? Voters who identify with no single party must also prioritize values before they vote. This process is vital to a democracy because it is an implicit acknowledgement of the need for tolerance and compromise in a polity in which others do not agree with us and we cannot force them to.

Single-issue movements do not obligate us to act this way. We pick and choose only the movements we support and avoid having to compromise along the way. The danger with them is excessive polarization, a diminishing recognition of the role of compromise, and a loss of syncretic partisan attachment or strong organizational bonds with others. Of course it makes sense—in moral terms—for everyone to be able to make his or her own statements; support exactly what he or she wants to endorse, nothing more or less; and lead exactly the life he or she wishes to have. But democracy is not, after all, about getting what you want. It is about having a debate about what everyone wants and settling it by some nonviolent principle of majority or plurality rule. This requires compromise, and it can be learned only in the actual interactions of people with one another.

The analogy of the cell phone is useful. The cell phone allows its owner to eschew commitment to a time or place. "Why set a time now? Just call me. If I'm not there, if I can't get it, I'll call you back, and we'll work it out." The inevitable result often is that it doesn't get worked out. By the time the call is made, other decisions have been made, we are in the thick of other engagements, and so the cell phone has liberated us, made us more flexible. We are finally free of the oppressive chains of obligation and commitment—and compromise.

Given the ubiquitous nature of television and the ever evolving state of communications, it seems inevitable that the problems faced by the advanced industrial states will readily complicate organization building in the developing states before their time. Access to the Internet extends to Africa, Latin America, and Asia (even China!)—and this type of communication at lower levels of political development has no historical precedent in the West. We can tell the story of the evolution of political parties and institutions in the West, but there is no predicting the way the high-tech revolution will affect emerging Third World democracies, how their access to a plethora of information about themselves and life in the First World will alter their experiences with political parties. We simply do not have the experience.

We return to the question of the proper organic sequence of development, whether new states can skip the stages passed through by the old. But if Sartori is correct, it would seem that the new democracies will not pass through the same stages as the old. The only question is how best to mitigate any negative consequences of this alternative path.[78]

The answers are unsurprisingly difficult to derive. We cannot predict the direction of technological change; if we could, the technology would exist already. Things move fast now, we think, but it was announced only in July 2000 that scientists had for the first time propelled something (light, as it happens) at a speed faster than that of light.[79] That is to say it is now possible, in admittedly limited circumstances, to move things faster than ever before thought possible. Meanwhile, the capability of computers continues to double every eighteen months.[80]

One must remain skeptical, however, of the degree to which technological advances in mass communication fundamentally alter the perceptions of people. After all, information's impact may depend as much on what it may mean to particular groups of information consumers as on the way it is accessed. To cite one reason why it might be too soon to declare the death of organization at the media's hands, consider the case, studied by da Silva, of two Brazilian communities exposed to a story about a workers' strike cast by the media in a deliberately negative light: "Workers in the south were upset about the obviously misleading coverage, and workers in the north wondered whether it was time to try organizing a strike."[81] The media's impact on viewers thus cannot be assumed without considering the position of the viewers themselves. Indeed, organizational commitments may determine the way news is interpreted. It remains an open question, however, whether the form and degree of interaction between citizens and the media in advanced countries has any particular effect on citizens' propensity to organize.

It is precisely this case that Robert Putnam has argued. He finds that the one factor explaining the decline in volunteering and other forms of civic activity is television.[82] "Other things being equal . . . each additional hour of television viewing per day," he argues, "means roughly a 10 percent reduction in most forms of civic activism—fewer public meetings, fewer local committee members, fewer letters to Congress, and so on."[83] Still, there are reasons to think that the effects of television are curvilinear, or certainly not linear. Television may contribute to an elevation of awareness and cognitive mobilization when viewers first tune in but may ultimately lead to a culture of apathy as viewing replaces other activities. The evidence suggests that the media's effect on individual citizens is conditional on the content and the context, not just the quantity. Putnam finds, for example, that "Americans who watch the news on television are *more* likely to read the daily newspaper than are other Americans, not *less* likely."[84] (Unfortunately, however, the number of people who choose to watch the news has been dropping.) Eric Uslaner has challenged Putnam's evidence, arguing that the prior condition of optimism or pessimism determines people's civic participation, not television. When optimism is controlled for in regression analysis, the effects of television appear spurious. Uslaner finds mixed effects of heavy viewing: some heavy watchers are substantially more pessimistic, while others are substantially more trusting. These effects cancel each other out, leaving television's overall effect ambiguous.[85]

In the 1989 presidential elections in Brazil, "video-politics" significantly contributed to the ultimate victory of Fernando Collor. Biased press coverage favored Collor, but Luis Inácio Lula da Silva (candidate of the Worker's Party) exploited a combination of free media time and information disseminated through the civil society to make an impressive showing. There is some limited evidence that attention to the media, particularly among the less educated, was circumscribed by preexisting choices of whom to support. That is, the media was, for some, a way of validating a decision rather than informing it. It seems, therefore, that those with less education were heavily influenced by organizational attachments and that the media helped to mobilize them in favor of the candidate they preferred, thus reinforcing, rather than replacing, organizational commitments.[86] Rokkan has suggested, following Tocqueville's lead, that readers of a newspaper where there are many newspapers are quasi-members of an organization. Thus the print media form part of an associational attachment. The evidence from Brazil suggests that television may work in a similar way.

It may be speculated that this is because of the format used. The free hour on Brazilian TV was a time for candidates to directly structure and mediate their own relationship to their following, rather than a time for the media to interpret that relationship. The free hour was not so much the fragmented stuff of "video-power" as an easier way of directly communicating with a large audience. It was used particularly well by Lula and Collor. This may be contrasted with the TV Globo–edited coverage of the debates between Lula and Collor, which was mediated and biased and had a registered negative effect on Lula. This latter phenomenon was a much clearer example of "video-politics" as Sartori defines it—replete with omissions, skewing, and fragmentation.

The argument advanced here is that the media does not have to be, nor is it only, a force for demobilization, delinkage, apathy, localization, or withdrawal from the complexities of organized participation. The media's effects depend on both the medium and the preexisting organizational context within which it is experienced. Rather than throwing up our hands in despair at the deleterious effects of cross-pressuring media on organizational capacity, we need to think creatively about how exposure to the media interacts with organizational structures not only to dampen but to enhance activism. This process has obviously happened to a certain degree in Brazil with the genesis of the free hour.

Nor is it just television that appears to have mixed effects on people's ability to organize. The cell phone, which we earlier derided for making life too flexible, has been instrumental in recent organizing efforts. Anecdotal evidence from the 1999 Seattle protests against the WTO suggests that cell phones were used extensively by organizers from around the country to coordinate. A rash of prison riots in São Paolo in February 2001 was apparently coordinated by cell phone.[87] Bolivian protests against water privatization relied on wireless connections, as well. While none of these is an example of technology promoting syncretic organizations, it is not hard to see how the cell phone could be used in that way. If it is not so employed, it is probably the fault not of the technology but of broader social phenomena.

While it is tempting to prescribe membership organizations as a solution to the problem of weak parties and overly elite-centered politics in developing democracies, there are good reasons to be skeptical of such a prescription under current technological conditions. Expanded media access does offer an opportunity to create better-informed and less apathetic electorates in new democracies, but it is not clear that this process can replicate earlier ones in the older democracies. Under the circumstances, new organizational forms may be needed to adequately inculcate habits of compromise while still respecting the awesome power of the media and communications technology to liberate citizens from their parochial contexts.

At the same time, there are some trends that run counter to those sketched above. For example, in line with modernization theory—which predicts that social change will result from technological advance, a burgeoning media industry, and a more differentiated workforce—secularization can be expected to emerge as well. Given that Protestantism and, more recently, Catholicism have played important roles in creating organizations, a lesser commitment to religion would not augur well for organizational capacity. In many of the new democracies, however, religion has played and continues to play an important role in spurring organization, much as it did in the early America Tocqueville described. Brazil and Korea both exemplify the continued role of religion in boosting political participation and associational activity.[88] If religion remains a salient feature of peoples' lives, the potential for a vibrant organizational life will remain high. An important difference between developing and developed democracies may be secularism's much greater strength in the latter.[89]

To conclude, political parties are vital to functioning democracies. Parties are vehicles for communication among important political actors, and they serve as uniquely syncretic organizations that socialize citizens into the give-and-take of democratic contestation. Organized parties act as guarantors of stability during democratic transitions and help to both establish the rules of the game and ensure that they are followed by relevant social actors.

Parties do not just happen; they must be organized carefully and thoughtfully. While new parties may be different than their predecessors and new party leaders may have to think in strategically distinct ways about party organization, there is no reason to think that parties should or will disappear as critical intermediaries in democratic societies. Nevertheless, as we have made clear, parties do not act alone. The vitality of another critical actor in democracies—civil society—is crucial in determining how parties function. If civil society per se is not a new actor in democracies, it has certainly become ever more internationalized, well funded, and institutionalized. In many states, civil society is far more developed than the party system. In chapter 4 we discuss what civil society is and why it matters, rounding out our treatment of institutions.

CHAPTER 4

CIVIL SOCIETY

CIVIL SOCIETY HAS PROBABLY BEEN the most gripping topic of discussion in democracy discussions in the past decade; this interest mirrors the focus on mass society theory in the post–World War II period, when analysts were trying to explain the origins of authoritarianism. There are many reasons for the renewed emphasis on civil society today. The third wave of democratization, seemingly driven in part by an explosion of civil society, has piqued researchers' curiosity. Neoliberalism's assault on the state has also opened up the study of civil society; if the central state's influence is to be reduced, something has to restrain it or take its place. This is not the first time that civil society has been at the top of the agenda. In the 1950s Lipset's *Agrarian Socialism* and *Union Democracy* helped set off the first surge of empirically based civil society studies. In *Agrarian Socialism*, Lipset explained the emergence of strong political movements in rural North America, from the Populists in the nineteenth-century United States, to the Cooperative Commonwealth Federation (CCF) and New Democrats in central Canada, as the result of myriad voluntary organizations—libraries, cooperatives, local phone companies, volunteer fire departments, and so forth—that made organization for political ends relatively easy. As noted in chapter 2, one of Lipset, Trow, and Coleman's central findings in *Union Democracy* was that democracy requires the existence of a network of independent voluntary associations that not only can train the electorate politically but can also form the backbone of a party system.[1]

This work corresponded with writings by theorists of mass society like William Kornhauser and Sigmund Neumann.[2] These scholars argued that a society lacking secondary associations was a "mass society," in which the potential for democracy was low and that for authoritarianism high. The first wave of civil and mass society analysts rooted their work in Alexis de Tocqueville's *Democracy in America*. Tocqueville, of course, had famously observed of American democracy that it seemed to rely on a level of associational activity that was unparalleled in France or the rest of Europe. Since the fall of communism in 1989, the analytical reputation of Marx among intellectuals has dropped, while that of Tocqueville has risen.

The study of civil society retreated in the 1970s and 1980s but then was reborn in the 1990s with the new and attractive concept of "social capital." A concept with a long history, social capital has been most elegantly elaborated by James Coleman, a coauthor of *Union Democracy* who wrote his dissertation with Lipset. According to Coleman, social capital comprises the resources that inhere in particular networks of people, rather than in the people themselves.[3] A classic example is the trust that is built up in a community of parents who watch out for one another's children. This trust is valuable because it makes parents feel secure that someone is taking care of their children and thus allows them to work or engage in other productive activity. If a family moves from one community to another, however, the parents lose this social capital because it exists not in themselves but in the network. This contrasts with the parents' educational achievements or child-rearing skills, which do reside in individuals and travel with them. Such individually "owned" skills are classically referred to as "human capital." Robert Putnam ignited a flurry of important, if critical, articles, new research, and even new Web

sites on social capital with his book *Making Democracy Work*. There
is now a Web page hosted by the World Bank that deals exclusively with the concept of social capital (www.socialcapital.org).

Why is civil society important for democracy? The many reasons that have been given can be collapsed into three broad categories. First, there is the social capital hypothesis, derived from
Tocqueville. This assumes that collective participant action facilitates democracy (as Gabriel Almond and Sidney Verba assert in
The Civic Culture). Since social capital reduces the costs associated with collective action and is reproduced and enlarged by
secondary associations, civil society is taken to be an important
contributor to democracy. Some have argued that social capital
facilitates broad interpersonal trust that lubricates the democratic system. One problem with the social capital thesis is that it
seems to confound cause and effect. That is, social capital is produced by associations, but associational activity would seem to
rely on preexisting social capital. The thesis is therefore potentially circular. At the very least, one would want to know where
social capital originates prior to its enlargement in associations.
It is also unclear whether we should focus on generalized social
trust, created by the general prevalence of social capital, or on
social capital only in specifically political or "democratic" associations. It is, therefore, an open question as to whether all social
capital is of equal value.

Second, the human capital hypothesis, also derived from Tocqueville, posits that the leadership skills necessary for participation in democratic politics—oratory, persuasion, compromise,
and the like—are built by secondary associations. Civil society
therefore represents a training ground for potential leaders in a
democracy. Implicit in this thesis is the notion that civil society,
since it is broader and more accessible to all citizens than strictly
political positions—party leader, legislator, or state employee—
offers opportunities to build leadership skills that citizens would

otherwise be denied.[4] This is the inverse of Tocqueville's original hypothesis, which was that political associations provided a broader training ground for subsequent work in civil society. "In politics, men combine for great undertakings, and the use they make of the principle of association in important affairs practically teaches them that it is their interest to help one another in those of less moment."[5]

Finally, there is the mediation hypothesis, according to which civil society is a mediating force between differentiated individuals and highly syncretic political parties and governments.[6] Individual interests are brought into the political system through their representation in civil society and through the subsequent interactions between secondary associations and political parties or government. Whereas the concept of social capital emphasizes social participation, often independent of the political system, the notion of mediation emphasizes interest representation in the political system. Through the representation of interests in civil society, citizens are able to influence party platforms and government policy. As a result, they become committed to the democratic system. The mediation concept also implies that civil associations help to both represent and moderate interests, by facilitating both cooperation and competition among citizens, groups, and the state. We would also include under mediation the direct role that organizations of civil society play in limiting the power of the state to trample citizen interests and rights.

If we assume that civil society does support democracy in these broad ways, it follows that democracy is not enhanced by just any civil society and that the quality of civil society is important aside from simply the quantity of associations, the apparent hubbub of associationalism. To determine what kind of civil society a successful democracy needs, we can perhaps narrow these broad concepts into more useful instruments.

SOCIAL CAPITAL

The concept of social capital has been best elaborated by James Coleman:

> Social capital is defined by its function. It is not a single entity, but a variety of different entities having two characteristics in common: They all consist of some aspect of a social structure, and they facilitate certain actions of individuals who are within the structure. . . . Unlike other forms of capital, social capital inheres in the structure of relations between persons and among persons. It is lodged neither in individuals nor in physical implements of production.[7]

Social capital refers to concepts such as trust, norms of reciprocity, and community "credit slips" that are generally intangible but vital to the functioning of a community. An individual who does a favor for a neighbor can expect the neighbor to do him a favor in the future. A member of a community expects that all members of that community will observe certain norms, even if she does not know everyone personally.[8] The mutual trust members build through community activities extends to periods of inactivity; this trust is bolstered by reputation, which is a powerful sanction on the behavior of those who know one another. These forms of social capital are augmented by association and iteration.

An extremely important concept related to social capital is social closure, or the degree to which different members of a community know one another. In Coleman's classic example, a community consisting of two parental units and their children is closed when the children's parents know one another, open when they do not. When the parents do know one another, they can enforce norms, draw on their trust of one another, and share resources. The members of a closed community can also rely on reputation to reduce the costs involved in obtaining information about one another and about whether to trust or not. As a result, the closed community has more social capital than the open community. Or, to put it another way, closure facilitates the production of social capital.[9]

It should be pointed out that social closure is not always good. It may lead to the replacement of meritocratic or universalistic procedures with nepotism and may encourage the group to close itself off from external information and exposure to other norms.[10] This is a matter of degree, of course. Any group must have some closure in order to be considered a group and to have any norms at all. While total closure implies an insupportable lack of liberty from social pressures, in the absence of any closure, the community as such ceases to exist and individuals must go it alone in a Hobbesian state of nature.

Social closure is, therefore, a relative, continuous variable. Its relationship to social capital may also be curvilinear. It can be hypothesized that up to some point, social closure increases social capital in a positive form. As social closure increases beyond this point, the likelihood of "unsocial" capital formation increases. All social capital, however, is probably accompanied by a certain degree of "unsocial" capital. Put another way, all forms of trust and loyalty are linked to a limited degree of corruption, if only because trust, loyalty, and family-like relationships require or press for nepotistic ties. Japanese values and behavior provide an example of a society with a strong emphasis on norms of reciprocity, where the need to pay community "credit slips" can produce corrupt behavior in the form of "pay-offs."[11]

Michael Woolcock has deftly distinguished between *integration* and *linkage* in a way that encompasses the distinction between social and unsocial capital. Integration is similar to closure: it measures the degree to which communities or organizations are integrated through intracommunity ties. Linkage is the degree to which members of organizations or communities are tied to other, external organizations or communities—the prevalence of extracommunity networks. As Woolcock argues, the balance between social and unsocial capital is determined by the balance between integration and linkage. Integration augments norms and trust but at the cost of fostering inefficiencies resulting from corruption or patronage. Linkage may weaken integration, but it offsets this cost by fostering efficiencies, the result of universalistic and rational criteria for action. Together, integration and linkage can augment the benefits of social capital while limiting its costs.[12]

One of the implications of Coleman's definition of social capital is that it is of only limited value in explaining democratic success, because social capital resides in specific social relations. If members of a group have developed internal social capital, it can be transferred to another group only if the new group is based on the structure of the old group. That is, if a bowling club decides to form an environmental group, than the social capital from the bowling club may be transferred to the environmental group. But one member of a bowling club takes no social capital with him to a meeting of an environmental group that is not founded organizationally on his bowling club. Therefore, social capital explains the persistence of organizational capacity only within units, not in the aggregate across society.[13]

Yet many now argue that social capital does have an aggregative effect. Robert Putnam, for example, in *Making Democracy Work*, argues that a "civic community," defined primarily by active participation in civic associations, contributes to democracy by encouraging collective action. How? Through iteration and interconnectedness of games; development of reputation; formation of models, or "templates," for collective action; and creation of norms of reciprocity.[14] Except for "templates," Putnam's theory relies on elements of social capital. This is problematic as it is not clear how norms or trust generated at the microlevel translate into norms or trust at the polity level. In this regard, the notion of templates is more compelling, but not much. Templates are models for social action that, once created, are used by others and make collective action easier to undertake. It is reasonable to assume that citizens who witness other citizens engaging in collective action will attempt to mimic this behavior. But why would people who don't know one another or have any other bond join together in collective action? If all it took for the average citizen to join together with his fellow, but unknown, citizens was to see this behavior modeled, the entire notion of social capital would be well-near worthless. But social capital itself is not in dispute. People do not simply come together to solve problems; though there are many models of collective action, dilemmas of collective action still persist. How do we preempt free riding or enforce sanctions? Social capital provides a partial solution. The notion of templates in and of itself has little to offer us on this point. [15]

Any theory connecting social capital and democracy thus faces at least two obstacles. First, how and when does microlevel social capital become transformed into macrolevel norms and trust? Second, in explaining the role of associations and social capital, the theory must avoid circularity. As it stands, the reigning theory seems to go something like this: Associations are good for democracy. They create social capital. Social capital is good for democracy because it stimulates association building. Associations are good for democracy.

This is rather unimpressive.

It is our position that, while social capital does play a role in democratic success, this role is exaggerated and virtually meaningless without reference to human capital and mediation. We reach this conclusion in attempting to overcome the aforementioned obstacles.

Can a coherent theory explain the ways in which microlevel social capital translates into state-level norms? Templates represent a start. Another part of the explanation for how intragroup behavior diffuses outward is what Woolcock calls linkage, whereby members of one group interact with those of other groups. It is important to understand the dilemma: according to Coleman, social capital exists within networks; therefore, an individual who leaves a social capital–rich area cannot take the social capital with him elsewhere.

Margaret Levi has proposed a way out of this dilemma: the psychological concepts of heuristics—learned but unproven shorthands that guide one's decision making—and projection—the supposition that others are similar to oneself. Because heuristics and projections allow people to transfer their expectations in one situation to others, both mechanisms could promote the metamorphosis of specific trust into generalized trust. Rather than seeking to identify direct pathways by which social capital located in one organization is then transferred to another—presumably because part of one organization forms the base for another—the logic of heuristics and projections allows us to make the jump from microlevel relations to macrolevel networks. The norms one learns in an association can be transformed into expectations at a social level.[16] This seems a more promising theoretical path to pursue.

While heuristics and projections advance our understanding of how the social capital developed in associations might contribute to democracy, they also blur the line between social and human capital. The ability and desire to utilize projections or heuristics presumably vary from individual to individual and are essentially traits located not in any social network but in individual actors. That which is projected, or that on which the heuristic is based, has its roots in social organizations, but the process of projecting remains an individual one.[17]

Furthermore, heuristics and projections add an unknown dimension to the theory because they rely on individuals from different backgrounds having the capacity to come together and transfer their trust and norms. Remember, social capital can be transferred, according to the original theory, if collective action is organizationally based on consistent, social capital–rich networks. With heuristics and projections, social capital transference is presumed to occur osmotically, since people who are from different social capital networks are allegedly using what they have learned therein to relate better to one another. Where norms are different, however, this process is not likely to be as simple as in the case of actors who can draw on standard social capital. It is not clear that heuristics and projections make association or trust among people who are *different* any easier than it would be without them. [18]

Clearly, the melding of social capital theory and heuristics and projections is problematic. If we want to say nothing more than that people who learn how to interact in collective-action situations are more likely to duplicate that behavior when faced with a different set of challenges and different actors, then we have really returned to the notion of human capital. That is, citizens who participate in civil society learn skills—compromise, leadership, negotiation, oratory—that are useful in a democracy, which demands a degree of citizen input for its healthy functioning. It would seem, however, that we are trying to get at something beyond human capital.

What is that something? Underlying both the social capital and heuristic-projection concepts lies the idea of interpersonal trust. While being trusting or nontrusting, as well as trustworthy or nontrustworthy, is an individual quality, trust is also something that exists within a network. Whether one's individual level of trust or trustworthiness is selectively beneficial depends upon the conditions of social trust. In a trusting society trust can be enormously profitable. In a "morally backward" society the opposite is true. Likewise, trust is selectively beneficial only where institutions and individuals are not only trusting but trustworthy. As Russell Hardin puts it, "If trust is merely expectations, then the claim that we should trust government is equivalent to some claim that we should expect government to do good. The latter would be a stupid claim much of the time. Should Martin Luther King and Ernest Hemingway have expected the FBI not to be spying on and harassing them even though they may have had evidence that it was?"[19] What is important is not simply that citizens be trusting but that the society as a whole be both trusting and worthy of that trust. Only under these conditions can trust be a wise investment. This state of society is not one that can be reached by individuals acting alone through their own human capital, but rather must be reached through collective action.

That said, the conditions of a trusting society cannot be deemed exclusively human or social. Trust always entails risk; that risk is greatly reduced in a trusting and trustworthy society, but getting to such a state in the first place always requires a leap of faith. Whether the decision is moral or strategic, opting to trust others for the first time is a distinctively individual choice. The outcome of this choice—cooperation or betrayal—determines the likelihood that the option to trust will be taken again. Thus the interaction between an individual human decision and a social response determines the likelihood of trust. And although that first leap of faith is individual, it is conditioned by the society's trustworthiness—again, a social condition. However, it is precisely here that the human capital variable assumes heightened importance. Remember that social capital exists within networks. The individual decision to trust within a trusting network is one in which the risks have been marginalized by social, not individual, action. The decision to trust outside this network demands individual determination and courage because no social network underwrites the risk. "A trusting person," Toshio Yamagishi and Midori Yamagishi point out, "is the one who overestimates the benignity of the partner's intentions beyond the level warranted by the prudent assessment of the available information."[20] The likelihood of individuals opting to trust outside the network over time will be conditioned by their success in doing so—again, a social condition. It is therefore not possible to disentangle the social and the human capital aspects of trust.

INTERPERSONAL TRUST

Theorists of social capital and democracy assume that the negotiation and compromise that democracy involves requires a high level of social trust. It is difficult, if not impossible, to negotiate with people one does not trust. Furthermore, democracy depends critically on whether the rules of the game, if followed, make it forever possible that the losers in one round will be the winners in the next round. These successive rounds may be elections or legislative sessions. Social trust is necessary in this context to assure the losers that the winners will give up power if they lose in the future.[21] Lacking this trust, the losers have no incentive to accept the results of any round. Diffuse interpersonal trust in those with whom we cooperate and compete is therefore taken to be critical to the success of a democratic polity.

Is it so critical? *Trust* is a curious word, prone to abuse. The kind of trust that inheres in social networks (social capital) is patently different from diffuse interpersonal trust. In the former case, trust is not a risky proposition, for the risks are underwritten by the social network. One trusts precisely because the risks are very low—others are unlikely to want to spoil their reputation, and they understand the benefits of cooperation within a network. Diffuse trust, in contrast, is not underwritten by a social network. But it may still be underwritten. For example, a system of courts and legal procedure makes it easier for us to trust others because we know that, as a last resort, we can rely on the judicial process to protect us (to marginalize risk). Yet if we know that effective sanctioning bodies exist to protect us, whether these be social networks or legal institutions, in what sense are we actually "trusting"? If trust exists, it is not because of individual willingness to assume the inherent risks but because of the institutions that will sanction these individuals if they violate our accords. It therefore seems that two kinds of trust are relevant to democracy: trust in social networks and trust in democratic institutions. The former allows us to associate with people we know or to whom we are connected directly by organizational ties; the latter, to interact politically and economically with people we do not know.

What then are the sources of these kinds of trust? Much ink has been spilled trying to demonstrate that network trust (social capital) both emerges from and enhances associational life. Although there is no way to find the beginning of this circle, it may reasonably be assumed that diffuse interpersonal trust feeds into it. The starting of a new association does usually mean that people who do not know one another will begin to interact with people who do. Some amount of blind trust brings people to associations like these, unless every association is only an off-shoot of people already organized in another association—with this infinite regress ending, if ever, only with the organization of the family.

Trust in institutions, in contrast, is rooted primarily in experience. We trust institutions that seem to work to continue to do so. Yet here again the specter of interpersonal trust arises, for two reasons. First, although we may say that we trust institutions in general, our ability to trust them in particular instances (when we interact with them) will rely not simply on some generalized conception of the institution but also on our actual interactions with the people who work there. So, for example, we may say that we trust the courts. Yet if we go to court and receive a court-appointed lawyer, we still have to be willing to entrust that individual with our personal information. Clearly, our trust in the court system conditions our willingness to do this, but so too does our ability to trust strangers. And so it goes with virtually every institution that we interact with. Second, it is nevertheless true that no matter how much trust we vest in the court system, none of us wants to end up in court suing our business partners, neighbors, or friends for violating pacts we have made with them. The legal process is costly and time-consuming, even if we win our case and retrieve our losses. It is simply impossible, large monetary rewards notwithstanding, to compensate someone for the time and anxiety involved in using the legal system. It follows that even if we put great trust in institutions, we still try to reduce the risks inherent in interacting with people. Without interpersonal trust we are unlikely to engage in many partnerships, because the risks are fairly high. Diffuse, interpersonal trust promotes interactions even where trust in institutions is also high.

A theoretical case, albeit a more tentative one than is often asserted, can be made that interpersonal trust does play an important role in a democracy, primarily through its interactions with existing social capital and its contributions to trust in institutions. While diffuse interpersonal trust alone hardly determines the success of democracy, it is hard to imagine how a society with extremely low levels of such trust could remain democratic.

Where then does diffuse interpersonal trust come from? We suspect that it has several sources. Social capital theorists assume that diffuse trust percolates up as an aggregate of microlevel, particular trust. But there is good reason to think that trust might also precipitate: aggregate, society-wide trust might be created by the behavior of elites and state institutions and then filter down to microlevel community trust. "A large body of social democratic theory," Margaret Levi has found, "claims an important role for the state in reducing the narrow and often risky personalized dependencies of people on each other."[22] The state can help to create an *environment* where people learn to trust one another and develop social capital. It also creates and earns—or destroys and squanders—generalized trust by its own *actions*. The state represents a type of potentially neutral, universalistic creature that, through good governance, can foster the trust and norms that Putnam describes.[23] But state action can also destroy trust and invalidate norms. As research by John A. Booth and Patricia Bayer Richard suggests, repressive government action has a highly significant effect on the levels of social and human capital in a society.[24]

Can it be determined whether trust is more likely built from above or below? Booth and Richards find that the effects of associationalism on levels of interpersonal trust are statistically significant but very small.[25] In Central America, at least, where they conducted research, top-down trust may be more important than bottom-up trust. In a study of the United States, Eric Uslaner reports that membership in civic associations has no impact on trust, though trust is a strong predictor of membership.[26] This study does not grapple with the notion of top-down trust but serves to weaken the case for bottom-up trust. Further damage is done to the theory of bottom-up trust by Dietland Stolle's survey of Germany and Sweden. She finds that short-term association memberships (one year) increase generalized interpersonal trust, but longer-term memberships (more than five years) actually decrease it. She concludes that tight intragroup bonds are detrimental to extragroup trust.[27]

Ronald Inglehart, analyzing forty-one countries across cultural and regional zones, concludes that democratic institutions have an insignificant effect on levels of interpersonal trust. Trust is strongly associated with *years of democracy* but, he argues, is a prior development. Nor does trust have an effect on the level of democracy or changes in the level of democracy; it affects only stability.[28] Thus, according to Inglehart, trust does not precipitate from the top down very much, either. In contrast, Muller and Seligson report that interpersonal trust is a product of democratic institutionalization. In their study, which covers a similar geographical area and uses indicators similar to Inglehart's, trust is also an insignificant predictor of *democracy levels* but is significantly influenced itself by exposure to democracy.[29] They find strong evidence of a top-down effect.

How do we explain this apparent contradiction? First, neither of these studies is conclusive. Both are constrained by data limitations and have limited samples. Still, Muller and Seligson's findings are more persuasive than Inglehart's. Both studies agree that trust is related to the stability, not the level of, democracy. They disagree as to the causal direction of the relationship. However, in arguing that experience with democratic institutions does not affect trust levels, Inglehart makes a curious choice. He regresses trust not on democratic stability but on democracy *levels* between 1972 and 1997 and finds no relationship. Muller and Seligson regress trust on democratic stability from 1900 to 1980 and find a significant relationship. Given the general agreement that the relationship between trust and democracy is relevant to democratic stability, Muller and Seligson's approach is more appropriate. Indeed, Inglehart's own subsequent analysis suggests the same result. Assuming that cultural variables influence democracy, Inglehart regresses democratic stability from 1920 to 1995 on two culture variables: trust and subjective well-being. He finds a very strong, statistically significant relationship. However, there is no reason to believe that the causation runs in the direction that Inglehart assumes. If it ran the other way, we would likely obtain the results that Muller and Seligson got. Inglehart's assumption that trust leads to democracy, not the other way round, is therefore questionable. There is evidence of a top-down effect, though that effect is limited.

As an aside, further evidence of a top-down effect of state institutions on trust can be gleaned from the remarkably low levels of diffuse interpersonal trust among African Americans. Blacks are less than half as likely to be trusting as whites. Orlando Patterson has explained this as the legacy of slavery and Jim Crow, a sordid tale of long-term state-supported discrimination: "Clearly, the distinctive historical experience of Afro-Americans as descendants of a slave population . . . and their subjection to herrenvolk democracy in the South; post-emancipation semi-serfdom in the share-cropping system; nationwide segregation, racism and economic discrimination . . . together largely explain the extraordinarily low levels of trust among all classes of the group."[30]

Taken together, these studies suggest that interpersonal trust is neither exclusively bottom-up nor top-down in nature; that is, it is neither solely created by civil society nor by democratic institutions.[31] Furthermore, neither the top-down nor bottom-up approach seems to account for a very high percentage of the variance in trust levels. Where, then, does trust originate?

It has long been theorized that greater wealth leads to greater levels of trust, because individuals who possess more wealth have more security and any trusting relationship poses less of a risk to their overall well-being. For the poor, the theory presumes, risky dependencies on other people must be curtailed because any misplaced trust can be catastrophic.[32] Inglehart suggests that cultural traditions and gross national product (GNP) per capita are the strongest determinants of levels of interpersonal trust. He claims that GNP per capita alone explains about 36 percent of the variance in levels of trust across societies; however, his regression suffers from omitted variable bias, as noted previously. The failure to include democratic stability means that it is possible that the effects of GNP per capita are really indirect effects of increased affluence on democratic stability.[33] Nevertheless, there is other evidence that prosperity increases trust. In his study of the United States, Uslaner reports that income and education both have significant positive effects on personal levels of trust.[34] Patterson also finds a strong correlation between class and trust in the U.S. case.[35] Our own regression analysis of the U.S. Social Capital Community Benchmark Survey data finds that income has an insignificant impact on trust but that education is highly significant ($p < .001$).[36]

We analyzed the U.S. Benchmark data to see if we could distinguish between bottom-up (associational) and top-down (state-influenced) trust creation, as well as to isolate other factors unrelated to these two processes. Using ordinary least squares (OLS) regression, we tested two dependent variables measuring generalized trust, using the same independent variables. The models and regression results are detailed in the appendix to this chapter. The survey data provided us with three variables that we used as metrics for bottom-up and top-down trust creation. The importance of associational involvement was measured using an index of the number of groups that respondents claimed to belong to (GRPINVL2). The top-down process is complex and more difficult to measure. How does one measure the state's ability to create conditions that encourage trust? How does one assess the actions of elite actors or the perceived efficacy of institutions that underwrite risk and make trust possible? We hypothesize that the state's role has an objective and a subjective component. That is, one can assess the actual capacity of the state to underwrite risk, to adjudicate fairly and equitably amongst parties, and to conduct its business with high standards. But one's subjective assessment of how the state performs on these measures is probably more important than its actual performance, measured "objectively." Respondents in the Benchmark survey were not given this question directly, but they were asked how much trust they had in both local and national government. Presumably, their responses to this question track (in part) their assessment of how trustworthy government is and how well it is creating an environment conducive to trusting interactions.

The reader may object that using trust in government to predict trust in general is really just a kind of autocorrelation, with trust predicting trust. There are both theoretical and practical grounds for rejecting this claim. We have already made a theoretical case that trust in institutions is distinct from interpersonal trust. Indeed, the argument can be made that the more trust one has in institutions, the less trust one requires in other people. It is therefore far from obvious that trust in local or national government will be positively associated with interpersonal trust. On practical grounds, one might argue that trust in government is just another kind of "trust in others," that government is simply another group, like neighbors, coworkers, or the generalized other. However, when all of these variables are intercorrelated, trust in government appears distinct. Consider Table 4.1 below.

TABLE 4.1
Correlation Matrix for Interpersonal Trust and Trust-in-Government Variables

	Trust Local Govt (0 = LOW)	Trust National Govt (0 = LOW)	Trust neighbors (0 = LOW)	Trust coreligionists (0 = LOW)	Trust shop clerks (0 = LOW)	Trust coworkers (0 = LOW)	TLOG5	TRSTREG
Trust local govt (0 = LOW)	1.00							
Trust national govt (0 = LOW)	0.51	1.00						
Trust neighbors (0 = LOW)	0.22	0.11	1.00					
Trust coreligionists (0 = LOW)	0.20	0.11	0.48	1.00				
Trust shop clerks (0 = LOW)	0.27	0.15	0.45	0.39	1.00			
Trust coworkers (0 = LOW)	0.25	0.13	0.41	0.46	0.44	1.00		
Dependent Variable								
TLOG5	0.25	0.17	0.39	0.32	0.38	0.37	1.00	
TRSTREG	0.31	0.16	0.79	0.74	0.78	0.76	0.47	1.00

SOURCE: Authors' analysis of U.S. Social Capital Community Benchmark Survey data

The four variables that make up our general trust scale—trust in neighbors, coworkers, coreligionists, and local shop clerks—are intercorrelated at the 0.4 to 0.5 range, while they are correlated with trust in government variables at the 0.1 to 0.3 range. Thus the interpersonal trust variables and the trust-in-government variables seem to form distinct clusters. When we correlate these variables with our dependent variables, we find that trust in government is correlated at less than a 0.31 level with the trust index (whose component parts are all correlated above 0.7), while the correlations with "tlog5," a single interpersonal trust question, show the same general pattern: correlations are above 0.3 for the interpersonal variables and below 0.3 for the government variables. In sum, for both theoretical and practical reasons, it is appropriate to view trust in institutions as an independent and distinct predictor of interpersonal trust.

In addition to the variables intended to measure bottom-up and top-down theories of trust formation, we have included several others of theoretical importance. As noted, Eric Uslaner has argued that optimism and pessimism are important predictors of trust. The Benchmark data include no direct question about optimism, but we used two proxies—self-reported happiness and health. Both of these variables tap into attitudes about the future that are similar to optimism. They also measure a person's self-confidence or sense of personal worth and strength, which might be expected to influence his or her willingness and ability to put trust in others. Another variable included is the number of people in their lives whom respondents say they can truly confide in (CONFIDER). Presumably, the more close friends one has, the more trustworthy one will expect people in general to be. However, it could also be the case that the more close friends one has, the more one expects that everyone outside one's intimate circle is not trustworthy. This would fall in line with expectations about in-group–versus–out-group attitudes—the more positive one feels about one's own in-group, the more negative one feels about out-groups. Thus, this variable has theoretically ambiguous implications. We have included hours of television watched on an average weekday, as several scholars have hypothesized that television is related to social capital and trust. Finally, we have inserted a number of standard demographic variables into the model.

What do our results tell us about the bottom-up–versus–top-down controversy? In one model, GRPINVLR, which measures the number of associations to which respondents belong, does not achieve significance; in the other, it does, but its effect is fairly small ($B = 0.167$). This means that someone who belongs to two groups is likely to be about 2 percent more trusting than someone who belongs to no groups. The trust-in-government variables fair better; both trust in local and trust in national government emerge as significant predictors in both models. Trust in local government seems more important. A person who feels local government can almost always be trusted scores between 21 and 37 percent higher on our trust measures than one who thinks local government can hardly ever be trusted. The effects of trust in national government are much weaker, ranging from less than 1 percent to about 19 percent. It would appear from this data that both bottom-up and top-down effects exist but that top-down effects may be a good deal stronger.

The variables that are most important in predicting interpersonal trust in both models are trust in local government, race, and happiness. Income is nonsignificant and quite weak. Blacks and Hispanics appear more likely to be distrustful than members of other groups. This probably has at least two explanations— historical cultural legacies, as explained by Orlando Patterson, and the effects of the perception or actual experience of discrimination. Because state institutions can mitigate (or fail to mitigate) the effects of discrimination, the fact that race is such a strong predictor of trust lends credence to top-down theories of trust formation. However, race also signals cultural legacies that may be the result of past, not current, state behavior. And minorities may simply feel discriminated against in their private lives, leading to distrust, even if the state is neutral or working actively in their defense. Thus race is not exclusively associated with a top-down notion of trust creation.

The interaction between race and trust can be further explored by looking at mean values of trust in government broken down by race. Tables 4.2 and 4.3 reveal significant differences by race, though they are not very large. Whites and Asians are more trusting of local government than Hispanics, who are more trusting than blacks. One could argue that this demonstrates the impact of past state-sponsored discrimination on attitudes about government, but Asian Americans have endured quite a bit of discrimination in the past. The puzzle deepens when we look at trust in national government. Since national government today implements affirmative action programs that benefit blacks and Hispanics and tend to hurt whites and Asians, one might expect that the ordering would reverse for trust in national government. Whites do indeed distrust national government, but blacks and Hispanics trust national government no more than local, and Asians are significantly more trusting of national government than everyone else. These tables suggest that the influence of race on trust is impacted not only by the state but apparently by sociocultural factors as well.

The most important of the variables yet to be discussed is happiness. Happier people are more likely to trust others. Happiness is an attitude reflecting one's whole life and worldview, as well as one's perceived prospects for the future. While one's present circumstances do affect happiness, the relationship is tenuous. Most Americans are happy or very happy, whether they are "not at all satisfied" with their current financial situation or "very satisfied." Happiness relates to one's socialization, upbringing, and general outlook—and is not particularly related to either state or associational factors. Closely related to happiness, but having a

TABLE 4.2
Mean Trust in Local Government By Race

	Mean	S.E.	Confidence Interval
Whites	1.43	0.02	1.41–1.44
Blacks	1.20	0.04	1.16–1.24
Asians	1.52	0.11	1.41–1.63
Hispanics	1.35	0.05	1.30–1.4

SOURCE: Authors' analysis of U.S. Social Capital Community Benchmark Survey data
Range: 0–3; 0 is lowest.

TABLE 4.3
Mean Trust in National Government By Race

	Mean	S.E.	Confidence Interval
Whites	1.09	0.02	1.07–1.10
Blacks	1.20	0.04	1.16–1.24
Asians	1.49	0.11	1.38–1.59
Hispanics	1.28	0.05	1.23–1.33

SOURCE: Author's analysis of U.S. Social Capital Community Benchmark Survey data
Range: 0–3; 0 is lowest.

lesser effect on trust, is the number of people one can confide in. Our results show that the more people one confides in, the more trusting they are in general. A person with two people he or she can confide in is about 5 percent more trusting than someone with nobody to confide in. This measure appears to relate more to one's own level of personal satisfaction and ability to trust than to an in-group–versus–out-group dichotomy.

Finally, the effects of television prove to be significant in one of our models, but very weak. A person who watches four hours of television is about 1.5 percent less trusting than someone who watches no television. In the other model, television is nowhere near significance.

In sum, the sources of trust, though not well understood, appear to be plentiful and diffuse. Clearly, the society's level of economic development plays a role, as does the state's capacity and judiciousness. Citizen interactions in civil society make a very small but important contribution to the generation of trust. The kind and quality of media access that the society has may also affect trust levels.[37] Cultural traditions are crucial, as well; if trust is a reflection of our values or worldview, it probably also has important wellsprings in the family and in the socialization process.[38] Regardless of the exact origins of interpersonal trust, however, civil society may play a role in diffusing it throughout society.

For trust to spread through society, it seems likely that citizens must have the opportunity to interact with others who are different from themselves. Social capital and social closure in groups help encourage individuals who hold similar beliefs or have similar interests to be trusting. But the real challenge to democracy is for citizens to trust those who are different, those who form the opposition. Here state and elite behavior surely plays a role. The rule of law is essential to creating a context of trust. However, "bringing the state back in," while important, does not answer the questions that remain logically prior: Why do elites trust each other in some societies but not in others?[39] How does elite behavior affect mass behavior and vice versa?[40] Why does the state act more responsibly in some societies than in others?

The last question may have multiple explanations that do not bear on the current discussion, but the others may indeed be related to social capital theory. The socialization of elites and other strategic actors in society, as well as the effect of elite behavior on the masses (or vice versa), can be in part explained by the heuristics-and-projections theory of social capital. In other words, it is possible to elaborate a partial theory of the bottom-up creation of trust by using social capital in conjunction with heuristics and projections (human capital). But we hypothesize that certain conditions must apply in order for this theory to have ramifications for democracy.

CONDITIONS FOR A SOCIAL CAPITAL THEORY OF CIVIL SOCIETY

Our revised theory of social capital argues that associational activity breeds social capital. Social capital in turn breeds more associational activity but also broader forms of social trust. Perhaps more accurately, social capital breeds expectations of trust and a desire to be trusting in order to reap the obvious benefits. Social trust is important to democracy because it facilitates compromise and negotiation.

A large body of theoretical and empirical literature on civil society hints at the important conditions for a social capital theory. We would argue that citizens must have many cross-cutting links to other citizens, particularly those who, while similar to them in some ways, are different in others. Furthermore, while all associations can breed trust and norms of reciprocity, the most important organizational attachments for democracy are those formed in specifically political organizations. Compromise on the soccer field does not necessarily translate into compromise in the halls of power.

Several kinds of diversity can be present in organizations. What we have earlier referred to as syncretism, or organizational purpose diversity, is the breadth and scope of issues that an organization deals with. Membership diversity may include a host of either ideological or structural divergences. An organization may also be diverse in its members' ideology—for example, the American Civil Liberties Union, which comprises people on the left and right dedicated to free speech. Or it may be diverse in its members' socioeconomic status, age, race, and/or regional origins. William Kornhauser argued in the 1960s, for example, that one of the more important functions of civil society associations is to encourage elite-mass interactions. [41]

We contend that a trust-promoting civil society includes a large number of associations with structurally diverse memberships and a large number of specifically politically oriented associations. The state of research on civil society, at least from a social capital perspective, is rather poor. There are wide lacunae in both theoretical understanding and empirical data. Nearly every article that deals with social capital employs a somewhat different definition of the term, rendering it nearly unusable. Nevertheless, a few studies have produced suggestive, though not definitive, results.

Limited evidence in support of our hypotheses comes from Dietland Stolle and Thomas Rochon's study of associations in Sweden, Germany, and the United States. Although this study suffers from some methodological weaknesses, the authors find a generally higher level of social capital among organizational sectors that had more membership diversity (measured in terms of education, occupation, religion, left-right ideology, age, gender, and in the United States, race). [42] They also find that human capital (as we have defined it) is more affected than social capital by all types of associational activity. [43]

Finally, in accord with the theoretical expectations of Max Weber and with Almond and Verba's findings in *The Civic Culture*, political, economic, and cultural interest groups have a more profound impact on the attitudes and behaviors of their members than recreational or other nonpolitical groups. As Stolle and Rochon put it, "Political skills and participation are more likely to be fostered in an association concerned with political ideas than in a bowling league." [44] This finding is also affirmed by the research of John A. Booth and Patricia B. Richards, who found that in Central America, more formal group activism contributed to the generation of skills and democratic norms, while communal activism (defined as "community development" and "local betterment" projects) tended to promote intragroup trust but had an insignificant impact on development of democratic norms and political knowledge. In other words, intragroup trust in apolitical groups is not necessarily transformed into political norms or trust in democratic processes.[45] However, while participation in formal, politically activist associations does translate into a greater appreciation for democratic norms, it is not significantly related to the development of interpersonal trust.[46] As a whole, then, civil society appears to be only weakly related to the development of trust and democratic norms.

And trust itself emerges as only peripherally related to a commitment to democratic norms. Actually, Eric Uslaner reports, using U.S. data, that "trusters" are more likely to view demographic out-groups positively (as being trustworthy) but are also more likely to view political out-groups negatively. In other words, trusting people are willing to work across demographic divides but are ideologically committed and apparently more likely to demonize the political opposition. This challenges the notion that trust in opponents (what we may call democratic trust or trust in institutions) and interpersonal trust track the same underlying phenomenon.[47] Recall that one of the alleged virtues of trust is that it allows people to rest assured that the opposition will play fair and concede power if it loses. Uslaner's findings suggest otherwise. James Gibson reports that in Russia, diffuse interpersonal trust has no relationship with support for democratic institutions or processes.[48] Likewise, Muller and Seligson's finding (reported above) that trust is created by democracy but has no effect on the level of democracy brings into question the relative importance of trust as a critical variable for democratization. Clearly, trust and democracy are highly correlated, but "level of trust" is apparently a variable of limited usefulness in explaining democracy.

Interpersonal trust is only weakly related to democracy. Social capital fares somewhat better, but not much. Our original theory posited that social capital bred associationalism, which in turn bred more social capital and wider interpersonal trust. It now seems that wider interpersonal trust is of only limited importance, which weakens the case for social capital as well. And without interpersonal trust, we have still not adequately escaped from the circularity of the social capital–associationalism argument. Social capital does play a role in stimulating associations, and associations are important for democracy, but their importance derives from a role generally unrelated to social capital.

On balance, while the concept of social capital has some relevance to democratic theory, we believe it receives exaggerated attention. Civil society is more important because it promotes human capital and because, rather than inculcating habits of trust or norms of reciprocity indirectly, civil society organizations and their members actively participate in the political process of mediation. The role that informal civil society apparently plays in increasing interpersonal trust is relatively small.[49] And interpersonal trust is of only limited significance to support for democratic norms and trust in democratic institutions and processes. Citizens learn to compromise and trust others through specifically political processes of negotiation and compromise that involve the state, political elites, political parties, and civil society. Rather than serving as the cornerstone of a theory of civil society, social capital should be viewed as simply one, rather small contributor to that theory.

THE THIRD HYPOTHESIS: MEDIATION

Before the spread of concepts like human and social capital (borrowed, obviously, from the discipline of economics), there was a broad understanding of the sociological and political importance of civil society. As noted earlier, civil society theory was until the late twentieth century dominated by the mass society school. These scholars claimed that a lack of civil society organizations leads to a lack of mediation between conflicting groups and between elites and masses, thus leaving few opportunities for cleavage to yield to consensus. Such conditions undermine the potential for democracy to succeed.

The academic revival of Tocqueville's emphasis on the importance of voluntary or secondary associations found early expression not only in Lipset, Trow, and Coleman's *Union Democracy* but also in the work of William Kornhauser, specifically his *Politics of Mass Society* (1959).[50] *Union Democracy* was unique for its time: most post–World War II theorists were concerned more with the conditions that fuel the rise of totalitarianism than with those that sustain democracy. Kornhauser was no exception. He sought a unified theory that would explain the conditions for movements like Nazism, fascism, and Poujadism (a rural right-wing protofascist movement in early-twentieth-century France).

While acknowledging the importance of economic conditions, Kornhauser argued that the rise of totalitarianism was primarily due to the evolution of a mass society, which he defined as "a situation in which an aggregate of individuals are related to one another only by way of their relation to a common authority, especially the state. That is, individuals are not directly related to one another in a variety of independent groups."[51] Kornhauser argued that the absence of intermediary institutions signaled a high degree of social alienation. This alienation led individuals to search for identity in more distant, national symbols. Since people were not connected to one another, they transferred their expectations from intermediate institutions to the state (or to other national organizations). Referring to Joseph Schumpeter, Kornhauser argued that this transference to distant objects led people to deny personal responsibility for the consequences of their actions. Thus deprived of the moderation that comes from social interaction, people were psychologically freed from reality to pursue extreme actions.[52]

The importance of intermediate institutions, then, from Kornhauser's perspective, is that they help people to confront the reality of their interests and actions. They create a space where individuals come into contact with other interests and must modify their own. Members of secondary associations develop identity and gain a sense of efficaciousness from their participation in meaningful discussion and action, thus acquiring and refining a political education. These organizations may operate as bases of opposition to central authority. They resist the hegemony of centralized mass movements. In short, they reduce the power of the central authority and promote the diffusion of power and influence. In our terms, associations mediate interactions between citizens; develop human capital in the form of tolerance, identity, and efficacy; and promote collective action through social capital formation.

Most of this was articulated or anticipated in *Democracy in America* and *Union Democracy*. Kornhauser's conception of the facilitating conditions for totalitarianism mirrored Lipset, Trow, and Coleman's conception of the facilitating conditions for democracy. Whereas Lipset and colleagues posited that intermediary groups were vital to the strength of democracy, Kornhauser drew on the civil society literature to argue that the very absence of these groups contributed to totalitarianism.

Yet Kornhauser added something vital to our conception of intermediate institutions. He sought to unify two disparate conceptions of mass society—the aristocratic and the democratic. In the first, the problem of mass society is that elites are too open to manipulation by the masses, too "accessible" to public opinion. In the second, democratic version of the theory of mass society, it is the masses, whose undifferentiated nature is encouraged by elites, who are open to manipulation. But for Kornhauser mass society means both sorts of manipulation. The absence of intermediary groups that channel and defuse the inherent tensions in the relation between elites and nonelites is the founding principle of the concept of mass society. According to Kornhauser,

Social groups larger than the family and smaller than the state operate to link elites and nonelites, so that the nature of these two groups shapes the political relation. Where intermediate groups do not exist or do not perform important social functions, elites and nonelites are directly dependent on one another: there is non-mediated access to elites and direct manipulation of nonelites. This kind of social arrangement leaves society vulnerable to anti-democratic movements based on mass support. Centralized national groups do not mitigate mass availability; neither do isolated primary groups. For the one relationship is too remote and the other is too weak to provide the individual with firm bases of attachment to society. This is the situation of the mass society. [53]

For Kornhauser, then, a vital role that mediating institutions play is in bringing together elites and nonelites. [54] Let us consider Kornhauser's vision more concretely. Kornhauser posited societies that consist of atomized individuals. Though they may have loose, nuclear family ties, they are essentially unrelated to one another in any way. As a result, there are only two "groups" in society: the state, composed of elites, and the masses, composed of everyone else. In this oversimplified conception, information travels from the state to the masses and back, but because there are no institutions to mediate its passage, this information is not subjected to discussion or interpretation by smaller-scale but somewhat integrated groups. By means of this unitary information pathway, elites can easily manipulate the masses but also must themselves respond to the feverish, unrefined messages emitted by those masses. A riot, or the threat of riot, by the masses over anything, from the most to the least rational demands, forces elites to bend to mass opinion because there are no institutions in society that constrain or channel mass impulses. Mass xenophobia, for example, demands strong action (expulsion, incarceration, genocide) from elites to head off riots. Elites are under heavy pressure to acquiesce to irrational mass demands under these circumstances.

If, in contrast, elites report that the country is being infiltrated by foreigners, then because the masses have no organizations to provide information to refute this claim, elites can easily manipulate mass opinion. As it happens, the ability of elites to manipulate the masses and vice versa constitutes a vicious circle in which demagogic irrationality and strong conformist pressures are likely to prevail. [55]

In this conception, associations perform two vital functions as a corollary to their overarching purpose—which, according to Kornhauser, is to foster elite-nonelite interactions. First, associations are spaces where information that is disseminated by the state, or by society, is considered and interpreted. Because of this meeting of minds, members learn more about current events than they otherwise would and their understanding of information is expanded and contested as they are confronted with new information and new perspectives on old information. This leads to a generalized skepticism, and the potential for public skepticism about the state and its policies. For Kornhauser this process was greatly augmented wherever elites and nonelites interacted. Such interaction increased the chances that differences would be exposed in associations and that these differences would directly bear on social and political issues.

Second, associations not only mediate but also generate preferences and conceptions. Associations have their own interests. For example, a nonprofit association has an interest in funding and regulatory issues that an individual does not have. Insofar as these new interests force members to consider new issues or alternative interpretations of state policy or information, they contribute to a differentiation of interests in society that weakens the hegemonic tendencies of the central state.

Consider the example of the state-supplied "news" that foreigners are infiltrating the country. While this is unlikely to serve any individual's self-interest, members of associations that have foreign members, transnational cultural and religious associations, labor unions that include noncitizens and those that exclude them, business roundtables that depend on alien workers, mutual aid associations that integrate foreign and native citizens—each of these has an interest in the issue of foreign "infiltration." In each, members are more likely to have a different view of the issue than they would if they had no affiliations. Some will undoubtedly view the government interpretation as correct; others will just as inevitably perceive it differently. Members' perceptions will be influenced not only by the opinions of other members but also by the way in which government policy or information affects their organization's well-being. Stirring up xenophobia will, for example, undermine those organizations that depend on foreign members. Although an individual may be agnostic or receptive to government propaganda on the subject of foreigners, as a member of an affected group, she may become highly partisan. By creating new interests, associations provide reasons why sectors of the public might be skeptical of state policy. Thus, while differentiation and contestation within associations lead to the possibility of skepticism, the interests generated by associations lend content to this skepticism (see Figure 4.1).

The paradigmatic case for the mass society theorists was Weimar Germany. They claimed that the low level of civil society in Weimar, coupled with a number of other problematic conditions—weak regime legitimacy, sharp economic depression, and so forth—led to the growth of mass society, which in turn facilitated the rise of the Nazis.[56] *Union Democracy* and *Political Man* used inverse reasoning to argue the opposite case: the presence of a strong civil society leads to a robust, pluralistic society, which facilitates democracy, as in the International Typographical Union and the United States.

In the 1980s, however, historians began to question the mass society theorists' assumptions about Weimar Germany. Whereas scholars like Kornhauser and Hannah Arendt portrayed Germany as fragmented and atomized, revisionist historians uncovered a very different Weimar—one that in some respects mirrored Tocqueville's America.[57] They argued that Weimar Germany

FIGURE 4.1
Impact of Associations on Mass Opinion Concerning Elite Policy and Information

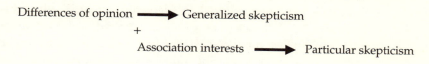

was transformed into the Third Reich, not because of, but rather in spite of a rich associational life.

How was this possible? And what does it mean for the mediation hypothesis? Evidence from Weimar means, according to the revisionist logic, a complete repudiation of civil society as mediator. In fact, Brent Hagtvet, surveying the literature on Weimar, has gone so far as to argue that "contrary to the claims of mass theory, it was the *high level of participation in secondary associations under conditions of superimposed segmentation which made for the rapid mobilization of people into the Nazi movement.*"[58] If this is true, then civil society facilitates authoritarian systems as well as democratic regimes and has little to offer students of democracy. Hypothesis three appears to be headed for the dustbin.[59]

We would argue, however, that the problem with hypothesis three is underspecification. The mere existence of a civil society is insufficient for a properly mediated democratic arrangement. The problem in Weimar was not the absence of civil society but rather the lack of strong ties between the existing civil society and the political system. Indeed, it was into this very breach that the Nazi party jumped. Hitler's success was based on his "finally bridging the gap between bourgeois civil society and party politics that had plagued Germany for half a century."[60] The existence of a strong civil society is a necessary but not sufficient condition for the existence of a mediated relationship between individuals and the state. The sufficient condition can be located in the relationship between the organizations of civil society and the political system, particularly political parties. In systems with weakly disciplined parties, civil society may need to rely more heavily on its relationship with the state bureaucracy itself, but if this link is too strong, it can undermine democracy. The bureaucracy and the civil society may play a democratic role only insofar as they have a mediated relationship with the institutions of democracy—again, primarily politicians and political parties.[61]

What is the nature of this relationship? Surely it can vary a great deal. In Europe, many civil society organizations have been formed by, managed by, or affiliated directly with political parties. In the United States, civil society associations have historically been much more fiercely independent of politics (though not religion), working with and lobbying political parties but trying to steer clear of official ties. Parties and civil society groups share members, ideas, and funds and participate in shifting alliances with each other. In general terms, the relationship between institutions of civil society and political parties should be characterized by productive tension, with neither dominating the other. Actors in civil society must perceive themselves as efficacious in their dealings with political parties; parties must be responsive but firm in forging compromises that do not alienate their own membership. The role of political parties as aggregators of interests that percolate up from society involves a great deal of mediation between parties and other secondary associations.

These civil society–party ties have been emphasized by Thomas Ertman in his superb review of the literature on democratization in Europe in the interwar period. As he puts it,

> Where parties and party competition stood at the center of political life before 1914 and the associational landscape was well developed (Britain, France, Scandinavia, Switzerland, Belgium, the Netherlands), the two came to reinforce each other in such a way as to further democratization and increase the durability of the resulting democratic regimes after 1918. Conversely, where the associational landscape was well developed but parties and party competition were not central to political life (Germany and

Italy), conservative political forces were fragmented and only weakly tied to bourgeois and agrarian associational networks. This situation created conditions favorable to the sudden success of far-right movements of agrarian and bourgeois defense under the crisis conditions of the interwar period. [62]

Thus, again, it is not the mere existence of either parties or a vibrant associational network alone that is important, but the relationship between them. To revise Kornhauser, then, democracy relies not only on the relationship between elites and nonelites but also on the relationship between differing sectors of the elite—the civil society elite and the political elite.

For this reason, one should be careful in assessing the impact of new NGOs (nongovernmental organizations) in the developing world. Although these suggest a flowering of civil society, we need to examine closely their relationship to the political system. The many cases in which this relationship is antagonistic and dysfunctional, with domestic NGOs turning to foreign organizations in order to circumvent the domestic regime, cannot be recipes for democratic success. While foreign funding may help open up domestic societies to ideas and views that would otherwise be stamped out by the state, a domestic civil society ultimately has to forge effective bonds with local political leaders and institutions. Fatalistic attitudes about the ability of the state or domestic political parties to address the concerns of civil society can be as detrimental to democracy as the institutions' actual failure. The relationship between civil society and democratic political institutions thus runs in two directions.

Public financing of NGOs may lead to their co-optation by government, in which case civil society is dominated from above by the state, rather than representing a two-way mediating structure between state and individuals. NGOs that receive financing from outside the community they purport to represent also may fail to truly mediate between their constituents and the state as a result of the mandates placed on them to insure continued funding.[63] This problem has been acute in many states, among them Botswana, as one study has revealed: "Government support has often encouraged social groups to become project oriented rather than developing permanent connections with their membership. In the long run, these organizations must come to grips with the need for more member financing of their activities if they are to concentrate on the advocacy function so critical to a vibrant civil society."[64] In this case, the relationship between civil society and the state may be too strong, effectively privileging the maintenance of that relationship over the accomplishment of constituent policy goals.

An important role that competitive party politics plays lies in encouraging civil institutions. On one hand, political competition breeds dependence on civil society. Politicians make promises to representatives of civil society in order to secure votes to win election. On the other hand, civil society needs political parties in order to influence the course of public policy as well as the implementation of the agenda propagated by the state bureaucracy. Competitive party politics insure that civil society both needs and is needed by the democratic political system.

Any assessment of the strength of civil society in developing democracies should focus not just on quantity but on quality. We take issue with what we believe is Robert Putnam's overemphasis on the civil at the expense of the political.[65] Civil society matters because of its relation to the polity. The political system, particularly political parties, play an aggregative role by pounding interests into compromises. While civil society can and does increase human and social capital, neither leadership skills nor networks of trust obviate the basic conflicts of interest that inhere in any society. Indeed, civil society actually augments conflict by giving rise to organizations that represent interests so that individuals are not left crying in the desert. As Michael Foley and Bob Edwards put it, "Talk about 'networks of civic engagement' glosses over the real, and often sharp, conflicts among groups in civil society. These conflicts, in the absence of *specifically political* settlements, may spill over into civil disruption and violence."[66]

Political parties, politicians, and state structures together must help to mediate these conflicting interests because civil society cannot do so alone. The quality of civil society is determined by the health of its relationship to domestic political institutions, because it is this relationship that bolsters democracy, not merely the existence of civic associations.[67] The development of social capital that accompanies the multiplication of collective movements and organizations that are not specifically political may help to bolster democracy, but it cannot replace the bonds between civil society and political institutions. Social capital can assist mediation but cannot trump it.

The importance of civil society to democracy is clear. As one among several critical institutional features of democracies, civil society promotes the socialization of democratic citizens, helps to bolster the skills necessary to participate actively in democracies, and builds networks of communication and trust that help to maintain connections between the political system and the average citizen. Most important from our perspective, civil society mediates the variegated interests of citizens through interactions with political parties. In this way, both civil society and parties are strengthened, and the efficacy of democracy is heightened. This vision of civil society and parties posits an idealized, stepwise path from individual interests in the citizenry; to collective interests analyzed and supported by civil society; to political parties, where these interests come into conflict with other interests and compromises are hammered out; and finally to government and legislative action, where compromise solutions are enacted. Thus civil society and political parties represent critical stages in the path from interest formation to government response. Without them, interests fall by the wayside, government becomes disconnected from citizens, and nondemocratic solutions become more attractive to disaffected denizens of democratic countries, threatening the stability of democracy.

CONCLUSION: FROM INSTITUTIONS TO SOCIETY

Thus far we have put forth our definition of democracy and explored the institutions that make this definition come alive. Executive-legislature and electoral systems determine how national elections translate societal interests into day-to-day politics. Political parties and civil society determine which interests have a chance to be represented at the national level and thus participate in democratic competition. All of these institutions together make democracy work. They are the stage and the players, the rules and the constraints.

Imagine a kickball field. It is well marcated, with fresh grass, clearly outlined dust bases, and brilliant white lines tracing the diamond. Now add two teams, organized, with distinctive jerseys. Assume the rules are known, fill the stadium with anxious parents, and sprinkle some referees and coaches around. Sounds good, but what actually happens when the whistle is blown to start play? Maybe the game starts as we hope and expect, or maybe the opposing sides and fans butcher each other, steal each other's resources, and head for the hills.

We don't know, because all that has been created so far is a set of instruments and regulations. Not all the circumstances in which the game is played (or violated) are known. Where are the players coming from? What do they think of the game? What are their interests in playing or abdicating?

This book has so far only set the stage for an intricate play; nothing has been said about what conditions actually make it likely that play ensues, that the players cooperate, that democracy happens. Nondemocratic societies often have many of the aforementioned institutions, such as political parties or legislatures. They don't work the same way as they do in democracies, but why not? What makes a society likely to employ democratic means of conflict resolution? What makes it likely to enjoy democratic stability? What are the socioeconomic and cultural preconditions that let the show go on?

In part II, we address these very issues. Neither economics, culture, nor institutional organization alone can explain democratization or democratic stability. Nevertheless, socioeconomic and cultural variables in tandem with institutional structures can increase the probability of democratic success, and social scientists now know something about how this works. In chapters 5 through 8 we summarize, analyze, and interpret this knowledge. We start with socioeconomic conditions, continuing an analysis that began around the time of Lipset's *Political Man*. We then move on to cultural variables, examining the kinds of issues that became important in Lipset's later work, particularly *First New Nation* and *American Exceptionalism*.

APPENDIX: DETERMINANTS OF TRUST

This appendix reproduces regression results from SPSS (Statistical Package for the Social Sciences) using U.S. Social Capital Community Benchmark Survey data. We attempted to measure generalized interpersonal trust in two ways. The social capital data include a variable called SOCTRUST that, for conceptual reasons, we have modified here. In the original data set, this variable is coded as a weighted mean of responses to six questions. Five of the questions ask how much trust one has in different groups: neighbors, coworkers, fellow congregants, local store employees, and police. The final question is the general one: Would you say that most people can be trusted or that you can't be too careful when dealing with others? From our perspective, bundling these questions together negates some important conceptual distinctions.

To begin with, the general question is distinct from the others in that it asks the respondent, not to think of any specific group of people, but rather to make a guess about people in general, which is primarily a group of people who are *unknown*. While one's answer to this question is undoubtedly related to one's experiences with known people, it is conceptually distinct enough to warrant separate analysis. We also believe that including the police in the average muddies the distinction between trust in other people and trust in institutions. Again, trust in police is related to the other questions but it is somewhat distinct because "the police" can mean either specific people or an institution. For many people who do not have contact with the police, this is undoubtedly a question about confidence in institutions. Since the distinction between trust in institutions and interpersonal trust is central to the debate over social capital, we want to maintain it.

In our own analysis, then, we measured trust using two different variable configurations. First, we measured trust as a mean of responses to four of the six questions, eliminating the question about trust in police and the general trust question. This variable we labeled "TRSTREG" and used as one measure of generalized trust in others. This allows us to measure one meaning of the word *general*, namely, "a sum of particulars." That is, with this measure, we consider a person to have general trust if she trusts many different groups of people. Such a person has a high level of general trust because she considers so many particular groups to be trustworthy.

Another way to measure general trust is to look only at the answer to the question about "most people." This question asks the respondent to directly assess his own level of general trust. Here *general* means "not particular" rather than "a sum of particulars." Respondents are saying, in some sense, whether they believe that any random individual is more likely to be trustworthy or untrustworthy. This question lends itself to a dichotomous yes—no scale. Respondents were asked whether most people could be trusted or not; if they responded "It depends," this was coded, but it was not offered to them as a choice.

The first variable (TRSTSCL), since it is a continuous scale, is suitable for multiple linear regression analysis. The second variable, coded as TRSTLOG in our data set, lends itself to logistic regression if we eliminate the small number of respondents who chose "It depends." Less than 7 percent of respondents chose this response. In our estimation, it is more appropriate to treat this as a dichotomous variable than as a continuous scale with "depends" as a middle category. We suspect that if the question had been asked differently, many more people might have chosen "It depends" or another middling category. It follows that the distribution of responses is skewed differently than it would be if the question had been asked in a different way. For example, if it had been phrased, "How much would you say other people can be trusted—not at all, a little, somewhat, a lot, or always?" the responses would probably follow more of a normal distribution. The way the question was asked and the distribution of responses seem to justify a logistic. For ease of interpretation and presentation, however, we have performed OLS regression on this indicator as well. This should not affect our coefficients, but it may bias our significance tests. To be certain, we ran these variables in a logistic regression, and the results were basically the same. We report our regressions (SPSS output) from these analyses in Tables 4.4 and 4.5. Interestingly, both regressions produce quite similar results.

The first model does better overall, having a much lower standard error of the estimate than the second model, but this is due to the binary response nature of the second model.

All variables have been scaled from 0 to 1 for ease of interpretation. The following variables have been included: age (AGEREG); income (INCREG2); gender dummy variable with male = 1 (male); married/nonmarried dummy variable with married = 1 (MARDUM); Asian dummy variable with Asian = 1 (asian); black dummy variable with black = 1 (non-hispanic black), Hispanic dummy with Hispanic = 1 (hispanic); education categories

TABLE 4.4
Regression: Trust Scale, TRSTSCL

A. MODEL SUMMARY

R	R-square	Adjusted R-square	Std. error of the estimate
0.576[a]	0.331	0.327	0.1777

[a]Predictors: (Consonant), CONFIDER, asian, MARDUM, male, TGOVNRE, TVHRSRE, AGEREG, non-hispanic black, GRPINVLR, HAPPYRE, hispanic, HEALTHRE, INCREG2, EDUCRE, TGOVLRE

B. ANOVA[a]

	Sum of squares	df	Mean square	F	Significan
Regression	38.452	15	2.563	81.159	0.000[b]
Residual	77.632	2458	3.159E-02		
Total	116.084	2473			

[a]Dependent Variable: TRSTSCL
[b]Predictors: (Constant), CONFIDER, asian, MARDUM, male, TGOVNRE, TVHRSRI AGEREG, non-hispanic black, GRPINVLR, HAPPYRE, hispanic, HEALTHRE, INCREG2, EDUCRE, TGOVLRE

C. COEFFICIENTS[a]

	Unstandardized coefficients		Standardized coefficients		
	B	Std. error	(Beta)	t	Significar
(Constant)	0.358	0.022		16.416	0.000
AGEREG	0.257	0.021	0.212	12.044	0.000
INCREG2	−4.20E-03	0.014	−0.006	−0.305	0.760
male	−2.00E-03	0.007	−0.046	−2.753	0.006
MARDUM	2.531E-02	0.008	0.057	3.282	0.001
asian	9.642E-03	0.025	0.007	0.386	0.699
non-hispanic black	−0.110	0.012	−0.161	−9.276	0.000
hispanic	−0.134	0.013	−0.184	−10.319	0.000
EDUCRE	5.603E-02	0.016	0.068	3.479	0.001
HAPPYRE	0.182	0.020	0.166	9.152	0.000
HEALTHRE	3.547E-02	0.015	0.043	2.350	0.019
TGOVLRE	0.216	0.023	0.186	9.456	0.000
TGOVNRE	7.069E-02	0.023	0.061	3.126	0.002
TVHRSRE	−4.91E-02	0.017	−0.052	−2.893	0.004
GRPINVLR	3.284E-02	0.026	0.023	1.254	0.210
CONFIDER	0.127	0.019	0.118	6.719	0.000

[a]Dependent variable: TRSTSCL

TABLE 4.5
Regression: Single Question, TRSTLOG

A. MODEL SUMMARY

R	R-square	Adjusted R-square	Std. error of the estimate
0.427[a]	0.182	0.177	0.4536

[a]Predictors: (Constant), CONFIDER, asian, MARDUM, male, TGOVNRE, TVHRSRE, AGEREG, non-hispanic black, GRPINVLR, HAPPYRE, hispanic, HEALTHRE, INCREG2, EDUCRE, TGOVLRE

B. ANOVA[a]

	Sum of squares	df	Mean square	F	Significance
Regression	104.894	15	6.993	33.987	0.000[b]
Residual	471.184	2290	0.206		
Total	576.078	2305			

[a]Dependent Variable: TRSTLOG
[b]Predictors: (Consonant), CONFIDER, asian, MARDUM, male, TGOVNRE, TVHRSRE, AGEREG, non-hispanic black, GRPINVLR, HAPPYRE, hispanic, HEALTHRE, INCREG2, EDUCRE, TGOVLRE

C. COEFFICIENTS[a]

	Unstandardized coefficients		Standardized coefficients		
	B	Std. error	(Beta)	t	Significance
(Constant)	−0.165	0.058		−2.864	0.004
AGEREG	0.122	0.057	0.044	2.166	0.030
INCREG2	2.795E-02	0.036	−0.017	−0.767	0.443
male	1.357E-03	0.019	−0.001	−0.071	0.944
MARDUM	1.227E-02	0.020	0.012	0.601	0.548
asian	−6.15E-03	0.064	−0.002	−0.097	0.923
non-hispanic black	−0.213	0.032	−0.134	−6.729	0.000
hispanic	−0.201	0.035	−0.119	−5.819	0.000
EDUCRE	0.238	0.043	0.125	5.545	0.000
HAPPYRE	0.299	0.053	0.118	5.678	0.000
HEALTHRE	0.134	0.040	0.070	3.330	0.001
TGOVLRE	0.365	0.061	0.136	5.943	0.000
TGOVNRE	0.192	0.062	0.070	3.119	0.002
TVHRSRE	−5.12E-02	0.046	−0.023	−1.118	0.264
GRPINVLR	0.167	0.069	0.050	2.424	0.015
CONFIDER	0.106	0.050	0.042	2.110	0.035

[a]Dependent variable: TRSTLOG

(EDUCRE); self-reported happiness (HAPPYRE); self-reported health (HEALTHRE); trust in local government (TGOVLRE); trust in national government (TGOVNRE); reported hours of TV watched per day (TVHRSRE); number of groups involved in (GRPINVLR); and number of persons confided in (CONFIDER).

PART II

MAKING DEMOCRACY HAPPEN (AND ENDURE)

CHAPTER 5

SOCIOECONOMICS

THAT ECONOMIC VARIABLES HAVE BEEN heavily investigated in the democracy literature, mostly because they lend themselves to better and easier quantitative testing, does not mean there is nothing left to learn about the political economy of democracy. Far from it. Still, as compared to other subfields of democratic studies, more can be said, and more concretely, about the economic correlates of democracy.

The most often investigated correlate of democracy, economic or otherwise, is the relationship between wealth (measured as gross domestic product [GDP] per capita) and survival of democracy. But there are other, less investigated areas of study, such as the association between income inequality and democracy and between free markets and democracy. In fact, all investigations of the relationship between economy and democracy are entangled, because the constellation of existing, consolidated democracies has made it difficult to distinguish the effects, say, of wealth from those of free-market systems, income distribution, or the extent of private property ownership. We should be wary about overgeneralizing from the existing cases. By exploring them in detail, however, we can perhaps observe processes that will give us clues about the relationship between economic and political variables.

The first point, and perhaps the only noncontroversial one, is the existence of a significantly positive correlation between democracy and GDP per capita.[1] The evidence of such a relationship has continued to mount since Lipset posited it over forty years ago in *Political Man*. Lipset's original cross-sectional work has been buttressed by increasingly sophisticated regression analyses of time series data. Today, a myriad of studies, all using different indicators and methodologies, point in the same direction: "the more well-to-do a nation, the greater the chances that it will sustain democracy."[2] Three of the most notable empirical studies of this relationship were published in 1996. Adam Przeworski summarized his own conclusions, similar to the others', with characteristic flair: "Above $6,000 [income per capita], democracies are impregnable and can expect to live forever."[3] This prognosis—a brasher but also better substantiated version of the conclusions Lipset originally reached in *Political Man*—is generally accepted.[4] As is shown below, this does not mean that there is anything like consensus on the underlying *theoretical* reasons for this empirical truth. As Harvard economist Robert Barro has written, "Given the strength of this empirical regularity, one would think that clear-cut theoretical analyses ought also to be attainable. (This seems to be a case where the analysis works in practice but not in theory)."[5]

Before examining the studies further, it may be helpful to trace the history of political scientists' thinking about the relationship between development and democracy. Modernization theory, which posited that economic and political development were inevitably linked and that economic development was destined to lead toward greater democratization around the world, was widely accepted in the 1950s and early 1960s. As noted, Lipset, among others, was associated with this work. Modernization theorists believed that changes in social structure—urbanization, increased education, diffusion of skills and wealth among a larger populace—led inevitably toward democratization as newly powerful social actors demanded representation in the political system.

In the 1970s, modernization theory came under heavy attack on both theoretical and empirical grounds. The notion associated with modernization theory that all countries would ultimately converge on a similar model of economy and polity came to be considered ethnocentric and unscientific. Dependency theorists began to argue that the world was divided into different classes of countries that filled different roles. The language of *core* and *periphery* was born. The new conventional wisdom was that less developed (or "dependent" or "periphery") countries would not follow the same path as wealthier countries (the "core"), in part because of their different cultures and in part because it was not in the financial interests of wealthy countries to allow poor countries to develop. Thus some found the predictions of modernization theory unlikely because of its Western capitalist bias, while others rejected the theory because, while it might be true that development led to democracy, the arrangement of the international system would prevent dependent countries from developing. In seeming synchronicity with these theoretical attacks, the fall of democracy in the relatively wealthy and industrialized states of the Southern Cone of South America seemed to disconfirm the predictions of modernization theory. These countries appeared to be getting wealthier and more authoritarian rather than converging on democratic regimes.

Perhaps the most vocal critic of modernization theory was Guillermo O'Donnell, whose exposition of bureaucratic authoritarianism became an instant classic in the 1970s. According to O'Donnell, who focused primarily on Argentina, authoritarianism was a logical outgrowth of the political economy of the import-substituting industrializers. The logic of his argument was that industrialization created a stronger and more mobilized working class whose demands for redistribution impeded further economic growth. Elites and the state pushed for greater economic integration with the world economy, greater labor flexibility, and a generally pro-business investment growth strategy, but newly mobilized labor movements got in the way. The overthrow of democratic regimes and the institution of bureaucratic authoritarianism was one way to demobilize labor and pursue the desired growth strategy. O'Donnell believed that, in the Southern Cone at least, this was a natural outgrowth of these countries having reached a middle range of economic development, having completed the "easy stage" of import substitution industrialization (ISI), so that they now needed to pursue new strategies. Thus the theory of bureaucratic authoritarianism seemed to suggest, for those who applied it to the world at large (O'Donnell was not among them), that as countries reached the middle income stage, there would be strong pressures toward authoritarianism.

Since the 1980s, the modernization perspective has enjoyed a resurgence. Bureaucratic authoritarian regimes have fallen, often in the midst of economic crisis. Middle-income countries, while often unstable, do not necessarily become authoritarian as a natural stage that must be passed through. The more and faster all countries at all levels grow economically, it appears, the more likely they will sustain democracy. The lessons culled from empirical studies of the past half century, capped by the 1996 studies discussed here, are unambiguous: economic development is associated with political democracy all the way up the income scale. The new modernization theory is somewhat less prone to accusations of ethnocentricity than the old, arguing for a more limited kind of convergence among countries and acknowledging the great institutional variety among capitalist democracies. However, many modernization theorists, including Lipset, have always recognized that convergence was a relative term; countries that appear to converge maintain distinctive cultures and social orders. Insofar as the convergence toward democracy is real, however, modernization theory has generally been validated.

Not everyone sees it this way. Rational choice theorists like Przeworski, while acknowledging that democracy and development are clearly related, see democracy in economistic terms.

Przeworski believes not that development leads teleologically toward democracy but only that once a democracy is established in a wealthy country, for any number of capricious political or institutional reasons, rational actors come to see this as a beneficial equilibrium state and defend it. This thinking departs from modernization theory's teleological or organic assumptions about changes in social structure that lead inevitably towards democratization.

Below we take a closer look at the recent studies that ostensibly validate the resurgence of the modernization perspective.

METHODOLOGICAL CRITIQUES OF THE 1996 STUDIES

In this section we discuss some limitations of the 1996 studies confirming the relationship between democracy and economic development. Those readers who lack a basic background in statistics may wish to skip to the next section.

Using multiple regression analysis to assess a large number of variables, Barro's 1996 study found that standard of living and level of economic development have statistically significant and positive effects on the *level of democracy*, using the Gastil (now Freedom House) freedom index. (According to this index, democracy levels, or the quality of democracy, increase when conditions associated with free and fair elections and an unrepressed civil society improve.) Specifically, Barro's model demonstrated that the following variables are favorably associated with observed levels of democracy: prior democracy, GDP, life expectancy, and female primary schooling. A dummy variable inserted for oil-producing countries was significantly negatively correlated. Not surprisingly, the most important predictor of democracy was prior democracy, much as yesterday's weather is the best predictor of today's. The full model predicted about two-thirds of the observed variations in democracy levels. The coefficient for log GDP was small, but positive and significant: 0.045 (0.017).[6]

Barro's evidence is encouraging but not conclusive. He looks at the relationship between democracy and economic development in three periods of unequal length (1965–75, 1975–85, 1985–90). The study uses varying (though highly correlated) democracy variables for the different periods because of information gaps.[7] The sample size is never more than 105 countries. Barro purports to measure democracy and economic development over ten-year periods using independent variables that have been lagged by five years or averaged. The method is reasonable enough, if rather arbitrary, but tells us very little about causation.[8] On one hand, a five-year average is essentially a single observation at an unreal point in time. On the other hand, a single observation five years prior, while a "true" observation, fails to indicate whether the variable is improving or deteriorating. In fact, insofar as two nations with the same average score over five years, or the same single lagged data point, could diverge—one improving while the other deteriorates—this method of measuring the independent variables is not particularly informative.[9]

The study of democracy is young, and the data available to carry out such research are limited. Fifty years from now scholars will likely have much more useful and significant samples to work with. Studies using current data should be accepted, but with qualified and healthy skepticism. Barro's study is comprehensive in its inclusion of a myriad of independent variables. It puts the available data to good use, but many unanswered questions remain. Specifically, we want to know what direct effects particular changes in the standard of living have on democracy levels, which involves annual tracking of the variables with (somewhat inevitably) arbitrary lag effects. Neither averages nor single-observation lags can conjure this kind of specificity. Without such specificity, it will be difficult to close the gap, identified by Barro, between theory and practice.

Fortunately, Barro's findings are supported by the other major 1996 study of levels of democracy, authored by John Londregan and Keith Poole. They use data running from 1952 to 1985 and employ the Gurr democracy index. Constructing a somewhat more complex, probit model, Londregan and Poole find that income has a small but positive and significant effect on *level of democracy*—essentially the same result as Barro. Their estimated coefficient is 0.119 (0.032).[10] However, the effect is even smaller when Europe is excluded.[11] Interestingly, neither the present nor the lagged growth rate has a statistically significant effect on democracy.[12] The Londregan and Poole study is important because it uses annual observations, rather than averages or single point lags, while injecting a one-year lagged GDP variable into the model. Further bolstering its specificity, the Londregan and Poole model uses country-specific fixed effects.

Of course, one may question the wisdom of using a lagged GDP variable of only one year to demonstrate a relationship between income and democracy. While the variable turns out to be significant and positive—adding to our understanding of democracy in practice—it does not contribute substantially to a theory of democratization. Any theory along the lines of modernization that posits gradual, long-term changes in democracy as a result of development needs a longer time frame than one year. The authors do concede that the changes in "democraticness" after one year of increased income, as identified by this study, are incremental and would be expected to accumulate only over longer periods of time. "Those expecting income growth to promote the development of democratic political institutions," they note, "must be very patient indeed."[13] In other words, this study, like Barro's, suggests that democracy stands to gain from higher income but provides inconclusive theoretical analysis to explain why. The study fails to reveal whether long-term income effects are hidden within the "prior democracy" variable. Systematic research of GDP per capita at a wide range of lag times to see which turn out to be more significant should help clarify the theoretical point.[14]

In their own probit model, Przeworski, Alvarez, Cheibub, and Limongi deliver substantially the same message, using a dichotomous variable and annual observations over an even longer period, 1950–1990. Their study, however, measures the *longevity of democracy* rather than its level. They explore regime survival rates at differing levels of income and find a rapidly rising life expectancy for democracy as per-capita income rises. Democracy survives on average 8.5 years for countries with less than $1,000 per-capita income; it extends to 100 years between $4,000 and $6,000. This important finding indicates that high income is correlated with the persistence of democracy, as distinct from the transition to democracy or the level of democracy.[15] At a minimum, this suggests that wealthy societies have access to resources that help to promote and stabilize democracy—*once democracies are established*—that poorer countries do not have. Because this study uses a dichotomous variable, however, it does not tell us much about the process of democratization (or its authoritarian counterpart) in countries that do not make the transition. Nor does it reveal what happens to democracy levels during the 8.5 or 100 years that democracies "live" in the Przeworski et al. model. Because there is no graded scale, there is no evidence of subtler changes in regime types.[16]

A final limitation of all these studies, from our perspective, is that none of their data sets goes beyond 1990. This is unfortunate, particularly because many changes have taken place since 1990, including the "second wave of independence" in Africa and the greatly increased number of poor democracies.[17] While these developments do not negate the findings of the studies reviewed here, they at least raise the possibility that the world has entered a new historical period in which the correlation may have weakened.[18] Of course, it is also possible that many of these poor democracies will not survive for long. A look at Table 5.1 suggests that a substantial increase in the number of poor democracies has brought poor countries much closer to the average

TABLE 5.1

Poor Democracies, 1990 and 2001

1990[†]	2001[*]
Comoros	Armenia
Gambia	Bangladesh
Honduras	Benin
India	Central African Republic
Pakistan	Georgia
Solomon Islands	Ghana
Sri Lanka	Guinea-Bissau
	Haiti
	India
	Indonesia
	Liberia
	Madagascar
	Malawi
	Mali
	Moldova
	Mongolia
	Mozambique
	Nepal
	Nicaragua
	Niger
	Nigeria
	Sao Tome & Principe
	Senegal
	Sierra Leone
	Solomon Islands
	Ukraine
Total: 7	26
Total poor: 49	64
Percent: 14%	41%

Sources: World Bank, *World Development Report 1992* (New York: Oxford University Press, 1992), and *World Development Report 2000–2001* (New York: Oxford University Press, 2000); Freedom House, *Freedom in the World* (Piscataway, NJ: Transaction, 1991, 1992, and 2001; Aili Piano and Arch Puddington, "Gains Offset Losses," *Journal of Democracy* 12 (January 2001): 90–91.

[†]Per-capita GDP under $755

[*]Poor defined as per-capita GDP under $610

democraticness of the world. Nevertheless, while 60 percent of the world's countries are democratic, only 40 percent of poor countries can claim that mantle. This is up from the figures a decade ago—about 45 percent of all countries versus 14 percent of poor countries. This represents almost a doubling of the ratio of poor democracies to all democracies, from about 1:3 to 2:3, over ten years.[19] Thus the correlation still holds, but there does seem to be considerable convergence.

ECONOMICS CONTINUED: BEYOND METHODOLOGY

While each of the 1996 studies suffers from weaknesses, taken together, they provide substantial evidence for the original Lipset hypothesis: "The more well-to-do a nation, the greater the chances that it will sustain democracy."[20] There is evidence that income lagged by a single year and income lagged by five years both positively affect democracy levels and that increasingly richer societies have progressively longer democratic lives. While none of these studies demonstrates a relationship between affluence and the likelihood of a transition to democracy, there is clearly a better chance of having both a more, and more consistently, democratic polity at high income levels. However, both Barro's study and Londregan and Poole's do *suggest* that transitions to democracy are more likely at higher levels. They do not look at anything called a "transition," but rather use continuous scales that show a positive relationship between an indicator of democracy and one for income. In other words, putting aside what we call the regime, countries are more likely to be democratic at higher incomes.

Furthermore, this relationship holds within what Samuel Huntington has called "civilizations." Huntington groups societies into roughly six civilizations: Western, Latin American, Slavic-Orthodox, Islamic, Confucian, and African. Henry Rowen finds a significant correlation between income and democracy within five of the six civilizations—with Islam being the sole outlier.[21] As Rowen notes, "The finding that income and democracy are correlated, with varying degrees of significance within every civilization but one, should help put to rest the notion that Western democracy is culture bound."[22] We will return later to the reasons why the relationship between Islam and democracy raises problems. The record does suggest that, of the two broad factors—economy and culture—economy, and specifically GDP per capita, is the more important variable. (It should be noted, however, that many scholars, from Max Weber to David Landes, have sought to explain economic development itself as a product of cultural legacies).

The underlying reasons for the correlation between income and democracy are still unclear. The available evidence supports some version of modernization theory—that wealthier countries develop psychologies, skills, a class stratification, or technologies that are conducive to democracy—but is inconclusive.[23] One challenge to this modernization approach is Przeworski and Fernando Limongi's finding that, above about $6,000 in per-capita income, the probability of an authoritarian regime becoming democratic begins to fall. This is not what one would expect if modernization theory is correct, because changes in the social structure conducive to democracy should intensify at high income levels, making a democratic transition ever more likely as countries climb the income ladder.[24] However, Przeworski and Limongi's findings are based on only a very few cases—authoritarian regimes in their data set spent sixty-two years above $6,000, while democratic regimes spent 740.[25] While these findings do not represent a serious threat to modernization theory, they do suggest the need for a more fine-tuned theory of why development should lead to democracy. By remaining confined to a purely mathematical explanation for the relationship between democracy and development, we are hard put to explain why, in spite of the robustness of that relationship, there is not, in Przeworski and Limongi's words, "some level of income at which one can be relatively sure that the country will throw off the dictatorship."[26] To clarify the reasons why development and democracy correlate, we look more closely at the relationship between capitalism and democracy, as well as the theory of modernization, below.

Economic development supports democracy in at least two ways. First, it contributes to increases in wealth, standard of living, and education, which in turn bolster democracy, as the data demonstrate. Second, it helps to legitimate new democracies, which generally have a weak title to rule at the outset. Material prosperity is the one thing that almost everyone expects and hopes for, and thus a system and governments that oversee higher levels of consumption will tend to receive greater support. However, it appears that democracy cannot be explained simply by growth (the evidence is inconclusive) but is strongly associated with absolute levels of development. What is it about affluence per se that makes democracy work more smoothly? And which, if any, of the factors associated with development can be fostered even in lieu of growth? Do all forms of prosperity help democracy equally well?

According to Przeworski's model, reflecting his rational choice perspective,[27] democracy represents an optimal equilibrium for affluent societies. In this characterization, it should not make much difference how the society became wealthy, how wealth is distributed, or what the productive base is for the society's economic growth.[28] Indeed, most cross-national studies find that there is an empirically strong relationship between GDP per capita and democracy regardless of any other economic variables, such as distribution or form of production.

There are two important exceptions to this generalization, however. First, although the oil-producing countries, particularly those of the Middle East, are relatively wealthy, they are almost all nondemocratic.[29] Second, although the effect of wealth on democracy holds up across world regions, it is strongest in Western Europe, which, along with the United States, can be considered the cradle of modern democracy.[30] This suggests that if we look closely at the economically developed Western polities, we might find something specific to them beyond simply GDP per capita that helps to explain the correlation.

What can we hypothesize about these two caveats? In the case of the oil-producing countries, it is reasonable to presume that single-commodity economies are not diverse enough to create distinct centers of power. Because power and wealth are concentrated in a single locus, often a monarchical state, there are few opportunities for an opposition to flourish. In a stratified system without an independent middle class, one would expect a limited base for political parties or civil society, both of which, as has been discussed, are themselves important correlates of democracy. In Barro's terms, "the income generated from natural resources such as oil may create less pressure for democratization than income associated with the accumulation of human and physical capital."[31] We argue, therefore, that one by-product of affluence, or more particularly, of economic development, is the creation of a more heterogeneous economy with decentralized pockets of wealth that can shift over time. A diverse, prosperous economy translates into a wide array of opportunities for an opposition to form and garner funding, independent of state patronage, and also provides nonpolitical foundations of security to the ruling elite and its followers.

What about Europe? Why are the effects of wealth on democracy stronger there than elsewhere? One could make a cultural argument about the democratic proclivities of Northern Europeans and North Americans (an argument that could be reversed for Islamic nations). Undoubtedly, culture has played a role, if for no other reason than the impact of geographical proximity on diffusion within Europe versus that from Europe to the rest of the world. We return to culture in chapter 7. From a superficial economic perspective, the most obvious tie that binds Europe and distinguishes it from much of the rest of the world is a long history of postfeudal capitalism.[32] We say "superficial" not because European countries are not capitalist but because they are so varied in their forms of capitalism.[33] Lumping Britain and Denmark together—countries that have very different degrees of state intervention in the economy—suggests that the meaning of *capitalism* is highly flexible, and indeed it is. But concepts that are loosely constructed often prove meaningless when subjected to analysis, so the superficial claim that capitalism and democracy are associated in Europe cannot be accepted without more careful investigation. This we do below. But first, a word about why we are bothering.

It seems likely that capitalism plays a role akin to that of single-commodity state-driven development, but in the opposite direction. That is, if and when capitalism produces decentralized bases of economic wealth and political power, it is a boon to democracy, for exactly the same reasons that single-commodity production is an obstacle. Diffusion of wealth engenders widespread human capital accumulation and creates a base for opposition organizations and for an active civil society. We want to be clear that we are not trying to prove an ideological tenet, but rather to find structural reasons why the putatively positive relationship between capitalism and democracy, at least in Europe, has existed to the present. A positive relationship between capitalism and democracy does not amount to a defense of existing capitalism in developing countries, because capitalism in developing countries may or may not be similar in its design and structures to that which blossomed in Europe. It is for this reason that we must define abstract terms such as *capitalism* and *democracy* specifically, rather than relying on their stylized versions. We have to identify structural relationships and then see whether these do apply in particular developing countries.

Below, we address the relationships of capitalism, free markets, income inequality, and economic reform to democracy. Since these themes are all interconnected, they are treated in tandem, though we also attempt to tease out some of their independent effects.

ECONOMICS CONTINUED: DEMOCRACY AND CAPITALISM

There is a long tradition of theorizing about the relationship between democracy and capitalism. One strand of thought is that advocated by classical liberals. For them, democracy and capitalism represent natural partner systems, since both seek to limit the power of the state and increase the power of individuals. Liberals did not believe, as some would argue today, that the coincidence between democracy and capitalism is inevitable, but rather that capitalism has been a necessary but insufficient condition for democracy. Economists like Milton Friedman and Friedrich Hayek have argued that the only way to protect individual freedom is to charter a weak state. Socialism, or any form of central planning, is therefore anathema to democracy because it gives the state enormous power and threatens the potential for independent thought or an independent opposition. [34]

Extrapolating from the position of classical liberals, some believe that democracy has been a by-product of middle-class liberalism. Although middle-class liberals played an important role at different times in the struggle for democracy—as in the late-eighteenth- and nineteenth-century revolutions (the American, the French, and those of 1848)—this view is seriously misleading if it ignores events of the twentieth century. Particularly in the interwar period, the bourgeois elements in much of Europe rejected democracy as counter to their interests. How, despite the contradictory postures the bourgeoisie took toward democracy at different points in European history, did democracy triumph there?

Some scholars have argued that the cause of democracy was propelled much more consistently by the working class than by bourgeois liberals. [35] Historical processes—particularly capitalist processes—that weakened the landed classes and strengthened the working class, as well as the bourgeoisie, were important to democratization in Europe. In the estimation of Evelyne Huber, Dietrich Rueschemeyer, and John Stephens, capitalist development "weakens the power of the landlord class and strengthens subordinate classes . . . [which] gain an unprecedented capacity for self-organization due to such developments as urbanization, factory production and new forms of communication and transportation."[36] This means that democracy was in some sense a by-product of capitalist development, which strengthened subordinate classes who were pro-democratic; only at a more advanced stage of both capitalism and democracy did the seemingly obvious, liberal theoretic basis for both come to be generally accepted. In other words, liberalism was strengthened by capitalist development; the success of this economic development ultimately encouraged a liberal impulse in politics.

This view is also misleading.[37] As we know from Robert Dahl's 1972 work, a historical process (though a rough and nonlinear one, with some reversals) of continuing contestation and expanding participation took place in most parts of the West. Political contestation first meant political conflict among the male elite propertied classes, then included the middle classes, then the working classes, and ultimately, women and minorities. In other words, a bourgeois liberal basis for political rights and competing parties predated the evolution of modern inclusive democracy and served the interests of the urban business class (personal and economic freedom and control), even if it often denied political rights to the working class and peasantry, which were more numerous. Liberal individualism informed both democracy and capitalism, but it was a circumscribed liberalism that applied only to certain groups in society. Nevertheless, in parts of Europe, a cultural acceptance of contestation (a degree of liberalism in politics) did predate universal adult suffrage.[38] If the liberal business strata were not always democratic in the modern sense, they were still possessed of protodemocratic impulses.[39]

Furthermore, bourgeois and middle-class sectors often were democratic in the modern sense, or at least believed that democracy could serve their own strategic interests. Strong bourgeois liberal parties played a critical role by incorporating labor movements into pluralist democratic contestation. As Gregory Luebbert has argued, strong liberal parties in some parts of Europe—notably England, France, and Switzerland—brought labor into democratic systems gradually, which was a boon to the survival of democracy, particularly in the interwar period. Liberals, and in some cases conservatives too, often mobilized worker or peasant support because they needed it in their non-class-related battles over issues such as religion. This pattern, which Ruth Collier has called "competitive support mobilization," applies to countries with long histories of democracy such as Chile and the Netherlands. It was precisely the weakness of bourgeois liberals in Germany, Italy, and Spain that helps to explain, in part, their capitulation to fascism.[40]

Barrington Moore has also pointed out that bourgeois revolutions, whether carried out primarily by democrats or not, played a vital role in weakening two of the most anti-democratic groups in traditional society: the nobility and the peasantry. In Moore's estimation, at the twilight of the feudal period, the only class whose interests were compatible with democracy was the modernizing bourgeoisie; the transformation, marginalization, or elimination of the classes that defined feudal traditionalism—lords and peasants—was essential to the eventual triumph of parliamentary democracy. Writing of England, Moore notes:

> The other main consequence [of productive capitalists robbing peasants of their lands] was the destruction of the peasantry. Brutal and heartless though the conclusion appears, there are strong grounds for holding that this contribution to peaceful democratic change may have been just as important as the strengthening of Parliament. It meant that modernization could proceed in England without the huge reservoir of conservative and reactionary

forces that existed at certain points in Germany and Japan, not to mention India. And it also of course meant that the possibility of peasant revolutions in the Russian and Chinese manner were taken off the historical agenda.[41]

The working classes were weak and numerically insignificant during the initial push for parliamentary democracy, from which they were generally excluded. In this first phase of the ongoing democratic revolution, the bourgeoisie fought to weaken the state and the state-sanctioned privileges of feudal lords, as well as to capture as much peasant land as it could. This set the stage for capitalist modernization and industrialization, which ultimately did create a working class that played an important role in the democratic revolution.

While the role of the working classes was vital in the final push for democracy, it is important not to romanticize them. Laborers were by no means always supportive of democracy. Democracy was often a compromise between the inclinations of the left and the right, of workers and the bourgeoisie.[42] Certainly the case of the Spanish Republic, described in great detail by Juan Linz, should dispel any notions that the working class was consistently pro-democratic. As Linz puts it, "Maximalist and Communist allies . . . were more concerned with achieving their demands than with the stability of the regime." The radicalism of the left in Spain was a major contributing factor to the democratic crisis there in the 1930s.[43] As Lipset has detailed, a strong authoritarian tendency within the working class has manifested itself in worker support for the Communists in Italy, Germany, and Spain, as well as for the populist authoritarianism of Juan Perón and Getúlio Vargas in Latin America.[44] Abundant survey data show a negative correlation between education and authoritarian attitudes, suggesting that working-class citizens are among the least supportive of democracy. In many countries, particularly those of Latin Europe and Latin America, the working class was dominated by anarchosyndicalists who rejected "bourgeois" democracy and colluded with nondemo-cratic allies.

Still, prior to the emergence of the Communists (ca. 1918), con-sistent advocates for democracy were often to be found among parties and unions supported by the working class, and capital-ism helped them in their organizational tasks. As Karl Marx noted, capitalist development led to the development of urban factories where organizing workers was facilitated and to enhanced intraclass communication that made it easier to circulate infor-mation among activists and their followers. Over time, growth in productivity led to increases in wages, which in turn led to greater independence for workers and enabled them to become involved in trade union activities and thus secure higher incomes and better working conditions. Strong worker organizations sub-sequently helped or led the final push for democracy in much of Europe.[45]

This analysis emphasizes continuous struggle amongst differ-ent groups eager for a share of power, rather than ascribing the leading role in democratization to any single class or class coali-tion. Nor have social classes been the only relevant actors. In her critique of Barrington Moore, Theda Skocpol has argued against a reductionist class analysis and for an autonomous state role.[46] According to Skocpol, although international capitalist develop-ment did lead toward a shift in the power of strategic actors, these were not exclusively class actors. An important type of strategic actor in her analysis is the state bureaucracy, whose interests are determined not only by its members' socioeconomic position in society but also largely by their desire to maintain their power within a robustly endowed state structure:

> Bureaucrats' positions in political and social life motivated them, especially in times of political crises, to call for such radi-cal reforms as equalization of mobility opportunities, political democracy, and (before the revolution at least) extension of civil liberties. Yet the primary orientation of these marginal elites was

toward a broad goal that they shared with all those, including traditionally prestigious bureaucrats, whose careers, livelihoods, and state identities were intertwined with state activities: extension and rationalization of state powers in the name of national welfare and prestige.[47]

J. Samuel Valenzuela has taken Skocpol's critique a step further, arguing that capitalist economic development empowers many groups in civil society, not simply the bourgeoisie or workers nor simply the state. It even empowers groups we might not expect to support democracy unless we examine their particular circumstances. Valenzuela finds that in Chile the main axis of competition leading to democratization was between religious and secular elements. Surprisingly, it was the Catholics, represented by the Conservative party, who made the biggest push for democracy in the nineteenth century. Why? Quite simply, because it was in their interests to break the stranglehold on power of the secular elements and because they had an ideological interest in mildly progressive social policies.[48] Thus the Conservatives pushed for more democracy to help them win more power.

Capitalist development helps to diffuse power and wealth throughout society. This is a structural phenomenon. It is not that landholders or secular business leaders decide to give up income or power willfully but rather that their power is weakened by the threat of, or actual, conflict. In many cases, the working-class achieves improvements in its wages through the heightened demand for its skills, but gains also reflect workers' increased ability to organize and fight for improved wages and benefits. There is nothing "natural" about these processes, but the growth of capitalism did affect the probability that landholders would be weakened, that the middle and working classes would become more assertive, and that nonincumbent groups, whether defined in terms of class or religion, would form liberalizing coalitions, thus fostering democracy. By diffusing physical and human capital throughout society and away from a single bastion, capitalism enhanced the organizational strength of actors—such as the state or religious groups, in addition to the more typical, class-based actors—in such a way as to increase the competition among them for power. While none of these groups—neither the bourgeoisie nor the working class, Catholics nor secularists, the state nor civil society—could always be counted on to support liberal politics, the structural impact of capitalism on the balance of power in society was a boon to democracy because democracy was one, increasingly preferable way to defuse the tensions inherent in the conflict among these groups. [49]

INCOME EQUALITY AND POVERTY

Another tradition, already alluded to, within liberal thought emphasizes not only the weakening of state control of the economy but also the prevalence of individuals who are financially independent and can espouse whatever views attract them. This logic is an extension of the "relative balance of power among competing groups" theory just described. Taking no position about the relative equality within society as a whole, that theory argues rather that strong competing groups determine political outcomes. Opposition groups tend to be strengthened by capitalist development insofar as it disperses resources more widely. However, this in no way precludes the coexistence, alongside these strong groups, of, for example, a very large and poor underclass.

Nevertheless, some thinkers have indeed argued that widespread destitution—or rather, the lack of a fairly self-sufficient, reasonably independent laboring or middle class—undercuts democracy. Thus Thomas Jefferson's affinity for the yeoman farmer—self-employed, robust, independent minded, all characteristics that were shared with artisans and self-employed businesspeople. According to this logic, an additional affinity between capitalism and democracy is rooted in the degree to which the majority of citizens have access to resources—access that was broadened as societies moved toward capitalist production, forming what might be called a "democratic stratum." Thus, while large competing groups—say, labor and bourgeoisie—may decide to foster democratic institutions to manage their conflicts, it is important that the wider society have the independence and resources to support a democratic transition and to participate in and defend the democratic system once in place. The "democratic stratum" both has a direct interest in representative institutions and tends to support democratic values. It forms the base for active civil society and political parties. It generally supports gradual reform and shies away from revolutionary rhetoric and actions. At the same time, it does not necessarily constitute a competing group or power bloc in the same way "the bourgeoisie," "labor" or even "the state" does. The "democratic stratum" does not necessarily lead the struggle for democracy, but it nevertheless weighs in and supports it.

The fruits of capitalist development—greater equality of wealth and a stronger middle class—appear to have been important facilitating conditions for democracy. Such was the case in the United States, which, even in its "protocapitalist" phase, did boast an expansive class of self-employed farmers and small entrepreneurs and very few landless peasants—a mix that Barrington Moore has emphasized as a tremendous asset. The survival of a huge deferential and exploited peasant mass is, he argued, a significant obstacle for democracy and a "reservoir for a peasant revolution leading to a communist dictatorship," as in Russia and China. [50] In the United States, most of those employed in agriculture, outside the South, owned or leased the land they worked. [51] Even Marx and Engels recognized that the unique pattern of individual, small landholding in the United States would stimulate egalitarian and potentially democratic values. [52] This was also true of other frontier societies like Canada and New Zealand, both of which became stable democracies. [53]

The argument here is that insofar as capitalist development leads to wider distributions of wealth, it generally benefits democracy by strengthening sources of political opposition with an interest in propagating democracy. The level of resource equality is a distinct attribute of a society that may or may not be associated with capitalism per se. If, however, capitalism leads under certain conditions to increased inequality and greater concentration of wealth in the hands of a few firms or individuals, then the liberal argument in favor of relative equality would work against free-market capitalism and in favor of redistributive measures. The importance of dispersion of wealth as a positive factor for democracy argues not only against state control of the economy but also against any concentration of power, including consolidated power in large corporations. Argentine-born sociologist Carlos Waisman has argued with respect to South America that overly concentrated private ownership has made democracy impossible there. [54] The state has been too weak (i.e., too lacking in autonomy) in relation to private landowners to permit true democracy. He concludes that the system of noncompetitive, highly controlled private ownership of the means of production has worked against democratization in South America; a strong, relatively unregulated but competitive market economy is essential. Private control of productive capacity without market competition leads to ineffective government, dominated by rent-seeking coalitions. [55] This empowerment of rent seekers damages the wider polity by consolidating power in inefficient industrial and labor groups and also reducing the pool of effective leaders with independent power bases.

Of course, advocates of liberal capitalism could argue that the problem Waisman identifies stems not from the free market but from the fact that the market is not truly free. In other words, liberal capitalists argue, the problem is not too much freedom but that political, corporate, or union forces have been allowed to co-opt the market. What is needed is not more regulation but more freedom. This brings us to the important distinction between capitalism and free markets. Lack of competition coupled with private ownership does not breed felicitous conditions for democracy. The ideal free market is also a competitive market, but this is not always the reality. Liberal capitalists may indeed be correct in their assessment, but in order to rectify the problem, the state may have to play a role in redistributing wealth and reconstituting a market. The central point remains: the importance of dispersed wealth argues against socialism, which consolidates power and wealth in the state, but does not necessarily argue for free-market capitalism. What matters is the dispersion of wealth and power on a continuous basis.

Let us here also distinguish between inequality generally and the existence of a financially independent "democratic stratum." Greater income equality does not really refer to the same thing as a strong, independent (middle) class. The important requirement for the Jeffersonians was a strong class of people who had enough resources to make themselves financially independent. If such a class exists, then the accumulation of more wealth at the top of society (an increase in inequality) does not necessarily have an adverse impact on democracy. Presumably, there is some minimum level of welfare that must be achieved by a broad swath of the population in order for many citizens to have access to political resources. In this sense, what is important is a relatively high minimum income.

There are, however, reasons to be skeptical about high minimum incomes obviating the issue of income inequality.[56] If any relationship between income and access to political resources exists, it may be that income inequality severely distorts such access. This does not necessarily mean that income inequality is anti-democratic. If there were no relationship between access to political resources and income, then income inequality would be irrelevant to democracy per se.[57] Since the degree to which income does enhance access to political resources varies from country to country, the importance of income inequality also presumably differs.[58]

Another aspect of the relationship between democracy and capitalism that Lipset has previously emphasized is the importance of a thriving private sector to prevent state power from becoming overly attractive.[59] In order for elected officials to be willing to turn the reins of power over to others when they lose elections, there must be an alternative source of high income or high status that can ease the transition from public life. This may be the private sector or an array of other public positions. Where the income gap between public sector service and private sector opportunities is very large, rational persons will be reluctant to abnegate power (the opportunity costs of freely giving up power are too high). Under these conditions, democracy becomes less likely. This thesis is often used to explain why poor countries are less successful as democracies: their private sectors are weak, and the state is the primary, almost sole, source of power and prestige. Although public sector jobs in wealthy countries could in theory pay high incomes and attract electorally unsuccessful incumbents, in most cases such jobs represent a major decline in status and income in relation to the opportunities available in the private sector. In the United States, a high-level public official can probably earn enough in the private sector after leaving government to at least partly compensate for a decline in prestige and political power. The predominant background of American elected officials has been the legal profession, and lawyers can gain considerable bargaining power when they return to the private sector. Even many nonlawyers are able to become highly paid lobbyists.

Ultimately, then, the strongest case for a positive relationship between capitalism and democracy is the effect that capitalism has on the relative power of strategic actors in society. Capitalism is good for democracy because it weakens the state, undermines its ability to politically or economically coerce citizens, circumscribes the potential of incumbents to hold onto power indefinitely, limits the attractiveness of state control as an object for capture by the ambitious, and offers jobs and incomes to those who lose public office. This is consistent with the capitalism's historical ability to weaken the traditional landlord stratum and to strengthen labor groups and the middle classes. Capitalist development weakens aristocracy-state alliances and enlarges and strengthens the bourgeoisie while facilitating organization among the working class, enabling workers to better unite for their interests (in large factories and urban industrial centers, for instance).[60] From both a theoretical and historical perspective, if with different emphases, there is agreement that capitalism alters the balance of power among strategic actors in society, increasing competition among them, and has therefore been conducive to democracy. This view is also compatible with a continuous measurement of capitalism, which stresses the degree of power that the state—a relevant strategic actor—controls relative to that held by the landed classes, the bourgeoisie, the working classes, or other groups, such as religious minorities. We thus avoid the false dichotomy between capitalist and noncapitalist (socialist) economies.

Finally, this view is compatible with the traditional emphasis in the literature on the middle class. A large middle class, as Aristotle argued, is a bulwark to democracy. The middle class has not always been a champion for democracy, but it has represented a stabilizing force within existing democracies. As argued above, the middle class(es) constitute a large body of citizens with economic and political skills and resources that can independently act as a check on the power of the state.

The available evidence on the relationship between economic development and democracy supports an expanded version of modernization theory. Increases in wealth lead to increases in both level and stability of democracy. The primary explanation for this is that economic development leads to the weakening of state-aristocracy alliances and to the empowering of the middle and working classes and other subordinate actors. Competition between powerful actors over political and economic goods tends to lead to democratic compromise because no class is strong enough on its own to destroy the others or to hold on to power through repression. Such compromise alone need not guarantee a democratic outcome, though it favors one. But the organization and empowerment of subordinate classes is facilitated by increases in urbanization and education, which lead, as Francis Fukuyama has argued, to a greater desire and capacity for political participation.[61] Thus, as Lipset originally argued in *Political Man*, economic development leads to psychological orientations that are more conducive to democracy, but this process is also heavily influenced by the economic power of strategic actors.[62]

The argument presented here is difficult to measure with quantitative data, but several studies have attempted to demonstrate its validity. Kenneth Bollen (1979) found that the greater the state control of the economy, the less likely a country was to be democratic.[63] Rueschemeyer, Stephens, and Stephens (1992) have extended their work on Europe to Latin America and the Caribbean and found similar relationships between capitalist development and democracy. Tatu Vanhanen (1997) has conducted a breathtaking study of democracy utilizing an Index of Power Resources (IPR). This index measures the concept described here as the balance of power among strategic actors. According to Vanhanen, where power is more widely dispersed among social actors, democracy is a more likely outcome. He argues from regression analysis on 172 countries from the nineteenth century to the present that his IPR is a better predictor of democracy than GDP per capita alone.[64] Another, more parsimonious attempt to measure the diffusion of power in society, or the relative well-being of society beyond simply GDP per capita, was conducted by Larry Diamond. Diamond uses the Physical Quality of Life Index (PQLI)—a measure of literacy, infant mortality, and life expectancy—in regressions with level of democracy for the 1960s to 1980s. He finds that this index is significantly related to democracy, much more strongly than with GNP per capita.[65] This suggests that high minimum incomes and diffuse well-being generated by modernization are positively associated with democracy. Other findings have also suggested that income inequality decreases the potential for democracy, but they are inconsistent and make use of limited data. [66]

In conclusion, we have tried to specify a structural relationship—a shift in the social balance of power—that underlies the abstraction of *capitalism*. One cannot be certain that all capitalist systems inevitably lead to this structural relationship. If, under certain circumstances, capitalism does not lead to the expected shifts in strategic-actor balance of power, then the relationship may not hold. Within the broad category of capitalism, then, we suspect that any type of capitalism that produces a shift in class balance of power as we have described it is conducive to democracy.

INTERLUDE: IS INCOME JUST A PROXY FOR EDUCATION?

One of the underlying reasons often posited for the relationship between economic development and democracy is the link between education and affluence. The evidence is clear that education levels are dramatically higher in wealthy countries than in poor ones. In 1997 the average level of secondary school enrollment in high-income countries was 96 percent. In low-income countries, by contrast, it was 51 percent. [67]

However, levels of education, though correlated with income and free markets, are independently associated with democracy. Henry Rowen reports that with each additional year in the population's average level of education, freedom scores, as measured by the Freedom House index, rise by a startling 6.6 percent. [68] A rise in formal education, paired with growing national incomes, has a noticeable positive effect on the attitudes and political expectations of newly educated generations. Almost three decades ago, Alex Inkeles and David Smith found on the basis of interviews with some six thousand men in six developing countries that "in large-scale complex societies no attribute of the person

predicts . . . attitudes, values and behavior more consistently or
more powerfully than the amount of education . . . received."[69]
Education itself seems likely to be part of the explanation, à la
Fukuyama, for why people feel that "recognition" through participation is important.[70]

Larry Diamond, surveying a number of studies of the importance of education in democratic consolidation, found that education strongly predicts a democratic political culture. This is true
not only in Western Europe but in post-Communist Europe and
in parts of Asia as well. The positive effects of education appear
not to be contingent upon culture but rather to be nigh universal,
as Inkeles and Smith also emphasized.[71]

More recently, survey research and reanalysis of older survey
data by Russell Farnen and Jos Meloen confirms that education
leads to more democratic (or as they put it, less authoritarian)
attitudes. They find this to hold true in different regions of the
world, in more and less developed nations, and in more and less
authoritarian/totalitarian states. They posit, following others,
that the impact of education in the country under investigation is
mediated by the level of development and political regime type.
This turns out to be true, with education leading to significantly
more anti-authoritarian attitudes in wealthy and democratic
countries. Remarkably, however, while education's impact is
weaker or stronger in different types of states, its pro-democratic
impact on attitudes is universal. As Farnen and Meloen put it,
"In almost all included countries and across all world regions,
there is a general decline in authoritarianism as people receive
more education and stay in school for a longer time."[72] Moreover, Norman Nie, Jane Junn, and Kenneth Stehlik-Barry analyzed data on education in several industrial democracies and
found a strong association between democracy and tolerant attitudes. When this analysis was extended to Hungary during its
nondemocratic era, education was even more strongly related to
tolerance than in the democratic sample.[73] Thus the evidence

that education's impact is tempered by the political economy of the regime under study is not conclusive. What does seem conclusive, however, is that education leads to more democratic attitudes.

In general, the cross-national literature that investigates the impact of education on democracy is relatively thin. While education may lead to more democratic attitudes around the world, the mechanism by which this occurs is still poorly understood. And even if it were fully understood, we would still lack an explanation for how these kinds of attitudes translate into democratization. It seems clear, however, that education acts as an independent correlate of democracy, distinct from, though related to, income. Income, in contrast, seems to have a theoretically and empirically distinct impact on democratization, apart from education.

CHAPTER 6

TRADITIONS, NORMS, AND EXPECTATIONS

WHILE ECONOMIC EXPLANATIONS OF regime type are both powerful and parsimonious, they are insufficient. The generally accepted relationship between development and democracy cannot explain the precise timing of democratic transitions or why many transitions fail multiple times before a given polity finally establishes a successful, enduring democracy. Economic development is only one of a number of conditions that help democracy succeed. Because it is (relatively) easy to measure, it often garners more attention than more abstract variables like culture. But the ease with which a variable is measured is no indication of its relative importance.

Returning to our kickball field analogy, we now know the rules of the game and the players, and we know that if the field is located in a relatively wealthy society, the game is more likely to begin and be played through. More likely, but there are no guarantees. We are still missing important information about whether play is more or less likely, likely to start earlier or later, likely to continue unabated or break down and then resume later. In this part of the book, we examine the final set of such factors that are of interest to us. Of course, there are many factors that we have left aside, as is natural in a book of this scope but we hope we touch upon the most important.

In this chapter, we turn from more easily identifiable and quantifiable structural conditions toward more qualitative and more difficult arenas of social change—culture and psychology. In the following sections, we tackle concepts that relate to societal values and norms that have a direct bearing on the political regime. The focus is on three such concepts: gradualism, culture, and legitimacy. We first explain briefly what we mean by these terms and then analyze them in greater detail.

Gradualism is an extremely important, if broad, concept. We mean by *gradualism* simply that it takes time for societies to change in order to evolve norms, stable institutions, and "rules of the game" that are widely respected ("legitimate") and that strategic actors can rely upon in their own calculations. Even with rapid economic change, a society's norms and political culture do not change overnight. As a result, the pace of political change can be a crucial variable explaining its success or failure, regardless of prevailing economic conditions.

By "culture in the political arena" we mean superordinate values from which behaviors, institutions, and values may be derived. Culture is a product not simply of ethereal, timeless values but of concrete historical processes. For example, postrevolutionary anti-statism (as in the United States) may foster institutions—such as a constitution of checks and balances—that serve to create and reinforce values, such as anti-statism. Various traditions may or may not have an impact on the acceptance of norms associated with democracy. In this section, we discuss the ever changing nature of certain cultural traditions, especially those tied to religion, and relate these changes to shifts in global politics. We elaborate more fully on the nature of democratic political culture and how it may relate to other aspects of national culture. Even when economic conditions suggest that a society is ripe for democratizing political reform, a society's political culture may reject liberalizing reforms, impeding democratization. Clearly, there is a relationship between economic change and political culture, as well—but this does not mean that economic development proceeds in lockstep with cultural change. To the contrary, rarely do cultural and economic variables shift at the same pace at the same time. This fact complicates democratization in countries with anti-democratic cultural legacies.

Finally, in chapter 8 we turn to the concept of regime legitimacy. *Legitimacy* refers to the degree to which society as a whole—elites and masses—considers the regime (as opposed to the current administration) to be the most appropriate for itself, the degree to which its members give it a "title to rule." The concept of legitimacy is obviously not culture bound. All societies take time in adopting norms, and all systems require that their political regime have legitimacy in the eyes of a broad swath of the population and elites. In the contemporary world, indicators of regime legitimacy can be assessed through public opinion polling. Legitimacy can be the product of a changing dynamic, particularly in new regimes or states or postrevolutionary polities. It can wax and wane over historical time. Again, economic development can lend regimes legitimacy (for authoritarian as well as democratic regimes), but regimes may also remain legitimate or illegitimate for some time in spite of economic performance. In the interim, the regime may be quite unstable. An illegitimate regime with good economic performance might not endure to reap the benefits of its economic stewardship.

In tackling these three aspects of democracy, we hope to both temper and integrate the emphasis on quantitative research in the social sciences that has emerged since World War II. Gradualism, culture, and legitimacy are all difficult to measure systematically, yet they play unambiguously important roles in democratization. At the same time, we do believe that more can be done to hone these concepts by using modeling and game theoretic techniques. We suggest a potential use for game theory in the section below on legitimacy.

TAKING IT EASY: THE IMPORTANCE OF
GRADUALISM IN DEMOCRATIZATION

It bears repeating that economic factors explain only part of the variance, or the causal process, in democracy's success. Democracy requires a supportive culture; acceptance by the citizenry and political elites of principles underlying freedom of speech, media, assembly, religion; acceptance of the rights of opposition parties, the rule of law, human rights, and the like. Such norms do not evolve overnight. Colonial histories and religious traditions may complicate the acceptance of democratic norms. Cultural changes are most effective politically if they occur gradually. Gradualism, considered as a noneconomic factor in democratization, is also linked to economics, for the wealthier a country, the more tenable gradualist processes will be. Wealthy countries tend to have status hierarchies that are less stark and relatively well-off working classes, both of which diminish the sense of inferiority or anxiety experienced by those of the middle and lower strata. As a result, the pressure for immediate shifts in status and income are reduced, and gradualism becomes more acceptable.[1]

Attempts to move rapidly from authoritarianism to democracy have failed repeatedly, from the French Revolution in 1789 to the Russian Revolution in February of 1917, from those in the new nations in Latin America in the early nineteenth century to most of those in Africa and Asia after World War II. Democratization scholars Juan Linz and Samuel Huntington have noted that the two waves of democratization prior to the contemporary third were followed by "reverse waves" that brought the revival of authoritarianism. Huntington has emphasized that only four of the seventeen countries that adopted democratic institutions between 1915 and 1921 were able to maintain them during the next two decades. He notes, as well, that breakdowns were frequent in the post–World War II world: of the thirty-two democratic countries as of 1958, one-third had become authoritarian by the mid-1970s.[2] The third wave (1974–) is also having problems, most notably perhaps in Pakistan and the former Soviet Union (FSU).[3] According to Freedom House data, freedom declined in 2000 in Russia, Georgia, Ukraine, and the Kirgiz Republic. Democracy has also struggled in former third-wave bright spots in Africa like Côte D'Ivoire and Nigeria. And the brief military coup in Ecuador showed that country's democracy to be of dubious strength.[4]

Virtually everywhere that democracy has been institutionalized, the process has been incremental. Rights have generally emerged in the give-and-take of political warfare over time. As Lipset, Trow, and Coleman emphasized over four decades ago, "Democratic rights have developed in societies largely through the struggles of various groups—class, religious, sectional, economic, professional, and so on—against one another and against the group which controls the state,"[5] not through a moral consensus on the virtues of democratic rights.

Relevant to this discussion is the peculiar finding that (until recently) democracy has been more likely in the former colonies of Britain than in those of other nations.[6] Myron Weiner pointed out that, in addition to the experiences of the Americas and Australasia in the nineteenth century, all former colonies with a population of at least one million (and almost all the smaller ones as well) that have had a continuous democratic experience were formerly ruled by Britain.[7] This relationship has ceased to be statistically significant since the transition to democracy in Latin America, but clearly a British colonial past has made a difference to democracy.

The factors underlying this relationship are not simple. Behind the British/non-British contrast is the fact that many former British-controlled areas—such as eastern North America before the Revolution; Australia and New Zealand in the nineteenth century; and India, Ireland, and Nigeria in more recent times—

had elections, embryonic parties, and the rule of law while still colonies of Britain. Weiner argues that "the commitment of the political elite to adversarial politics within bounded rules . . . is a necessary condition for a democratic system, and it is one more likely to have been instilled by the British than by other colonial elites."[8] In contrast, the areas controlled by the Spanish, Portuguese, French, Dutch, and Belgians, and obviously the former Soviet-controlled countries as well, did not allow for the gradual incorporation of "elected" native "outgroups" into the polity prior to independence and in subsequent efforts at democratic transition. Hence democratization could occur more gradually and more successfully in former British areas than elsewhere; their preindependence experiences provided a kind of socialization process, helping to ease the transition to freedom. This agrees with Dahl's argument that polities with high levels of contestation and low levels of participation will democratize more easily than those in the reverse condition.[9] It is easier to increase participation—a legal matter—than to foster contestation—a matter of political culture. Those countries that had experience with the political culture of democracy prior to the departure of the British should have had an easier time, as in fact they largely did, extending democracy over the state once the British left.

Thus, long-enduring British rule allowed for the gradual emergence and expansion of democratic institutions to incorporate larger and larger segments of the population and assume increasingly significant responsibilities. During its final eight decades of colonization, India went through several phases of constitutional reform that opened government to indigenous representation and scrutiny while successively broadening the basis of participation. Though initially quite superficial, the reform process in 1909 brought the direct election of Indian representatives to provincial and national councils. In 1919 new reforms granted provincial legislative councils substantial autonomous powers while expanding the franchise and giving elected representatives certain administrative responsibilities in the ministries. The dramatic reforms of the Government of India Act of 1935 extended the franchise to only a sixth of the population, but these provisions for self-government in the provinces and widespread electoral competition were to prove invaluable in preparing Indians, and the Indian National Congress, for the rigors of democratic politics and governance. Of course, one cannot overemphasize the importance for Indian democracy of the existence and growth of the Congress for six decades preceding independence in 1947, as not just a nationalist organization but a political party democratic in its procedures and goals, conciliatory in its approach to conflict, and increasingly incorporative of rural and urban mass groups. Nor can one ignore the ways that cross-cutting cleavages—caste, class, religion, and language—provided the basis for parties and moderated contestation. Finally, the extraordinary caliber of leadership in India, as characterized by Gandhi and Nehru, was critical. The contrast with Pakistan—where political parties were less active and had less experience in government, where cross-cutting cleavages were less potent, and where the process of obtaining separation from India stunted the development of competition between parties—suggests the usefulness of this kind of preindependence development of democratic political institutions. [10]

Jamaica—over the past three decades, one of the most stable postcolonial democracies—may be another instructive example of the impact of lengthy British colonial rule. During the nineteenth century, it evolved a very limited, exclusive parliamentary structure. Although this structure was long dominated by aristocratic white settlers and then interrupted by revolt and repression, it slowly broadened to incorporate middle-class groups between 1884 and 1944, when the British granted universal adult suffrage and considerable self-governance. There followed eighteen years of two-party competition and gradual colonial withdrawal leading to independence in 1962. This staging, which handed over actual administration of the colony to indigenous ministers in 1953 and granted full internal self-government in 1959, was perhaps the ultimate expression of British colonial democratic design. Carl Stone observes, "The main idea behind this incremental process of advance to full democracy was the insistence by the British on having the emergent local leadership serve an apprenticeship in parliamentary government to ensure that they ran the system for some time under British supervision with a view to ensuring conformity to the rules of the game of British parliamentary democracy."[11]

In the United States, the original colonies had elected legislatures decades before the Revolution. They survived the Revolution and served as the basis for the institutions of the modern United States. This may be contrasted with Latin America, where centralized control of the colonies from Spain and Portugal substituted for British-style decentralized autonomy. In Latin America the colonies had little experience with self-governance or democratic culture at independence.

It may be objected that this promise of colonial experience has not been born out in most of Britain's former colonies in Africa. Among these one might number the notoriously unstable Nigeria and the once peaceful but increasingly troubled Kenya and Zimbabwe. Two observations must be made, however. First, it is still true that the few success stories of the African continent are primarily former British colonies: among these are Botswana and Mauritius. Second, the British colonial experience in Africa was comparatively shorter, less pervasive, and more divisive than it was in Asia or the Caribbean.

Several factors converged to fate Britain's colonial endeavors in Africa to more likely democratic failure, a point that Larry Diamond has elaborated. The British policy of deliberately encouraging ethnic attachments and the use of ethnic languages played into much more complex and volatile circumstances in Africa than in some Asian and especially Caribbean circumstances. The policy of indirect rule translated into an explicit formula of divide and rule. Throughout their empire, but with pronounced and possibly more deleterious results in Africa, the British selected certain ethnicities and races for special preference in military or administrative service; for example, northern tribes were recruited to the military in Uganda. Separate and differential administration of different portions of a colony engendered and permitted the accumulation of volatile cleavages. As Diamond has noted, "In Uganda and Nigeria, the tension and lack of integration between a far more economically and educationally advanced south and a politically or militarily advantaged north would constitute the most destructive element of Britain's colonial legacy," and with the approach of independence, the British insisted on preserving their anomalous and unstable federal structures despite dangerous signs. [12]

Related to this, because Britain established comprehensive colonial governance in Africa only after 1900, it had considerably less time to foster limited democratic institutions and norms and indigenous skill and experience in modern politics and administration. Furthermore, it was forced, by nationalist agitation and global anti-colonial sentiment after World War II, to begin the process of decolonization earlier and to push it along more quickly than it had planned. Throughout British Africa, William Tordoff has written, "nationalist pressure, particularly following the Gold Coast riots of 1948, quickened the tempo of constitutional reform," and as the pattern of constitutional advance was repeated from one African colony to the next, the British retreat became more hurried (for example, eliminating in East Africa the multitiered indirect elections that had been used in West Africa), and the "curve of reform" kept shortening. [13]

Finally, the British (and other Europeans') colonial presence was often highly uneven—very intensive and active, culturally and economically, in the coastal areas but scarcely present in many large sections of the interior. This not only left many areas with little real contact with British values and institutions but also created diffuse inequalities in education, professional training, and economic development that exacerbated ethnic differences (the gap between southern and northern Nigeria being a classic example).

It is still the case, in spite of these flaws, that Britain's colonial legacy was more conducive to democracy than that of other colonizers. However, the French also stand out in the relative access to democratic praxis granted during their reign when compared to the Belgians and the Portuguese. Although French colonies had less experience with self-government than British colonies, the French occasionally allowed some indigenous elites to participate in the French Chamber of Deputies and in local government. Senegal, the one French colony in which the elite was provided a long and significant exposure to political life, has today a reasonably functioning democracy. Further evidence of a Francophone effect in Africa includes the national conferences held in many former French colonies in Africa during the 1990s. These national representative bodies intended to reform the political system had in general a profound impact on the degree of political liberalization in countries where they took place; however, only sometimes did they result in full-blown democratization.[14] In other words, Francophone states were more likely to have national conferences, more apt to try liberalization, but only somewhat more disposed to see this process result in democracy—indicative of the somewhat more ambiguous legacy of the French as compared to the British.

In other parts of Africa and the rest of the colonial world, the speed of transition to independence provided virtually no time for democratic institutions to develop and strengthen. This was particularly true for former Belgian (Congo, Burundi, and Rwanda) and Portuguese (Angola, Mozambique, and Guinea-Bissau) colonies. In some newly independent countries, like those formerly controlled by the Portuguese, the liberation from colonial rule was achieved through armed struggle leading to violence and destruction of democratic institutions. In Latin America too, the bloody wars of independence, often followed by long periods of civil war, destroyed budding political and administrative institutions and obstructed the task of state building (though this was not true in Brazil). In the United States, by contrast, after the War of Independence, the colonial legacy was preserved and built upon rather than destroyed. The state and local governments continued to operate as self-governing units, their legitimacy derived from colonial charters.[15]

But gradualism is not simply a matter of political culture or adaptive institutions; it also relates to the pace of economic change and its impact on the political system. The West was fortunate in this regard. Economies grew much more slowly in Europe and North America than they are currently growing in the more successful developing countries. Western growth rates in the nineteenth century tended to be between 1 and 2 percent per annum.[16] Today most developing Third World polities, as distinct from the impoverished, purely agrarian Fourth World, have had much higher annual rates, with some reaching 10 percent.

Historical evidence from many European countries suggests that wherever industrialization occurred rapidly, introducing sharp discontinuities between the preindustrial and industrial situations, extremist working-class movements emerged.[17] The best example of this relationship is the Russian Revolution. The population engaged in industry in Czarist Russia jumped from sixteen million in 1897 to twenty-six million in 1913.[18] Leon Trotsky, in his *History of the Russian Revolution,* showed how an increase in the strike rate and in union militancy paralleled the growth of industry. The revolutionary Marxist left wing in Germany before World War I also derived its support from workers in the rapidly growing industries. It retained considerable support within the Social Democratic party, while the moderate sections of the party were based on more stable, established industries.[19] The variations in the working-class politics of the three major Scandinavian countries have also been accounted for in large measure by the different timing and pace of industrialization. Denmark experienced gradual economic and urban growth; the Danish Social Democratic movement and trade unions remained reformist and moderate. The few left-wing groups in the country were based mainly on the rapidly expanding industries.

In Sweden, manufacturing industry grew very rapidly from 1900 to 1914, causing a sudden increase in the number of unskilled workers, largely recruited from rural areas, and an expansion of industrial rather than craft unions. At the same time, a left-wing movement arose within the trade unions and the Social Democratic party that opposed the moderate policies both had developed before the great industrial expansion. A strong, quite radical, anarchosyndicalist movement also emerged in this period. Here too it was the rapidly expanding industries that formed the base of aggressive left-wing movements.

Norway, the last of the three Scandinavian countries to industrialize, had the highest rate of growth of all three between 1905 and 1920 and experienced the greatest radicalization during and shortly after World War I. Edward Bull, a Norwegian historian, has explained the variations among the countries by a central "macro variable" that he defined as *the suddenness of the changes brought about by industrialization.* As Stein Rokkan and Henry Valen explain, Bull "developed a general proposition: . . . the *slower* the growth of industry and the more of its labor force that can be recruited from already established urban communities, the less leftist the reactions of the workers and less radical their party; the more sudden the growth of industry and the more of its labor force has to be recruited from agriculture and fisheries, the more leftist the workers and the more revolutionary their party."[20]

Britain and Belgium have both had moderate labor and socialist movements. They were the first two nations to industrialize in

Europe; hence, the worst of the social strains occasioned by rapid industrialization and urbanization occurred before the emergence of modern labor movements and Marxist parties.

One can also illustrate the relationship between rapid industrialization and working-class extremism in Latin America. Those Latin American countries that experienced rapid industrial growth had large-scale pseudofascist movements. The working classes, suffering from tensions inherent in rapid industrialization, provided the primary base of support for the movements of Perón in Argentina and Vargas in Brazil. These movements, like the Communist ones, appealed to the "displaced masses" of these industrializing countries.

Substantial evidence from the older democracies thus demonstrates that rapid industrialization often leads to severe social and political pressures that may explode in anti-democratic, revolutionary movements. This would seem to urge pessimism regarding the likelihood of stable democracy emerging in newly industrializing states. It should be noted, however, that aggregate evidence gathered from nations since World War II suggests that the high levels of economic growth experienced by developing countries have *not* been detrimental to democracy. In fact, Adam Przeworski has argued that "democracies are always more likely to survive when they grow faster than 5 percent annually than when they grow slower."[21] Perhaps the global decline in the attractiveness of the far left—signified by the end of the Cold War and the shift rightward by most leftist parties—is part of the explanation. At any rate, the revolutionary tensions present in the older democracies seem to have mitigated since World War II.

In addition to the pace of change, scholars have also speculated about the importance of the sequence of change. Historical sequencing is interwoven with debates over many of the conditions for democracy. For example, those who posit a close relationship between capitalism and democracy worry that the modern state has too much power in new democracies to allow for the healthy development of a private sector. Others are concerned, as is discussed earlier, about the nature of technological change in developing countries and its impact on the media, which now is a much more significant, independent sociopolitical force than it was in the older democracies. Yet, as Amartya Sen's quote that opens this volume suggests, the global zeitgeist in favor of democracy may contribute to significant demonstration effects that help diffuse democracy to places where it never existed before (see the following section on culture). As mentioned above, Dahl has argued that nations with high levels of contestation that ultimately widen participation are more likely to succeed as democracies than those that follow the opposite course. Finally, some have argued that the formation of political parties with enduring affective ties before the onset of industrialization is a boon to democracy, because it allows the working class to be incorporated more easily into an existing party system. We will not deal with historical sequencing as a distinct type of condition for democracy, though we have touched upon it in previous sections and will continue to do so.

Suffice it to note here that Bollen's research (1979) has suggested that the timing of development is insignificant in comparison with level of socioeconomic development and proportion of the economy controlled by the state. Although this work is limited in scope, we are inclined to believe that while historical sequencing may be important, it is rarely determinant and is subject to abuse conceptually as a kind of ad hoc catchall category for all cases in which economic or other structural variables seem insufficient to account for democratization or its absence at any particular time.[22]

Summing up, the pace of political and economic change can play a major role in the long-term success of democratization. Historically, gradual economic and political change have been a boon to young democracies, while the dislocations caused by sudden transformations have often proven too much for democracy to handle. This has been true across a wide variety of countries and eras, though it has been particularly important in periods when countries were moving from pre-industrial to industrialized status. Although the historical record would seem to counsel pessimism regarding many developing nations that are currently in the midst of wrenching changes, we end this section with a bit of optimism born of Przeworski's evidence on the positive effects of rapid growth in the postwar era.

Let us now move from gradualism to culture. Gradualism, as we have noted, is important not only because of the economic havoc that fast-paced transformations can wreak but also because widespread cultural resistance to change can hamper attempts to move from one kind of societal logic to another. For most non-democratic societies, the norms of authoritarian rule cannot be disbanded from one day to the next. The constitutional basis for democracy may be established with the stroke of a pen, but people's behaviors and attitudes—about government, about their fellow citizens, about the meaning of elections or political parties—take time to change. The likelihood of these changes, and the rapidity with which they take place, is highly contingent upon a given society's dominant culture. In the next section, we explore what is known about the cultural correlates of democracy and democratization and argue that, even given optimal economic preconditions, overcoming cultural resistance to democratic norms may take a long time and many failed attempts.

Perhaps the most controversial and interesting area of social science research, cultural analysis can often be the most frustrating as well. All of these characteristics stem from the difficulty with which culture is specified and measured. Nevertheless, culture is an important correlate of democracy, and we enter wholeheartedly into the debate.

CHAPTER 7

CULTURE: RELIGION AND REGION

ARE THERE CULTURAL PREREQUISITES for democracy? It once appeared certain that there were: the Protestant European nations, particularly the British and their overseas colonies (e.g., North America), were the first to democratize (and to develop capitalism). Catholic states once seemed somewhat impervious to democracy and resistant to free-market economies. Islam was even more demophobic. Some states in East Asia rejected democracy as their elites claimed it was dissonant with "Asian values."

Today, the overall picture looks different. Spain, Portugal, and most of Latin America have had relatively free, competitive elections. Taiwan and South Korea have been transformed into vital democracies. Indonesia may be limping along, but its electoral institutions survive. Even Lee Kuan Yew, former authoritarian ruler and founding father of Singapore, has begun to moderate his own rhetoric about "Asian values" and the need for autocracy, proclaiming, in a recent article for *Newsweek,* that Singapore must create a "bohemian" quarter where messiness and innovation can prevail. [1]

Still, democracy and Islam remain at odds. [2] Democracy in Catholic Latin America looks tenuous in many places. Even if many countries are now turning to democracy that, on the basis of cultural analysis, would not have been expected to do so earlier, this shift may speak to the power of diffusion and demonstration effects to overcome cultural obstacles, as well as the more recent exercise of coercive power by Western-controlled supranational organizations (such as the International Monetary Fund and World Bank) that demand democratic processes as a condition of membership and/or economic assistance. [3]

In sum, culture matters. It has mattered in the past, and it appears still to matter. What is it about culture that matters? How much difference does culture make? Surely culture can play only a limited role in democratization, because culturally diverse countries can and have embraced democracy. But what explains this embrace?

Democracy implies a particular political culture, a democratic culture. This culture consists of acceptance of the rule of law, tolerance of opposition, respect for differences of opinion and a reluctance to insist on the absolute nature of truth, legitimacy of national institutions (a title to rule), and acceptance of uncertainty. Democratic culture also consists of attitudes about the relationship between state and society that Gabriel Almond and Sidney Verba characterized as the "civic culture." The civic culture is a mix of three roles, "participant," "subject," and "parochial": civic citizens are capable of actively challenging the polity (participant), but also of accepting its authority (subject) and of retaining a strong sense of responsibility to their own communities and families outside the realm of divisive politics (parochial). These three roles encourage moderate conflict accompanied by allegiance to the democratic regime and prevent a hyperparticipant culture from forming and overburdening the state. [4]

Not all cultures are equally receptive to the democratic political culture. Protestantism, with its early acceptance of secular progress, individual achievement, and pluralism proved to be an ideal match. Catholicism, until recently, resisted the notion of a secular realm where truth and public policies are contested and religion does not hold sway. Pierre Trudeau, the late scholar and longtime prime minister of Canada, once argued, in relation to why pre-1960s Quebec was not democratic while English Canada was, that since Catholics are "authoritarian in spiritual matters, and since the dividing line between the spiritual and the temporal may be very fine or even confused, they are often disinclined to seek solution in temporal affairs through the mere counting of heads."[5] Religious values have impeded the permeation of democratic values and can continue to do so. But religious values are not immutable, and indeed, Catholicism has been transformed greatly over the course of the twentieth century.

Some scholars have argued that in Islam the concept of secularism—the existence of a nonreligious public sphere of life—does not exist. Islamic society's religious code is the highest authority. "The heart of the matter," Mohamed Elhachmi Hamdi argues, "is that no Islamic state can be legitimate in the eyes of its subjects without obeying the main teachings of the shari'a. A secular government might coerce obedience, but Muslims will not abandon their belief that state affairs should be supervised by the just teachings of the holy law."[6] The failure of modern Islam to discern a secular realm means that the frame of reference in Islamic polities conflicts with the democratic political culture described here. Islam, if this description holds, proscribes tolerance of opposition and the acceptance of either relative truth or uncertainty.[7] Islam too can change, of course, and adapt itself to the requisites of democratic culture. So far, there is sparse evidence that it has.

This characterization of Islam as lacking any acceptance of an independent secular realm has also been applied to Confucianism and Orthodox Christianity, and the converse hypothesis—that cultures which do sanction an independent secular sphere are conducive to democracy—has been used to explain the success of the overwhelmingly Hindu, Indian democratic system. As Shmuel Eisenstadt has argued:

> The most salient feature of Indian civilization, from the point of view of our discussion, is that it is probably the only complete, highly differentiated civilization which throughout history has

maintained its cultural identity without being tied to a given
political framework. . . . [T]o a much greater degree than in many
other historical imperial civilizations, [Indian] politics were conceived in secular forms. . . . Because of the relative dissociation
between the cultural and the political order, the process of modernization could get underway in India without being hampered
by too specific a traditional-cultural orientation toward the political sphere.[8]

It seems clear that diverse cultures may share similar attitudes
about secularism that may conduce to or obstruct democracy.

Cultures are not monolithic. Within each, as Amartya Sen has
noted, it is possible to find "heterogeneity of values."[9] In particular, Sen identifies liberal traditions within Confucianism, Buddhism, and Islam that belie the dominant view of these cultures
as illiberal and authoritarian: "To see Asian history in terms of a
narrow category of authoritarian values does little justice to the
rich varieties of thought in Asian intellectual traditions. Dubious
history does nothing to vindicate dubious politics."[10] For the
most part, there are liberal traditions within all cultures, but it is
precisely the *majority attitude of the people—and of the politically
relevant elites—toward this heterogeneity that is important.* Where
heterogeneity is shunned and tolerance for dissent is low, it does
not particularly matter that a few dissident voices are crying in
the wilderness. Liberal Catholics have surely been around for
many generations, but Catholicism as a whole did not begin to
accept liberalism until very recently.[11] Through an often tortuous
transformation, what was heterodox can become mainstream.
The process is a long one, but it can happen.

Our attitude about culture, then, is no different from our generalized posture: pessoptimism. Culture matters, particularly in
the short run. But in the long run, most cultures appear to have
the potential to converge with democratic culture. Convergence
is an arduous process that is proscribed not by culture per se but
rather by the dominant view within a given culture at a given
time. As Abdou Filali-Ansary has written, "If great numbers of

Muslims today invoke religion rather than democracy as the alternative to despotism, and others consider democracy itself (at least implicitly) as a kind of new religious belief, this is not because of some special characteristics either of Islam or Muslims. It is rather because of the particular historical circumstances"[12] that have led to the particular current definition of Islam and Islamic principles. In the next section, we analyze the evolution of Catholicism as a paradigmatic case of convergence with democratic culture.

CATHOLICISM AND DEMOCRACY

Samuel Huntington noted in *The Third Wave* that "overall, roughly three quarters of the countries that transited to democracy between 1974 and 1989 were Catholic countries."[13] This was in sharp contrast to the earlier waves of democracy, which created a world in which Protestantism correlated very highly with democracy and Catholicism appeared incompatible with it. What happened? To explain why this original relationship no longer holds, both Huntington and Catholic scholar George Weigel have relied on a number of arguments that describe changes in "cultural principles" or the institutional structure of the church.

Huntington argues that the Catholic Church, for a variety of reasons, underwent significant doctrinal changes that led to political realignment. Whereas the Church had been a force for the status quo and for authority and authoritarianism, it reversed course in the 1960s and became a force for democracy and social justice and "almost invariably opposed authoritarian regimes."[14]

Papal biographer George Weigel identifies historical and institutional factors in the nineteenth century Catholic Church that were anti-liberal. He cites the effects of the French Revolution, specifically the anti-clerical Jacobin chaos, which led Catholics to recoil from liberalism, and in order to shore up civilization and order, to institute an authoritarian, centralized bureaucratic structure in the Church. Furthermore, Weigel asserts that the perceived conceptual links between liberalism, Darwinism, and socialism threatened the Church's intrinsic nature through their revolutionary commitment to rationalism and critical thought.[15] In rejecting these ideological assaults on its authority, the Catholic Church failed to confront modernity, continuing a tradition of deeming the progressively more expansive "lay world" to be of "religious unimportance."[16] In this, Catholicism lagged behind Protestantism, which in the nineteenth century embraced modernity and reformulated "Christian meaning" in what scholar of Catholicism Thomas O'Dea has called "one of the great achievements of the Western mind."[17] Catholics would continue to strongly oppose liberalism until the twentieth century.

If developments in the nineteenth century led the Church to oppose liberalism and socialism, how did events in the twentieth lead it to the opposite stance? Its experience in the United States forced the Church to reconsider its position vis-à-vis political regime types, because in that country Catholics flourished under the protection of American civil liberties and the separation of church and state. Whereas this was a happy but idiosyncratic fact at the end of the nineteenth century, the subsequent terrors of totalitarianism in the twentieth century enhanced the reputation of liberal democracy in the Church's view and helped to create an institutional commitment on its part to democratic governance.

Of more interest to controversies over cultural values, however, were changes in the Church's theology. Pope Pius XI would profoundly influence the direction of Catholic doctrine with a letter written in 1931. The "principle of subsidiarity" established in this letter incorporated into Catholicism a number of the values traditionally associated with Protestantism (and typically alleged to be responsible for the latter's affinity with both capitalism and democracy), including individualism, personal liberty, and popular participation. While no overt political regime was specified by these teachings, neither was it a great leap from acceptance of these first principles to acceptance of and support for democracy.

The critical transformation in Church doctrine that paved the way for the impressive commitment of Catholicism to democracy in the second half of the twentieth century came with Vatican II (1962–65). Under the intellectual leadership of American theologian John Courtney Murray, Catholicism incorporated a radical redefinition of the relationship between church and state. By effectively severing the ties between them and emphasizing personal freedom to pursue religion, the traditional connection between Catholicism and monarchy was fully replaced with a new commitment to a limited, secular state buoyed by civil rights and liberties.[18]

This history is meant to suggest that the revised relationship between Catholicism and democracy may be attributable to the changing nature of Catholicism. Yet variations in the nature of the Catholic Church or of Catholic "principles" would not be expected to have had an immediate impact on the cultural legacy described by Pierre Trudeau. Does the institutional shift of the Church from siding with authoritarian to democratic governments really have an effect on the *personal values* of Catholics? Likewise, do papal letters or conferences declaring new Catholic values make millions of Catholics worldwide *more democratic* personally? Perhaps they do over time.

But if cultural values, deeply embedded and largely accepted without skepticism, heavily influence a people's capacity for democratic governance, then an institutional shift in the Church should have no real short-term effects on the personal values of Catholics. The same could be said for doctrinal shifts. The niceties of Catholic doctrine may be important to the clergy and may have long-term effects on Catholic society, but how important is this "elite culture" in determining the democratic capacity of the mass of Catholics?[19] Simple shifts in Catholic doctrine should have no short-term effects on, for example, the acceptance of authority or levels of secularism amongst a group of people. More important are changes among the rank and file and lower clergy. Some of these changes may be a result of top-down religious inculcation, while some may have independent sources (e.g., modernization) that then cause religious change to percolate up.

Three different processes are being labeled "cultural."[20] The first process (originally claimed by cultural determinists seeking to explain the failure of Catholics to democratize) involved inculcating the masses with religious values deemed antithetical to democracy. The second and third processes, now employed to explain the failure of the first, were (1) organizational shifts that aligned the church with new institutional allies in society and (2) changes in elite interpretations of Catholic principles. Yet it is only by showing that the second and third process translated into the first that this argument has coherence. If deeply held personal cultural values impeded democracy among Catholics in the past, then only the rejection of those values, or the recent acceptance of new ones, could alter that. [21]

Of course, in the long run, one would expect shifts within the value structure of the religion to have an effect on its adherents, because the long-term process of acculturation is being posited as the determining factor in the first place. And indeed, Weigel's assessment of Catholicism explores changes in the religion over the course of a century (1865–1965). Surely, institutional and doctrinal shifts within the religion could have influenced "mass culture" over such a long period. At the same time, it is possible that some of these elite-level shifts reflected changes in mass culture, rather than the other way round. While Weigel's work does not illuminate the complex relationship between institutional or elite positions and changes in "mass culture," it lends credence to the notion that in the long term, religious or cultural values are not fixed and can be made compatible with democracy, or any other system.

But Weigel's is not the last word on the subject. Where Weigel's history is silent, other scholars who have examined religious change in Latin America are vocal. These scholars identify the missing contemporary link between elite and mass culture as liberation theology. The lines of causality are unclear when it comes to liberation theology: it appears to have had its roots both in institutional changes at the elite level as well as popular agitation and discontent at the grass roots. Liberation theology established a new and dynamic relationship between the masses and Church elites that radically altered the cultures of both. South of the Rio Grande, liberation theology, by promoting contestation and participation, transformed Catholicism on a mass level, making it eminently more compatible with democracy than it had been in the past. This occurred in spite of the fact that many of the "liberationists" were leftist authoritarians.

Liberation theology could be many things to many people. It was strongest in Latin America and in many ways was a specific historical response to the spiritual and political needs of Latin Americans. It is therefore neither all nor even most of the story behind the transformation of Catholicism. Yet it is a good example of how changes in the Catholic Church as an institution allowed for radical departures from the Church's historical role, and a new cultural commitment to democracy, in an area that has been a stronghold not only of Catholicism but also of authoritarianism.

Liberation theology was made possible by the specific changes that took place with Vatican II. In particular, two broad transformations are relevant here. First, the Church finally confronted modernity and recognized the importance of a secular sphere of life. As O'Dea describes the new position, "While temporal affairs do 'depend on God,' and man cannot participate in them 'without reference to their Creator,' nevertheless a sphere of legitimate autonomous human action in the world is proclaimed."[22] Thus were science and faith reconciled, through the notion that both derive from God and both illuminate God. This marked the first time that the Church had tried to co-opt, rather than reject, the secular world. And this, in turn, has allowed the Church to support development and human welfare as legitimate ends.

Second, Vatican II signaled to the international Church that it was time to investigate innovative approaches to reconciling the secular and religious worlds. Having lost considerable ground due to its failure to "modernize," the Church now needed to innovate in order to compete in the religious marketplace. Central to the Church's innovation strategy was decentralization. The Vatican thus reaffirmed and stimulated a process that had begun prior to the Second Council—the formation of smaller "base" communities and local institutions. In Latin America this process translated into the now famous CEBs (ecclesial-base communities), national bishops' conferences, and a Latin American bishops' conference (CELAM). Each of these, while still under the authority of the Vatican, represented a new level of independence and input into the meaning of Catholicism from below.

It was out of these twin reforms—acceptance of the secular and of some decentralization—that liberation theology was born. The critical addition brought by liberation theology was the "preferential option for the poor," which essentially decreed that the poor to whom the Church should attend were not just the spiritually impoverished but the materially impoverished as well. A number of innovations in Church praxis and ideology followed. Many clergy went to live among the poor in Latin America, to influence and to be influenced by them.[23] The Bible was translated, often for the first time, into the vernacular of "the people." This had an enormous impact on the level of participation among the poor in religious activity. As David Levine explains the rationale, "If all can read and comment on the Bible, the value of popular insights is enhanced and traditional distinctions of rank in religious life are undercut. Equal access to the Bible can be a great leveler, as the experience of the Puritan revolution in seventeenth-century England reminds us."[24] Base communities were founded by clergy to encourage participation in frequent discussions of Bible topics. In Brazil the founding of CEBs and the national bishops' conference led to the creation of other church-related civic and political groups, such as the Workers' Pastoral Commission (CPO) and the Indian Missionary Council (CIMI). Liberation theologists, and Catholics generally, took the newfound relationship between religion and human welfare to mean a necessary expansion of church organizations and services.

The net effect of these changes was that the institutional and elite-level transformations of values that made Catholicism less hostile to democracy were directly transmitted to the grass roots. Liberation theology filled in the theoretical gap that would have otherwise existed between elite, institutional changes and mass culture. It therefore helps to illuminate the long process by which Catholicism and democracy were reconciled on a mass level.

CULTURAL STABILITY AND CHANGE

The relationship between regime type and culture is actually a compound of two distinct questions: First, what kind of culture would invent a democracy and establish it independently? And second, what kind of culture can sustain a democracy once it has been established?

The original Weberian hypothesis concerning Protestantism and capitalism, modified to include democracy, suggested reasons for the invention of democracy in Europe and North America and its early development there. But it does not mean that cultures elsewhere cannot adapt themselves to democracy. Furthermore, the demonstration effects that emanate once a democracy exists in an area make it much easier for other, culturally distinct countries to attempt democracy. Once democracy has been invented, the wheel need not be completely reinvented by each subsequent state that decides to democratize. The process is much like the spread of capitalism.

It is possible that particular institutional changes led to the implementation of democracy in Catholic countries, but the lack of cultural change on a mass level may doom these democracies in the intermediate or long term. Institutional changes may lead to democracy's implementation, but the lack of value changes may lead to instability. Some societies, however, might never have invented democracy or capitalism, but their cultures may prove highly compatible with them. In these cases, institutional changes may take root relatively easily in seemingly foreign soil.

Japan provides an excellent example of the latter. It may not have had cultural values conducive to the organic development of democracy, but democracy was imposed from outside, and Japan had the values to support it once democracy had been established. Indeed, Francis Fukuyama believes that Confucianism could be a particularly strong pillar of democracy throughout East Asia: "Confucian values might work quite well in a liberal society (as they clearly do for many Asian immigrants to the United States), where they can serve as a counterbalance to the larger society's atomizing tendencies."[25] Again, this point seems to apply to capitalism as well; analysts like Fukuyama and Robert Bellah have argued that countries might never have naturally adapted to capitalism, even though many of their values are consonant with it. Once exposed to capitalism, these countries, like Japan, prove highly successful practitioners. Bellah argues that the religious emphasis in feudal Tokugawa Japan contained behavioral principles akin to those Weber pointed to in Calvinism.[26]

Other scholars, confronting the pitiful record of Islam vis-à-vis democracy, have made similar arguments regarding the future of democracy among Muslims. In arguing for the compatibility between democracy and Islam, Robin Wright claims that "Islam is not lacking in tenets and practices that are compatible with pluralism. Among these are the traditions of *ijtihad* (interpretation), *ijma* (consensus), and *shura* (consultation)."[27] While the historical record implies that religion has precluded the organic growth of democracy in Islamic nations, Wright believes that many of the important democratic principles are in waiting within

the culture.[28] She quotes the Muslim scholar Rachid al-Ghan-
nouchi to this effect: "Once the Islamists are given a chance to
comprehend the values of Western modernity, such as democracy
and human rights, they will search within Islam for a place for
these values where they will implant them, nurse them, and cherish them, just as the Westerners did before, when they implanted
such values in much less fertile soil."[29] The implication here is that
Muslims may not conjure up democracy on their own, but after
having tried it out (via borrowing or imposition), they will find it
highly compatible with their own traditions.

Postmodern discourse tends to elevate culture to the point that
its preservation is lauded as a goal in and of itself, without reference to other principles. In this environment, cultural change is
regarded with suspicion. Yet culture is constantly, and furiously,
changing. It is functionally integrated and molded by human
hands. Therefore, there is no a priori superstructure called culture that cannot be adapted to circumstance. All the pieces of a
culture can interact freely and independently and can act upon
one another as frequently as they are acted upon. They can therefore be as much effect as cause.

There is a tendency to think, and the literature consistently so
argues, that religion is a cause of democracy or of the lack thereof.
Even those who reject this view, such as Adam Przeworski and
his colleagues, argue simply that religion is not a cause once other
factors are accounted for. But religion should not be viewed
strictly as either a cause or not a cause.

Lee Kuan Yew, culturalist par excellence, has argued that religion can actually be seen as an effect: "If you look at the fast-
growing countries—Korea, Thailand, Hong Kong and Singapore—there's been one remarkable phenomenon: the rise of
religion. Koreans have taken to Christianity in large numbers, I
think some 25 percent. This is a country that was never colonized
by a Christian nation. The old customs and religions—ancestor
worship, shamanism—no longer completely satisfy."[30]

Cultural values and attributes are not preexisting and immutable. They are the results of historical developments, of dynamic, ongoing processes. Culture can therefore never be taken to be a permanent obstacle to democracy. As Przeworski writes, paraphrasing John Stuart Mill, "People may be unprepared for democracy but they can be taught to behave as democrats."[31] Cultures can change and become compatible with democracy; the power of experience can overcome cultural obstacles and transform individuals into democrats.

Curiously, after introducing it to much potential advantage, Przeworski ultimately leaves this argument aside. He identifies five possible interpretations of the relationship between culture and democracy. The first three he claims are not falsifiable with available evidence, and the fifth is the "noncultural" argument, to which he subscribes. But number four is Mill's, which Przeworski evades (though he later uses Mill to argue against "strong" culturalists).[32] Mill neither argues that culture does not exist nor that culture is irrelevant; he simply states that culture is not fixed. It is true, he says, that some societies are more inclined to be democratic than others, but this does not matter. Everyone can become democratic.

Yes, but they may have to change a part of their culture. They may have to give up their authoritarian tendencies, their nonsecularism—even, perhaps, their belief in the good of society over the good of the individual. In other words, though Przeworski is not clear about what democracy's cultural values are, people may have to substitute the values of good democrats for their own values when these conflict. That they are capable of doing so, Przeworski adamantly argues, is without doubt.

But this is not a noncultural view but a universalist cultural view. That is, it does not posit the unimportance of culture in determining the success of democracy. Rather, it contends that all cultures can change to look like the culture of democracy. There *is* a culture of democracy—a culture rooted in secularism, tolerance, liberal individualism, respect for and obeisance to the rule of law—and any culture that wishes to become democratic must swallow these values and adapt them to its own. But if cultures *must* change to become democratic, then culture per se must be an important factor in the success or failure of democracy.

If culture were truly unimportant, why would anyone have to change their own to become a democrat?

EXCURSIS ON DEMOCRATIC CULTURE

We have said that a democratic culture is one that encompasses secularism, tolerance, and respect for the rule of law. Obviously, however, these values are counterbalanced by others in every democratic (and nondemocratic) society on the globe. As Tocqueville noted and contemporary survey data continue to report, the United States is one of the most religious countries in Christendom. [33] It also has pockets of intolerance and communitarian credos that stand in sharp contrast to its democratic culture. As with all cultural values, those that constitute a democratic culture are in perennial tension with other, often less democratic values. Stable democracy depends on the relative, not the absolute, primacy of democratic values, particularly among elites. While elements of these values may be found in any society, it is apparently not the existence of democratic values but their predominance that is important.

Although the relative predominance of democratic values bodes well for democratic stability, secularism, tolerance, and respect for the rule of law are compatible with other regime types as well. Some scholars have argued that democracy requires still other norms, specifically related to how citizens perceive government, civil society, and political struggle. These norms define the role of the state and citizens and allow democratic processes to proceed on a day-to-day basis.

Gabriel Almond and Sidney Verba did pathbreaking work on the empirical study of political culture in *The Civic Culture,* published nearly four decades ago. They argued that a democratic political culture mixes and balances parochial, subject, and participant roles. The *parochial* represents primary group associations, such as the family and the village, that are not distinctly political and that are divorced from the modern administrative state. The *subject* is represented by the citizen who perceives, evaluates, and generally accepts the administrative order (output) of the state. The *participant* is actively engaged in the political process (input) by which administrative rules are decided. Civic culture is a mix of these three roles; civic citizens are capable not only of actively challenging the polity but also of accepting its authority and of retaining a strong sense of responsibility to their own communities and families outside the realm of divisive politics. These three roles serve to encourage moderate conflict and a flexible, pluralistic political culture.[34] As Almond and Verba put it, "The maintenance of . . . more traditional attitudes and their fusion with the participant orientations lead to a balanced political culture in which political activity, involvement, and rationality exist but are balanced by passivity, traditionality, and commitment to parochial values."[35]

Implicit in this developmental definition of civic culture is the assumption that democratic political culture is a form of consciousness. The participant-subject-parochial citizen understands the importance not only of participation but also of submission and recognizes that while it is important to interact with the state, it is not the be-all and end-all of existence. Citizens have overlapping obligations and consider their interactions with the state as only one subset of these. Because they are tied to primary associations and a generalized loyalty to the administrative state, only a limited degree of political participation in and conflict with the state is realistic. Most people most of the time will accept the administrative outputs of the state; they will reserve activism—high degrees of participation—for what they perceive as gross cases of abuse or neglect.

Consciousness does not stop with an awareness of the need for moderation or the need for parochial affiliations and participant activity in political groups. Civic culture also involves consciousness of the links among these three aspects of political culture. Almond and Verba found that general social attitudes—for example, interpersonal trust—did not necessarily translate into political participation—for example, forming groups to affect policy. That is, citizens did not necessarily perceive the potential links between their parochial ties and political participation. They did so only in the United States and Britain, the most advanced and consolidated democracies in the study. Almond and Verba concluded that the development of democratic systems coincides with the development of a political consciousness that is integrated (congruent) with the social structure in a seamless continuum. While politics do not supercede parochial ties, these ties are not isolated and prevented from fostering political ends.[36] At the same time, politics are forced to moderate and conform to a pattern (exemplified by parochial institutions) of close ties, limited conflict, and tolerance. A democratic culture permeates the entire social structure; since everything is open to political use, conflict must be moderate to avoid the disintegration of parochial and subject allegiances.

In their attempt to measure political culture, Almond and Verba operationalized the culture variable in varied ways. They looked at knowledge of, attitudes about, and expectations of government, arguing that the norms of the civic culture included being informed and positive about government and having high expectations of equal treatment before the law. They argued that the democratic citizen is necessarily an open partisan, "emotionally involved in electoral contests but not so intensely partisan as to cut himself off from relations with members of the opposing party."[37] He or she feels an obligation to participate in local affairs and has high levels of interpersonal trust that translate into political participation.

While not taking a definitive stance on the direction of causality—civic culture to democracy or vice versa—Almond and Verba did argue persuasively that the extent of civic culture could be predicted by structural and historical factors. Variations in the level of civic culture were associated with differing political structures in the countries studied. But there was also strong evidence that some aspects of the civic culture were powerfully associated with education levels, across national borders. [38]

The Civic Culture came in for a great deal of criticism, some of it quite justified, on the same grounds as modernization theory generally. Many believed that Almond and Verba's conception was biased toward the Anglo-American model of liberal democracy, while others took issue with their lack of historicism. *The Civic Culture*, cross-sectional as it was, did not explain changes over time in the case studies. Scholars in the neo-Marxist vein found Almond and Verba too unwilling to explore what these critics deemed the "middle-class" biases in their conception of culture or the structural implications of their study. [39] Yet the conceptual framework of *The Civic Culture* remains vibrant. As Carole Pateman notes in her critique, Almond and Verba did not specify the exact nature of the balance among their three orientations—subject, parochial, and participant. [40] Although they were criticized for putting too much emphasis on the parochial and subject roles, the balance that Almond and Verba implied can be discarded without losing their categories. In our view, Almond and Verba were right to point out the perils of hyperparticipation, and it is definitely not necessary for the maintenance of democracy that citizens as a whole be overly prone to participation. Indeed, it is possible that the class-based divergence between elite participation and mass apathy that Pateman notes is functional for democracy, though it is obviously not progressive. This may raise normative concerns about democracy, but it does not mean that the conception of civic culture is flawed.

Almond and Verba's conception of democratic political culture has a different flavor than the standard induction of "tolerance, moderation, secularism, and respect for the rule of law."
"Civic culture" deals primarily with the orientation of citizens
toward political institutions and the state. It does not follow from
their definition that citizens must be particularly tolerant or
moderate in their daily lives or in their attitudes about strangers
or outside groups. Because citizens must be both passive and
activist, it is enough that they not be *actively* intolerant or immoderate. That is, if citizens act like subjects when their government
is tolerant or moderate and reserve their participation for times
when their government is either radically unresponsive or
immoderate in its policies, then as long as elites practice tolerance and moderation, democracy will be safe. The same could be
said for respect for the rule of law. Elites must have respect for
the law because they are in a position to break it with some
impunity. The average citizen must have not so much a respect
for the law as a fear of punishment for breaking it that is
grounded in a realistic assessment of the power and province of
institutions like courts and the police.

In our view, the kind of *political culture* discussed by others is
primarily important for elites and is distinct from Almond and
Verba's *civic culture*. This is the only defensible position given the
widespread indications that mass citizenries tend to be intolerant
and immoderate. Consider James Gibson's findings from a survey done in 1987 in the United States, which are consistent with
similar studies. Given a list of widely disparate groups, such as
"Ku Klux Klan," "blacks"—as well as "other" followed by a
blank in which they could write their own description—respondents were asked to identify their most disliked groups and rank
order them. They were then asked what basic civil and political
rights they would extend to this most disliked group. All of the
rights about which they were queried are protected under the
U.S. Constitution already, though respondents were not informed

of this. Only 6.3 percent of Americans would extend all of these basic rights to their most disliked group. The item that most directly related to a minimalist definition of democracy was "run for office." About 27 percent of Americans felt that their most disliked group should be allowed to run for office. This rose only to 36 percent for respondents' fourth most disliked group. Only one of the listed rights was extended by a majority of Americans to their most disliked group: the right to make phone calls untapped. [41]

It is therefore possible to take a two-pronged approach to democratic political culture. First, the much heralded values of moderation, tolerance, secularism, and respect for the rule of law apply primarily to elites in democratic systems. Second, the vision of *civic culture* comprising parochial, subject, participant orientations advanced by Almond and Verba has broader applicability. It applies to the majority of citizens; if most citizens have weak parochial ties and take a participatory stance toward the state, the result will likely be overload, hostility, and zero-sum politics. Because Almond and Verba's conception itself relies on the idea of moderation, we cannot consider our two prongs to be completely distinct. [42] At the very least, it can be said that societies as a whole must be willing to accept moderation and tolerance on the part of their elected representatives and state bureaucrats, even if they themselves do not really subscribe to these values. In this sense, elite behavior must be based on mass attitudes that are, at best, tolerant and moderate themselves and, at worst, acquiescent or apathetic about elite attempts to be tolerant and moderate. To some extent, then, our two prongs of political culture answer two different questions. First, how should strategic political actors act in a democracy? And second, how should society be oriented toward the political system in a democracy? Political culture (tolerance, moderation, and respect for the rule of law) answers the first question, and civic culture (à la Almond and Verba) answers the second.

Democratic political and civic culture are necessary, but not sufficient, aspects of democracy. When tolerance, compromise, gradualism, respect for the rule of law, and aspects of the civic culture come into conflict with the larger culture of a society, something has to give. Since political culture applies specifically to the workings of the political system and, most often, to the behavior of elites, it is possible for citizens to adopt a specific political culture that is different from the larger social environment. Almond and Verba found that such variations did in fact occur in the less democratic nations in their original five-nation study. However, as they argued, democracy seems to require an overarching structure, the civic culture, that allows for the continued importance of parochial and subject ties but adapts them to the needs of a participant political culture. Democracy respects the parochial but simultaneously demands moderation from it. Democracy's survival, then, is improbable where the broader culture is in continual conflict with the democratic political culture, as is the case in most Islamic countries today. Where the broader culture is not "civic"—that is, comprises anti-democratic values—culture clash is inevitable. The closer the broader culture is to the democratic political culture, the more easily democratic norms will be accepted as legitimate, but the results of such clashes are indeterminate.

CULTURAL THEORY AND RATIONAL CHOICE

It is at this point worth tackling one more argument by Przeworski against considering culture as a causal factor in democratization or democratic stability. According to Przeworski, writing from a rational choice perspective that assumes self-interested behavior on the part of major social actors, democracy represents a kind of equilibrium for rational actors. Their obeisance to the results of elections may appear to have a "cultural" aspect to it—respect for the rule of law, compromise, and so forth—but is in fact a thin veneer that deflects attention from their true motivations:

democracy is in the best interests of democratic elites. According to Przeworski, then, "equilibrium culture"—his name for the operation of democratic rules, such as the rule of law—is not the cause but rather the effect of a panoply of rational choices that lead all major actors to accept democracy. [43]

This argument is intriguing. From an anthropological perspective, it is not unreasonable to claim that all cultures grow out of rational reactions to the environmental context a group or society faces. For example, in societies where the cost of having children is much less than the benefits of their labor, families will be large. In modern, urban societies like our own, where the costs of child rearing are great and the benefits are much fewer, families will tend to be smaller. Although cultural theory does not claim to supercede rational interest analysis, culturalists are interested in the following conundɪums: If actors are rational, why do individuals that move from one society to another not immediately conform? When environmental conditions change, why do people often stay the same? Culturalists note that, in the short term at least, adherence to cultural norms often trumps rationality. Habituation beats self-interest—not all the time and certainly not over the long term. Ultimately, of course, actors may readjust their "cultures" to fit the rational needs of their environments.

In the meantime, however, heuristics often suffice. Indeed, this is precisely the point of culture: it is a mechanism that allows us to make assumptions about what others will do in our own societies that reduce transaction costs and uncertainty. We are reluctant to transform our culture because we cannot be sure that we will reach another equilibrium that provides the same level of certainty. If we change our behavior in response to changing conditions, can we be sure others will, as well? Can we be sure that others see the changes that we see? If others do not change but we do, will we lose out during the period of disequilibrium? [44] In the long run, societies will tend to reach equilibrium, but in the meantime, it is exceptionally difficult to predict behavior. The major difference between the culturalist and rational choice schools is, How long is the meantime?[45]

Democracy may represent an equilibrium culture, a "rational choice," but this culture is broadened and deepened beyond the constraints of rationality by iteration and the accretion of moral attachments to it. Rationality cannot explain what the classic public choice dilemma manifests: why people vote when the probability that their own vote will affect the outcome is basically infinitesimal. Self-interest is hard put to explicate why political minorities vest importance in symbolic gestures or expend energy on hopeless political campaigns. Groups, regions, or nations, though faced with the same conditions, may act very differently. The German and American economies were both pulverized in the 1930s by the Great Depression, with similarly high levels of unemployment and bankruptcies. The electorate of one supplied mass support for extremist anti-system parties; that of the other looked for moderate changes and rejected extremism. Cultural variations are more useful than rational choice in explaining these differences.

In the main, however, we agree with Robert Bates, Rui J. P. De Figueiredo, Jr., and Barry Weingast that rational choice theory and culturalist interpretations can work together to explain human behavior.[46] Bates and colleagues, along with Dennis Chong, argue that rational choice theory can be used to explore value formation.[47] In this way, rational choice theory can inform culturalist interpretations. Bates et al. recognize, as well, that under conditions of uncertainty or instability, rational choices are often jettisoned in favor of actions that are conditioned by preexisting cultural worldviews. From this perspective, Przeworski's "equilibrium culture" of democracy may represent a rational equilibrium, but this equilibrium has to be worked out over time as strategic actors build up trust, uncertainty diminishes, and the political system stabilizes. "Equilibrium culture" becomes rational only over time; rationality cannot uniformly predict it. Together, culturalist and rationalist approaches may bear more fruit than either one on its own.

CONCLUDING THOUGHTS ON CULTURE

We agree with Przeworski that no culture can be said to be absolutely antithetical to democracy. But if cultures must change to become democratic or allow for democracy, then it must be true that certain cultures are more closely allied with democratic values than others. As a result, culture may be an obstacle to the development of democracy, but not a fixed one. Culture may help to describe the pace with which countries change or, alternatively, may describe the probability of change. While culture never represents an insurmountable obstacle to democracy, it may make democratization, like capitalism or industrialism, more or less likely.

The debate over culture's effects on regime type has only infrequently been well marcated. The confusing and powerful word *culture* has been used in myriad ways to make arguments that depend on the word's fundamentally different, noncomparable connotations. In many cases, semantics are utilized, intentionally or unintentionally, to construct suspect arguments. Meanwhile, the processes of cultural diffusion that produce particular attitudes or values are not well understood, nor is it known exactly how susceptible attitudes or values are to change. Likewise, Przeworski is correct, as is Lee Kuan Yew, to remind us that cultural values can be the dependent factors, the product of other variables, not just the independent source of particular behaviors. Dynamic interactions between culture and society or among various parts of a cultural system make cultural change an extremely complex phenomenon. The fact that the process can rarely be quantified does not make it any less real.

While culture may provide one part of the explanation for democratic success or failure, a distinction must be drawn between its short- and long-term effects. *If we want to focus on how successful democracy is once it has been established,* cultural effects can be significant in the short term but should generally be considered close to zero in the long term. This is tantamount to saying that any people, society, or culture can ultimately maintain a democratic polity but that the process will be much more difficult for some cultures than others. Because the process of cultural change is long, arduous, and gradual, some states will take a very long time to achieve democratization. But all of them can do it. This is not to say that all cultures will establish democracy. Here, only those variables that affect the longevity and quality of democracy are being addressed. Cultures may be more or less likely to adopt democracy on their own, but history has shown that democracy may be established for many reasons—including conquest, imposition, and endogenous compromise. Our argument is simply that if any culture, bounded in a state, adopts democracy, it can be successful over the long term.

There is a culture associated with democracy, and this culture, whether it is universally subscribed to or not, whether it is developed before a democratic transition or after, whether it evolves at the same pace in all nations or not, whether it is a product of economic development or experience, must emerge in the long run in order for democracy to survive.

CHAPTER 8

REFLECTIONS ON LEGITIMACY

WE HAVE DEMONSTRATED THE IMPORTANCE of economic development for democratic longevity. We have also argued that cultural change is often a critical variable for democratic success. But another variable is specific to political institutions and crucial for democracy: legitimacy. The concept of legitimacy is relevant to all regimes across all cultures—not just to democracies. Lack of legitimacy may trump cultural, economic, or institutional variables. A well-designed system in a relatively wealthy country that is deemed illegitimate by a large segment of the population and elites (e.g., Weimar Germany) can crumble in the face of crises that legitimate regimes may be able to withstand. The degree to which a regime is legitimate may be affected by cultural expectations but also depends on economic and institutional factors that are not culture bound. Legitimacy is therefore a bridge between cultural factors and institutional variables. This chapter touches on the sources and importance of legitimacy.

Stable political systems, even authoritarian ones, cannot rely primarily on force. The alternative to force is legitimacy, a broadly accepted systemic "title to rule." Legitimacy is not equivalent to "satisfaction" with the current regime—a positive evaluation of social or economic policies, for example; legitimacy should persist in spite of underperformance.[1] Legitimacy means that the society as a whole believes that the existing political institutions are the most appropriate, regardless of how it feels about the specific people who hold office at any given time. Those in power have gained their position through processes accepted as proper by almost all significant actors or potential actors in the political process.

Regime legitimacy is difficult to measure; the best we can do generally is to rely on survey questions that directly ask citizens whether a democratic (or other) regime is the preferred regime type. Larry Diamond, as mentioned above, argues that a consolidated democracy ought to have robust support (two-thirds or more of the population) for democracy as the preferred regime type.[2] In nonauthoritarian systems, legitimacy is correlated strongly with the level of democracy in a country; the more democratic a nation is, the more legitimate the political system tends to be. Political factors—civil and political liberties—are more important than simple economic performance in predicting the legitimacy of the democratic regime in a nation.[3] This does not mean that legitimacy is the source of democratic success. Most likely, democracy and legitimacy reinforce one another through a complex feedback mechanism. Legitimacy may be viewed as a stock of credibility that can delay or reduce the intensity of crises for a democracy. When times are good, legitimacy slowly accumulates. When times are bad, legitimacy is expended. But it lags behind temporary conditions, so that in times of crisis, a legitimate regime is able to slowly expend its legitimacy, while illegitimate regimes are likely to fall quickly.

Legitimacy involves a normative judgment that cannot be explained entirely in terms of other judgments or observed political or material conditions. For example, Linz and Stepan find that, in Portugal and Greece, despite economic deterioration in the early years of democracy in both states (the late 1970s), regime legitimacy generally grew or remained high. "What the Portuguese case reveals clearly is that democracy became consolidated during a period of deep economic hardship but not of political despair or system blame."[4] In Southern Europe, the legitimacy of democracy is delinked from attitudes about past authoritarian regimes. Linz and Stepan argue that citizens discriminate between the past and future, allowing for benign interpretations of actions taken by past authoritarian regimes while still believing that democracy represents the best regime for the future. The recent data from Spain and Portugal support this view of legitimacy.[5] Why does legitimacy matter?

LEGITIMACY AND THE PRISONERS' DILEMMA

To explore the importance of legitimacy in more depth, we introduce a concept from game theory: the prisoners' dilemma. The prisoners' dilemma is a paradigmatic case of the problem of collective action, which, briefly, is the problem of how actors in society who do not know one another can reasonably work together to improve collective welfare. The model assumes that actors are self-interested and ignorant of other actors' choices. Imagine two prisoners who have been arrested for the same crime. Both prisoners are offered the same deal: if both keep quiet, they will get a short jail term (lesser conviction); if both confess, they get a long jail term; if one confesses and the other does not, the one who confessed goes free and the other serves a long jail term alone. The two are being held in separate cells where they cannot communicate with each other. Each player then faces the following options:

1. *Say nothing.* If the other prisoner also says nothing, a collective optimum is achieved, because both prisoners get light terms. If the other player "defects" (confesses), however, then the first player gets the worst outcome (the "sucker's payoff"), conviction alone while the other player goes free.
2. *Confess.* If the other prisoner says nothing, then the first prisoner goes free, an individual optimum, and the other player gets the worst outcome. If the other prisoner also confesses, both prisoners are convicted, but with lighter sentences than either alone.

The best outcome for any individual player is to defect, but since both players are likely to do so, they will always achieve a collectively suboptimal outcome. They would both be better off if they "cooperated" (said nothing), but this outcome is extremely unlikely because it presupposes trust in another rational self-interested actor with whom one cannot negotiate in good faith. Since neither prisoner can be sure that the other prisoner will refuse to confess, both players are likely to confess (defect). By following their own best strategies given the circumstances, a suboptimal result ensues. One can infer, then, that there is a deficit of trust—in the sense of reasonable expectations that the other player will not take advantage of one's attempt to cooperate—in the prisoners' dilemma that leads to worse outcomes.[6] This example approximates the collective action dilemma in many situations, including the case of democracy.[7]

In a democracy, legitimacy can help to resolve the collective action dilemma. How? Let us consider democracy itself to be a collective good. Democracy depends on the interactions of many actors whose actions are unpredictable. Although democracy may be a collectively optimal equilibrium, some actors could potentially gain more by standing outside the democratic game and attempting to achieve power by force. Imagine that at time t, society is democratic, and all actors have to determine whether at time $t + 1$ to continue to play democratically or to revolt. If democracy is a collective good and if regime outcome is represented as a classic prisoners' dilemma, those actors who want to defect will particularly benefit if other players act democratically while they themselves revolt. If no actor believes that any other actor will cooperate, then all actors will defect. If some actors comply (operate democratically rather than preparing for revolt), then defectors will easily take control of the state (they have been preparing for revolt while others have been acting democratically in good faith), and those who cooperated will get the "sucker's payoff"—in this case, servitude under a nondemocratic state.

However, if all players defect, the result will be bloody conflict, destruction of capital, and many political losers. Therefore, unless an actor is certain that he or she will win the ensuing struggle for power if he or she defects, democracy remains a collectively optimal equilibrium. As with any collective action problem, however, the recognition that a particular outcome is collectively optimal does not easily translate into the achievement of that outcome. If actors do not know or cannot trust one another, they are likely to fall short of collective optima.

Widespread legitimacy acts as a kind of informant, breaking down the constraints of the prisoners' dilemma (in which actors have no reliable information about the actions of other actors). If all actors recognize the democratic regime as legitimate, they are encouraged not only to cooperate but to trust that other actors will also cooperate. Legitimacy carries signals to actors—signals that there is a bias toward cooperation among other actors—that make cooperation a less risky choice. A rational actor under conditions of widespread legitimacy may conclude with reasonable certainty that "I do not need to prepare to revolt, because no other major actors are preparing to do so." It is precisely this information that is missing in the prisoners' dilemma. For an explanation of why legitimacy might work even though it sends signals that could be exploited by defectors rather then cooperators, see the appendix to this chapter.

In addition to bringing the costs of cooperation down, legitimacy also makes defection more costly. In spite of our simplified model, society does not consist only of individual actors. It also consists of collective actors, some with more weight than others. One of these is the state. Those in control know that the state can enhance its own legitimacy by crushing illegitimate defectors. In fact, citizens ascribe legitimacy to the state in part because they believe that the state will stand up to others that are considered illegitimate; when it fails to do this, legitimacy is lost. As Juan Linz notes, quoting John F. Kennedy, "A democratic leader—in fact, any leader—must be able to say: 'My obligation under the Constitution and the statutes was and is to implement the orders of the legitimate authority with whatever means are necessary and with as little force and civil disorder as the circumstances permit and to be prepared to back them up with whatever other civil or military enforcement might have been required.'"[8]

Under conditions of legitimacy, therefore, the state can count on support (cooperation) in its efforts to destroy defectors. Defectors in turn can assume that the state will not just lie down in front of them. They can expect a particularly costly struggle for power, which should serve as a disincentive to defect in the first place.

Legitimacy is also important in nondemocratic regimes. A major collective actor in authoritarian regimes is the military. The actions of the military, particularly its willingness to lend support to a repressive regime, are linked to the degree of legitimacy that authoritarianism is afforded in a given society. If the military believes that its own professional interests will be undermined by cooperating with an illegitimate, nondemocratic regime, it may defect, thereby significantly weakening the nondemocratic regime. A case in point was the military defection from the authoritarian government of Ivory Coast in October 2000. When protesters took to the streets after a sham election, the Ivorian military sided with opposition leader Laurent Gbagbo and abandoned dictator Robert Guei. The military may also defect from unpopular democratically elected leaders in the name of democracy, allowing new democrats to replace the old, who are perceived as threatening a legitimate system. This is basically what happened to Joseph Estrada in the Philippines in January 2001. The military supported popular protests that led to the fall of Estrada and his replacement by his vice president.

In addition to affecting the constraints of the prisoners' dilemma, the extent of legitimacy influences the political calculus of actors. Indeed, to say that the system is highly legitimate is equivalent to saying that many strategic actors will cooperate for what may be an irrationally long period before they begin to defect. As Linz argues, modifying Albert Hirschman, legitimacy translates into optimism about the opportunities for reform within existing institutions that make actors more inclined to cooperate—as long as they are not overly concerned about defection. In this way, legitimacy affects not the *constraints* of the prisoners' dilemma but rather the incidence of cooperators versus defectors in the game.[9]

Legitimacy is, of course, only one of many important variables that enter into the calculations of individual and collective actors in society. The importance of legitimacy, like many such variables, depends on actors' perceptions. No regime is ever completely legitimate in the eyes of all citizens. The degree of legitimacy, then, and its impact on actors' decisions, is largely a subjective question.

Having discussed briefly the importance of legitimacy to all regimes, but particularly to democratic regimes, we now explore the sources and variants of legitimacy. Max Weber pioneered legitimacy theory, identifying three types of legitimacy: traditional, rational-legal, and charismatic.[10] Traditional authority derives its legitimacy from a time before collective memory—it has "always" existed. The best example is a traditional monarchy. Rational-legal authority involves an acceptance of the "rules of the game," a good example of which is the legitimacy accorded to the American Constitution. Finally, charismatic legitimacy is derived from a leader who radiates a "cult of personality." This is obviously the most volatile and short-term type of legitimacy and the least conducive to democracy. Of course, these three types of legitimacy need not exist in their pure forms; states may derive legitimacy from a combination of sources.

The sources of legitimacy must appeal above all to the sensibilities of elite political actors. Elites may take it upon themselves to justify system legitimacy to the wider society. If an important segment, such as the intellectuals, does not believe the system is legitimate, however, it can foster subversion of the regime.[11] This is not to belittle the significance of legitimacy among the masses. If on one hand many citizens come to reject democracy, they may be open to parties that expressly repudiate democracy—such as the communists or fascists during the 1930s—making possible a shift of power from pro-democratic to anti-democratic elites. On the other hand, it is fair to say that elites who consider democracy illegitimate can have a much more profound destabilizing effect on a regime than mass protest by nonelites.[12] Elite actors manifest their belief in the legitimacy of the system through their political actions; nonelites are infrequently called on to legitimate the regime.[13]

How have the three types of legitimacy affected the acceptance of democracy?

Strikingly, traditional legitimacy has played a significant role in the institutionalization of democracy. The Northern European and British Commonwealth nations and the Low Countries developed democratic institutions while retaining traditional legitimacy— that is, continuing their monarchies. In 1959 Lipset reported what he called an "absurd fact," that all the stable democracies then existing were kingdoms, except for the United States, Switzerland, and at the time, Uruguay.[14] The survival of the monarchy reflected the fact that democracy had evolved gradually in lieu of a violent break with the absolutist past, at least in Europe.

Traditional legitimacy does not pertain only to kings and queens. Botswana provides a stellar example of the use of traditional legitimacy in the African context. Elites in Botswana combined democratic adaptation with traditional deference in preserving the protodemocratic institution of the kgotla while entrenching a multiparty democracy. The *kgotla* was a traditional community meeting of all adult males, presided over by a chief or headman. "Traditionally," John Holm reports, "these leaders did not make major decisions without consulting the *kgotla* and, if possible, achieving a consensus."[15] Although the democratic character of this and other Tswana cultural traditions has been romanticized, the *kgotla* did function historically to impede the growth of autocratic tendencies and lack of accountability.[16] While the ruling party undermined the authority of chiefs and transferred most of their substantive powers to modern institutions, it wisely retained and even amplified the use of the *kgotla* for public consultation and debate on major policies. The preservation of the institution of chief (*kgosi*) has been crucial in the process of utilizing and modernizing tradition to legitimate a new democratic regime. The chiefs have been instrumental not only in convening the *kgotla* but in expanding it to incorporate women, moderate disputes, promote tolerance and accommodation; in short, they have performed a vital role in lending strength and legitimacy to the democratic system.[17]

The record shows that the overthrow of monarchies and other traditional legitimators reduces the chances for democratic survival. A comparison of the consequences of deposing the German kaiser after World War I with those that followed the retention of the emperor in post–World War II Japan furnishes a good example. Japanese nationalists, unlike pre-Hitler German rightists, adhered to occupation-dictated rules. The Weimar Republic never could attain legitimacy in the eyes of the German right, while Japanese conservatives who despised the MacArthur constitution obeyed it since the Emperor proclaimed and thereby legitimized it.[18]

New republics, even with symbolic presidents who try to act out the role of constitutional monarchs, as in Weimar Germany or Fourth Republic France, will, ceteris paribus, be more unstable than polities that retain powerless royalty. The danger to continuity is even greater when the head of state is also a policy-making executive, as in Latin America, where symbolic authority and effective power are combined in one person. Without a legitimating symbolic head of state, it is difficult for the public to separate feelings toward the regime from those held toward the policy makers. Yet this is the critical distinction that must be made in a democracy, for it legitimizes the concept of a loyal opposition. Without acceptance of the difference between the source of authority (or the abstract polity) and the policy-making office-holders who temporarily hold that authority, any opposition may appear to be against the system and threaten the polity's very foundations. The chronic difficulties in institutionalizing democracy in many Latin American presidential regimes for close to two centuries may reflect the difficulties that inhere in the absence of a distinction between the source and the agents of authority.

The United States presents a special case. Despite combining symbolic authority and power in the Presidency, the American Constitution has been so hallowed by prolonged effectiveness and ideology for over two hundred years, that it, rather than those who occupy the offices it specifies, has become the legitimate source of authority. But this example of constitutional legal-rational legitimacy took many decades to develop. It was in no way predetermined that the country would survive the many secession crises and brutal civil war that plagued the United States during its first century. [19]

Rational-legal legitimacy, the acceptance of basic law, does not exist in new systems, since the law has previously been identified by much of the population with the interests of a foreign exploiter or a deposed domestic dictator. Efforts to construct rational-legal legitimacy necessarily involve extending the rule of the law and the prestige of the courts, which should be as independent of the rest of the polity as possible. In new democracies, these requirements imply, as Bruce Ackerman notes, the need to draw up a "liberal" constitution as soon as possible. Ultimately, the constitution can provide a basis for legitimacy, for limitations on state power, and for political and economic rights. Since most governing postrevolutionary coalitions suffer from disintegrative pressures once the object of the revolution (i.e., the old regime) has been removed, it is important to formulate a constitution in the fleeting moments before these pressures take hold, while there is still an opportunity for a mobilized and unified society to accomplish common ends.[20]

South Africa has attempted to follow this strategy by fleshing out its constitution through intensive dialogue in the form of town meetings. The Truth and Reconciliation Commission, which aired the many offenses committed by all sides under apartheid, also represented an attempt to stimulate rational-legal legitimacy for the new regime, by positioning the African National Congress (ANC)–led government as a force for both justice and for inclusion. The South African case is particularly relevant to the rest of Africa, where legitimacy most often has had to be forged in new, ethnolinguistically fragmented states, with a weak sense of nationalism, against a backdrop of military coups and authoritarian governments. Artificial boundaries constructed by colonial powers undermine a sense of nationhood, in spite of a common colonial experience. In many of the former colonies, the extent to which the former colonial power played different ethnic groups off against one another has seriously eroded the potential for national unity. Most of the early leaders of postcolonial states tapped into charisma as a basis for their legitimacy, and most of these in turn became increasingly authoritarian. As charismatic legitimacy is a weak foundation for democracy, and traditional legitimacy is difficult to come by in states with no unifying "tradition," it should come as no surprise that ethnolinguistic fractionalization, characteristic of most of sub-Saharan Africa, has inhibited the development of political legitimacy.

LEGITIMACY, ETHNIC FRAGMENTATION, AND CONFLICT

Legitimacy is facilitated by cultural homogeneity, but as noted, most postcolonial states are highly fragmented. Although legitimacy is difficult to foster under conditions of cultural heterogeneity, elites can choose to exacerbate or ameliorate these conditions. It is not impossible to deal with ethnic differences in the construction of legitimacy, but it requires sophisticated statecraft and the use of both symbolic and concrete gestures to forge a demos.

Political actors in Africa have often exacerbated ethnic conflict in order to create or find a loyal base. Although the whole of Kenya, for example, was subjected to British rule, differential treatment by the colonial rulers led to heightened conflict among its ethnic groups—particularly between the largest ethnicities, the Luo and the Kikuyu, on one hand, and the smaller ones, like the Kalenjin, on the other. Political maneuvering by Jomo Kenyatta, Kenya's first president and a Kikuyu himself, eventually isolated the Luo while bringing some of the smaller ethnic groups into a governing coalition through the use of patronage. [21] The effect of this was to create blocs—the Luo versus the Kikuyu and their allies—that were mutually hostile and suspicious of one another and to exacerbate the ethnic sources of conflict, beyond partisan ideological tensions. This ethnic conflict tended to undermine the legitimacy of the postcolonial regime amongst various sectors of Kenyan society. Power politics was privileged over the forging of national unity. An increasingly polarized atmosphere was also stimulated by an increasingly dictatorial approach to governance and a gradual erosion of the electoral system inherited from the British. Kenyatta's successor, Daniel arap Moi, continued to exploit ethnic divisions in his ever more authoritarian state. To create a viable national identity, Kenya needed either to look into or beyond its past and create a legitimating myth that would help tie its disparate sections together. Its failure to do so encouraged violence and economic deterioration. The regime has been low in legitimacy, and the government has been unable to handle the tensions created by economic crises. Kenya's bright immediate, postcolonial prospects deteriorated into authoritarianism.

An alternative to this course can be seen in Kenya's neighbor to the south, Tanzania. Julius Nyerere, Tanzania's founding father, pursued disastrous, pseudosocialist economic policies that have left Tanzanians much poorer than Kenyans (and he also insisted for many years on the moral superiority of a one-party state). Yet Nyerere understood the importance of national unity and the need for national legitimacy in a country as fissiparous as any in East Africa. In order to forge a national consensus, Nyerere determined that everyone in Tanzania would speak Kiswahili, a coastal language composed of shards of the Arabic and Bantu language families. Today, virtually everyone in Tanzania does indeed speak Kiswahili and pays minor attention to ethnic dialects. Everyone in mainland Tanzania is a Tanzanian first.[22] Unlike Kenya, Tanzania has suffered from little ethnic violence. Through the creation of a common language, Nyerere used his own charisma and an invented tradition to create the foundations for a legitimate nation-state. Although Tanzania is among the poorest countries in the world, Nyerere's cultural policies may have increased the potential for democracy in the future. The evolution of multiparty politics in Tanzania does not so far carry ethnic connotations that could be used to undermine the legitimacy of opposition leaders, as has happened in Kenya, Zimbabwe, and other African states.[23] The evolution of a more unified demos ought to make multiparty politics easier to accept.

Where legitimacy is inherently weak or low, as it is in new states or postrevolutionary ones, it is best stimulated by prolonged effectiveness—that is, the actual performance of the government, the extent to which it satisfies the basic needs of most of the population and of key power groups (such as the military and economic leaders).[24] For most people effectiveness is a judgment largely based on economic performance and the consequent effect on standards of living. In the short run, however, this generalization is of little help to new systems. For them, the best immediate institutional advice is to perpetuate or create a source of national authority distinct from the agent of authority. This is not easily done, although post-Franco Spain seems to have facilitated it with a revived constitutional monarchy. In the wake of an attempted coup in the early 1980s, the king was able to persuade the military to return to the barracks. Alternatively, a symbolic but powerless elected head of state may help foster political legitimacy, as in post–World War II France, Germany, and Italy. The history of the latter two and of other new democracies suggests that it is possible to acquire a kind of inoculation against authoritarianism as a reaction to the viciousness of the previous dictatorial regimes, as seems to have occurred in some Third Wave Latin American and new, post-Communist democracies.

Before leaving the theme of legitimacy, we note a complicating factor in determining the extent of democratic legitimacy and its impact. One interesting trend that has been prevalent in parts of Latin America is the notion that democracy is the most legitimate regime type but, because of democratic failures, military action must be condoned to remove one democratic government and replace it with another.[25] For example, in Brazil, both military elites and many citizens have long believed that the military is the guardian, or like the former emperor, the "moderating power," within democratic politics. According to the logic of this "legitimacy," the military plays a role in politics that is limited but accepted in the same way as other institutions are, like the judicial branch. This kind of legitimacy is problematic, of course, for reasons that Brazil itself manifested when the military decided to hold onto power from the 1960s to the 1980s, pursuing a more transformative project than simply assisting democratic regime change. Nevertheless, it presents a problem for students of legitimacy, because it implies that some actors may believe democracy is the most legitimate regime type *and* that the military may need to intervene. The coup in Ecuador in 2000 may have been an example on some level, with some citizens feeling that it was necessary to remove the current administration by military force—to replace it, though, not with a military government but with another democratic one. It is probably fair to say that these types of attitudes represent an intermediate phase between democratic illegitimacy and democratic legitimacy that should fade if democratic systems mature. Finer-tuned survey research is needed to tease out the real meaning of legitimacy to respondents.

Legitimacy thus presents some of the same measurement difficulties as are associated with the other variables discussed in this part of the book, gradualism and culture. Perhaps one of the most important areas of research to be mapped out by future generations of democracy students is in fine-tuning our ability to measure, quantitatively or otherwise, these more difficult to operationalize variables that play a vital role in democratization and democratic stability. While the pace of economic growth is relatively easy to measure, simple annual changes in GDP per capita may mask significant differences in where growth is happening and what impact it has. Likewise, the pace of political change presents difficult measurement problems, and little work has been done to study this phenomenon systematically across countries. Culture requires more systematic study, as well. The advent of the World Values Survey has made it possible to begin cross-national study of cultural variation, as have the various public opinion "barometers" now in existence around the world. Unfortunately, we lack historical data on public opinion in these regions, but as the discipline moves forward, questions can be honed and normalized to make comparisons easier. Finally, as pointed out in this chapter, the study of legitimacy requires some hard thinking about the appropriate survey instruments to get at the right issue. How contingent are our respondents' attitudes about legitimacy? Do people across cultures and regions really mean the same thing when they profess to ascribe legitimacy to particular regime types? This remains unclear.

We hope that the issues raised in these chapters will be part of the future research agenda of social scientists interested in democracy. The difficulties of measuring legitimacy, culture, and to a lesser extent, pace of political and economic change should not inhibit their study. These variables are simply too important to ignore.

APPENDIX: LEGITIMACY AND THE PRISONERS' DILEMMA

In this appendix we explore further the mechanism by which legitimacy makes the survival of democracy more likely. We return to the prisoners' dilemma, which, again, has four outcomes:

- T: player A defects, player B cooperates; player A achieves individual optimum
- R: player A and player B cooperate; collective optimum
- P: player A and player B defect; collective suboptimum
- S: player A cooperates, player B defects; individual worst outcome for A

Consider: player A and player B are in a prisoners' dilemma. Neither's preferences are known to the other.

Player A assumes that player B has the same preferences as himself. These are $T > R > P > S$. Player A then chooses to follow the strategy "defect." Why? If he follows this strategy and he is right about player B's preferences being the same as his, he will achieve P. If he is wrong about player B and player B's real preferences put cooperation at the top, say $R > T > P > S$, then he will get T, his preferred outcome. Player A has to choose to defect, because he otherwise risks S, his worst outcome.

Player B is in the same position if his preferences look like those of player A. If he really prefers the cooperative outcome R, he is still foolish to choose to cooperate unless he believes that player A also prefers R. Otherwise, he risks S—also his least preferred outcome. Therefore, a rational player who assumes that other players are first and foremost self-interested, even if he is not, will also defect to avoid S.

Under what conditions will the players achieve R instead of P? If the players were able to communicate and create a pact, they could make an agreement to cooperate and achieve R, but the pact would hold only if there was significant trust between the players, since each player would have an incentive to violate the pact. But the incentive to violate the pact in the prisoners' dilemma is based on the assumption that there are no effective sanctions for defection. This assumption in turn is based on the idea that this is a one-shot dilemma. In the case of interactions among social actors over time, however, there are many cases of prisoners' dilemmas that are iterative.

In fact, if the prisoners' dilemma is iterative, then the calculations of the prisoners could be very different. Returning to the prisoners' dilemma above, if the players participate in the dilemma once a day, they will quickly learn each other's preferences. Under the assumptions we have outlined, rational, self-interested, and clever actors will always prefer to defect, achieving P rather than S. However, if the dilemma is iterative, both actors have an incentive to try to achieve a better outcome than P. The only way to achieve a better outcome is to cooperate simultaneously. If the players were able to communicate to each other their desire to cooperate, they could obtain R instead of P and both achieve a collective optimum together.

How does the logic behind this optimum work? If the players agree to cooperate to obtain R, it is still in both players' interests to defect at the last moment, because now both players have compelling reason to believe that the other player will cooperate, and they would be able to obtain T by defecting—their individual optimum. This strategy will work on day 1 for player A, but it will fail on day 2, because player B will recognize that he has been betrayed. Both players will return to defection as their default strategy. Alternatively, if both players try to defect on day 1, they will return to P on day 1 itself.

Although it may take some adjustment, it remains the case that both players can achieve more in the long run by cooperating and achieving R than by defecting once and achieving P in subsequent attempts. As long as both players are farsighted, then, they will prefer to cooperate if they can be sure that the other player will cooperate. The question in the case of iterative dilemmas, therefore, is what are the conditions that facilitate reaching a pact that allows the players to cooperate?

In large societies with many actors, it is not possible to form direct pacts with all of the relevant players. Nor is there any way to directly enforce sanctions against the many unknown people who may defect from collective action. What is needed, therefore, is some form of informal understanding that can be assumed among many people who do not know one another. This informal understanding either takes the place of or is a result of repeated bouts of prisoners' dilemma in which all actors defect as a learning tool that leads to the ultimate achievement of outcome R.[26] It sends a signal to all players that outcome R is desired and that the relevant players are ready to cooperate. This understanding is what is known as "legitimacy." Legitimacy also implies, moreover, that T is not a stable outcome for those who would subvert the regime. Even if defectors are able to capture the state at time t, their actions will be considered illegitimate, they can expect resistance, and they will ultimately be forced back into outcome P, having lost the opportunity to obtain outcome R. If indeed R is preferable to P over time, legitimacy is a heuristic device for communicating the desirability of R to all strategic actors in a society.

The prisoners' dilemma is a useful device for thinking about regime types because, in an abstract sense, the players really are prisoners. That is, they cannot "exit" from play, but are constrained to live in society under some regime type that will be at least minimally coercive. The option to exit, then, cannot confer the ability to impose sanctions on players. Sanctions can be imposed only through continued play, and with the prospect of violent coercion.

CHAPTER 9

CONCLUSION

DEFENDING DEMOCRACY:
DEVELOPMENT, PEACE, AND SECURITY

WE HAVE DEALT WITH THE DETAILS of democracy: what constitutes democracy, how it works, what makes it last. In closing, we want to talk about why democracy is worth the trouble, informing, we hope, the urgent work of democratizers around the world. There are basically three valuable consequences of democracy that we should not lose sight of: (1) Democracy is a tool for fuller political development than mere economic development. (2) Democracy tends to encourage domestic peace. (3) Democracy tends to promote international peace.

There is a wide-ranging debate about the degree to which democracy affects economic growth, which is far more controversial than the question of whether economic development affects democracy. For some time, the so-called "Pinochet effect" school of thought had a strong following in this subfield. The assumption was that dictatorships were better than democracies at pushing through structural reforms, controlling present consumption in order to increase investment, and thus facilitating economic growth. This view was popularized by, among others, Samuel Huntington.[1] It is no longer in vogue (though it seems to linger in Putin's Russia). A paradigm shift of epic proportions has occurred, to the extent that many will maintain, in spite of Pinochet's record in Chile, that the only way to develop is through democracy.[2] Both of these views were and are too proximate. The theoretical assumptions behind both of them are weak or easily contradicted.[3] Nevertheless, one may take a middle road that is satisfactory. Economic development can happen with or without democracy, but political development, almost by definition, requires practice with democracy.

There is no authoritarian quid pro quo for modernization.[4] But if modernization means economic development and democracy, then citizens must see not only their standard of living rise (what we generally call development) but also their political self-actualization increase (what we may call political development). There is ample evidence that democracy, a democratic culture, and learning to play by democratic rules are the result not simply of structural determinants but of practice with democracy. Although the structural correlates improve the chances that democracy will be tried, and will be successful if and when tried, only actual practice with democracy can make it a reality.

In this sense, we agree with Alain Touraine that the definition of development has to be widened to take into consideration not only economic conditions but political ones as well. Like Touraine, we see this as a project that, while not exactly liberal, does agree in principle with the liberal understanding of positive liberty. The classical liberals have always understood that there is no such thing as freedom where economic autonomy is lacking. Political and economic freedom are linked and interdependent. Ergo, *development* means not only improvement in living standards but people's ability to have some input in the process by which their lives change materially. People cannot simply be developed; they have to develop themselves. While this view does not preach an abandonment of state intervention, as the most rabid liberals would have it, it is quintessentially liberal.[5] It assumes freedom to be the ability to make individual choices about both the political and the economic, between which there is not really any clear division. Touraine has put it thus: "If . . . we define development as the political management of the social tensions between economic investment and social participation, then democracy will be seen as the precondition for that management and not simply as its result."[6]

Development implies participation. Otherwise, it is not really development. In accord with this argument, there is some reason to expect that democracy might limit the worst excesses of poverty. Why? Amartya Sen has suggested that the electoral consequences of mass starvation may be too great for democratic leaders to ignore, while authoritarian leaders are able to use military coercion to avoid the inevitable protests that come with such macrolevel disasters. Sen has found that no democracy with a reasonably free press has ever suffered from a major famine.[7] Along these same lines, a recent study by Thomas D. Zweifel and Patricio Navia reports a statistically significant positive impact of democracy on infant mortality rates.[8] This empirical evidence supports a limited "worst-case avoidance" defense of democracy, rather than the broader, "democracy as quid pro quo for development" argument.[9]

Development also should mean freedom from arbitrary violence. Here the democracies do have a definitive advantage over the nondemocracies. Internal coercive violence is lower in democracies. On the heels of Sen's argument about famines, which are almost ubiquitously political phenomena, it follows that the political costs of condoning large-scale violence are too high for elected leaders to absorb. This does not mean that there is no violence in democracies, but only that, on balance, the levels of internal violence tend to be lower.[10]

But it is not just internal violence that is eschewed by democracies. R. J. Rummel reports that democracies have never gone to war with one another in modern times.[11] Democracies are also unlikely to target one another in lower-level bilateral disputes short of war; less than 7 percent of bilateral disputes between

1816 and 1992 were between democracies.[12] This does not mean that democracies do not wage war—or that they avoid reciprocation of hostilities—only that they do not wage war with other democracies. Furthermore, disputes among full democracies tend not to relate to the often intractable issue of territory and have tended to be shorter in duration in contemporary times.[13] The more democratic the globe, then, the more peaceful it is likely to be. Democracy may not be a necessary condition for security and peace, but it appears to be a nearly sufficient one.

SUMMING UP

Before moving on to the case study section of the book, we summarize the lessons learned in parts I and II. The reader will want to bear in mind the analysis presented in chapters 1 through 8 when examining our assessment of the specific cases of the United States and Latin America. Although part III, "Hemispheric Divide," can stand alone and was originally delivered as a distinct lecture from the rest of this book, it is our hope that the broad lines of attack we have sketched here serve to elucidate the successes and failures of democratic experiments in the United States and Latin America.

An understanding of the correlates of democracy inevitably leads to "pessoptimism" about democratic prospects in the world. There is much recent good news to report, but all of it is tempered by other, less sanguine reports and the knowledge of how tenuous the experiment with democracy can be.

We have argued that the success of democracy can be explained only by employing a multivariate analysis. Although our search for a model of how democracy works explores many aspects of social systems, it is far from exhaustive. And although we offer as many insights as the preceding page span allows, we admit that a multivariate analysis of this type does not yield an equation that can explain all of democracy's success stories nor predict where it will be succeed in the near future. Indeed, it cannot even be said with certainty which of the multiple factors we have identified is the most important; so much depends, as it does in baking, on the exact quantities of each ingredient and their synergistic effects on one another.

Our model of democratic success is primarily endogenous. We do not emphasize international factors, though neither do we ignore them entirely. We therefore start with a contentious assumption—that domestic political regimes can be explained primarily by domestic political factors. This point is certainly debatable. However, it is also impossible to demonstrate, without reference to numerous and dubious counterfactuals, that where international factors did play a role in the breakdown of democracy, *but for* those international pressures democracy would have survived. In fact it is impossible to prove that international factors are or are not determinant, a point we do not care to debate here. What we believe, and this is the important issue, is that even where international factors do play a role, they are conditioned by domestic political factors. Thus, a critical break or juncture in the domestic political system must occur, as in the case of Chile in 1973, that allows for international factors to play a role. International factors conceivably can exert the extra pressure needed to topple, or undermine the consolidation of, a regime, but this occurs almost always where domestic factors have already created the conditions for breakdown or failure to consolidate.

What then are the domestic factors that determine the success or failure of democracy? Surveying the robust literature on the role of economic development, we find that perhaps the single most studied and most important factor in the literature on democracy is economic prosperity. While economic development almost certainly leads toward democracy, it is important to specify both the reasons for this and the type of economic development we mean. The main impact of economic development, particularly capitalist economic development—that is, a relatively significant, diffuse, and competitive private sector—is the dispersion of skills, power, and resources away from a single center toward new groups. Over time the advanced democracies have developed thriving economies with a bewildering array of powerful groups vying for political power—the bourgeoisie, religious groups, state employees, labor unions, and more recently, welfare-state interest groups. Democracy has offered these competing groups an opportunity to share power without the cost of destructive internecine warfare. What has made democratic compromise possible is the growth in the resources available to these groups to pressure one another. And this diffusion of resources has been a by-product of capitalist development. This offers one reason why, although many Middle Eastern oil-rich countries have prospered, they have not democratized. The model of development they have followed, conditioned on the exploitation of a single primary export controlled by the state, has not led to the creation of independent sources of wealth or power in these countries. Thus, while they have grown wealthier, they have not fundamentally changed the relationship between state and society that exists in most poor countries, in which the state is the main locus of power and wealth.

We put considerable emphasis in this book on the role of culture, which has probably been referred to almost as frequently as economic development but is much less well understood. Although culture cannot entirely be distinguished from the socioeconomic structure that underlies it, this does not mean that it has no independent weight. As we argue, culture can both influence and be influenced by socio-economic structures. But there is no one-to-one correlation, meaning that culture has independent effects. We analyze the culture of Catholic Latin America and of the Islamic world and demonstrate how, in the historical trajectory of these regions, certain attitudes were either missing or directly in conflict with a democratic culture. In Latin America a virtual revolution within the Vatican, along with the innovations of liberation theology, have restructured Catholicism significantly, allowing for more democratic, individualistic, participatory, and contentious values to prosper. In Islam, however, while there are potential inroads for democracy in the cultural heritage, legacies of complete opposition to secularism and tolerance continue to inhibit the development of values consonant with democratic praxis. There is a democratic culture, and cultures that are not compatible with its tenets—acceptance of a secular sphere, tolerance of opposition and contention, for example—have to change in some measure to incorporate these principles if they are to make successful democracies.

Elite and mass culture are not always consonant. In this regard, elites must be willing to stick to the rules of the game, must manifest tolerance and acceptance of electoral defeat—even though mass opinion may often be hostile to these values. Where this hostility exists, the general population must at least acquiesce in or be apathetic to the extension of democratic values and liberties by elites. One could argue that in many Islamic countries today, the population neither holds democratic values nor is apathetic about the behavior of their elites in this regard. Part of the reason for this stems from the failure of these societies to delineate secular and religious spheres where different rules apply. As long as the public political sphere is seen as a stage where religious values are preeminent, it is unlikely that citizens will greet elite actions with the apathy required of them if they hold antidemocratic values themselves.

Because of the great dislocations involved in economic and cultural change, it seems that the slower the pace at which societies move between different stages of liberalization, the more stable and successful their democracies tend to be. Although recent evidence suggests that rapid economic growth can be a consistently powerful aid to democratic consolidation, rapid changes can threaten the degree to which important social actors perceive the political system to be legitimate, creating a pool of discontented, semiloyal or disloyal citizens willing to support the overthrow of democracy. New and weak regimes must search out ways to build legitimacy with the population to protect democracy from downturns or dissatisfaction with either rapid change or stagnation. Successful strategies have included the creation or reinforcement of traditional sources of legitimacy, such as monarchies (Spain) or traditional councils (Botswana). Where this is not realistic, broad participation in the creation of new symbols for the regime (e.g., the constitution in South Africa) can also be efficacious.

In analyzing political institutions, we find that too much has been made of the distinction between presidential and parliamentary regimes and too little of intervening variables, such as the electoral system. While some presidential systems do encourage a zero-sum approach to politics, this is also true of some parliamentary systems. At the same time, perhaps the distinguishing feature of failed presidential systems, most of which have been in Latin America, is the infelicitous combination of presidentialism with proportional representation (PR) that has lead to the extreme fragmentation of power at the national level and to executives' frequent resort to decree powers in order to bypass chaotic legislatures. A better model for presidentialism is that of the United States, where the president is a weak office but the electoral scheme is a plurality rather than a PR system. This allows for "manufactured" majorities of moderate ideological tendencies with the flexibility to pass legislation.

Our discussion of political parties and civil society mirrors in some way our discussion of economic development. We argue that successful democratic systems are those in which centers of power and influence are diffuse. These centers of power include political parties and civil society groups. We also argue, though we do not discuss it in great detail, that federalism contributes to this same end, by creating power blocs at a subnational level that diffuse resources and political power.

Political parties have tended to be most successful when they have been linked to deep social cleavages, such as class and religion, though the United States is exceptional in this regard. Ties to enduring cleavages have ensured parties a reliable support base while simultaneously allowing citizens to express their identities and interests in concrete ways that tie them to the political system. In the past, parties provided important outlets for entertainment, segmented social spaces, and sources of political information. With technological change and transformations in class structure, parties find it ever more difficult to organize the way they used to. No longer do citizens need to join organizations like parties for social or informational purposes. The impact of technological change on organization is ambiguous, however, because technology also assists organizers in their tasks, even as it undermines some of the old purposes of joining organizations. Undoubtedly, party organizers in new democracies face considerable challenges in following the models of older democracies, but cleavages still represent the most promising avenue for organizing.

Perhaps the most ambitious part of this book looks at the role of civil society in democracies. The topic of civil society has exploded in recent years not only within political science but in the social sciences generally. A great deal of useful and provocative research has fomented new theorizing and discourse. Yet civil society theory remains poorly specified, with authors using the concept of civil society, as well as the new term *social capital*, with abandon—signifying different things at different times and complicating the process of knowledge accumulation. We have tried to rationalize the literature on civil society by mooring it to older conceptions, dating back to Tocqueville, and the more recent work of Lipset and Kornhauser.

We argue that civil society theory has three broad strands. Social capital theory has received the most attention of late, though we find this focus unwarranted theoretically or empirically. Whereas social capital theory emphasizes the importance of organizational life in creating and enforcing social norms and patterns of behavior conducive to democracy, human capital theory emphasizes the role that organizational membership plays in inculcating skills and norms that are conducive to individual participation in democracy. Finally, interest mediation theory emphasizes the direct role that interest groups in civil society play in representing the interests of citizens in the political system, particularly through the ties that civil society maintains with political parties.

Our review of the theoretical and empirical literature, as well as our own analysis of the U.S. Social Capital Community Benchmark Survey data, finds that social capital is an overemphasized branch of the overall theory of civil society. Far more important are the roles played by both human capital and interest mediation. The most important aspect of civil society for a democracy is that it have creatively tense but efficacious links to the political party system. As we note earlier and develop further in the Latin American section of this book, the relationship between civil society and political parties in many new democracies falls far short of this ideal. This is not always because of the weaknesses in civil society—it is often a result of the weaknesses in the party system.

What does all of this mean for the future of democracy? Our attitude toward democratic prospects is conditioned by our expectations. The state of democracy in Africa could not have been much worse than it was until the 1990s; however, there are now a few bright signs across the continent—including Nigeria, Senegal, South Africa, and Tanzania—that draw our attention. In contrast, the high hopes we hold for Latin America have been dampened by events in the nineties and after in Colombia, Venezuela, and Haiti. In Asia the news is mixed. Indonesia survives, but rumbles of discontent are everywhere. Taiwan is still in the cradle of its democracy, but the collapse of President Chen Shui-bian's grand coalition has ambiguous portents. Democracy in Russia and the FSU is under siege, yet progress does continue. Nor is democracy fully secure in the developed world.

In parts I and II we focus mainly on the lessons from old democracies that are relevant to new democracies. But this should not be taken to mean that the old democracies have completed the process of democratization. Even using our minimal definition, it should be evident that the old democracies can make their democratic processes both more inclusive and more competitive. A report at the dawn of the millennium by the International Helsinki Federation for Human Rights suggests that abuse of civil rights is unacceptably high in a number of the advanced democracies, including several European states and the United States (not just the more obvious cases of deterioration of both political and civil rights in the former Soviet Union). [14]

Building democracy in this century remains a formidable task, but it is one for which solid foundations were laid in the last one. There is broad consensus on the need to follow capitalist market-oriented growth strategies around the world, and this bodes well for democracy in the coming century. This is true even though the pendulum has shifted perhaps too far toward a neoliberal version of capitalist development. Current capitalist systems need correcting, but citizens around the globe understand that there is no going back to socialism. Cultural changes occurring throughout the world bode well for democracy, though there is little evidence that the Islamic regions are due for serious cultural rethinking any time soon. In the current atmosphere, this seems as unlikely as ever. The explosion of civil society in the past two decades was and remains exciting—but it has not been coupled with encouraging developments in the realm of political parties. Civil society and parties must grow together for democracy to succeed, and it remains to be seen whether political parties in new democracies can adapt to and establish effective linkage with the newly active civil societies they encounter. In terms of economy, culture, and institutions, progress has been made—but we may witness a few steps backward on the path toward better and stronger democracies.

The road toward democratization and consolidation in the coming century will doubtless be long and winding, with many stops, starts, and reverses. But if the denizens of the earth are able one day to truly call this first century of the third millennium the Democratic Century, it will have been well worth the trouble.

PART III

HEMISPHERIC DIVIDE: THE UNITED STATES AND LATIN AMERICA

CHAPTER 10

THE ARGUMENT AND CASES

WHY HAS NORTH AMERICA EXPERIENCED years of successful democracy while Latin America has struggled?

Parts I and II of this book define democracy, explore its inner workings, and try to explain what makes democracy happen and endure. We have addressed the correlates of democracy—socioeconomic, cultural, institutional—broadly, generalizing from existing cases and taking advantage of many cross-national studies. In part III, a different method is employed—testing the general theories presented earlier by examining a comparative case.

Here we look at Latin America in relation to the United States. Because this case study is rooted primarily in a historical analysis of these regions, the emphasis is somewhat different from our general model. The application of general theory to specific cases always leads to caveats, details that are unaccounted for in the general theory, and occasionally even contradictions between what has actually happened and what the theory predicts. Good theories, of course, minimize these problems; ideally the reader will find that our own theories explain much of the difference between the United States and Latin America, even as they do not explain everything. Although this part of the book was originally written as an independent lecture, we have made a concerted effort to make explicit the connections between the theories elaborated in parts I and II, and the following case study.

So let us start with the central question at the heart of this part of the book. Although both the United States and Latin America were originally colonized by European powers and though both gained their independence in nearly the same era, we cannot but be impressed by the divergences in history, culture, society, and economy of these two parts of the New World. As Douglass North, William Summerhill, and Barry Weingast put it, "During the late eighteenth and the first half of the nineteenth century, the United States created a stable political economy and was well on its way to becoming the richest economy in the world. . . . In contrast, after independence most of Spain's former colonies on the mainland imploded in a costly and deadly spiral of warfare. . . . Destructive conflict, rooted in the independence struggles and disputes over early republican state-building, diverted capital and labor from production and consigned the new nations to a path of stunningly poor performance in comparison to the United States."[1]

One divergence in particular concerns us here: why did North America develop a stable democratic political system while its Latin American neighbors did not and continue to struggle to do so? While the United States and Canada, despite the latter's separatism problems, have established long-lasting democracies, Latin American countries, with a few notable exceptions, have been led for most of their history by dictators. This has occurred despite the Latin American countries' apparent advantages early in the New World's history. They possessed enormous mineral wealth, plenty of land, and became more urbanized than their North American neighbors. How then do we explain the differences in the ways these two regions developed politically and economically?

It is our contention that historical conditions rooted in the different colonial experiences of North and Latin America inaugurated a Weberian "loading of the dice"[2] that made it more likely that North America would become and remain democratic and, simultaneously, increased the chances that Latin American efforts at democracy would be faltering, insecure, and often fleeting. These varying historical conditions were not controlling; we do not mean to imply that any political outcomes were foregone by the time the colonial powers departed from the New World. But the colonial histories of North and Latin America are powerful legacies that have shaped the economic, political, social, and cultural paths that the regions have followed. An analysis of these historical legacies will thus inform our consideration of the structural and institutional variables we identified in part I.

THE ARGUMENT

To assist the reader in following part III, we sketch the argument here. It is our basic contention that the history of democracy in Latin and North America was significantly affected by the histories of Spain, Portugal, and Britain prior to their colonization of the Americas; by these European nations' initial patterns of colonization; by their subsequent incorporation of these new colonies into their broader political economies; and finally, by the wars for independence that created the new nations of North and Latin America. Additionally, the continuing political, economic, and cultural legacies affected the development of important institutions, such as political parties and civil society.

Britain and Iberia had divergent histories that translated into very different cultural legacies. Inevitably, these legacies affected the colonization and independence processes, but it is striking that they continue to have a significant impact even today on both regions. The main differences between the two European regions were political-institutional, economic, and cultural. In Britain the evolution of limited representative institutions and the early triumph of industrialization led to a society more mobile, more republican, more dynamic and entrepreneurial, and more modern than that of Spain or Portugal.

Although most of the colonists from both Britain and Iberia wanted to get rich, only in North America did the bulk of them come to live permanently. From the beginning, British colonists were fleeing to the New World to stay, not to return quickly with wealth to the motherland. Spanish colonists came to conquer, collect, and evangelize and then to return home. As it happened, it was Latin America that ended up containing relatively easy-to-exploit mineral wealth, while North America was less well endowed with specie. The North American landscape, however, could be molded to the uses of agriculture. Although parts of Latin America also had agricultural potential (e.g., Argentina, Chile), North Americans quickly adapted themselves to the pursuit of agriculture because they had come to stay, while Latins ignored the potentially time-consuming task of developing land and continued their search for quick riches.

In the end, the seeming lack of material wealth in North America was propitious for the development of autonomous political institutions because the British simply did not worry much about their colonies. They left them alone to develop. Spain, in contrast, had a great deal of interest in gold and silver in Latin America and attempted to exercise stricter control over that bounty.

Nevertheless, one cannot explain the differential institutions in North and Latin America entirely in terms of factor endowments, for they bore a striking resemblance to institutions in Britain and Iberia. Left to their own devices, North Americans created representative bodies modeled extremely closely on the British bicameral parliamentary system. Spain developed a system of centralized, hierarchical viceroyalties that ruled the vast domains in Latin America—regardless of factor endowments. Britain left its colonies alone, in part because they were unlikely to provide much material wealth but also because traditions of decentralization and autonomy ran deep in the British ethos. Spain tightened its grip on its colonies, in part to control their vast wealth, but also because centralized control was the order of the day in Spanish political culture.

One can see this differential in the economic policies of the two empires, as well. After all, while the British colonies contained little material wealth, they quickly began to supply agricultural products. Thus trade became an important aspect of both the North and Latin American political economies. Here too Britain took a more decentralized, laissez-faire approach, with lower taxes and fewer regulations on colonial trade. Spain, in contrast, created a set of tight regulations that often led to inefficiencies in production and trade. This had extremely negative consequences for Latin America. First, it impeded colonial development, skewed incentives, and promoted an unequal distribution of property. Second, it created a legacy of statist economic control and arbitrary interventionism that has persisted until today and has undermined development for several centuries.

As a result of these legacies, North America had representative political institutions that were strong, independent, and local; experience in governance; and relatively egalitarian land distribution by the time of the American Revolution. Conversely, Latin America had no such institutions, hardly any local experience with government, and quite unequal distributions of property. On top of this, Latin Americans inherited an Iberian Catholic cultural tradition that emphasized unity, authority, hierarchy, and centralized control, while Anglo-Americans inherited a British Protestant cultural tradition of individualism, pluralism, decentralization, and skepticism toward authority. In short, the culture of Protestant Britannia was more liberal than that of Catholic Iberia.

While liberalism may be an important correlate of democracy, it is evident that countries need not be as liberal as the United States to have successful democracies. Consider, for example, the corporatist social democratic states of Northern Europe and Scandinavia. The lack of liberalism in Latin America was important but by no means determining.

The historical failure of Latin American economic development did undermine democracy. As noted in part II, national wealth is the single most consistent predictor of democratic success. Latin America's failure to develop economically consistently upped the ante in distribution struggles, casting political disputes in zero-sum terms. This made democratic compromise difficult.

The independence wars and state consolidation of the early nineteenth century represented a critical juncture in Latin American history, when problems of regime legitimacy severely undermined the capabilities of Latin American nations to develop politically or economically. This problem was solved in the United States relatively quickly. Here, the natures of the historical relationships between colony and motherland, the framing of the Revolution, and the cultural and institutional preparedness of the colonists for self-government explain why independence was managed so much more successfully by North than Latin Americanists.

Finally, it is striking that even in those countries in Latin America where democracy seemed to make significant headway toward institutionalization, regimes still fell. Have Latin American institutions been particularly weak or consistently flawed? We argue that there are both structural and cultural reasons why even ostensibly strong institutions—such as those in Uruguay and Chile—were unable to resist the tendency in the region toward military intervention and authoritarian rule. Skewed patterns of development, weak middle and working classes, gross inequality, cultural dispositions that favored the alienation of power from the people to strongman rulers, and hierarchical, organic social organization—these are among the most salient reasons we offer for why political parties in Latin America failed to provide stability and why the relationship between civil society and the party system has been plagued with difficulties. Even when Latin Americans tried, as they did many times, to establish democracies, these have been damned by institutional problems.

A WORD ABOUT THE CASES

Although *Latin America* can refer to everything south of the Rio Grande, we have limited our selection of cases somewhat for various reasons. First, we decided to focus on South America rather than all of Latin America simply in order to reduce the number of cases to a manageable level. We also believe that South America has developed more independently of the imperial influence of the United States than have countries farther north. Although external, or international, factors clearly can play an important role in democratization, we largely ignore them in the first part of this manuscript, preferring to pursue a primarily endogenous theory of democratization and democratic stability. Our analysis is therefore limited to countries where most of the outcomes can be explained by endogenous factors. We believe, in turn, that this situation approximates the vast majority of countries in the world, though there are exceptions. To attempt to explain regime outcomes in Central America without a significant emphasis on external factors would be disingenuous. Of the Central American nations, Dietrich Rueschemeyer, Evelyne Huber Stephens, and John D. Stephens have written: "To a greater extent than South America and Mexico, they were shaped by external economic and political forces. . . . The ex-Spanish Central American countries had come under U.S. domination by the turn of the century already. Essentially, this meant that no government could consolidate its rule if it was not acceptable to the United States."[3] We would not go quite so far. The United States has played an important role in political outcomes throughout Latin America, broadly defined, but only in Central America has this role been so dominant. Thus for reasons of both analytical consistency and convenience, our analysis is limited primarily to South America.

We make two exceptions. Recognizing its general importance and following scholars such as David and Ruth Collier and

Rueschemeyer, Stephens, and Stephens, who have included Mexico in comparative analyses with South America, we include Mexico in our analysis.[4] And we also include Costa Rica, because of its undeniable success in democratization and because excluding it would prejudice our analysis. Further, because we put a great deal of emphasis in the following analysis on the colonial heritage of Latin America and because Costa Rica shares this heritage but is also a democratic success story, we wanted to see if the country challenged our multivariate analysis.

We have focused on the United States in our analysis of North America, eschewing, for the most part the history of Canada. This is again a matter of limiting the scope of our work. Lipset has written extensively about Canada in other venues, including a broad comparative study of Canada and the United States.[5]

CASE SUMMARIES

To assist the reader with the analysis, which presumes some knowledge of the history of the individual countries in the region, we briefly outline the political histories of our cases in the following section, emphasizing issues that come up later in the book. Readers with some background in Latin American politics may prefer to skip these summaries now but refer back to them as they move into the comparative analysis that follows.

The summaries draw on a wide range of sources, but we are particularly indebted to the authors listed in the endnote.[6]

Argentina

Argentina, like most of Latin America, spent the better part of the nineteenth century engaged in civil conflict with an incompletely centralized, institutionalized state. Yet by the late nineteenth century, Argentina was on its way to becoming one of the wealthier countries not just in Latin America but in the world. Argentina's levels of education and its standard of living rivaled or exceeded those of the advanced countries of Europe by the early part of the twentieth century. All indications were that Argentina would also develop a political economy similar to the advanced European states, with the eventual consolidation of a middle-class capitalist democracy. Yet between 1930 and the mid-1980s, there were multiple military coups, and just under half of those years were spent under dictatorship. Rather than progressing toward the advanced industrial world, Argentina consistently regressed toward the rest of Latin America. A coup in the late 1970s led to one of the most brutal military regimes on a continent well-known for its military interventions.

Argentina has been riven geographically since the days of the Spanish conquest. It has been most heavily settled and developed in the coastal regions, known as the littoral, while the grassy pampas of the interior were owned by large landholders but went underutilized. There has also been an exceptionally high level of immigration to Argentina, mostly from Southern Europe, that was partially the result of a deliberate strategy to stimulate the country's development and improve its culture. Finally, whereas industrial development in much of Latin America has been largely driven by foreign capital or backward linkage through import substitution, Argentina has followed a more traditional pattern of forward linkage, with major landholders expanding into manufacturing.

Oligarchic landholder control of the state went basically unchallenged until the formation of the Radical party in the late nineteenth century. This middle-class-based party was given a boost in 1912 with passage of the Sáenz Peña reform, which extended the suffrage and revised the electoral system. In 1916 the Radicals came to power, which they held until a coup in 1930. Fleeting attempts to incorporate the very large, mobilized, anarchist working classes were quashed by the elite landholding classes. The 1930 coup was precipitated by fear on the part of elites that their economic interests were being undermined by a combination of middle-class political dominance through the Radical party and the advent of the Great Depression. Conservative politicians alternated in power during the 1930s and early 1940s, but they were not freely elected.

In 1943 a military faction including Juan Perón overthrew the government. Perón, who served as labor secretary in the new government, understood the importance of incorporating the working classes into the political system. He used his post to grant new powers and privileges to labor, thus establishing a personal following within the labor movement that helped propel him to the presidency in 1946. Perón held power until the mid-1950s but did not build any organizational apparatus to sustain him, relying on personalistic appeals to unions and nationalism. His election in 1946 was free and fair, but by 1951 he had turned to active suppression of the opposition. He was overthrown by the military in 1955, and the weakly institutionalized Peronist party was suppressed, as were others with direct ties to him.

During his tenure Perón tried to create a state corporate model based on organized bourgeois and labor groups, with employment as his primary goal. In the end, he succeeded in mobilizing these groups but failed to integrate them into the broader political system or any party. His strategy proved alienating to the landed upper classes and middle classes, ending in military takeover. Perón's top-down style, his creation of a party that deified him, and his emphasis on state corporatism and appeals to nationalism have led some commentators to dub the Peronist party "fascist," but this seems to overstate both the ideological coherence and organizational success of Peronism.

Perón was sent into exile by the military but continued to be actively involved in the Peronist movement in Argentina. In his absence, however, Augusto Vandor, a leading Peronist unionist began accruing power and working toward the creation of a Peronist party that would present candidates for election in Perón's stead, an idea that Perón himself greeted with little enthusiasm. As it turned out, the average Peronist sided with

Perón, symbolizing an enduring problem in Argentina—the preference for personalism over party building, and intense factionalism within the major parties. Vandor's efforts failed.

In 1966 another military coup led to seven years of rotating military rule, during which time strikes, demonstrations, and leftist guerilla activity accelerated. By 1973 the country was ripe for another try at Peronism with Perón. Perón only finished a year in office before he died, but his wife, Isabel, took over upon his death. Isabel did not have the force of personality to hold the weakly institutionalized Peronist fractions together, and continued violence and economic instability inspired another military coup in 1976.

This time, the military took a far more aggressive and violent tack, and about nine thousand people "disappeared" during the its campaign of repression. The regime attempted to follow a more free-market approach to development, but economic crises, violence, and an embarrassing war with Britain over the Falkland Islands were the major hallmarks of the military's strategy. The excesses of the military's "dirty war" against internal subversives greatly improved the image of liberal democracy in the minds of most Argentinians and their political parties. In 1983 the Radical party returned to power under Raul Alfonsín, inaugurating a new democratic era and a nascent two-party system with the Peronists, now known as the Partido Justicialista (PJ), in opposition. Since then, the two parties have become near catchalls, despite their divergent histories, with few programmatic or ideological differences between them. This was substantially achieved by Carlos Menem of the PJ, who in the 1990s dramatically ended Peronism's traditionally more statist policy orientation in favor of a neoliberal approach. Several smaller parties also entered the scene in the 1980s, some on the left and some on the right, but none large enough to compete for the presidency with the Radicals or the PJ.

Bolivia

Bolivia has had relatively little prolonged experience with democracy, but has been remarkable for its economic policy (if not for its high levels of economic development). One of the few countries in Latin America to actually undertake land reform on a scale that could be considered revolutionary, more recently it has also become a leader in pursuing neoliberal policies. In spite of a distinguished economic record, Bolivia has never achieved political stability, and its political institutions remain weak.

Bolivia spent most of the nineteenth century in turmoil after its independence in 1825. In the 1880s, relative political stability finally developed concomitantly with a two-party system. While Bolivia developed a limited democracy in the early twentieth century, its party system remained elitist and politics remained personalistic, with control of the state attractive primarily as a source of patronage. Unfortunately, state patronage would remain the animating factor in nearly every government in Bolivia's history, with a few notable but fleeting exceptions.

Although Bolivia had an established political order and reasonably functioning elite democracy by the early twentieth century, the growth of the urban middle classes and working classes posed a problem that ultimately proved insoluble. Starting in the 1930s, Bolivia entered a period of significant instability as violence escalated against the status quo.

In the 1940s, a new kind of party appeared that would play a substantial role in Bolivia, the Movimiento Nacional Revolucionario (MNR). The MNR was not linked to a single sector, though it was rooted in the growing but insecure middle class. Rather than rely on class as an organizing principle, however, the MNR professed a broader, "nationalistic" agenda: a multiclass attack on foreign capital and the domestic oligarchy. Like the other Andean countries, Bolivia had a large unincorporated indigenous population, to which the MNR also directed itself. The MNR came to power in 1952 and undertook a substantial political and economic revolution. Mines were nationalized and agricultural lands were redistributed. At the same time, universal suffrage was finally introduced. However, the MNR was no fan of liberal democracy. Like the PRI in Mexico, the MNR hoped to create a single-party bureaucratic state system. While the MNR originally professed to be anti–foreign capital, it nevertheless adopted adjustment policies prescribed by the IMF in the mid-1950s. And while the MNR was Bolivia's first mass party with any substantial organization outside the Congress, it nevertheless reverted to a patronage basis for government operations. Economic growth was not strong enough to provide everyone with the plum jobs and patronage they demanded, however, nor was the MNR able to control the demands of the labor or military organizations that it had helped to build. The intense conflicts over patronage and policy led to the military overthrow of the MNR in 1964.

Over the next two decades, military coups were the normal means of succession in Bolivia. The MNR's failure to channel the demands of working-class Bolivians or incorporate major labor organizations was replicated by military government after military government. This was not for lack of trying, as both Generals Ovando and Torres attempted to encourage labor participation. Nevertheless, these experiments were halted in 1971 when General Hugo Banzer came to power. While Banzer managed to suppress the left, his government descended into the same chaotic war over patronage as nearly all of Bolivia's regimes. Bolivia remained a state without effective institutional means for expressing class or other cleavages.

Democracy returned to Bolivia in 1982, and a peaceful transfer of power, the first in over two decades, followed in 1984, when Victor Paz Estenssoro, the founder of the MNR, assumed the presidency. His regime was marked by a shift away from the MNR's more traditionally statist tendencies toward neoliberal stabilization, which proved quite successful in ending hyperinflation.

Since the 1980s, political parties have been surpassed by organizations of civil society that have attempted to take their cause directly to the executive without mediation by parties or the legislature. This has exacerbated hyperpresidentialism and the highly personalistic nature of Bolivian politics, which revolved in the 1990s around Paz Zamora of the leftish Movimiento de Izquierda Revolucionaria (MIR) party, Paz Estenssoro (before his retirement), and Banzer (before his death), who was reelected in 1997.

Brazil

The only Portuguese colony in Latin America, Brazil has both the largest area and largest economy of our cases. The imperial legacy of Portugal has been different from that of Spain, but in many ways the history of democracy in Brazil is perhaps more similar than different from the rest of Latin America. Particularly salient in modern Brazilian history (at least since late in the Old Republic) has been the role of the military, which generally believed, and was affirmed in this by many civilians, that it had a duty to act as an escape valve when democracy became corrupted. Brazil stands out as a case of late catchall party development and extreme party fragmentation and instability, particularly for a country with a relatively developed economy.

Brazil achieved independence in 1822 but was the only country in South America to revert to a monarchical form of government after independence. In large part, the epicenter of the Portuguese empire moved from Portugal to Brazil during the late eighteenth and early nineteenth century. Brazil's transition to independence was far more orderly than that of the rest of Latin America, because it occurred under the umbrella of the Portuguese monarchy, without the ensuing anarchy that plagued most of the region.

The First Republic was established in 1889, which meant that Brazil's first stab at stable democracy occurred at nearly the same time that other Latin American countries were establishing political order and elite democracy for the first time. Under the "Old

Republic," political power alternated between powerful leaders from the states of São Paulo and Minas Gerais. The republic lasted until 1930, when a dispute over succession allowed Getúlio Vargas, hailing from Rio Grande do Sul, to take power, which he held continuously until 1945. Vargas was democratically elected at the outset, but the regime entered a distinctly dictatorial phase in 1938, the Estado Novo (New State), with Vargas jettisoning a ban on consecutive terms and proscribing political parties.

Under Vargas, Brazil turned toward intensive industrialization, and the working class expanded rapidly. Labor was organized into Vargas-controlled unions, reflecting Vargas's simultaneously corporatist and charismatic approach to sociopolitical organization. By the time he was forced from power by the military in 1945 and Brazil returned to a kind of democratic contestation, he had created two political parties to compete. The first, the Social Democratic Party (PSD) was composed of governmental elites from the Vargas regime, with patronage as the glue that held them together. The other, the Labor Party (PTB), was formed by the Vargas labor unions. Opposition to all things Vargas was concentrated in a third party, the National Democratic Union (UDN).

Democratic-style politics persisted from 1945 to 1964, but the military intervened at critical junctures, including a coup in 1955. Vargas was elected president again in 1950 but committed suicide in 1954. Although the political system experienced some maturation during this time, fundamental economic problems were not resolved, and by the 1960s, inflation was rampant, and an increasingly strong and mobilized labor movement was threatening the political order. Enter the military.

In 1964, driven not only by its historical self-conception as democratic escape valve but also by new counterinsurgent national security doctrines, the military overthrew the leftish Joao Goulart, then tried, like Vargas, to establish a two-party system from above. This experiment was of limited success, as Vargas's earlier one had been, in terms of concentrating or institutionalizing a party system, and it undermined what democratic institutionalization had taken place since 1945. However, the military did succeed in stabilizing the regime, accelerating economic growth and industrialization, and staging a gradual and peaceful exit from power by the mid-1980s. While economic growth benefited a broad swath of Brazilian society, it increased inequality and allowed poverty to continue to fester, particularly in the northeast.

Brazil has been plagued by weak nonstate institutions confronting a powerful bureaucratic state, and as Scott Mainwaring has argued, Brazil's institutional rules have often exacerbated this situation. Presidentialism and proportional representation with open lists have encouraged personalism and fragmentation. Nevertheless, democracy has strengthened in Brazil in the past decade, particularly under Fernando Enrique Cardoso, a sociologist and, in a prior incarnation, a leading dependency theorist. Brazil has not only weathered serious economic crises but also, through constitutional and legislative reform, managed to begin to reduce the fragmentation and increase the discipline of its party system.[7]

Chile

Chile's political history is quite distinct when compared with other Latin American nations, so much so that one may speak of a kind of Chilean exceptionalism. Even so, Chile, like many of its neighbors, descended into brutal authoritarianism in the 1970s. Today, however, Chile again continues on a somewhat unique trajectory, its economy generally far better off than its neighbors' have been in the late 1990s and its politics defined largely by the continuing strength of authoritarian-regime supporters and allies.

Chile was one of the first nations to achieve political stability after independence from Spain. While other countries engaged in seemingly unending civil war for most of the nineteenth century, Chile had established political order by the 1830s. By the 1870s, Chile had created a fairly stable system of oligarchical republican rule with a limited franchise. By the 1890s, suffrage had been considerably expanded. In this regard, the historiography is curious. Secular liberal control of the state apparatus and increasing state autonomy led religious conservative activists to try to overthrow the state. In this they were unsuccessful—so they turned toward peaceful attempts at democratization. Thus a distinctive scenario unfolded, with conservatives pushing for a larger franchise that they hoped to control, while liberals clung to the limited oligarchy they already controlled. The conservatives won the battle, but the liberals won the war, maintaining control of the presidency throughout the parliamentary republic. Meanwhile rapid urbanization and industrialization fueled the growth of left-oriented working-class parties, which obtained representation in Congress in the 1920s. Thus was born the most ideologically rigid and polarized, cleavage-based party system in Latin America. Democratic politics persisted for several decades, and notable progress was made in terms of legislating social reform. While organizations shifted over time, Chile nevertheless maintained a party system with a very distinct trichotomy—left, right, and center—and high levels of partisanship that were far more similar to patterns in Europe than those in other Latin American nations. That is, until the Pinochet dictatorship, stretching from 1973 to 1990.

The origins of the Pinochet regime have been debated hotly, particularly because this was Chile's longest period of sustained authoritarian rule in over a century and a half. Like many Latin American nations (and non–Latin American ones, for that matter), Chile struggled to integrate its working class into the political system. On some level, the failure of Chilean democracy must be traced to a system that could not sustain the election of a socialist president, which occurred for the first time in Chilean history in 1970. Essentially, rightist elements in Chile, as in other Latin American nations, were unwilling to support democracy if it led to the victory of the left. Others have persuasively argued, however, following Arturo Valenzuela, that the failure of democracy in Chile was primarily political and that both the left and right share the blame. In this telling, Chilean democracy failed because of hyperpresidentialism, because the center was unable or unwilling to forge compromise between right and left, and because, in the lead-up to the 1970 election, political forces were mobilized on both sides of the ideological spectrum that political parties like the Christian Democrats were unable be harness (a civil society–political party mismatch of the kind we describe in part I). Furthermore, Salvador Allende, elected with just over a third of the vote, used decree powers to pursue a fairly revolutionary program as if he had a mandate for far-reaching change; this he did not have. Thus, according to this interpretation, the failure of Chilean democracy has to be located in the failure of Chile's political leaders and institutions to channel political tendencies into moderate and civilized debate and reform.

In any event, the Pinochet government implemented perhaps the most extensive economic reforms of any Latin American regime, adhering fairly quickly to a strict monetarist, free-market model and reversing most of the nationalization undertaken by Allende. While the free-market model met with some success, the state failed to play a sufficient regulatory role to insure the fairness and efficiency of the privatization process, and with economic crisis in the early 1980s, Pinochet was forced to backpedal toward a more centrist model of capitalist development. Nevertheless, the Pinochet regime, unlike military regimes in nations such as Argentina, is associated with a highly successful economic reform project, a fact that may contribute to the relatively low premium put on democracy in Chile today.

Since Pinochet was voted out at the end of the 1980s, the government has been controlled by a coalition of left and center parties known as the Concertacíon that have attempted to inject some social reforms into the economy they inherited (which is at least partially responsible for the phenomenal drop in poverty in the last decade). Nevertheless, the preponderance of leftist influence in post-Pinochet governments—capped by the triumph of Socialist president Ricardo Lagos in the last presidential election— has not challenged the basic outlines of the economy.[8]

Colombia

Two parties have traditionally warred with each other in Colombia since independence, the Liberals and the Conservatives. As in much of Latin America, these caudillo-led parties were not particularly ideological or cleavage based, though they did have faint undertones of nineteenth-century European liberalism and conservatism. They should be considered clientelistic, catchall parties. While civil war was a fairly constant fact of life from the early nineteenth into the twentieth century, a period of stability and economic growth (driven by coffee exports) was reached between 1910 and the middle of the century.

Still, by the 1940s, violence escalated to new levels. At least part of the problem, as in other parts of Latin America, stemmed from efforts to incorporate the new labor interests that the industrialization process had created into the political system. Alfonso Lopez, a Liberal who ascended to the presidency in the 1930s, made an attempt to bring labor into the fold and supported the organization of a trade union federation. This caused considerable consternation among capitalists and landowners and precipitated a return to violence. Nevertheless, the breakdown of the regime was as much a result of political competition and polarization among elites as the result of class struggle. La violencia of the 1940s and 1950s left about 200,000 dead; finally, in 1958, a temporary peace was restored with the formation of the National Front. During the era of the National Front, a type of consociationalism was established that dictated alternation of the presidency each term between the two parties, as well as splitting up other offices equally between them. This arrangement, while less than optimal from a democratic standpoint, had some important successes. It brought relative stability to Colombia and relatively consistent and substantial economic growth rates.

At the same time, lack of political competition severed the links between state and society, allowing the state to become somewhat arbitrary and self-serving. Attempts to incorporate labor and popular movements continued to fail. Over time, both the state and new social movements lost their ties to the political system, opening the door to further violence and praetorian politics. It was in this period that many of the guerilla groups, such as the Revolutionary Armed Forces of Colombia (FARC) and the National Liberation Army (ELN), that still dominate Colombian politics today were formed. Bipartisan arrangements persisted into the mid-1980s, though violence has continued to the present. Also in the 1980s, a new, cleavage-based left-wing party, Union Patriotica, appeared on the scene. Its tenure was short-lived, however. Accused of representing the left-wing guerillas, it was literally wiped out, with over one thousand of its members assassinated in the late 1980s. In 1991 a national referendum, provoked by a student-led social movement, yielded a new, more democratic constitution for Colombia. Although this ended the coalition system that had led to praetorianism in the first place, the level of violence in Colombia was so high that it could not be tempered by the constitution alone.

Present-day Colombia presents difficult classification problems. It is considered by some to be a quasi-democracy and by others to be authoritarian. In our estimation, a fundamental requirement for a democracy is a state. The compromised nature of the Colombian state, the regime's failure to exercise a monopoly of coercion over the territory of Colombia, means that Colombia cannot be considered a democracy. Furthermore, the excessive violence engendered by both election campaigns and the attempts of left-leaning groups to participate in politics means that elections cannot truly be considered free and fair.

Costa Rica

Costa Rica is arguably the most successful democracy in Latin America today, marked by continuous democratic contestation for over fifty years. Although it has a reputation for uniqueness among Latin American countries, it shares many traits with the rest of Latin America, as well. For example, while Costa Rica is indeed distinctive in the relative lack of violence subsequent to its independence and in its relatively egalitarian patterns of land distribution, predemocratic oligarchical competition did not really start any earlier than it did in many other Latin American nations, and there have been ample coups and periods of nondemocratic rule and repression. Even in egalitarian Costa Rica, a 1917 military coup was basically orchestrated by the landholding class as a response to mildly progressive state reforms. Nevertheless, it is true that Costa Rica stood apart as a model liberal regime through most of the twentieth century. When other Latin American nations were falling to coups in the 1960s and 1970s, Costa Rica's democracy continued to thrive.

Oligarchical rule in the nineteenth century gave way to restricted democracy in the late 1880s. The Liberal Republic, lasting until the 1940s, was marked by peaceful contestation and democratic transitions, with the sole exception of a 1917–19 dictatorship. The original cleavage in Costa Rica was a secular/religious one, but over time—again distinctive in Latin America—civil society expanded considerably, giving voice to new pressure groups with issues ranging from education to economic policy. Costa Rican politics during this time were dominated by the Republican party, but the rise of organized labor and communist groups became a defining axis of politics by the 1930s. In 1936 conservative coffee oligarchs co-opted the Republican party and pushed against social reform, but when one of their leaders, Rafael Calderón, came to power, he began to mobilize labor and clerical forces for reform, pushing through, inter alia, controversial social security legislation. In addition to his domestic policies, Calderón's alliance with the United States in World War II also divided the (mostly pro-Axis) oligarchy.

This division led to a great deal of consternation on the right. Oligarchic forces aligned against Calderón, as did reform-minded sectors of the middle class that did not like Calderon's autocratic style or unholy alliance with communism. In 1948 José Figueres, a leader of the middle-class social democratic opposition, led a successful six-week offensive against the government after it appeared that the legislature was nullifying that year's election results to insure another Calderón victory. Figueres seized power for eighteen months and instituted important reforms—a wealth tax, bank nationalizations, and political rights for women—while simultaneously demobilizing the labor movement. The liberationists ultimately ceded power to the conservative Unidad coalition, backed by the coffee oligarchy, after Figueres's reformist policies were met with a backlash in congressional elections. But Figueres subsequently formed the National Liberation Party (PLN), which would dominate Costa Rican politics for the next half century.

Although the various players were not necessarily committed democrats, after 1948 democracy seemed to represent the best way to preserve the interests of both the PLN and the Unidad coalition. The PLN maintained until the last decade or so what most consider a social democratic platform and has regularly alternated in power with some version of the more classically liberal (and socially Christian) Unidad coalition, although both parties may be considered catchalls in their steadily weakening programmatic agendas. While the PLN is often referred to as social democratic, this label perhaps implies too much affinity with its European brethren. The PLN has never had strong roots in the working class and has since its inception fused social democratic reformism with strong liberal tendencies. In this regard, it is rather distinct from the labor-oriented social democratic parties of Europe.

In part because of the PLN's consistent control of the legislature over the last half century, Costa Rica has developed a European-style welfare state unique in Latin America. In general, Costa Rica's economic structure and class development have been more similar to Europe's or the United States' than to those of most of Latin America. Agricultural interests concentrated landholding over time, without destroying the middle-income peasantry. Industrial development in Costa Rica was driven by forward rather than backward linkage—from the landholding class outward. The middle classes have expanded significantly over time. Nevertheless, one should avoid making too much of these similarities, as Costa Rica still has a larger agricultural class, more income inequality, and more poverty than the advanced countries.

Since the advent of a debt crisis in the 1980s, Costa Rica and its party system have converged on a more neoliberal direction for economic reform. In the last few years, public safety has deteriorated considerably, which some blame on the large influx of immigrants from neighboring Central American countries as a result of recent hurricanes. Although there are signs of unrest, there are no significant threats to Costa Rican democracy at the moment. Nevertheless, some commentators have questioned whether, in the wake of the debt crisis and in light of the PLN's long history of labor demobilization, Costa Rican civil society has not become dangerously delinked from the party system and government apparatus. If so, this does not bode well for the future.[9]

Ecuador

Ecuadorian politics have traditionally been defined by a geographic division, with the highlands around Quito representing traditional conservative landholding interests while liberalism has found more support in the coastal region around Guayaquil. Interestingly, the unassimilated and very large Indian population of Ecuador has been concentrated near Quito, while a more mestizo and less rigidly defined culture has been centered around Guayaquil. Ecuador has little sustained experience with democracy and has generally been defined by organizationally weak political parties and somewhat praetorian politics.

As in much of Latin America, Ecuador did not achieve a semblance of political order until late in the nineteenth century. After establishing a relatively centralized state under the Conservative party in the 1860s and 1870s, the Liberal party, based in Guayaquil, assumed power in the aftermath of the 1895–96 civil war and held it until the midtwentieth century, using troops when necessary to maintain its power in the face of unrest among the lower classes. From the 1950s until the 1970s, Ecuador was marked by alternating civilian administrations and coups. In 1970 Jose Maria Velasco Ibarra, elected for his fifth (nonconsecutive) term in 1968, himself orchestrated an *autogolpe* (regime overthrow) and seized dictatorial powers, only to be overthrown by the military in 1972. During the 1970s, the military abetted long-overdue modernization in the Ecuadorian economy, using petrodollars to finance agrarian reform and an expansion of the industrial sector. Democracy returned to Ecuador in 1979 with the election of Jaime Roldos Aguilera and has muddled along since. Brief scuttles between civilian government and the military continued in the 1980s. In 1987 President Léon Febres Cordero was kidnapped for the better part of a day until he agreed to amnesty for a dissident general. Economic crisis in the 1990s led to increased political unrest; dramatic economic reforms, including eventual dollarization; and the mobilization of new social movements and groups, particularly among the indigenous population. A short-lived coup supported by indigenous groups and sectors of the military in 2000 was quickly reversed after the head of the armed forces, Carlos Mendoza, who had originally supported the coup, backed down under international pressure and allowed the former elected vice president to assume the presidency.

Elite divisions between Liberals and Conservatives date back to the nineteenth century, but the contemporary Ecuadorian political system was established in the twentieth century. With the advent of a degree of economic modernization and growth in the middle classes, the traditional parties began to splinter, giving way to an increasingly schism-prone and party-heavy political system. A remarkable feature of Ecuadorian politics has been the lack of linkage between political parties and organized civil society, such that Catherine Conaghan refers to the Ecuadorian political system as one of "floating politicians and floating voters."[10] Parties in Ecuador, most of them fleeting and riven by internal divisions, have served primarily as electoral vehicles for individual political leaders with little organizational weight of their own.

It is difficult to explain why Ecuador has been particularly distinctive in this way, but several hypotheses can be suggested. One points to the extremely large, unassimilated population of Indians and their concentration in and around the center of power. Ethnic divisions in Ecuador have certainly contributed to an unwillingness on the part of the conservative Quito elite to engage in party building of the kind necessary to build durable institutions. At the same time, late and weak economic modernization in Ecuador delayed pressures for democratization, via the working or middle class, such that by the late 1960s, literacy restrictions still limited the franchise to less than 20 percent of the population. This limited the desirability of organizing political parties outside elite centers of power. Inevitably, leadership must also be indicted, for leaders could have tried to organize parties and push for democratization. But, as Conaghan argues, they chose to eschew party building, following the mold of Ibarra, the populist anti-party leader who dominated Ecuadorian politics from the 1930s to the early 1970s.[11]

Mexico

Mexico, though long known for its admirable stability, has had precious little experience with democracy. With the transition to democracy in 2000, however, Mexico has come to be seen as a bright spot in Latin America, especially as previous success stories, like Venezuela and Argentina, have come to seem far less stable.

In the nineteenth century, Mexican politics revolved around power struggles between Conservatives and Liberals, with the focus on the clerical/anti-clerical axis. As in much of Latin America, the first part of the nineteenth century was marked by fairly chronic instability, and Mexico suffered losses of territory and military defeat at the hands of the United States. There was also a short-lived attempt to reestablish imperial hegemony in Mexico by Napoleon, who imposed the Austrian emperor Maximilian, a move welcomed by some royalists in Mexico. In the late 1860s, the Liberals triumphed with a new constitution that fortified the liberal secular tradition under Benito Juárez, and Maximilian was executed. However, the Reform period of relative democracy was quite short-lived. In the 1870s, the traditional parties atrophied under the *porfiriato*, the dictatorship of Porfirio Díaz, which lasted from 1876 to 1911. The *porfiriato* was a time of economic development and relative stability in Mexico, but by the second decade of the twentieth century, political elites were tired of Díaz and sought greater power and mobility for themselves.

The bloody Mexican Revolution featured caudillo warfare and extremely high casualties, ending only in 1917 with the promulgation of a new, seemingly progressive constitution. Nevertheless, in the revolution's aftermath, violent contestation between regional bosses continued, and political leaders continued to search for a way to institutionalize the transfer of power among elites and reduce the incidence of bloodshed. This quest led Plutarco Calles to form the National Revolutionary Party in 1929, which would later change its name to the PRI (Partido Revolucianario Institucional). The party apparatus worked as planned, but it did not quell demands for social reform from the broader society.

In 1934 Lázaro Cárdenas, a leftish reformer, seized the presidency and instituted agrarian reform, nationalization of foreign oil industries, and wage hikes for labor. He incorporated mass organization into the party and gave it a revolutionary leftist bent. He also created sectors within the party that incorporated labor, the rural poor, the "popular" middle class, and the military. His successors would move the party back toward the right but continue to build on his mobilization efforts, turning the PRI into one of the most effective and stable corporatist electoral machines in Latin America. Over time, the PRI instituted bureaucratic controls that removed the process of determining leadership from the political sphere and to a technocratic sphere. The PRI successfully incorporated labor and the poor, established good relations with business, and marginalized the church.

In 1939 the Partido Acción Nacional (PAN) emerged to contest Cárdenas's turn to the left and to promote a more clerical-based but economically libertarian agenda. Although for many years the PAN met with little success at the national level, its representation in Congress continued to grow. In 2000 the PAN became the first party to seize executive power from the PRI since its formation seven decades before. Vicente Fox, the PAN candidate, assumed the presidency, after perhaps the most competitive, (relatively) free and fair elections in Mexican history.

The PRI's electoral dominance over its seventy years in power gradually eroded, though the most striking drop in its competitiveness came during the 1970s and 1980s. The party's success in fostering economic development and stability created new pressure groups—more urbane and middle class—and a clamoring for broader access to power. In the 1980s, leftish elements of the party, displeased with the PRI's turn toward neoliberalism, began exiting to form new groupings. In 1989, led by popular PRI-dissident Cuauhtémoc Cárdenas, son of the former president, the left merged into a new party, the Partido de la Revolución Democrática (PRD). Cárdenas had run for president in 1988 against PRI candidate Carlos Salinas de Gortari and lost, but sentiment was widespread that he would have won if the vote counting had been fairly executed.

While this election marked a low point for the PRI, it bounced back in the next couple of years as economic growth picked up, and it was not seriously challenged at the executive level until it finally lost the 2000 election. Nevertheless, uneven economic growth and the peso crisis of 1995, coupled with continued social and political dissatisfaction, did cost the PRI congressional seats and gubernatorial races throughout the 1990s. Furthermore, electoral reforms in 1996 laid the groundwork for the PRI's eventual defeat at the presidential level.

Although Mexico is an overwhelmingly mestizo society, with a great deal of national attention paid to the mixture of European and Indian elements in the national culture, unassimilated indigenous groups persist, particularly in the southern states of Oaxaca and Chiapas. In recent years, these groups have organized to press their demands for autonomy, land reform, and constitutional reform, most notably in the form of the Zapatista movement. Violence among indigenous groups, paramilitaries, and government partisans has contributed to political instability in Mexico, though this has generally been limited to the southern regions.[12]

Paraguay

Paraguay is probably the least discussed and researched case of political change in Latin America, and it has generally come to be associated with entrenched militarism and authoritarianism. It has had almost no experience with prolonged electoral competition in which parties peacefully transfer power, although it has not always lived up to its stereotype as dominated by a particularly repressive series of regimes either.

In the late nineteenth century, two elite parties emerged in Paraguay, the Liberals and Colorados. Like their sister parties in

Uruguay and Colombia, these parties were formed relatively early and developed strong webs of clientelism but little programmatic content. Universal suffrage was established in Paraguay prior to the formation of the parties, however, so they did not develop first as completely elite parties and then as mass-based parties. The enduring strength of these clientelistic parties is no doubt tied to the late modernization of Paraguay and the lack of diversification in a predominantly agricultural economy that preserved rural patronage relations well into the second half of the twentieth century.

Paraguay has been marked by several long periods of continuous rule by a single leader or party. From 1887 to 1904 the Colorados held power; from 1904 to 1936 it was the Liberals. In the late 1920s, relatively competitive elections were in place, with about a tenth of the population casting votes. In 1936 a brief authoritarian interlude was initiated by a more socially reformist brand of liberals (called the Febreristas) interested in land reform and regulation of the market. They were overthrown by the military, which ruled directly from 1940 to 1946 and then in concert with the Colorado party thereafter. In 1954 Alfredo Stroessner came to power; he held it until 1989, making him a uniquely enduring dictator.

Stroessner co-opted the Colorado party and turned it into a personalistic vehicle. Over the next decades, he would legalize various factions of the Liberal party to present a "multiparty" face to the world, but by keeping these factions weak and independent, he pitted them against each other and weakened any potential threat from the Liberals. Paraguay has had totalitarian, fascist tendencies, with the Colorado party used to mobilize residents for the provision of services and their integration into the political system. In many ways, the party supplanted the state, which follows the ultimate logic of fascism. In other ways, Paraguay's one-party regime was similar to that of Mexico's PRI, where a level of bureaucracy separated the state and the party so that a state did exist apart from the party. Of course, in Paraguay one man controlled the government for over thirty years, while in Mexico the party and bureaucracy controlled policy but individuals came and went. Through the 1970s, Stroessner succeeded in attracting foreign capital and increasing annual economic growth to quite high levels.

In the 1980s, dissension from within the ranks crippled the Colorado party. These divisions had political origins not only in different factions of the party—the *tradicionalistas* and the *militantes*—but also in a changing international environment, with dictatorships increasingly less acceptable to allies such as the United States, economic crisis which made enemies out of old supporters like the commercial class, and rancor over who would succeed the ailing Stroessner. The instability of the late 1980s ultimately led to a coup against Stroessner and a return to a semicompetitive electoral regime at the outset of the 1990s. With this return to semicompetitive elections, the Liberals came to occupy a central role, and a new party—Encuentro Nacional—has also risen to rival the old. Paraguay still suffers from relatively flawed elections, however, and the military continued to threaten and attempt coups throughout the 1990s. Much of the tension between military and civilian government in the 1990s revolved around General Lino Oviedo, who led the coup against Stroessner but then illegally involved himself in vote recounts, campaign propaganda, and ultimately a 1996 attempted coup. Nevertheless, in 2000 a vice presidential candidate who was not a member of the long-ruling Colorado party won a post in a relatively free and fair election, perhaps setting the country on a new course. [13]

Peru

Although Peru was one of the wealthiest outposts of the Spanish empire, it has had a fairly unimpressive experience with democracy, and its economic indicators have also been among the continent's poorest. Although the last few years have seen consistent moves toward greater democratization, the country's future is uncertain.

Like much of Latin America, the postindependence (1824) nineteenth century was dominated by civil strife and oligarchical control. Not until 1895 was a civilian regime of any duration established. The limited-suffrage "Aristocratic Republic" lasted from 1895 to 1914 without interruption, propelled by export-led development. Peru's first oligarchic political party, the Civilistas, was established in the 1870s and was the source of much of its leadership in the ensuing half century. As in other Andean countries but to a greater extent in Peru, the number of whites and creoles was vastly outnumbered by the indigenous population. From before independence, this created persistent fear among elites that the indigenous would mobilize against them.

In the 1920s, a new party was formed based in the working class, student, and some middle-class elements under the leadership of Haya de la Torre. APRA (Alianza Popular Revolucionaria Americana) competed for power in the 1931 election and lost. It retained a radical and sometimes violent stance through the 1930s and was viewed as substantially threatening to the oligarchy, which forbade it from direct participation in further elections for president. From 1945 to 1948 APRA was involved in an alliance with the president, Jose Luis Bustamente, that helped to promote import-substituting industrialization and leftist state-centered reform. A military coup in 1948 turned APRA out of government, but the new regime, while pushing export-led growth, did not wholly turn against state-centered development.

Civilian government returned to Peru in 1956, and in 1962, APRA was allowed to compete in elections again. However, military fears that it might actually win led to a brief coup, and new elections in 1963 were won by the candidate of the reformist, but not radical, Acción Popular (AP), Fernando Belaunde. Belaunde followed through on part of his reform agenda but was in part blocked by APRA in the congress, which, though ostensibly committed to reform, was concerned about being supplanted by a successful AP.

In 1968 a reformist military coup occurred, signaling a departure from military-oligarchic alliances and bringing Juan Velasco Alvarado to power. The Velasco regime pursued wide-ranging reform, nationalizing industries, promoting education, and undertaking agrarian reform. It stimulated labor participation and trade union organizing but created no new political party regime of its own. Social reform alienated rightist elements within and outside the military, and economic difficulties led by the late 1970s to broader social unrest. After several rotations in the leadership of the military regime, democracy was finally reestablished in 1980 with the advent of universal suffrage and AP's Belaunde returned to power.

The 1980s were marked by the regionwide debt crisis and the rise of the extremely violent guerilla movement Sendero Luminoso (Shining Path). Belaunde was unsuccessful in dealing with either. In 1985 Alan García, the first APRA leader ever to assume the executive, took the mantle of power and proceeded to shift policies drastically to the left. His policies also proved ineffective— hyperinflation raged and the guerillas continued their ascent as well. In 1990 Alberto Fujimori, a dark horse with a flash party vehicle, Cambio 90, came from out of nowhere with a vaguely reformist platform to seize the presidency, defeating renowned novelist Mario Vargas Llosa. Once in power, Fujimori adopted harsh neoliberal reforms and built up the state's national security apparatus in a successful bid to consolidate power and defeat the guerillas. In 1992 Fujimori conducted an *autogolpe*, ending constitutional rule. Democracy was reconstituted in the 1995 elections, which Fujimori won easily. His popularity derived from his slaying of both the guerilla movement and hyperinflation.

Toward the end of the 1990s, Fujimori's government began to look more and more authoritarian as he angled for a constitutionally dubious third term in office and the power of Vladimiro

Montesinos, his intelligence chief, grew rapidly. In the 2000 election, Alejandro Toledo, a U.S.-trained economist from an indigenous background, alleged that he had actually won the balloting but that Fujimori had rigged the outcome. Fujimori's grip on power began to erode with revelations of high-level corruption and intimidation among his security services, led by Vladimiro Montesinos. Fujimori called new elections before he resigned from the government and fled to Japan. In the elections on April 8, 2001, exit polls showed that Alejandro Toledo had won the first round of balloting in Peru's presidential elections. Since the election of Toledo, Peru has more firmly returned to the democratic camp.

Uruguay

Like Chile, Uruguay had a long and admirable record of competitive democratic elections that was interrupted by a military regime in the 1970s. Like Argentina's, Uruguay's standard of living was, in the late nineteenth and early twentieth century, not simply among the highest in Latin America but among the highest in the world. Nevertheless, while it has not sunk to the depths of its larger and wealthier neighbor to the south, Uruguay has—in the last half century—regressed considerably toward the levels of the rest of Latin America, rather than keeping pace with the rest of the developed world. Uruguay still stands apart from its neighbors in many ways, however, and its military regime was shorter and/or less brutal than that of Chile, Argentina, and for the most part, the rest of Latin America.

Uruguay's clientelistic party system is quite old, with both the Colorados and Blancos dating to the first half of the nineteenth century. These parties, like those of Colombia, were much more clearly defined by patronage networks and electoral orientation than by program. There was a loose association between the more urban, Montevideo-oriented commercial networks controlled by the Colorados, on one hand, and the Blanco's more geographically dispersed, rural networks, on the other. As in Colombia, distinctive types of pacts and coparticipatory arrangements marked the history of party conflict. But Uruguay's political system has been marked by several unique attributes. First, for much of the twentieth century, Uruguay experimented with a collegial executive rather than a single leader. Second, Uruguay's electoral system, the "double simultaneous vote," was a completely original mechanism that basically allowed parties to conduct primaries and elections in a single contest. Voters chose lists of candidates, headed by presidential contenders, but all of the votes for each list were pooled to determine the winning party, and then the list with the most votes from that party was elected. This system had the curious result of allowing a contender who won a plurality of votes to lose the presidency because he happened to be from the wrong party (i.e., the party that gained fewer votes overall for its lists). This arrangement, combined with proportional representation (as in most of Latin America) contributed to intraparty fragmentation and reinforced the clientelistic, nonprogrammatic nature of Uruguayan politics while simultaneously encouraging continued bipartisanism. Finally, Uruguayan politics were marked by the generally middle-class progressive orientation of the country, which had a weak landholding class from the outset and few obvious cleavages.

Uruguayan democracy dates from the beginning of the twentieth century. Under the auspices of José Batlle y Ordoñez, Uruguay enacted progressive social policies, achieved substantial economic growth, and experimented with constitutional reform. The 1930s brought depression and a military coup (in 1933). This coup initiated a period of nondemocratic rule by the Colorado party that lasted just under a decade. Although technically a dictatorship, the Colorados' rule was marked by no large-scale repression or military terrorizing. The return to democracy in 1942 marked a period not only of political liberalization but also of successful economic growth within an import substitution model.

By the late 1950s, however, it was clear that that economic model had reached its limits in Uruguay. GDP actually fell from the 1950s to the 1960s, and Uruguayan policy makers failed to generate a significant response. Indeed, the bloated state and the parties' vested interests in maintaining it were major sources of the economic trouble in the first place, making it unlikely they would be able to reform themselves. Martín Rama, an Uruguayan economist, has argued that stagnation in Uruguay was driven by the lack of state autonomy and by the incredible power of public employees, labor unions, and industrialists within the political system.[14] Economic atrophy led to increasing political polarization; constitutional reforms that centralized power in the president; the breakdown of the two-party system and the rise of a third leftist party, Frente Amplio; and ultimately, political violence as the left-wing Tupamoros urban guerilla movement grew through the 1960s. The cumulative impact of these changes was to transform politics into a zero-sum game, elevate security concerns to preeminence, and increase voter apathy about the importance of democracy—opening the way for the coup of 1973.

The years following the military coup were undoubtedly repressive, but military control was neither as enduring nor as brutal as in Chile, where a coup occurred at the same time. The military exhibited considerable obeisance to democratic norms, allowing a completely fair counting of the votes in the 1980 plebiscite, and it never outlawed Uruguayan political parties, which played a critical role in the transition to democracy. Democracy was restored in the mid-1980s, and the first peaceful transition from one party to another took place in 1989. In the postauthoritarian party system, the Blancos and Colorados have maintained themselves as reduced but significant party actors, alongside the Frente Amplio and a center-left splinter group, Nuevo Espacio.[15]

Venezuela

For many years, Venezuela was considered a model of democratic success in Latin America, as a fairly institutionalized, moderate, two-party system functioned smoothly between the early 1960s and the late 1980s. Since then, however, Venezuela has come to be a source of much consternation for those concerned about the continent's democratic prospects. Venezuela's party system has come under serious attack, and there were short-lived coup attempts in 1992 and again in 2002.

As in much of Latin America during the nineteenth century, civil factions sparred with one another continuously in Venezuela. Civil order was not established until the twentieth century, and then it was consolidated under the heavy hand of Juan Vicente Gomez, whose iron fist guided Venezuela toward modernity until his death in the 1930s.

Liberalization followed the death of Gomez, and out of the ashes of student revolts against the regime in the 1920s was born one of Latin America's most impressive political parties, Acción Democratica (AD). In the 1930s and 1940s, the party's titular head, Romulo Betancourt, dedicated AD to organizing throughout the country—among peasants, workers, teachers, students, and feminists. By 1945 AD had established itself as the farthest-reaching and most comprehensive organization in Venezuela. In that year a coup replaced the military regime with an AD-led coalition that lasted three years. During the *trienio*, AD's nearly total political dominance led to heavy-handedness. In particular, AD leaders underestimated the importance of other interests in society—especially business and military conservatives and the Catholic Church—as they pursued a left-liberalizing agenda. As a result, the *trienio* ended with a bloody coup against AD in 1948, and democracy was squelched for another decade.

During the dictatorship, AD was banned and other parties began to mobilize. In what has become a famed case study for scholars of pacted transitions, these new parties—COPEI (Comité de Organización Politica Electoral Independiente), a center-right party, and URD (Unión Republicana Democrática), a left party, along with AD—agreed, at the Pact of Punto Fijo, to a common minimum program and respect for democratic process. A coalition government led by AD was formed in 1958, and a fairly long era of peaceful democratic politics was initiated. After a relatively short time, Venezuelan politics evolved into a two-party system with AD and COPEI dominating the electoral scene. Both parties had strong roots in civil society, an expansive organization, and respected leadership that had learned from the mistakes of the past, particularly the *trienio*.

Although AD had started as a left party (albeit an anti-communist one) and COPEI had loosely started as a center-right Christian democratic party, both were always multiclass parties with broad constituencies, and they evolved toward moderate, catchall platforms over time. Although Venezuela entered a period of continuous, fairly smooth democratic contestation and economic growth in the 1960s, by the 1980s, cracks were beginning to appear in the facade of the model democracy.

There were at least two clear sources of trouble. One was the failure of Venezuela to undertake serious social or economic reform. Redistributive struggles had been papered over, particularly in the 1970s, by fast and loose access to petrodollars as the price of oil shot up. With the collapse of oil prices in the 1980s, Venezuela's failure to diversify its economy meant that social conflicts resurfaced with no easy fix. Repeated failed attempts at reform undermined the credibility of the party system. The party system also began to "cartelize" over time as the parties, without credible opposition from outside, became insulated from social demands and began to collude rather than compete with one another.[16] Once the economic situation had deteriorated such that it could no longer be ignored, president and AD partisan Carlos Andres Perez finally had to implement an IMF package in 1989, which led to street violence and chronic instability for the rest of his term.

The party system fell into such ill repute that in 1993 the founder of COPEI, Rafael Calderón, actually ran and won on an anti-party platform. The election of Hugo Chavez in 1998, who had led a failed coup against Perez in 1992, signaled that the party system was in deep trouble. Chavez's own attempts to implement a vague "Bolivarian Revolution" by wiping out the party system, bringing labor under his control, and appointing military friends to plum government jobs have not portended democratic renewal. A coup attempt in 2002 against Chavez was condemned by the international community (though rather belatedly by the United States), and Chavez was quickly returned to power, but unrest has continued. Venezuela's democratic future remains uncertain. [17]

DEMOCRATIC STABILITY

It is self-evident that North American polities have been more stable and democratic than the Latin American systems. Most of Latin America went democratic during the third wave, whose crowning achievement was probably the election in Mexico that brought Vicente Fox to power in 2000. The North American countries have effectively had no regime changes for over two hundred years. By contrast, in Latin America regime change has been the order of the day. Table 10.1, adapted from research by Rueschemeyer, Stephens, and Stephens, illustrates the point, covering the period between 1900 and 1990. Although this table is imperfect (particular entries may be debated), it conveys the general trends accurately.

The table underestimates the years Latin American countries have spent under democracy because its coverage stops at 1990. The third wave is reflected in this chart, because most Latin American nations made the transition well before 1990. However, some countries (e.g., Chile) had not, and many of the other

TABLE 10.1
Durations of Democratic and Authoritarian Rule in Latin America

	Years of		Cumulative years under	
	Authoritarianism	Restricted or full Democracy	Authoriatrian Regime*	Democratic Regime*
Argentina	before 1912	1912–30	12	18
	1930–46	1946–51	28	23
	1951–58	1958–62	35	27
	1962–63	1963–66	36	30
	1966–73	1973–76	43	33
	1976–83	1983–	50	40
Brazil	before 1930–45	1945–64	45	19
	1964–85	1985–	66	24
Bolivia	before 1930–52	1952–64	52	12
	1964–82	1982–	70	20
Chile	before 1920	1920–24	20	4
	1924–32	1932–73	28	45
	1973–89	1990–	45	45
Colombia	before 1936	1936–49	36	13
	1949–58	1958–90	45	45
Ecuador	before 1916–48	1948–61	48	13
	1961–78	1978–	65	25
Mexico	up to 2000	2000–	90	0
Paraguay	up to 2001		90	0
Peru	before 1930 to 39	1939–48	39	9
	1948–56	1956–62	47	15
	1962–63	1963–68	48	20
	1968–80	1980–90	60	30
Uruguay	before 1903	1903–33	3	30
	1933–42	1942–73	12	61
	1973–84	1984–	23	67
Venezuela	before 1935 to 45	1945–48	45	3
	1948–58	1958–	55	35

Source: Dietrich Rueschemeyer, Evelyne Huber Stephens and John D. Stephens, *Capitalist Development and Democracy* (Chicago: University of Chicago Press, 1992), 160, table 5.1. Adjustments have been made to convert their five categories into two.
*Calculations based on start year of 1900, end year of 1990.

countries in the table have experienced at least another ten years of democratic consolidation since the table was constructed. Furthermore, Costa Rica is not included in the chart, and its absence significantly reduces the number of years spent under democracy.[18] Even taking these caveats into consideration, however, it is clear that Latin America has historically been far less stable and democratic.

Using Ted Gurr's polity dataset, which has a finer quantitative ranking of democracies, the United States has never scored lower than an 8 out of 10 on its democracy scale since 1810. Canada achieved this distinction in 1888. This cannot be said of any Latin American country prior to 1969, when Venezuela reached this level of democracy. And prior to the 1980s, no other country in Latin America had shifted fully to democracy.[19]

Having established that democracy in Latin America has been far less stable than in the United States, we now try to explain this remarkable phenomenon. We begin our analysis with the colonial period.

CHAPTER 11

THE COLONIAL LEGACY

BEGINNING AT THE BEGINNING:
DIFFERENCES IN THE MOTHER COUNTRIES

THE DIFFERENCES BETWEEN THE COLONIAL experiences of North and Latin America are rooted in the differential histories of the mother countries, as well as in the different objective conditions that the colonists confronted in the New World. The values, political culture, and institutions that were prevalent in the mother countries at the time of colonization were transferred to the New World and were modified to suit the situations that Britons and Iberians found themselves in. In this chapter we look at the divergent histories of the European powers and their initial colonizing experiences. This sets the stage for a consideration of the wider political economy and culture of the colonies themselves.

Spain brought a distinctly violent tradition of development to the New World. Spain's social and political structure was an outgrowth of the prolonged wars of the Reconquista against the Moors. Spain never developed the classic manorial system that existed in other parts of Europe.[1] Ricardo Lasso Guevara notes that whereas in Continental Europe persistent feudal wars gradually evolved into a more productive and peaceful agricultural and pastoral economy, in Spain this process was delayed. As the Spaniards drove the Moors out of the peninsula, feudal rights were obtained to the lands that had been conquered. The struggle on the peninsula ended in 1492, just as the military struggle in the New World began. Precisely at the time when the Spanish might have been expected to turn toward a more agriculturally centered existence, vast new conquest opportunities presented themselves in the Americas. Thus Spain never relinquished feudal, militaristic tendencies, and these were transferred intact to the Americas.[2] According to Lasso Guevara,

> Castile had prolonged from the tenth century the *caballeresca* structure and feudal warlord as a consequence of its fight against the infidels. This fight terminated, as is known, in 1492, but it would reinitiate almost immediately the armed action against a new and different type of infidel, the American Indian. . . . In this manner, the Spain that moved to America not only came with the same prejudices and intolerance, but it also included the system of encomiendas [landholders entrusted with Indian laborers] and medieval mitas [obligatory work to which the Indians were subjected] still used in the peninsula for the exploitation of the earth.[3]

Spain transferred from Iberia to Spanish America not only the goals of conquest and subjugation but the methods, that is, the Spanish system of governance. Spain maintained a fairly high degree of control over its colonies and extended its political institutions across their breadth. The Spanish state remained centralized and authoritarian. The Cortes (the legislature) in Spain never achieved the kind of autonomy won by England's Parliament. Timothy Anna has argued that the ideology of Spanish absolutism was underwritten by Thomism, a political philosophy of governance which implied that:

> the people had formed a contract with the monarch, by which they vested power in him, unconditional power. That is, the people did not merely delegate authority to their prince; they alienated it to him utterly. By contract, then, the prince was superior to the people. But the prince must, according to all precepts of Thomism, rule justly and in the best interests of the people . . . for [Thomist philosopher Francisco] Suárez also taught that the law of the prince loses its force if it is unjust. . . . In other words, Spanish kings depended for their authority on the right to rule, but

were not bound by a law, even so sweeping a law as the first written constitution of the monarchy, if, in their role as interpreter of the nations' wishes, they felt the call of a higher ethic.[4]

In short, there were no institutional checks on the power of the Spanish monarch, as these were deemed unnecessary. It would be a mistake to conclude by reference to Thomism that the Spanish empire represented a smoothly functioning unitary system with all power flowing from the monarch. Quite the contrary: it was not possible for the Spanish monarchy to completely control either mainland Spain or the New World colonies. Thus developed "the longstanding tradition," Anna argues, "that colonial, or peninsular, officials refused to obey or implement laws or decrees of the crown that were perceived as being inappropriate to local conditions"—a tradition accepted by officials and crown alike.[5] Indeed, the Bourbon reforms of the late eighteenth century were designed to curb these practices, which were deemed irrational, counterproductive, and detrimental to monarchical sovereignty.

What is remarkable, however, about the Spanish system is that there were no *institutionalized* limitations on monarchical sovereignty before the Bourbon reforms, only *informal* ones. While collegiality may have generally reigned on the peninsula and de facto decentralization did delimit boundaries of executive power, there were no *institutions* to protect Spaniards from capricious rulers who might divine different policies than those acceptable to society. The lack of such institutions contributed in no small part to the difficulty colonials had in responding coherently to the Bourbon reforms (or to the overthrow of the monarchy in 1808) and their delay in initiating Latin American independence struggles.

Portugal also had a strong tradition of Thomistic, corporate thought. Thus Brazil inherited a legal system that privileged state control of interest groups, such as labor unions, over an independent, pluralistic civil society in the Anglo tradition. Both Portugal and Spain took the Church's organic vision of society to heart, in which order was maintained through the acceptance of hierarchy and every class and corporate group played its proper role, promoting harmony and welfare. The cerebrum of the organism, the executive, was to be in control, and there would be little need for competitive politics. "In organic-state thought," the ruler or rulers take the role of the brain and are supposed to see that the *general will* or national interest prevails over the specific interests of which the society is composed. . . . The prevalence of this view reinforces the dominant position of the state elites, because they can discredit specific interest groups or opposition forces for trying to deform the national interest in order to achieve their own private gain."[6] Thus Spain's political institutions were top-heavy, putting little emphasis on the participation or collective decision making that might have been effective precursors to democratic praxis.

England's political history was very different. Much earlier than other societies, England shifted away from a social order dominated by war toward one based on productive enterprise. As Alan MacFarlane notes, "It is arguable that the presence of cash, towns and markets, trade and . . . other factors . . . already separated England in the thirteenth century from other rural societies."[7] Cottage industries and by-employments proliferated, as well as a fairly developed bureaucracy. MacFarlane finds evidence of a burgeoning meritocracy and of a strong commercial impulse. Different members of the same family rose and fell on their efforts, not on their birth alone, and marriage occurred later in life so that young men could establish themselves.[8] MacFarlane concludes: "The majority of ordinary people in England from at least the thirteenth century were rampant individualists, highly mobile both geographically and socially, economically 'rational,' market-oriented and acquisitive, ego-centered in kinship and social life."[9]

Traditions of political participation also ran deep through British history. Lasso Guevara notes that England was exceptional, different from the Continent, as early as the twelfth century. He writes: "Another aspect that demonstrates characteristics of true exception for those times was the active participation of the community in public matters, to the point that the life of the population would appear to depend more on the civic dynamics of the citizens than of the king or his representatives. Not only in the participation of the population in the administration of justice, but also in the maintenance of roads and bridges, and up to the formation of militias for the protection of life and households of all those associated."[10]

In stark contrast to the absolutism of Spain and Portugal, Parliament became dominant in England early on. This was the result of a long process that began with the Magna Carta of 1215. Historically, Britain had a weak state bureaucracy and little control over its aristocracy. In part, this was due to its island nation status and the fact that its monopoly of violence was consolidated not in a standing army but in the navy. Douglass North and Robert Thomas write: "The key to the story, which contrasts so sharply with the case of France, . . . was the inability of the Crown successfully to enlarge fiscal revenues through effective control of the economy. Success would have required a large bureaucracy which owed its loyalty to the king, the effective ability of the guilds to control apprenticeship and industrial regulation, and a court system responsible to royal control. All of these elements essential to success were missing in England."[11]

By the time of the American Revolution, Britain had been significantly transformed into a constitutional pseudorepublic. As Gordon Wood notes,

> The English thought they lived in a republicanized monarchy, and they were right. Their famous "limited" or "mixed" monarchy was in fact a republicanized one. . . . Nearly everyone agreed

that the substantial element of republicanism in the English constitution was a crucial source of its strength. Some Englishmen were even willing to admit that the English constitution was republican. Thomas Wentworth in 1710 said that the arrangement of "king, lords and commons, each a check upon the other," was "calculated for the good of the whole," which meant "that it may more properly be called a commonwealth than a monarchy."[12]

Thus a pluralist, individualist, even loosely republican, British heritage was transplanted to North America, where it would later be crucial for the development of democracy in the United States. Meanwhile, neither Spain nor Portugal provided any significant philosophical or ideological legacy dedicated to self-governance or individualism.

These differences were rooted not only in political history but in cultural traditions. As we argue in part I, Protestantism was conducive to democratic practice because it put less emphasis on ownership of absolute truth and encouraged its adherents to work hard and exercise their energies in this world. Latin Catholicism, in contrast, inculcated obedience to authority and an emphasis on absolute truth, lessons hardly conducive to the acceptance of pluralism or an opposition.

DISCOVERY AND INITIAL CONDITIONS

Latin and North America differ greatly in their European foundings. The former was settled by Spanish and Portuguese, who were primarily interested in getting rich quickly by extracting valuable minerals. Those who came over were at best *sojourners*, people who expected to return to their homelands. The English-speaking colonies, in contrast, were formed by *settlers*, largely residents of the British Isles who expected to settle or to remain in the New World by becoming farmers or tradesmen and freely practicing religions that were persecuted in Britain. Both areas, it should be noted, brought over workers who became slaves, primarily in the tropical and subtropical areas. Colonists in each region not only arrived with different missions but faced different circumstances.

The regions' indigenous populations differed. In particular, the Indian communities of North America were quite different from those of Mexico and Peru. As Octavio Paz notes, "The northern part of the continent was settled by nomadic, warrior nations; Mesoamerica, on the other hand, was the home of . . . agricultural civilization[s] with complex social and political institutions, dominated by warlike theocracies that invented refined and cruel rituals, great art."[13] Given these variations, centralized, concerted military force was vital in parts of Latin America to a much greater degree than in North America. Because North American colonists did not face empires, they relied on loose, decentralized militias that engaged in the more limited violence that ensued during the early years of settlement.

The British and Iberian attitudes toward native peoples were fundamentally different. For the most part, the British viewed indigenous people as an obstacle to be removed; for the Iberians, conquest was entangled with the urge to proselytize. Again in the words of Octavio Paz: "Conquest and evangelization: these two words, [are] deeply Spanish and Catholic. . . . Conquest means not only the occupation of foreign territories and the subjugation of their inhabitants but also the conversion of the conquered. The conversion legitimized the conquest. This politico-religious philosophy was diametrically opposed to that of English colonizing."[14]

These factors—stronger, unified Indian groups and a desire for both conquest and integration—would lead to another important difference between the societies of many Latin American countries and those of North America: the persistence of a large body of indigenous peoples in Latin America—particularly the Andean countries—that have been only partially integrated into the polity. The English in North America, by contrast, made scant attempts to absorb the indigenous. North American colonists considered it their right to expel the Indians and take their lands. Thus, native peoples were virtually wiped out or otherwise marginalized to the point that they had little impact on the major institutions of society. The United States has not witnessed the kind of upheavals that have taken place in Chiapas, Mexico (the Zapatista rebellion); Cochabamba, Bolivia; or most recently, Ecuador, where native peoples joined with part of the army in an attempted overthrow of the government in 2000. Unassimilated indigenous peoples have posed an enduring challenge to political stability in major parts of Latin America.

POLITICAL ORGANIZATION AND INSTITUTIONS

The relations between the new colonies and their mother countries varied considerably. The British gave considerable autonomy to their regions. Salvador de Madariaga, the famed Spanish historian, has noted that one of the most important events in world history occurred in 1629, when the Massachusetts Bay Company was given a charter by King Charles to settle in the Massachusetts Bay area. [15] As Daniel Friedenberg notes, this "royal charter confirm[ed the stockholders'] rights and allow[ed] a government resident in America, which was to be nominally subordinate to the company. Three hundred-fifty settlers were sent over, and later that same year the financial interest of the company, whose investment policy was still controlled by Puritans or their sympathizers, was transferred to the colonists." [16]

As Madariaga emphasizes, this was the first time in the modern world that self-governing colonies had been established. Anglo-Americans elected legislatures in most of the colonies. There were limits on local representation that would be unacceptable today, of course: The governors were still appointed by the throne and held considerable power. Most legislatures were bicameral, with one house appointed by the governor and the other elected from the propertied classes. Nevertheless, as Max Savelle explains, "in America there existed at the beginning of the eighteenth century a functioning structure of representative political institutions that made the British empire unique among the European empires in the hemisphere."[17] Today, visitors to Williamsburg or Boston may still visit the buildings in which the colonial legislatures operated.

Though the governors were usually sent from Britain to the United States to represent the interests of the mother country, they often came with the intent of accumulating land in the United States. It was thus in their interest, in common with the American landholders, to work together with the legislature to protect the rights of landholders in the colonies, to limit quitrents to the crown, and to join companies that speculated in western land. These governors acquired extensive knowledge of American conditions and allowed Anglo-American property holders to exercise considerable autonomy vis-à-vis the crown. It was precisely because of this autonomy that, when the crown determined to squeeze its colonists for revenues to fund the military in the 1760s and attempted to restrain colonial land speculation (through the Quebec Act of 1774), Americans became rebellious. Accustomed to being left alone to carry out their affairs with the generally sympathetic governors' offices, they were not amenable to new constraints by the crown.

Conversely, Spain and Portugal sought all along to control their colonies from Lisbon and Madrid. The Latin American colonial experience was much more centrally controlled, hierarchical, and paternalistic, reflecting Iberian values. There were no elections and no elected assemblies of significance, except at the municipal level. The officials largely came directly from the motherlands (though the Portuguese relied substantially on the Brazilian born to administer the colony). The crown attempted to exercise absolute control over the administration and revenues of the colonies. The crown retained direct colonial administration in its own hands through the Conselho Ultramarino (Overseas Council) in Portugal and the Consejo de Indias (Council of the Indies) in Spain. There was little representation for the colonists, even those descended from Spaniards, the *criollos* (creoles). Spanish American government was based on six viceroyalties, defined as extensions of the crown. The only check on the power of the viceroyalties was also exercised by the central Spanish government through the *audiencias*, councils of officials appointed by the crown to watch over the viceroys in Latin America. Thus a system of checks and balances was put in place, but with the crown as the source of both sides of the balance.

The members of the Council of the Indies rarely had experience in Latin America. While they were not democratically elected, *audiencia* members at least spent time in Latin America. Contrary to what we might expect, however, they were not pulled into Council positions. Mario Góngora notes that only one member of the *audiencia* was appointed to the Council in the sixteenth century, only six between 1600 and 1629, and no more for the rest of the seventeenth century, "so that it was not easy for the supreme organ of government to become familiar with the problems with which it had to deal."[18]

Even the conquistadors remained under total control of the crown. Unlike their North American counterparts, who received grants from the crown, the conquistadors were not free entrepreneurs under private contracts. Instead they were required to request privileges from the crown.[19] While they assumed most of the risks, they were not automatically assured of any of the gains.

Stephen Clissold describes how the Spanish crown was quick to perceive and prevent the seeds of self-government from forming. While initially the *cabildos* (town councils) were elected by the *vecinos*, or house-holders, the crown was determined to prevent a challenge to its rule and sought to eliminate the efforts at local control. "Laws were accordingly issued," Clissold writes, "to prevent any form of consultation or association between the separate *cabildos*, to which the Crown increasingly appointed its own nominees. Offices ceased to be filled by election and were put up for sale. Eventually they became little more than sinecures which were often held in Spain and delegated to hirelings or simply allowed to lapse. Only in the remoter areas, well away from the centers of colonial administration, did the *cabildos* continue to attract some degree of popular participation."[20]

Latin American–born whites, or *criollos*, were also excluded from government in practice. Although under the law they were termed Spaniards, few were given official responsibilities. Creoles held only four of all the viceroyalties, 14 of the 602 captaincies-general, governorships, and presidencies, and 105 of the 706 bishoprics and archbishoprics.[21] One exception to this pattern existed in Argentina, which, because of its paucity of minerals and general strategic unimportance, developed considerable autonomy from Spain. There, creoles did participate; indeed, they basically dominated government. However, this idiosyncratic situation changed rapidly with the foundation of the Viceroyalty of Río de la Plata in 1776, following the emergence of a significant agricultural sector in Argentina and the decline of silver production in Peru. Just as the American Revolution was beginning, creoles in Argentina were blocked from political participation when the Spanish crown attempted to tighten the screws on its more autonomous colonies. Thus Argentina, although originally unique, wound up with the same form of imperial control as the rest of Latin America.[22]

The creoles' lack of governing experience had a devastating effect on subsequent efforts at state building after independence. Morse writes:

> After independence it was the Creoles who took over the organization and leadership of the new republics. Although habituated to the attitude of command, they had been accorded no generously defined functions and responsibilities in the colonial world. They had been born into a vast, tradition-bound, seemingly permanent Hispano-Catholic society, highly layered and compartmented, in which status, after the conquest years, was a matter more of definition than of achievement. Yet in the anarchic

fragments of that society there was suddenly thrust upon them the role of forging new nations.[23]

The English, in contrast, had given much of their authority to the original proprietors, thus encouraging the invention and development of representative institutions. As noted above, most North American colonies had miniature Parliaments. The Anglo-American colonists were therefore able to learn and develop democratic practices that their Latin American counterparts were prohibited from experimenting with. When independence came, the human capital (experience, knowledge, skills) that had been acquired in the North American colonies was absorbed by the United States. In contrast, in Latin American, human capital, such as it was, was largely reabsorbed by Spain, since few locals had been allowed to gain administrative experience in the former colonies.

Thus independence represented a much greater rupture with the past in Latin America than it did in North America. New institutions had to be created from scratch and manned by inexperienced practitioners. The struggles for independence failed to integrate Latin American polities with national identities to the same degree as the United States achieved during the American Revolution. Thus these new institutions had to take root in unstable systems that were rupturing along new fault lines. "The defeat of Spanish forces in the 1820s throughout Spanish America," North, Summerhill, and Weingast argue, "resulted in the fragmentation of Spain's former colonies into new republics. These in turn virtually collapsed under the weight of the challenges of what historians refer to as 'state building.' They lacked self-enforcing institutions that constrained predatory action. In the face of widespread violence, political organization disintegrated into smaller units, typically organized around a caudillo for protection."[24]

If colonial legacies were important to the subsequent histories of both North and Latin America, "critical junctures" could still shift the regions in new directions. Major cataclysmic events such as war, depression, religious schisms (like the Protestant Reformation) can bump polities off their most likely trajectory. Indeed, the struggles for independence, shared by North and Latin America alike, had major effects on both. Revolutions in both North and Latin America were fought in the name of liberal principles. Yet the American Revolution was infinitely more successful in fomenting nationalism, democratizing politics, and forging new values than any revolution in Latin America. Why?

INDEPENDENCE AND STATE CONSOLIDATION

While the United States consolidated its borders and its culture through military and ideological warfare with Britain, the same could not be said of most of Latin America, which remained fractured after its wars for independence. Although the Latin American struggles were generally fought in the name of the same liberal values as the American Revolution, there was a disconnect between these values and the existing institutions in Latin America (and in Iberia). In the United States, by contrast, these liberal values corresponded to a very real mix of decentralized, republican institutions. Thus the independence wars had very different effects in Latin America and the United States. Whereas the United States consolidated political order under a relatively unified nationalist ideology after the American Revolution, the Latin American states in general devolved into bloody civil wars that dragged on for decades.

Historians continue to debate whether the American Revolution was in any sense a real revolution. Although more property was lost in, and more emigrants fled from, the American Revolution than in or from the French, the latter is generally considered a truly radical revolution, while the former is often deemed conservative. Against this grain, scholars such as Gordon Wood have argued that the American Revolution was radical in its social and political ramifications.[25] We do not here join the debate over the Revolution's true significance. For our purposes, scholars like Jack Greene and Gordon Wood, who disagree about the Revolution, agree on one central point: North America was exceptional. Greene believes that American exceptionalism was a product not of the Revolution but of the unique combination of British values and the American condition, which completely predated the Revolution; whereas Wood finds much of American uniqueness traceable directly to the ideas and values generated by the Revolution: "It was the Revolution, more than any other single event, that made America into the most liberal, democratic, and modern nation in the world."[26] Regardless of the precise role of the Revolution, however, it is clear that the fusion of British and American values and institutions led to a uniquely egalitarian, meritocratic, and—in the wake of the Revolution— nationalist ethos that bound Americans together in a way that would simply not repeat itself anywhere in Latin America.

Greene attempts to locate colonial America within the broader context of the British Empire. The fundamental fact about the empire was that it was always a loose alliance of Britons who had gone out to make their claim on the world as British citizens, basically with their own private resources. Their allegiance to Britain was ideational, a relationship of social and political identity; in both concrete economic and political terms, they were quite autonomous.[27] This depiction in fact fits quite well with that of Gordon Wood, who argues:

> Most colonial leaders in the mid-eighteenth century thought of themselves not as Americans but as Britons. They read much the same literature, the same law books, the same history, as their brethren at home read, and they drew most of their conceptions of society and their values from their reading. Whatever sense of unity the disparate colonies of North America had came from their common tie to the British crown and from their membership in the British empire. . . .
>
> Many of the characteristics for which the eighteenth-century colonists were noted were in truth English characteristics or exaggerations of English characteristics. . . .

Englishmen on both sides of the Atlantic bragged of their independence. . . .

America had a reputation for egalitarianism but so too did England. . . .

In the mid-eighteenth century Englishmen on both sides of the Atlantic made new efforts to embellish royal authority.[28]

The list goes on, but the point is clear: pre-Revolutionary America was distinct from Europe and from the Spanish New World settlements, but it was distinct precisely because it was British. If the wars for independence in North and Latin America had accomplished nothing other than the severing of direct political and economic ties to Europe, the United States in its Britishness and Latin America in its Spanishness would still have been very different places, with liberty, autonomy, and political participation far more respected in the North than in the South.

Yet even if one were to accept Greene's position on the conservative nature of the Revolution, it is clear that the American war for independence forged a nationalist identity that has stood the test of time, while the same cannot be said for Latin America. Although the (much later) U.S. Civil War did threaten the consolidated North American state, Latin American nations faced multiple civil wars and armed threats to their consolidation *even as their independence wars were winding down*. In other words, nationalism was simply not so strong a force in Latin America as it became in the United States. Severance from the Spanish monarchy resulted in multiple crises of legitimacy throughout Latin America, where neither existing institutions nor new constitutions were able to consolidate the former legitimacy of the monarchy. Identity was often stronger at either the regional or supranational level, since nation-states were not the operative context for political order in the colonial period. Thus wars were fought not only to preserve local autonomy but also to create supranational autonomy, as in the short-lived Peru-Bolivia Confederation (1836–39). Several futile attempts were made to import legitimacy by installing European princes as heads of nation-states (as in

Argentina, Chile, and Mexico),[29] but in the end, the only type of legitimacy that had any success in Latin America was charismatic, manifest in strongman *caudillos* who were able to create dedicated followings and, however temporarily, monopolize force.[30]

In part, the anarchy that followed independence reflected the weakness of the Spanish nation-state as compared to Britain. Although Britain was certainly taxed by its quest for worldwide domination, the strength of its state apparatus at the end of the eighteenth century is manifest in its empire's trajectory over the nineteenth century, when it established global predominance. Spain, in contrast, was falling apart at the beginning of the nineteenth century. Revolution in Latin America was precipitated in part by the French invasion of Spain and the Spanish monarchy's abdication of the throne.[31] Indeed, Spain, not Britain, actually offered its colonies an opportunity to participate in national institutions (the Cortes), precisely because it was not strong enough to do otherwise. This in turn complicated the relationship between Spanish Americans and the Spanish nation-state. In Latin America, as Jaime E. Rodriguez O. notes, civil war broke out between those who believed that the newly constituted Cortes (which included colonials) and national institutions of Spain remained legitimate, and those who believed that the abdication of the throne meant that the only remaining source of legitimacy was local autonomy, the so-called *juntas* (local governing bodies) formed all over the Spanish world after the fall of the monarchy.[32]

Of course, no such reforms were undertaken in North America as those that brought colonials into the Cortes in Spain. It was thus not possible to argue that the British were truly taking North American colonists' interests into consideration. The American public was divided over the American Revolution, with many colonists supporting the British. Some estimates have put the number of loyalists at around 20 percent of the white population.[33] This did not lead to civil war, however. American Tories were hard put to refute the revolutionary principle of "no taxation without representation," since the British offered little remedy. If some brand of republicanism was the very essence of Britishness, then Britain's alleged abrogation of this principle was very serious indeed. The revolutionaries ultimately won the moral argument definitively in the United States, unlike in Latin America. That argument followed a distinct logic: representation is of fundamental importance; we are not being represented; either we must be represented or we must declare independence.

In the Spanish world, claims that representation was a legitimating principle were weaker, and thus the fact that representation was not given to the colonials at first was not as egregious. In the event, the admission of colonials to the Cortes undermined a logic of independence for the sake of principles of representation. In other words, neither of the Americans' first two logical arguments really applied to Latin America—representation was not so important, and the colonials were ultimately given representation. Spanish American colonials, however, desired autonomy from excessive oversight as much as self-respecting landholders anywhere would. In Spanish America, then, there were real social divisions over the appropriate relationship between the crown and the colonies that were not entirely resolved either before, during, or after the wars of independence.

Arthur P. Whitaker notes that the same stresses that led to revolution in the United States existed in Latin America as well, but they did not really provoke revolt:

> Despite differences of detail, there is a basic similarity between the measures by which the British government of George III provoked the American Revolution and the celebrated reforms of Charles III of Spain and the Marques of Pombal of Portugal. All three were seeking to solve the worldwide imperial problems by a further centralization of power, by more effective law enforcement, and by raising additional revenue. The parallels come to an abrupt end when we turn to consider the American responses. Within a decade the British North American colonies had declared their independence, and within another seven years

they had won it. Spanish America and Brazil, on the other hand, remained quiescent, they had no such liberties to lose. Their independence came 30 to 40 years later and under widely different circumstances.[34]

Timothy E. Anna argues that the Spanish Empire collapsed because it ultimately lost what he calls "authority," a concept very similar to what we mean by *legitimacy*. He writes that "the crucial point is that everything, from the authoritarian power of the viceroys to the role of the monarch himself, was based on the single principle—strong and weak at the same time—of the acceptance of authority, the right to rule, of the monarch."[35] He argues from the Mexican case that Spain retained its legitimacy through both the Hidalgo rebellion of 1810 and the Morelos rebellion of 1813–1814. Neither of these rebellions gained much popular support, and the idea of Mexican independence still seemed chimerical until the 1820s. But the incessant turmoil *in Spain*, as evidenced by the establishment of the Republic; the restoration of Ferdinand VII, who abolished the Constitution; and then the restoration of the Constitution in 1820, led to a crisis of legitimacy, at least in Mexico. Anna writes:

> The Constitution served to point out to Mexicans the emptiness of the imperial ethos. The Spanish sovereign was not divinely endowed to possess absolute authority. If he were, he would not be reduced to a figurehead by the Cortes. The great fear was not of the Constitution, but that viceregal despotism might at any moment reassert itself, as it had [before], to deny Mexicans their constitutional guarantees. The general thrust of Iturbide's rebellion, as expressed in its propaganda, was to overthrow viceregal government, not the Constitution. . . .[36]
>
> Authority slipped out of Spain's grasp because of the countless contradictions between the imperial ethos and the actual fact of Spanish administration. One moment advocating constitutional reform, the next moment advocating absolutism, then returning to constitutional reform; teasing Mexican political aspirations with the hollow promise of reform but not the reality; forced by the European war to squeeze every penny out of New Spain but refusing ever to reward its generosity—Spain toyed with Mexican

loyalty until the habits of centuries were broken and aspirations that in 1808 were hardly spoken aloud became the public consensus of 1821. [37]

Thus, without a ready replacement, the legitimacy of the Spanish Empire crumbled. What was to follow in Mexico, and the rest of Latin America, was unclear. In Latin America independence was more a break from Spain and Portugal than a transformation of the social order. In many of the new countries, the postindependence period was thoroughly chaotic for nearly thirty years, during which all but Chile and Costa Rica experienced constant change in rulers. Semifeudal systems were perpetuated and power was lodged in regionally based *caudillos*. In the end, wars of independence proved to be conservative movements "aimed at preserving oligarchic privilege and the status quo." [38]

Octavio Paz referred to the constitutions created in Latin America following independence as "constitution lies." He argued that the liberal and democratic constitutions

> merely served as modern trappings for the survivals of the colonial system. This liberal, democratic ideology, far from expressing our concrete historical situation, disguised it, and the political lie established itself almost constitutionally. The moral damage it has caused is incalculable; it has affected profound areas of our existence. We move about in this lie with complete naturalness. For over a hundred years we have suffered from regimes that have been at the service of feudal oligarchies but have utilized the language of freedom. [39]

THE LEGACY OF INDEPENDENCE

Why did so many of the initial attempts to set up republics in Latin America fail? Three primary causes have been identified here: the weak tradition of representative government in Spain and Spanish thought, a lack of experience with representative government in Latin America, and lack of legitimacy of the new states created by independence.

Simón Bolívar recognized that both Spain and Latin America lacked the experience in governance and democratic culture that North Americans exemplified. In the "Jamaican Letter" of September 6, 1815, Bolívar wrote:

> Venezuela has been the clearest example of the inefficacy of the democratic and federal form for our infant states. . . . As long as our compatriots do not acquire the talents and political virtues that distinguish our brothers of the North, wholly popular systems, far from being favorable, I fear will bring our ruin. Unfortunately, these qualities, in the grade that they are required, appear to be very far from us; and to the contrary, we are dominated by vices that we contracted under the direction of a nation like the Spanish, that only has excelled in ferocity, ambition, vengeance and greed. [40]

Later he would ask, "Wouldn't it be very difficult to apply in Spain the code of political, civil, and religious liberty of England? Well it is even more difficult to adapt to Venezuela the laws of North America."[41] Bolívar even quipped that "it would be better for [Latin] America to adopt the Koran than the government of the United States, although it is the best in the world."[42]

Douglass North made a very similar point:

> Although the Wars of Independence turned out to be a struggle for control of the bureaucracy and consequent polity and economy between local colonial control and imperial control, nevertheless the struggle was imbued with the ideological overtones that stemmed from the U.S. and French revolutions. As a consequence, independence brought U.S.-inspired constitutions, but the results were radically different.
>
> In the case of the United States, the Constitutions embodied the ongoing heritage of first British and then colonial economic and political policies, complemented by a consistent ideological modeling of the issues. In the case of Latin America, an alien set of rules was imposed on a long heritage of centralized bureaucratic controls and accompanying ideological perceptions of the issues. In consequence, Latin American federal schemes and efforts at decentralization did not work after the first few years of independence. The gradual reversion, country by country, to

bureaucratic centralized control characterized Latin America in the nineteenth and the twentieth centuries. The persistence of the institutional pattern that had been imposed by Spain and Portugal continued to play a fundamental role in the evolution of Latin American policies and perceptions and to distinguish that continent's history, despite the imposition after independence of a set of rules similar to the British institutional tradition that shaped the path of North America. [43]

The problem for Latin Americans stemmed from the fact that the institutions they had inherited from Spain assumed central control and the center had suddenly dissolved. Whereas the colonial legislatures of British America could continue in modified form in the United States without British governors, a system based almost entirely on viceroyalties loyal to the crown could not continue in any form without a crown—without some form of central authority that was viewed as legitimate. As Timothy Anna writes, "The greatest loss involved in the disintegration of the Spanish authority in America, . . . was that the independent states had no unanimously accepted authority to take its place." [44] Since virtually all preindependence power was vested in centralized institutions, it is not surprising that warfare broke out in Latin America for control of their commanding heights. After all, that was the only power to be had, and with no real tradition of representative power sharing among local elites, it was the only evident power worth having. *Indeed, without the power of the crown to inhibit the viceroys, central control of independent Latin American states actually meant even greater power and status to the local authority than it had during colonial times.* [45] It was without a doubt power worth fighting for. Thus, the rapid failure of the first republican institutions was precipitated by and led to internal warfare, which while nominally based in ideology, largely involved power grabs. Carlos Rangel asserts:

We see Spanish America spending the balance of the nineteenth century in internecine strife, civil wars, and coups d'état. Theoretically, these confrontations were motivated by ideological

considerations, including the false distinction between Central-
ism and Federalism, and the overblown dichotomy between conservatives and liberals. In reality, however, they were no more
than power struggles for the same unchanging prizes: control
over government and the public treasury, the only reward understood in politically backward societies.[46]

While the warriors of nineteenth-century Latin America may
not have been as cynical as Rangel suggests, there is no question
that struggles involving vexing issues like clericalism and liberalism were entangled with more primitive desires for power and
authority, though whether this renders Latin America particularly distinct is another question altogether. In sum, while the
problem of the proper balance between church and state and the
issue of free trade did motivate nineteenth-century ideologists in
Latin America, the particular form that warring parties followed
was determined largely by their desire for power, their weak
sense of nationalism, and the power vacuum at the center of
most new Latin American polities.

By 1850 some semblance of postindependence order had generally been established in most of Spanish America, though it
was not until the 1870s and 1880s that the political situation was
stabilized in many states. Wiarda and Kline argue that either
landed and commercial wealth gradually consolidated and joined
with strong oligarchic rule—as in Argentina, Brazil, and Chile—
or strong *caudillos* came to power in the name of order and progress, as with Porfirio Díaz in Mexico.[47] Neither of these two
models would be precursors to successful democratic governance.

Costa Rica was more isolated from the Spanish Empire than
our other cases, and its transition was less violent and anarchic.
It achieved independence peacefully as a by-product of Central
American secession from Mexico. The lack of a strong conservative royalist sector in Costa Rica allowed a fairly homogeneous,
reformist liberal regime to consolidate power in the aftermath of
independence. Nevertheless, the military played an important

role in power transitions in Costa Rica throughout the nineteenth century, and there was much nondemocratic squabbling within the coffee elite over control of the state. Stability was achieved only a little earlier than in the rest of Latin America.

Brazil's history was rather different. In large part this was due to the very weak position of Portugal at the end of the eighteenth century and on. Whereas the fall of the Spanish crown to Napoleon was an interlude in Spain, in Portugal the Napoleonic conquest meant that the entire state apparatus actually moved to Brazil, which at that point seemed to have more potential as the base for an empire. The monarchy eventually returned to Portugal, but shortly thereafter the imperial family more or less peacefully split Brazil from Portugal in the 1820s, and stable rule continued until the formation of the republic in the 1880s. Probably the most significant difference between Brazil and Spanish Latin America was not in the degree of centralization, or the type of landholding patterns, or the tradition of authoritarianism—in all these ways, Brazil was very similar to its Spanish neighbors. What was most different about Brazil was that its independence was achieved through its complete usurpation of the Portuguese empire. Not only did the metropolis move from Lisbon to Rio de Janeiro, but the eventual split was accomplished within the context of the old symbols of empire. Dom Pedro, direct heir to the Portuguese throne, stayed in, and became the emperor of, Brazil, thus giving that country what the rest of Latin America seemed to lack: "a symbol of legitimate authority and a powerful instrument of political and social stability and of national unity."[48] The relative ease with which Brazil split from Portugal unleashed no destabilizing power struggles, nor did it stimulate forceful ideological demands for liberty or democracy.

In concluding this section on the wars of independence in North and Latin America, we draw attention to the importance of individual action. Social scientists are often criticized for over-determining outcomes based on structural factors and ignoring the roles of individuals. Individuals can play an important role in history, albeit within a context that is structurally wrought. As Lipset has emphasized, George Washington exemplifies how social conditions combined with personal leadership can lead to certain outcomes that might otherwise be impossible.[49]

In considering the differences between the "revolutions" in North and Latin America, we cannot help but be struck by the measured seriousness with which North Americans took principles of republicanism as compared to their Latin American counterparts. North Americans moved to collapse the old distinctions of birth in order to erect a new social order on the basis of merit, achievement, refinement, and education. Yet the consolidation of this new order was never certain through the course of the American Revolution. Perhaps the moment at which it became clear that this order was real, not simply imagined, was when George Washington resigned the presidency after two terms and withdrew from public life. As Gordon Wood notes:

> His retirement had a profound effect everywhere in the Western world. It was extraordinary, it was unprecedented in modern times—a victorious general surrendering his arms and returning to his farm. Cromwell, William of Orange, Marlborough—all had sought political rewards commensurate with their military achievements. Though it was widely thought that Washington could have become king or dictator, he wanted nothing of the kind. . . .
>
> Washington was not naïve. He was well aware of the effect his resignation would have. He was trying to live up to the age's image of a classical disinterested patriot who devotes his life to his country, and he knew at once that he had acquired instant fame as a modern Cincinnatus.[50]

Thus cultural ideas about the value of republican government informed Washington's individual decision to relinquish power, and Washington's actions gave life to those very same republican notions. Individual action interacted with social structures— existing republican institutions, widely circulating republican ideals—to consolidate American democracy. One searches in vain for a comparable figure in Latin America's early postcolonial history.

In sum, following the wars of independence in Latin America, one of the primary conditions for successful democracy—the existence of a secure unit that represents the demos—was very weak. Or as some scholars have put it, the wars for independence failed to create the foundations for political order based on a consensus among political elites, as the war had in the United States.[51] Divided societies had only slowly come to militate for independence, and ensuing independence wars did not generate the kind of nationalism that infected the United States through the American Revolution. Democracy cannot easily take root where political instability reigns and the nation-state is a weakly defined territorial and cultural unit without legitimacy—as was the case in postindependence Latin America. Latin Americans, then, not only had to invent democratic institutions from scratch but had to do so under highly inauspicious circumstances.

The lack of consensus among elites does not even broach the fact that many of the Latin American nations with significant indigenous populations—particularly Peru, Ecuador, and Bolivia—failed completely to provide these nonelite populations with a semblance of national identity. These groups remained apart from the symbols and institutions of their respective nations through most of their histories, and are still struggling today for incorporation. This ethnic dimension further increased the instability of national governments and detracted from attempts to create truly national institutions.

INTERLUDE: THE IMPORTANCE OF CULTURE

In Part II we describe at length the problematic relationship between Catholicism and democracy and how this relationship has changed over time. To that analysis we add here that the cultural differences between Latin America and North America not only were theological but also were embedded in the different intellectual traditions and colonial styles of the Spanish and British, as well as the ideologies of those who fomented the colonial wars of independence. Having already enumerated a number of cultural differences between the regions, we respond below to critics of culturalist approaches by examining the interaction between culture and development.

While studying the United States in the 1830s, Alexis de Tocqueville compared its success to the failure of democracy in Latin America: "I have remarked that the maintenance of democratic institutions in the United States is attributable to the circumstances, the laws, and the customs of that country. . . . Other inhabitants of America have the same physical conditions of prosperity as the Anglo-Americans, but without their laws and their customs; and these people are miserable. The laws and customs of the Anglo-Americans are therefore that special and predominant cause of their greatness which is the object of my inquiry."[52]

Domingo F. Sarmiento, before he was president of Argentina, traveled throughout the United States in the mid-nineteenth century. Extolling the virtues of the United States in comparison to what he perceived was the backwardness of his own country, as well as the rest of Latin America, he asked: "Why did the Saxon race happen upon this part of the world, so admirably suited to its industrial instincts? And why did South America, where there were gold and silver mines and gentle submissive Indians, fall to the lot of the Spanish race—a region made to order for its proud laziness, backwardness, and industrial ineptitude?"[53]

He admired the fact that the masses of the U.S. population had acquired a political consciousness. "It is a feat that comes from four centuries of preparation; it is the practice of doctrines and measures that Europe rebuffed and conquered, and which with the Pilgrims, the Puritans, the Quakers, *habeas corpus*, parliament, the jury, the depopulated lands, the great distances, the isolation, the savage nature, independence, etc., . . . has been developing, perfecting, strengthening."[54]

What is it then that defines North and Latin Americans? Many of the differences between them have already been noted in detail. North Americans are characterized by individualism, lack of trust in authority and government, a high value placed on work both as a good and as a focal point of their organization, a belief in meritocracy, and a propensity to look at issues in terms of rights and/or of morals. Much of this can be subsumed under what is called the American Creed, composed of the values of liberty, egalitarianism, individualism, populism, and laissez-faire. [55]

There is no corresponding Latin American Creed to which Latin Americans aspire, however. There are, of course, important values that most Latin Americans share. There is more of an emphasis on hierarchy and concentration of power in the state. Latin American society has been much more paternalistic. Personalism and kinship ties have been highly valued, often more than they merit. A review of recent survey data suggests a few ways in which Latin American attitudes differ today from North Americans'. U.S. citizens are more likely to believe that efficient work should be rewarded with higher pay (86 percent of U.S. respondents versus 74 percent of Latin American respondents) and that determination (41 percent versus 28 percent) and independence (44 percent versus 31 percent) are important values. U.S. respondents are also more likely to say that politics are a very important aspect of life (59 percent versus 33 percent). [56] These data are only suggestive; they cannot tell us about the value differences over the respective histories of either region. Nevertheless, there are good reasons to believe that value differences have persisted for many years between North and Latin Americans.

Have these value differences had concrete impacts? Many critics of culturalist explanations complain that culturalists rarely operationalize their variables or that they rarely show any real impact of values on actions. Furthermore, while skeptics admit that cultures do vary, culture is often deemed epiphenomenal, a result of other factors, such as class structure, level of socioeconomic development, or the organization of political institutions. In our estimation, cultural factors are relevant and do have real-world effects. Culture clearly does interact with other variables and may be created by economic and social factors, but it also influences these factors.

One realm in which cultural values in Latin America have historically had an important impact is that of educational practices. Many Latin Americans prize degrees in prestige fields like law and medicine, even though these are not the disciplines most relevant to economic development. [57] This is related to the Latin American emphasis on aristocratic values and the ideal of a cultivated gentry. As early as Spanish colonial times, manual and technical work were devalued in favor of humanistic education. Thus, in the 1950s, while 34 percent of West Europeans were studying science and technology and 23 percent of non-Communist Asia was doing the same, only 16 percent of Latin Americans were in these fields. [58] Education was viewed as a means not to greater productivity but to greater status. As Lipset has argued:

> The high prestige of the university in Latin America is to some extent linked to its identification with the elite, with the assumption that professors and graduates, "doctors," are gentlemen. However, such an identity is not dependent on the universities' contribution to society, and is clearly dysfunctional in any society which seeks to develop economically, or make contributions to the world of science and scholarship. And it may be suggested that the resistance to "modernizing" the curriculum and to "professionalizing" the professoriate stems from the desire to maintain the diffuse elitist character of the role of the intellectual. [59]

The most successful businesspeople in contemporary Latin American cultures have often been immigrants or other social "deviants," suggesting that mainstream values have tended to retard economic development. This contrasts with North America, where dominant values have emphasized pragmatism, frugality, achievement, and the value of work. Thus in North America, mainstream Protestants constituted the bulk of the industrial class. A study of U.S. business leaders in 1870 found that 86 percent of them came from "colonial families," who dated their arrival in the United States to before 1777. [60] Conversely, Latin American industrialists were disproportionately drawn from marginal groups.

The cultural values of Latin Americans thus tended to promote ascription and humanism and to look askance at technical achievement and hard work, at least when compared to the United States and Canada. These values were reinforced by the inegalitarian distribution of land and lack of economic opportunity for lower-class Latin Americans. As a result, economic development was slow, and defenders of democracy were few and far between. In North America, by contrast, an emphasis on pragmatism and rewards for achievement was reinforced by a far more egalitarian distribution of land, which contributed to the creation of a massive middle class that has fueled innovative economic growth and defended democracy.

Another important criticism of cultural arguments is that cultures are left powerless to change. In a frequent critique of culturalist arguments about democracy, skeptics note that Latin Americans are prevented from becoming democratic by their "culture," which is then traced back several hundred years, as we do here. But, continues the critique, as it is not possible to change something that took place several hundred years ago, what hope does culturalist analysis allow, other than for a wholesale imperialist project to wash out indigenous "anti-democratic" values?

This critique of cultural arguments misses the main point, however. Cultures do change, and it is not always some exogenous shock that allows them to do so. In part I of this book, we describe changes in Catholicism that came both from above and below in response to the conditions of poverty that many Catholics were experiencing. Catholicism underwent major changes over the course of the twentieth century, changes that were not imposed by any exogenous force but came from within Catholicism itself.

Culturalists allow for the prospects of such change; they believe only that it is slow and arduous.

To take an example of such internal cultural changes from another part of the world, consider the policies undertaken by the Meiji elites in Japan, who sought to prevent a Western takeover. State officials decided to award titles and honors to previously deprecated commercial elites, with the express purpose of providing incentives to economic development. Although state actors were motivated by external competition with foreign powers, they still implemented policies of their own design and for their own ends. And Japan developed successfully. Japanese elites decided that they would not remain victims of their past, and they did not. Thus, in spite of cultural obstacles to development, societies can restructure their own cultures and develop their own societies. Cultural analysis does not translate into eternal underdevelopment.

It may be noted here that liberalism has been a very weak cultural tradition among Latin American elites. As Atilio A. Borón notes, Latin American conservatives have fought to the bitter end, right up until today, to preclude mass participation, protect their status and wealth, and privilege their own interests through repression and military rule: "The enlightenment that illuminated so many spirits in eighteenth-century Europe, and which prompted remarkable humanitarian progress in the West, failed to reach this part of the globe. Latin American conservatives remained primitive and barbarous, and only a few of them regarded the reading of Kant, Hume, and Bentham as a worthy enterprise."[61]

The Latin American right has easily discarded the notion that equality and liberty have any intrinsic value. This is surely a cultural predisposition, however much it is rooted in enabling structural conditions.[62] But as Borón observes, conservatives with a minimal legacy of liberalism can transform themselves if they so wish. This is precisely what happened to the right in Spain under Franco, led brilliantly by Adolfo Suarez into the era of competitive democratic politics. One can observe that Spanish liberalism was weak and truncated for many generations, but Suarez's leadership both exploited existing sentiments and generated cultural change. In his hands, Spanish elite culture was malleable. The weakness of liberalism in Latin America comes into focus when the region's polities are compared to other poor countries that have been more successful with democracy. Indeed, the most spectacular poor democracy of all, India, puts to shame structuralist arguments that weak economies simply cannot support liberal politics. But in India, in stark contrast with Latin America, a strong tradition of liberalism and pluralism date back to the early part of the nineteenth century. While homegrown Latin American liberalism did play a role in the independence wars of the same historical period, liberalism nevertheless was and has remained a weak tradition amongst Latin American elites.

Culturalist explanations, therefore, do not condemn anyone to underdevelopment or authoritarianism. Since the 1950s, Latin America has changed in many ways that have made it more conducive to democracy. We have discussed some of these changes—the transformation of Catholicism, for example—and discuss others below, including decreases in poverty, statism, and agricultural dominance of the economy. There are others, such as a widespread distaste for authoritarianism in the wake of the repressive and callous dictatorships of the 1970s and 1980s. Nevertheless, culture has played, and continues to play, a role in Latin American politics, often limiting the efficacy of democracy. That role will be noted in the following chapters on economics and institutions.

CHAPTER 12

ECONOMICS: UNDERDEVELOPMENT
AND OVERREGULATION

IF WEALTH LEADS TO DEMOCRACY, then clearly Latin America has trailed North America rather consistently. Lipset stressed in *Political Man* that the average per-capita income in "European and English-speaking Stable Democracies" was US$695, whereas in Latin American "Democracies and Unstable Dictatorships," per-capita income was US$171.[1] Those data were from the 1940s. More recent data from a slightly later period confirm the general trends: GDP per capita in the United States in 1950 was about $8,700; in Latin America GDP per capita was about $2,200.[2] Median income in Latin America was closer to $1,500.[3] Do these numbers give short shrift to outliers that were closer to U.S. GDP per capita? Not really. The countries whose per-capita incomes were closest to that of the United States still registered levels that were less than 55 percent of the U.S. figure. Still, three countries did stand out in 1950 from the rest of Latin America, with levels of income more than double the median: Argentina, Uruguay, and Venezuela. All three nonetheless experienced military dictatorships sometime between 1950 and 1990.

What is the story today? The most recent data in the source we use (Penn World Tables 5.6 [PWT]) are for 1990. Although more recent data would be preferable, using the same source allows us to use a standardized set of data points. Virtually all of Latin America has become democratic by now; third-wave states include

Argentina (1984), Bolivia (1982), Brazil (1985), Chile (1990), Ecuador (1979), Peru (1980), Uruguay (1985), and Mexico (2000). The only state that has not quite made it is Paraguay, though Colombia is clearly limping along.[4] Except for Mexico, transitions to democracy in these states all took place by 1990. If there is a relationship between GDP per capita and democratization, we ought to be able to see it in the PWT dataset.

The statistics from 1990 document that the United States bounded ahead of Latin America, with no Latin country approaching even 40 percent of U.S. GDP per capita. However, incomes have risen substantially in Latin America. Average income in 1990 was about $3,350; median income was $3,300. Venezuela, Argentina, and Uruguay still topped the list, but they looked less spectacular in relation to the rest. The range was 4,982; in 1950 it was 3,605. Although the range had increased absolutely, it was only 1.5 times the median; in 1950 it was 2.4 times the median. In other words, there were several countries that remained very poor in Latin America in 1990, but the majority had moved closer together toward a higher per-capita income. This can also be seen in the fact that the median and the mean are much closer together in 1990 than in 1950, meaning that there are fewer outliers nudging up the mean.

By 1990 Latin America had grown wealthier and more democratic than in 1950, but it still lagged substantially behind the United States both politically and economically. Most of Latin America's democracies are young. According to Adam Przeworski and his colleagues, democracy does not become impregnable until the $6,000-per-capita income mark (calculated from the PWT data). In 1990 only Venezuela had reached this level, though by some measures, it had fallen below the threshold again by 1999. Current events in Venezuela suggest that democracy is not at all assured there.

Though the data are not strictly comparable because of different measurement techniques, estimates of the most recent income levels can at least permit identification of any distinctive trends in the last decade. According to Economist Intelligence Unit figures, growth continued over the 1990s, producing two more countries above the income threshold of $6,000, Uruguay and Argentina. There appears, however, to have been little real growth in GDP per capita in Venezuela over the 1990s.[5] Indeed, in 1998–99, GDP per capita fell significantly in Venezuela. (See Table 12.1).

Clearly, a major difference persists between the levels of afflu-ence the United States and Latin America have reached. This variation has accompanied much greater instability and author-itarianism in Latin America than North America.

This cross-historical, aggregated approach conceals some impor-tant variations over time in Latin America, however. Argentina, Chile, Uruguay, and Venezuela have all reached levels of eco-nomic development over the course of their histories that should have stabilized democracy, yet only in Venezuela has democracy not completely broken down. Mitchell Seligson has concluded that Latin America as a region seems not to conform very well to the predictions of a strictly economics-based approach.[6]

But economic factors are not just a matter of GDP per capita, a point Seligson recognizes. In chapter 5 we argue that democracy is facilitated by capitalism, relative economic egalitarianism, high minimum standards of living, and consistent economic growth over time. With a more holistic economic approach, perhaps we can better understand Latin American political history.

MODES OF PRODUCTION AND EQUALITY

How do the economic systems of Latin America compare with those of North America? Historically, North America developed in a very different manner from Latin America. Driven largely by individual entrepreneurs, the process in North America was much more decentralized than in Latin America. Land was more evenly distributed in the United States and Canada than in most of Latin America, where massive haciendas dominated the landscape. As

TABLE 12.1

GDP per Capita in Latin America and Selected Organization for Economic Cooperation and Development (OECD) Countries, 1999 and 2000

	1999	2000
Argentina	$7,676	$7,676
Brazil	3,105	3,394
Bolivia	1,000	1,000
Chile	4,867	5,000
Colombia	2,048	1,976
Costa Rica	4,000	4,000
Ecuador	1,167	1,167
Mexico	4,948	5,808
Paraguay	1,600	1,333
Peru	2,040	2,077
Uruguay	7,000	6,667
Venezuela	4,292	5,042
Latin America	3,645	3,762
United States	34,050	36,063
Canada	21,138	22,705
France	24,268	21,648
UK	24,310	24,175
Netherlands	25,215	22,950
Japan	35,669	37,507

SOURCE: Economist Intelligence Unit, 2002, http://www.eiu.com.

it is difficult to find consistent statistical data from Latin America prior to World War II, this section relies on a combination of impressionistic, qualitative historical accounts with some empirical data.

In Latin America life was much more hierarchically organized than in North America. While North Americans mainly lived on small farms, the Latin American colonies initially were built on the *encomienda* system, which developed from Reconquista practice.

The *encomendero* was *encomendado*, or "entrusted," with the Christian instruction of a group of Indians who in turn would work for the *encomendero*. His responsibilities and privileges were proclaimed in the 1512 Laws of Burgos, which mandated that the *encomendero* give the Indians food and housing and some education and specified the amount and conditions of work. Of course, the system was susceptible to abuse, and the conditions of *encomiendas* differed greatly.[7]

Two aspects of the *encomienda* system should be highlighted. First, it limited the powers of the *encomendero* in terms of controlling the Indians. Domestic servitude by the Indians was not allowed, only productive work such as in mining and farming. Mario Góngora writes, "The assumption was that the natives owed the king service, and the king ceded that service to a Spaniard, as a privilege which remained legally guaranteed and was to last for two natural lives."[8] In the end, therefore, the *encomienda* system continued the crown's strong hierarchical control over all aspects of life in Latin America. In other words, the *encomendero* did not actually own his land or his workers but was granted them temporarily. Thus the principle of private property was weak in Latin America.

The *encomienda* system also discouraged the development of a work ethic in Latin America. "The basic presupposition underlying the system of the *encomienda* based on personal service," Góngora explains, "was that Europeans were not to perform labour on the land or in the mines."[9] In this way, the *encomienda* system exhibited the same debilitating tendencies as slavery in the American South. Unlike the American South, however, the *encomienda* system was not balanced (or ultimately destroyed) by a culturally and economically distinct, work-oriented North.

The *encomienda* system was later replaced by a system of *repartimiento* and *mita* (forced labor on a shift basis, mainly in South America). Once again the crown maintained control over the labor of the Indians. In the *repartimiento* system the viceroy and *repartidores* judges would decide what projects would employ labor, the hours of work, and the number of workmen. Generally they were only for public works or for private undertakings that might be beneficial to the entire community.[10] Góngora writes:

> From the standpoint of social history, the replacement by about the mid-sixteenth century of the *encomienda* involving personal service by the system of *mita* and *repartimiento* is extremely important, because it demonstrates the strength of the Crown's reluctance to permit the growth of a feudal nobility, a reluctance displayed by its tendency to supply a labour force for landowners, mine-owners and operators of textile works through the medium of administrative arrangements, without conferring any permanent or hereditary privileges. The Crown thus transformed the upper strata of society, and placed the *encomendero* who occasionally benefited from the *repartimiento* on the same level as any other miner or landowner.[11]

Ultimately, the hacienda system, similar to sharecropping, emerged in much of the region. The landowner advanced poor Indians food and wages in return for work. Many would work for the same *patrón* for the rest of their lives as the estate owner continuously advanced them food or wages and the Indians were unable to work off their debts. Children would also often become indebted to the *patrón*. In this manner, the landowner acquired a permanent supply of labor.

Haciendas were in large part economically and socially self-sufficient. The workers would look toward the *patrón* to settle their disputes and provide some sort of education, including religious instruction.[12] As Wiarda and Kline describe it, "the *hacienda* was a self-contained unit socially, economically, politically, religiously. The *hacendado* had absolute sway. . . . The large estate was thus both a capitalist enterprise and a feudal one. It helped perpetuate the two-class, exploitative, authoritarian structure first established during the colonial period."[13] Ultimately, as historian Richard Morse explains, the hacienda differed from earlier systems because "the Indians enjoyed no tutelage from the state and in effect were under the jurisdiction, and at the mercy, of the *hacendado*."[14] Therefore, the hacienda system moved away from state control of the labor force toward private, but no less coercive, labor control.

Russell Fitzgibbon and Julio Fernandez write that this *latifundismo* (pattern of large landholdings) worked against the political education of the masses: "In a *latifundio* agriculture the peasant is imprisoned in a system which requires blind obedience to a landed elite. The totalitarian character of the system discourages freedom of choice and socializes the peasant to believe in total submission and unquestioned loyalty to the power elite."[15]

Carlos Rangel asserts that the effects of such a system endure long after it is abolished; even freed peasants have difficulty abandoning the pattern of dependency. "[The peasant's] new status as owner of his land," Rangel argues, "will not change him overnight; he will continue to look for some paternalistic control; it is in this relation that he will now stand, as peon and as *voter*, to a political party or to a government locally represented by a cacique. . . . The peasant still has the attitude of a slave; he still expects others to make his decisions for him, and prays only that these new masters will be less demanding and better-intentioned toward him than the former landowners."[16]

Not only does the slave or peasant become dependent on the landowner, but white society develops the belief that work is suitable only for slaves. Rangel writes, "In a slave society, the ownership of a plantation, a hacienda, and slaves becomes the highest social ambition and the earmark of a self-styled aristocracy. Any other activity or vocation seems unworthy of respect. . . . The doctor, the lawyer, the financier, the industrialist, the businessman—all dream of becoming planters one day, of ending their lives as gentry or country gentlemen, the owners of land and slaves."[17]

Latin America's systems of landholding would also have repercussions on the extension of inhabited lands. Latin America was largely divided up into large landholdings of which only a small part may in fact have been cultivated. Whereas in the United States, pioneers pushed back the wilderness at the frontiers and earned ownership of the cleared land, in Latin America, virgin land, when available, lay far from occupied areas due to the system of *latifundias*, whereby large tracts of land were owned but remained idle. This made it difficult for individuals to reach and maintain virgin lands. Stephen Clissold concludes, "Latin America has consequently never known, apart from certain exceptional regions, the 'moving frontier' which played such a part in the development of the United States."[18]

Some parts of Latin America are similar geographically to the United States and might have been expected to develop in similar ways. Perhaps the most obvious example is Argentina, whose interior pampas are quite similar to the North American prairies. One can only speculate about the reasons that the pampa region did not take on the characteristics of the American frontier, but among the most likely factors are historical Spanish/British cultural differences in the approach to settlement and development.

First, the Spaniards who came to Argentina, as with all Spanish who came to Latin America at the outset, were not looking for agricultural work but rather to discover precious specie that they could quickly convert into wealth. Thus, unlike their North American counterparts, they were unimpressed by vast lands that might be used for agricultural production and settlement. "The sixteenth century Spaniards found these grasslands even more uninviting," James Scobie explains, "and soon discovered the subjugation of their inhabitants both unprofitable and impossible. Conquistadors who had ranged over a hemisphere in search of gold and souls carefully skirted the rim of the pampas."[19]

The Spaniards, like the Puritans, favored an organized approach to development. However, the Spanish model was very different from the New England township model. In Argentina, Scobie writes, "the conquistador carefully chose a site with an eye to its defense, its water supply, and the presence of friendly Indians.

He laid out a rectangular gridwork of streets and a central plaza on which faced lots for a church and a municipal building," thus establishing a predictable arrangement of colonists. But "at this stage, relations with the native population assumed vital importance to the settlement's survival. . . . Thus, upon establishment of a city, Indians were assigned to the principal Spanish leaders" under the *encomienda* system.[20] The establishment of towns in Argentina, then, as in most of Latin America, was a precursor to the creation of a system of missionary-inspired slavery, rather than the cultural heart of a diffuse spread of moderate-sized family homesteads worked by their owners—as was true of the townships in New England. This pattern of development can be explained only by the desire of Spanish colonists to follow a feudal-aristocratic model established in Spain and transferred readily to other parts of the New World—a model based on the delegation of production to others under the colonists' management. "They fought campaigns and engaged in administration of government, religion and commerce, but they never sullied their hands with manual labor."[21]

Edmund Urbanski argues that a fundamental difference between the North Americans and Latin Americans was in their attitude toward work. Both cultures were ambitious, but the Spanish set out to conquer other peoples and extract the surplus from their work, while the North Americans took the land for themselves and were prepared to work it themselves.[22] This attitude on the part of the North Americans stimulated in turn greater ingenuity and a frontier sensibility that Latin Americans lacked. Given the relative anarchy of the frontier, anyone willing to work and clear land under dangerous conditions could have a go at it with little if any oversight. What made the North American frontier unique was the decentralized nature of settlement and the ultimate rule of the frontiersmen.

Squatters—or pioneers—successfully settled and developed land throughout the North American West in spite of the efforts of first the British and then the U.S. Congress to eject them. Under the British, several attempts—the Proclamation of 1763, the Quebec Act of 1774—were made to control the development of land. But the crown's weak hold over its governors and the powerful landed interests in America rendered these policies utterly symbolic. Subsequently, the U.S. government tried many times to forcefully expel squatters, destroying their property, "burning their cabins, rooting up their potatoes and other crops, destroying their fences, and forcing them to flee," but in the end, this violence proved fruitless.[23] There was continuous tension between squatters and large landholding families. Neither the British nor the Americans were able to marshal effective central control over land development as the Spanish did. A weaker central government in the United States was simply incapable of taking on the squatters. As Hernando de Soto notes, Congress ultimately acquiesced to settler demands and, accepting the situation on the ground, enshrined "preemption" in American law. Preemption meant that if squatters improved the land they claimed as their own, they would have the first right to purchase that land. This idea was later enshrined in the famous Homestead Act of 1862 but had already formed the working basis for property rights many years before.[24] Initially, Congress had rejected squatting as illegal activity, but after many unsuccessful attempts to control the practice, it finally legalized squatting throughout the country in 1841.[25] Legally sanctioned preemption created incentives to settlement and investment in rather dangerous frontier circumstances.

The chaotic history of land law and tenure in the United States, reflecting local initiative, contrasts with the more centralized process in Latin America. Adam Smith noted that the Latin American colonies were marked by a deleterious concentration of landholdings: "In the Spanish and Portuguese colonies, what is called the right of *majorazzo* takes place in the succession of all those great estates to which any title of honour is annexed. Such estates go all to one person, and are in effect entailed and unalienable."[26]

Recognizing the Church's part, he continued, "In the colonies of all those [Latin] nations too, the ecclesiastical government is extremely oppressive. Tithes take place in all of them, and are levied with the utmost rigour in those of Spain and Portugal . . . Over and above all this, the clergy are, in all of them, the greatest engrossers of land."[27] Conversely, in North America, Smith asserted, "the engrossing of uncultivated land, though it has by no means been prevented altogether, has been more restrained in the English colonies than in any other."[28] Smith argued that North American land patterns encouraged rural development: "The labour of the English colonists, therefore, being more employed in the improvement and cultivation of land, is likely to afford a greater and more valuable produce, than that of the other [Latin] nations, which by the engrossing of land, is more or less diverted toward other employments."[29]

Landholding in North America was far from egalitarian, but it constituted a significant improvement over patterns in Europe and Latin America. Unfortunately, there is only limited documentation on this latter point, since the North American data are generally far more sophisticated than those that exist for Latin America. Historical research has shown that opportunities for landholding were between two and five times as great on the U.S. frontier as in Europe at the turn of the nineteenth century.[30] The average property-holding proportion (proportion of those holding property to the total population) for the country was about 0.5. Lee Soltow's findings suggest that landholding patterns were not terribly distinct from one region of the United States to another; even in the South, landholding was more egalitarian than in Europe.[31] Nevertheless, tenancy was widespread in the United States; the yeoman farmer of Jefferson's ideal was, while a real phenomenon, far from ubiquitous.[32]

Notwithstanding the significant inequality in land ownership in the early United States, it still appears that property owning was more widespread there than in Europe or Latin America.

Most North American property owners held enough land both to support themselves and, in the New England states at least, to participate actively in political life. Soltow has estimated that in Kentucky in 1800, about 4 percent of landholders held less than fifty acres, and 1 percent held less than twenty acres. Presumably, then, the vast majority of landholders were self-sufficient. The Gini coefficient—a measure of inequality—for land distribution among landholders in the United States was about 0.588 in 1798—substantial, but not extreme. [33]

This relative economic equality translated into relative political equality as well. For example, over 90 percent of colonial Massachusetts residents were able to meet the property qualification for voting. Around the time of the Revolution, a resident needed little more than a barn, a home, and about five acres of land (or equivalent property) to vote. Robert Brown remarks of land distribution in Northampton that "the tax lists show that almost all of the people were property owners, that the spread in the amount of property owned was not wide, and the vast majority of men were farmers. . . . A list of shops in Northampton in 1773 reveals that workers other than farmers were not day laborers who worked for wages, but skilled artisans who worked for themselves. . . . Furthermore, the fact that most of them owned substantial amounts of real estate indicates that they were both farmers and artisans." [34]

In sum, while economic inequality in North America was high in prerevolutionary times, two important conditions held. First, a large proportion of the population could support itself and thus was able, à la Jefferson, to exercise an independent voice in politics, an important condition facilitating democracy. Second, social and political opportunities for participation existed in the anglophone colonies and the early United States to a much greater degree than they did in Latin America.

It is not possible to directly compare landholder inequality or absolute wealth in North and Latin America in the colonial or early independence years. However, Tatu Vanhanen has made a heroic effort to compare landholding patterns in most of the world from the 1850s to the present. Vanhanen looks specifically at the proportion of family farms as a percentage of the total. Family farms are those that are held by a single family and that provide at least a subsistence so that farmers are not dependent on others for their livelihood. Thus Vanhanen's index provides a fairly long-term measure of the proportion of independent citizen—farmers from a time when many societies were still predominantly agricultural. As he notes, "The higher the percentage of family farms, the more widely economic power resources based on the ownership or control of agricultural land are usually distributed."[35] Vanhanen's index is reported in Table 12.2 for selected years.

Clearly, Latin America has had a weaker independent farming sector than North America or, for that matter, other states in Europe. The quality of the data makes comparing individual countries problematic, yet they capture fairly well the overall trends and certainly the region to region disparities.[36] It should also be noted that Costa Rica stands far enough apart from the rest of Latin America to represent a truly distinctive landholding pattern.

Another way to break this data down, one that also suffers from weaknesses, is to examine Gini coefficients of inequality in land ownership. Strictly speaking, this metric assesses overall inequality, while Vanhanen's measures the strength of a middling, politically independent class but nothing more. Are most of the nonfamily farms much bigger than family farms in which wealth is highly concentrated? Or, at the other extreme, are the nonfamily farms impoverished, enabling families to eke out only a meager income that must supplemented by working as paid laborers? These questions can be better answered with inequality data.

While strictly comparable data on inequality for North and Latin America do not exist for the colonial period or even the

TABLE 12.2

Family Farm Index*: North America, Latin America, and Selected OECD Countries, 1850–1979

	1850–59	1870–79	1900–09	1920–29	1950–59	1970–79	Average†
Argentina	5	5	8	11	18	24	12
Bolivia	2	2	2	2	3	25	6
Brazil	3	3	4	7	14	19	8
Chile	1	1	2	4	6	17	5
Colombia	3	3	5	10	17	22	10
Costa Rica	25	20	15	15	25	27	21
Ecuador	10	10	10	14	23	29	16
Mexico	2	2	1	5	29	42	14
Paraguay	4	4	4	4	6	7	5
Peru	2	2	2	2	7	13	5
Uruguay	8	8	10	15	21	24	14
Venezuela	2	2	2	2	4	17	5
United States	60	60	60	60	72	72	64
Canada	—	63	64	55	64	64	62
France	28	29	29	35	70	67	43
Sweden	35	35	35	50	79	75	52

SOURCE: Tatu Vanhanen, Prospects of Democracy (London: Routledge, 1997).
*Index is percentage of family-owned farms to total farms.
†Simple average of values shown, calculated by authors.

nineteenth century, more reliable comparisons of equality and opportunity have been made from the post–World War II period. Given changes in the economies of both regions, it may be asked whether landholding patterns have meaning any longer. Certainly, to understand inequality today requires measurements not only of landholding but of cash incomes. Nevertheless, as Table 12.3 reveals, the agricultural sector of the economy was very important in Latin America well into the twentieth century.

Given that so many Latin Americans are still working in agriculture, indicators of inequality in land distribution are still useful

TABLE 12.3

*Proportion of Labor Force in Agriculture, Latin America
and the United States, 1950–2000*

	1950	1960	1970	1980	1990	2000
Argentina	0.25	0.21	0.16	0.13	0.12	0.1
Bolivia	0.56	0.55	0.55	0.53	0.47	0.44
Brazil	0.62	0.55	0.47	0.37	0.23	0.17
Chile	0.33	0.3	0.24	0.21	0.19	0.16
Colombia	0.59	0.52	0.45	0.4	0.27	0.2
Costa Rica	0.58	0.51	0.43	0.35	0.26	0.2
Ecuador	0.65	0.59	0.51	0.4	0.33	0.26
Mexico	0.6	0.55	0.44	0.36	0.28	0.21
Paraguay	0.58	0.52	0.48	0.4	0.36	0.3
Peru	0.24	0.21	0.19	0.17	0.14	0.13
Uruguay	0.43	0.33	0.26	0.15	0.12	0.08
Venezuela	0.48	0.43	0.38	0.32	0.26	0.22
Latin America	0.49	0.44	0.38	0.32	0.25	0.21
United States	0.12	0.07	0.04	0.03	0.03	0.02

SOURCE: Food and Agricultural Organization, Statistical Databases (FAO-STAT), Long-Term Indicators (Agriculture), Data available at http://apps.fao.org/default.htm. Authors' calculations.

in measuring total socioeconomic inequality and opportunity. In 1950 nearly one in two Latin Americans still worked in agriculture; in 1980 one in every three worked on farms; by 1990 the figure had fallen to nearly one in four but was still substantial and about nine times the American proportion. The countries in boldface in Table 12.3 are those in which the level of labor force participation in agriculture is consistently higher than the average. Measures of Gini coefficients for land distribution in these countries are of particular interest. The available findings for these and other Latin American and OECD (Organization for Economic Cooperation and Development) countries are presented in Table

12.4. Although quite a bit of data is missing in Table 12.4, the general picture is clear: land distribution in Latin America has been highly inegalitarian—especially in those countries that are still predominantly agricultural—when compared to the United States.

Though the composite figures in the last column of Table 12.4 are only impressionistic and should be used with caution, they identify basic trends. Historically, land has consistently been more evenly distributed in the United States than in Latin America. However, several surprising findings emerge from this table. Based on the available information, Mexico has had the most egalitarian distribution of land among our cases, and it appears to be more egalitarian even than the United States. As expected, Costa Rica has a better-than-average distribution of land, but this is less impressive given that both Bolivia and Ecuador compare favorably. However, since the table is biased toward more recent periods, what is really of interest is the historical pattern. The earliest period for which most of our cases have information is the 1950s. In this decade, the only country with a distribution of land more egalitarian than Costa Rica was Mexico. In general, as the composite figures suggest, Latin America was in a similar relative position to the United States in the 1950s.

One last way of looking at inequality in distribution of land is to compare the area of land and income derived from large holdings (*latifundias*) with those from smallholdings (*minifundias*). One scholar found that in a sample of Latin American countries between 1950 and 1960, there was at least three hundred and in some cases *as much as sixteen hundred times as much land in* latifundias *as* minifundias, and between 35 and 165 times as much income per *latifundia* as per *minifundia*.[37]

While the many holes in all these data sets preclude us from definitive conclusions, taken together, they provide substantial evidence for the view that landholding was far more egalitarian in the United States than in Latin America from the earliest years of the American republic until the present.

TABLE 12.4.

Gini Coefficient of Land Distribution by Decade, 1940–1990

			1960s		1970s		1980s		
	1941–50	1951–60	Gini coeff.	Year	Gini coeff.	Year	Gini coeff.	Year	Composite
Argentina	—	0.86	0.87	1961–70	—	—	0.86	1981–90	0.87
Bolivia	—	—	—	—	—	—	0.77	1981–90	0.77
Brazil	0.83	—	0.85	1960	0.84	1970	0.86	1980	0.85
Chile	—	0.93	—	—	—	—	0.64	1987	0.79
Colombia	0.81	—	0.87	1960	0.86	1970–71	0.77	1981–90	0.83
Costa Rica	—	0.78	0.79	1961–70	0.81	1971–80	—	—	0.8
Ecuador	—	0.86	—	—	0.82	1971–80	0.69	1980	0.79
Mexico	0.59	0.62	0.75	1961–70	—	—	—	—	0.65
Paraguay	—	0.86	—	—	0.93	1971–80	0.94	1981	0.91
Peru	—	—	0.94	1961–70	0.91	1971–80	—	—	0.92
Uruguay	—	0.82	0.83	1960	0.82	1970	0.84	1980	0.83
Venezuela	—	—	0.94	1961	0.91	1971–80	—	—	0.92
Latin America	—	—	—	—	—	—	—	—	0.83
United States	0.7	0.71	0.72	1961–70	0.75	1971–80	0.7536	1981–90	0.73
Canada	—	0.53	0.54	1961–70	0.51	1971	—	—	0.53
France	—	—	0.52	1961–70	0.58	1979	0.58	1981–90	0.56
UK	0.72	0.72	0.69	1961–70	0.68	1971–80	0.6214	1981–90	0.69
Netherlands	0.55	0.55	0.48	1961–70	0.7	1971–80	0.5	1981–90	0.56
Japan	0.39	0.41	0.42	1961–70	0.52	1971–80	0.38	1981–90	0.43

SOURCES: International Fund for Agricultural Development, *Rural Poverty Report* (New York, 2001), 117–19 (all dicennial averages); *Statistical Abstract of Latin America (SALA)* 37 (2001)

THE STATUS OF MARKETS: LACKING OR CONSTRAINED

What does this distribution of land tell us about patterns of economic production and social conditions in Latin American? Latin American landholding historically has had many feudal attributes. Although private ownership of land has been prevalent, only recently has land become part of a broadly capitalist system, as is agriculture in the United States. What does this mean? Capitalism involves not only private ownership but also a cash economy in which workers receive wages, owners receive rents, and a market exists in which goods are traded, lending incentives to productive investment. In a capitalist system private wealth can be accumulated (saved or invested) and converted into productive enterprise.

Although the United States did not start out with complex markets or strong incentives to productive investment, it has always had a land tenure system that encouraged individuals to improve their land. In addition, ample incentives encouraged landowners to produce various kinds of goods for local markets. As Gordon Wood points out, "Many . . . farmers engaged in domestic industry and marketing not simply to make ends meet but also to bolster their income and raise their living standards. Even farmers who were not growing crops for export abroad were nonetheless scrambling to create goods to exchange in local markets—putting their wives and children to work spinning cloth or weaving hats, dressing deer skins and beaver pelts, making hoops and barrels, distilling rum or cider, and fabricating whatever they might sell to local stores."[38]

Latin America has long had a system, closer to plantation farming, in which landowners lent their land to tenants who worked it in return for a part of the crop. This sharecropping system involved little currency or production for markets. Land was disproportionately concentrated in the hands of large landholders who lived a leisurely existence, collecting their share of crops at the end of each harvest. The sharecroppers, unable to accumulate wealth, had little incentive to improve their productivity. As Ronald Clark has noted of Bolivia, "Before the Revolution of 1952, Bolivia's peasants lived under conditions approximating serfdom, while the society, the economy and the political system were dominated by a relative few who owned and controlled the land and other resources. Most peasants lived under a tenure system which granted them access to small plots in return for heavy—and unpaid—farm labor and personal service obligations to their landlords."[39]

Furthermore, land was often viewed as a status symbol rather than an input to production. As one study of Argentina puts it:

> Insofar as the entrepreneurial bourgeoisie moved up in the social scale, they were absorbed by the old upper classes. They lost their dynamic power, and without the ability to create a new ideology of their own, they accepted the existing scale of social prestige, the values and system of stratification of the traditional rural sectors. When they could, they bought estancias [ranches] not only for economic reasons, but for prestige, and became cattle raisers themselves. [40]

Lack of commercial opportunities inhibited the creation of an independent entrepreneurial class and did little to spur the demise of the peasant class in Latin America. Semifeudal arrangements— never present in North America except in the South—have persisted until very recent times in Latin America. In contrast, broad private ownership in the United States constituted a logical foundation for capitalist enterprise.

Where smallholdings have existed in Latin America, they have often been sufficient only for subsistence farming. About two-thirds of the peasants in the 1960s in Colombia owned either no land at all or barely enough land to feed their families. Smallholding peasants were not oriented toward capitalist production because they simply did not have enough land.[41] Ernest Feder estimated that this was true for Latin America in general in the

1970s, with two-thirds or more of the region's rural populations working *minifundias* or owning no land in many countries. In Ecuador and Peru, for example, he reported proportions above 0.85. [42] Thus ownership patterns in Latin America consistently inhibited the development of commercial incentives and the development of a market-oriented acquisitive mentality on the part of average landholders.

But markets in Latin America were not just constrained by traditional structures of ownership. They were also directly undermined by the organization of colonial society. A pervasive urban bias in Latin America that began in the colonial era persists to this day. Spanish colonists settled mainly in cities, while North American colonists settled as farmers, in rural areas. This, as Lasso Guevara describes it, shaped how the Anglo- and Latin Americans ultimately viewed land: "While in the North the urban areas were established to serve the countryside, the reverse occurred in Latin America" [43] In the latter, urban centers were administrative entrepots from which colonial officers attempted to control native Indian populations. The Spanish thus established a pattern of development that entrenched them in centralized management and distribution of land resources. This model inhibited the development of capitalist enterprise.

Both the Portuguese and Spanish Empires tightly regulated commerce and production—the Portuguese through the Conselho Ultramarino, the Spanish through the Casa de Contratación. Both empires (Spain to an extreme extent) prohibited other nations from engaging in direct trade with their colonies. Neither of these Iberian countries (nor its overseas colonies) had a large manufacturing sector, and therefore both imported goods from Northern Europe for delivery to the colonies in return for raw materials. [44] Colonial authorities acted to inhibit the development of commerce that, from the mother countries' perspective, was or could become unmanageable.

Central regulation of ports in particular led to gross inefficiencies. The decision to prevent shipping of Argentine goods from Río de la Plata for many years meant that goods had to travel overland to Peru on their way to Europe.[45] Adam Smith argued that Spanish and Portuguese port restrictions encouraged the creation of oligopolistic trade concerns that inflicted heavy costs on the colonies. Merchants found it in their interest to act in concert, resulting in collusion. Colonists were therefore ill supplied and faced high prices for imports and low prices for exports.[46]

While the Anglo-American colonies also faced mercantilist policies by the British, they faced fewer restrictions. The British system allowed them to trade with any country in the Atlantic community as long as they observed the Navigation Acts (which required that all goods be carried in British or American ships and that some goods go through British ports). There was some colonial manufacturing, mainly for internal needs, of silver ware, woolens, and furniture. Anglo-American merchants also held a large share of illicit international trade, including trade to other colonies, for example. Savelle writes that this "contributed mightily to the expansion of their capital wealth."[47]

Adam Smith also recognized these Anglo-American advantages, arguing that they encouraged competition and prevented the collusion evident in the Spanish and Portuguese colonies. Colonists were therefore able to buy and sell at more reasonable prices. Furthermore, many goods (including grains, lumber, salt, provisions, fish, sugar, and rum) could be exported to other countries, provided they were carried in British or colonially owned ships.[48] There was also some freedom of trade between British North American colonies and the British West Indies.[49] The result, Adams observed, was that "the English colonies have been more favoured, and have been allowed a more extensive market, than those of any other European nation."[50] Smith emphasized that because the English colonies also had more moderate taxes, "a greater proportion of this produce belongs to themselves, which they may store up and employ in putting into motion a still greater quantity of labour."[51]

Contemporary Chilean scholar Claudio Véliz argues that the extreme control over the economy maintained by the Spanish monarchy was due to a mistrust and suspicion of economic motivations that could disturb the harmony, balance, and health of the Christian realm:

> The Catholic monarchs saw one shining truth surrounded by the shadows of many errors, pitfalls, and temptations that could, if ignored and allowed to persist, threaten the well-being of the larger community; they did not feel free to abdicate responsibility of directing things economic because they were convinced that this was the only way effectively to frustrate the egoistic appetites nourished by greed and ambition and thus to prevent them from disrupting the efficient functioning of the incipient but well-ordered Christian society in the Indies or from usurping precedence over the legitimate interests of the Crown.[52]

Ralph Woodward, Jr., has argued that the differences between British and Spanish economic regulation in the Americas were due not only to cultural divergences but also to the relative strength of the Spanish bureaucratic state in relation to the British state. Thus many of the distinctions between North and Latin America evolved from the inability or unwillingness of the British state to enforce stricter controls over trade and production, an approach the Spanish did not shy away from. As Woodward argues, "In both systems, of course, it was a case of the government using the merchants as a means of developing its power and wealth, but the difference was the degree to which the merchants were controlled, regulated, and watched over by the Crown. . . . In theory and in law the English commercial system was nearly as closed as the Spanish, but the individual merchants and shippers were much less restricted and controlled, and in practice the English system in North America went virtually unenforced until after 1763."[53]

Another difference Woodward has identified lay in the constitution of the "private" commercial sector in both regions. In Latin

America, power and privilege were entrenched in *fueros*, reserved domains of authority granted by the state. The military and Church both benefited from these reserved domains, as did the merchants. Thus the Spanish formed *consulados*, which were basically private monopolies subsidized by the state to promote economic development. These *consulados* steered development toward their own interests in a way that was alien to the more pluralistic and open markets of the North.[54] The merchant class in North America, by comparison, basically had to fend for itself. Commercial conditions were closer to the ideal competitive market, in which competition yields diffuse benefits rather than concentrated profits.

Latin American countries have subsequently found it difficult to abandon the notion, inherited from the Spanish colonial legacy, that the economy must be controlled by the state in order to preserve the national interest. In the immediate postindependence years, those countries that were able to establish political order did so by avoiding what North, Summerhill and Weingast term "market-sustaining federalism." States such as Brazil and Chile concentrated power at the top and left the door open to arbitrary intervention in, and regulation of, commercial markets. "Instead of competing for mobile factors of production," they argue, "provincial elites competed for pork and protection within national legislatures." Rent seeking replaced decentralized competition for productive investment ("market-sustaining federalism"). As a result, long-term economic growth was hindered by post-independence governments much as it had been by Spanish colonial authorities. This pattern held until the twentieth century in most of Latin America.[55]

Ultimately, Latin America turned toward industrial capitalism, like the Northern countries, but with a great deal less success. During the nineteenth and twentieth centuries, feudal structures eroded and were gradually replaced by more market-oriented structures, though statism was omnipresent. More liberalized attempts to spur development at the end of the nineteenth century were jettisoned in the twentieth century. From the 1930s to the 1970s, many Latin American countries attempted to pursue capital-intensive import substitution industrialization (ISI), only to abandon this policy by the 1980s in favor of more market-driven development strategies. [56] How capitalist has Latin America actually been in comparison to the United States?

This question immediately begs another: how do we measure capitalism? There is no good single indicator. Arguing for the simplest possible interpretation of capitalism, we may distinguish economic systems on the basis of who owns the means of production and conditions of exchange. The most capitalist systems have virtually no state-owned enterprises; the most socialist have virtually no privately owned enterprise. Most polities fall in between. It is worth noting that governments may substantially imitate state ownership of privately owned firms by burdening them with extensive regulations, price controls, and hiring quotas and by eliminating or circumscribing competitors. Therefore, formal ownership of the means of production is an imperfect metric for degree of capitalism. Although the freedom of markets is also distinct from capitalism per se, measuring both state ownership and market freedom together constitutes a better approximation of degree of capitalism than either alone. Finally, as noted earlier, the question in Latin America is not just between capitalism and socialism but between capitalism and semifeudalism. Thus it is not just private ownership that matters but also the extent of markets, the number of workers in agriculture, and the proportion who receive wages. In the modern period, Latin American agriculture has both shrunk and become predominantly capitalist. Thus, for this period at least, we can focus on ownership of the means of production and regulation of markets. Our interest in Latin American versus North American capitalism is founded on our analysis in part II of the importance of capitalism to democracy. We hypothesize that a generally capitalist orientation is healthy for democracy.

Unfortunately, the data on either resource ownership or market regulation are scarce, at least prior to the 1960s. Below we analyze the extant data.

"Overall" economic freedom scores in Table 12.5 represent the entire panoply of regulations and restrictions that governments place on the free flow of commerce and currency. "SOEs" is a composite rating that takes into account the total number of state-owned enterprises and the quantity of government investment as a proportion of total investment. Scores for both measurements range from 1 to 10, with 10 representing the most "capitalist." The last two rows of entries in the table makes clear that the United States has been consistently more capitalist by these measures than Latin America. Overall, values hover around 8 for the United States and 5 for Latin America. Only in the 1990s was there momentum toward closing this gap. More important for our purposes, from 1970 to 1990, little real movement occurred in either region; the United States barely increased its capitalist ratings, and Latin America saw no increase at all. Thus the gap between the two regions held up consistently for a long period.

These aggregate trends should not be allowed to obscure consistent real movement toward capitalism in some countries, notably Chile, Ecuador, and Bolivia. Costa Rica and Venezuela performed favorably over much of the period, though Venezuela seems to have been closing its markets while other Latin American countries were opening theirs. One surprise in this table is the anomaly of Paraguay. A generally strong performer, Paraguay was able to keep its markets relatively open over the period by investing the large sums of development aid it received in return for doing so. If most of Latin America is more capitalist in 1997 than in 1970, however, this is primarily because of a worldwide shift toward market economies in the 1990s, not because of any consistent move away from statism before that time.

Although aggregate data on economic freedom are desirable, it must be acknowledged that there are no such comparable

TABLE 12.5
Level of "Capitalism" in Latin America and the United States, 1970–1997

	Economic freedom	1970	1975	1980	1985	1990	1995	1997
Argentina	Overall	6.6	3.2	4.8	3.8	4.9	7.9	8.4
	SOEs	4	4	4	4	6	8	10
Bolivia	Overall	—	—	4	4	6.5	7.9	8
	SOEs	2	4	2	2	0	2	4
Brazil	Overall	5.6	4.5	4.1	3.2	4.4	5.4	5.9
	SOEs	4	4	2	4	6	6	6
Chile	Overall	3.7	3.7	5.9	6	7.4	8.2	8.2
	SOEs	4	2	4	4	6	7	7
Colombia	Overall	5.1	4.7	4.6	5.2	5.1	6.4	5.6
	SOEs	4	4	2	2	2	4	4
Costa Rica	Overall	—	6.7	5.8	5.4	6.8	6.6	—
	SOEs	6	6	4	4	6	4	—
Ecuador	Overall	3.9	5.8	6	4.5	5.3	6.7	7
	SOEs	4	4	4	4	4	4	4
Mexico	Overall	7	5.7	4.9	4.5	6.4	7.4	7.7
	SOEs	4	2	2	2	4	6	6
Paraguay	Overall	—	—	6.2	6	6.3	7.8	7.6
	SOEs	8	8	8	6	7	7	7
Peru	Overall	4.7	3.5	3.4	2.3	3.7	7.5	7.9
	SOEs	6	4	4	4	6	8	8
Uruguay	Overall	—	6.5	6.3	6.8	6.9	7.2	7.4
	SOEs	6	6	6	6	6	6	6
Venezuela	Overall	7.8	6.5	6.9	5.8	5.8	4.5	6
	SOEs	7	4	2	0	0	0	2
Latin America	Overall	5.6	4.9	5.2	4.6	5.8	7	7.2
	SOEs	4.9	4.3	3.7	3.5	4.4	5.2	5.8
United States	Overall	8	8.1	8.5	8.6	8.8	8.9	9
	SOEs	7	7	8	8	8	8	8

SOURCE: Economic Freedom Network, *Economic Freedom of the World: 2000 Annual Report*, www. freetheworld.com; results for Costa Rica, from *2002 Annual Report*.
NOTE: SOE stands for "state-owned enterprise."

quantitative data on the degree of capitalism in Latin American countries over the whole historical period that is of interest. Furthermore, data of this type do not entirely elucidate the complex structural relationships that scholars like Barrington Moore and Dietrich Rueschemeyer, John Stephens, and Evelyne Huber have drawn our attention to. As we argued in part I, the triumph of democracy in capitalist systems owes much to the shifts in the relative power of strategic actors in society brought about by capitalist development. In particular, we drew attention to the rise of a bourgeoisie and ultimately a working class linked to democratic reforms and to a decline of the rural sectors—landlords and peasants—that were more supportive of authoritarian forms of governance. Yet the process of capitalist development in Latin America has been quite different from those processes in Europe and the English-speaking former settlement colonies. It is therefore one thing to say that Latin America has been less capitalist than the United States since 1970 and to assume on the basis of qualitative evidence, as we have, that these differences extend far back into history. It is another thing, however, to determine exactly to what degree Latin America has been less capitalist than the United States and identify the ramifications.

It is worth noting in this regard that statist European nations like Sweden have not been very much more capitalist than Latin America over the last thirty years. Summary rankings for Sweden, Denmark, and France are presented in Table 12.6. All three European countries—among the most statist in Europe—show overall ratings that top the average for Latin America, but there is a strong government presence in the SOE sector. In this regard at least, France is no more capitalist (and in some cases less so) than Ecuador, Peru, Argentina, Brazil, Chile, or Uruguay. However, over the period in question, France still exhibits higher overall scores (as do Sweden and Denmark) than any country in Latin America. A comparison of Latin American countries with the most statist countries in Europe, therefore, reveals that the "capitalist" countries of Europe, often governed by Social Democrats, are still more capitalist than those of Latin America. However, the differences, at least according to our crude quantitative measures, are not enormous. And, even more suggestive, the average SOEs score for the statist European countries in 1970 was actually lower than the Latin American average, though this has reversed for every period since then. But these data raise intriguing questions about the differences prior to the years covered by our data set. Some scholars have argued, for example, that the most significant difference between the social democracies of Europe and the states of Latin America is not in their degree of capitalism per se but in the sequencing of the growth of their states and the institutionalization of democracy. By this logic, the European states grew *after* representative institutions had been consolidated that were able to limit and channel this growth with some accountability. This did not happen in Latin America. [57] A more subtle consideration of qualitative factors would seem to be in order.

One important difference between the capitalist systems in Latin America and in Europe is particularly relevant here, because it concerns the relative power of strategic actors: the working class was relatively weaker in Latin America in relation to the middle class than in Europe. This was so because of a long-surviving rural peasantry in Latin America combined with a focus, during the period of ISI, on capital-intensive industries that stunted growth in the size of the working class. ISI required a managerial class, though, and a large state bureaucracy, so that, ironically, the industrialization process created a state sector as much as a private industrial one. According to Rueschemeyer, Stephens, and Huber,

> This pattern was set by the growth of the export economy, as this caused growth of the state and urbanization before any significant industrialization (with the above mentioned exceptions of Argentina and Uruguay), and it was perpetuated during the ISI

TABLE 12.6

Level of "Capitalism" in Some Statist European Countries, 1970–97

	Economic freedom	1970	1975	1980	1985	1990	1995	1997
Sweden	Overall	6.2	6.2	6.3	7	7.5	7.9	8
	SOEs	2	4	4	6	6	6	6
Denmark	Overall	7.6	6.7	6.8	6.9	7.7	8.1	8.4
	SOEs	6	6	6	6	6	7	7
France	Overall	7.3	6.3	6.3	6.4	7.8	8.1	8
	SOEs	4	4	4	4	4	4	4
Statist Average	Overall	7	6.4	6.5	6.8	7.7	8	8.1
	SOEs	4	4.7	4.7	5.3	5.3	5.7	5.7
Latin America	Overall	5.6	4.9	5.2	4.6	5.8	7	7.2
	SOEs	4.9	4.3	3.7	3.5	4.4	5.2	5.8

SOURCE: Economic Freedom Network, *Economic Freedom in the World: 2000 Annual Report.*

phase. Urbanization and state expansion brought forth middle classes of state employees, private white collar employees, professionals and intellectuals, artisans, shopkeepers and small entrepreneurs. Late and dependent industrialization, though, did not lead to a corresponding formation of an industrial working class and labor movement. Even when ISI was undergoing significant growth, labor absorption by industry remained limited.[58]

In general, this pattern of development would be expected to produce weaker support for full political democracy than would be found in the advanced industrial states of Europe or the United States.[59] In Europe the middle classes pushed for parliamentary democracy, while the working classes together with middle-class elements made the final push for full modern democracy. A weaker working class should result in more restricted democracies, regimes with parliamentary forms and procedures that are exclusive or capable of weathering only limited degrees of contestation. In particular, the persistence of large numbers of unorganized peasants (i.e., a persistent agricultural sector) in lieu of a strong working class did not augur well for democracy in Latin America. Again, it is not that working classes are inherently prodemocratic but that the weakness of an important strategic actor that would have competed for power with elite upper-class actors made democratic outcomes less likely. If democracy is an equilibrium produced by actors that are in conflict but cannot destroy one another, then it is more likely to exist where the power of strategic actors is nearly equal. The weakness of the Latin American working class meant that opposition to landed upper-class hegemony was more limited. To understand this numerical weakness in comparative terms around the time when European countries were democratizing, consider Table 12.7, which reports the size of the industrial working class in Latin America, the United States, and several OECD countries in the 1920s. Though only rough estimates, these figures tell the general story.

The relative weakness of the working class in Latin America was clearly connected to the persistence of a peasant class, as detailed above in Tables 12.2 and 12.3. Regarding the issue of land and income distribution, two important points come to mind. At the outset, we would expect more equal distribution of land to be a boon to democracy, as it clearly was in the United States. A large body of medium-sized landowners creates the conditions for entrepreneurial activity, an active civil society, and a body of citizens who are economically independent enough to form an opposition to the state. Therefore, the fact that land distribution in the nineteenth century was much more inegalitarian, that a much smaller proportion owned property, was connected to Latin America's failures to democratize. In the industrial and postindustrial eras, agriculture becomes the work of a specialized and numerically smaller group of people. More egalitarian modern societies might have less egalitarian distributions of land than in the past

TABLE 12.7

Estimated Size of the Working Class in Latin America,
the United States, and Selected OECD Countries, 1920s

	Working-class population	Percentage of economically active population
Argentina	340,000	8.3
Uruguay	39,000	7.0
Chile	82,000	6.1
Brazil	380,000	3.7
Mexico	160,000	3.2
Colombia	47,000	1.8
Venezuela	12,000	1.5
Latin America	—	4.5
United States	10,880,000	29.7
Canada	530,453	16.7
France	5,869,000	27.4
Netherlands	738,000	27.1
United Kingdom	7,000,000	36.2
Sweden	787,000	30.2

SOURCES: Ruth Berins Collier and David Collier, *Shaping the Political Arena* (Princeton: Princeton University Press, 1991), 67; B. R. Mitchell, ed., *International Historical Statistics: The Americas; International Historical Statistics: Europe 1750–1993* (New York: Stockton Press, 1998). Historical Statistics of Canada (www.statcan.ca).

NOTE: Latin American figures represent factory employment, 1925; OECD figures, manufacturing employment, 1920.

but more equal distributions of cash income. The most recent income inequality data from the 1990s, shown in Table 12.8, bears this out. The table contains Gini coefficients that measure the dispersion of wealth in a country. Latin American income inequality is generally higher than that of the United States.

Again, the United States has relatively high income inequality when compared to the OECD sample but generally lower

TABLE 12.8
Income Inequality, 1990s

	Gini Coeff.			Gini Coeff.	
	Income	Year		Income	Year
Argentina	—	—		—	—
Bolivia	42	1990		42	1998
Brazil	63.4	1989		60	1998
Chile	56.5	1994		57	1998
Colombia	51.3	1991		57	1998
Costa Rica	47	1996		—	—
Ecuador	46.6	1994		—	—
Mexico	53.7	1995		47.6	1998
Paraguay	—	—		59	1998
Peru	44.9	1994		46	1998
Uruguay	—	—		—	—
Venezuela	53.8	1990		47	1998
Latin America	51	—		52.6	1998
United States	45.6	1994		40	1998
Canada	31.5	1994		—	—
France	32.7	1995		—	—
United Kingdom	36.1	1991		—	—
Japan	24.9	1993		—	—

SOURCE: World Bank, World Development Report (New York: Oxford University Press, 2000, 2001); Social Watch, www.socwatch.org.uy.

inequality when compared to Latin America as a whole. Per our discussion in part I, however, income inequality per se may not be directly related to democracy. While relatively high minimum incomes can facilitate democracy by fostering a relatively independent class of citizens who can form an opposition, it does not follow that an increase in income at the top of society (leading to an increase in inequality) is necessarily detrimental. Therefore, we should examine not only inequality but relative poverty.

POVERTY

As with most social phenomena, poverty is difficult to measure, though one instinctively knows what it is. The simplest measure available is cash income. However, income is a poor proxy for poverty if it is not tied to an index of purchasing power. After all, a dollar in the United States does not buy the same amount as a dollar elsewhere. Purchasing power parity measures present various problems of their own; for our purposes, not the least of these is that they are unavailable for many years. However, the same can be said for nearly all of our metrics. Poverty is not really just about income, however. As is now widely accepted, poverty is multidimensional, subsuming lack of education, lack of access to basic resources or assets, poor health conditions, and other factors. Although it is broadly true that people with high incomes can afford more quality health care, education, and resources than people with low incomes, it does not follow that this relationship is linear or monotonic. For this reason and because of the many gaps in the data, it is wiser to look at a broader array of indicators rather than simply cash incomes. This is done in Table 12.9.

Clearly, we face comparability problems with this data. The only metric available for both developing and developed countries is the composite Human Development Index (HDI), devised by the United Nations. This measure averages GDP per capita, longevity at birth, and educational opportunity. Using this metric, the United States has clearly outperformed Latin America. The percentage of the population living below the national poverty level can also be examined and compared with the purchasing power parity figure of $14.40 for the United States because that number is based on the U.S. national poverty line. Again, though poverty is considerable in the United States, it is generally much lower than in Latin America, with the possible exception of Uruguay, which reports no national poverty

TABLE 12.9

Measures of Poverty and Well-Being, Late Twentieth Century

	Proportion of population in poverty					HDI (1975)	HDI (UNDP) (1998)	Percent below $14.40 (1989–95) PPP 1985	Percent below 50% of median (1987–97)
	Below $1	Below $2	Year	National	Year				
Argentina	—	—		0.26	1990's	0.837			
Bolivia	0.11	0.39	1990	—		0.781	0.643		
Brazil	0.05	0.17	1997	0.17	1990	0.512	0.747		
Chile	0.04	0.2	1994	0.21	1994	0.639	0.826		
Colombia	0.11	0.29	1996	0.18	1992	0.702	0.764		
Costa Rica	0.1	0.26	1996			0.657	0.797		
Ecuador	0.2	0.52	1995	0.35	1994	0.62	0.722		
Paraguay	0.19	0.39	1995	0.22	1991	0.66	0.736		
Peru	0.16	0.41	1996	0.49	1997	0.635	0.737		
Uruguay	0.02	0.07	1989	—		0.753	0.825		
Venezuela	0.15	0.36	1996	0.31	1989	0.714	0.77		
Latin America	0.11	0.31		0.27		0.67	0.76		
United States						0.862	0.929	14.1	17.3
Canada						0.865	0.935	5.9	10.6
France						0.844	0.917	12	8.4
United Kingdom						0.837	0.918	13.1	10.6
Netherlands						0.857	0.925	14.4	6.2
Japan						0.849	0.924	3.7	11.8
OECD							0.893		

SOURCE: United Nations, *Human Development Report, 2000* (New York: Oxford University Press, 2000).

NOTE: *HDI* Stands for Human Development Index; *UNDP*, for United Nations Development Program; *PPP*, for purchasing power parity line. Argentina, Chile, and Costa Rica also stand out as having achieved fairly high levels of human development as of 1998.

In sum, U.S. society has historically offered more widespread opportunity than Latin America's. It has obviously not been egalitarian in any absolute sense, but North Americans have had a greater chance of owning land, supporting themselves, and escaping poverty both in the early part of American history and in more recent years. Thus, economic trends established in the early colonial period in both Latin America and North America have continued, though with modification, into the present period.

CHAPTER 13

INSTITUTIONS

LATIN AMERICAN DEMOCRATIC INSTITUTIONS have been hampered by their hypercentralization, overwhelming concentrations of power, and emphasis on hierarchy rather than meritocracy. These political legacies of Spanish colonial structure and immediate postindependence rule have impeded the proper functioning of the Tocquevillian triad, elucidated in part I. According to that previous discussion, the triad—parties, civil society, federalism—is important to democracy because it represents a cohesive set of institutions that considerably undermine central power and attempt to garner prestige and authority for themselves. In so doing, they open up space for political competition. They prevent hegemony and encourage the creation and protection of democratic rules that protect incumbent and opposition alike. Yet these institutions must work together properly to insure the Tocquevillian triad's effectiveness.

Because Latin American political parties have often been weak or shifting; because they have had inefficacious relationships with civil society; because in the few cases in which parties have been strong, they have dominated civil society; and because federalism has only rarely been successful, Latin America has been plagued by diminished space for public consultation and contestation. In addition, the combination of weak civil societies or

weak parties with a strong executive—both de jure and de facto—
has contributed to frequent bouts of authoritarian rule.

It is clear that political institutions in Latin America have not
played the role they are supposed to play to insure successful,
stable democracies. But why? Of course, one can rely on cultural
explanations, making the argument that Latins have a propensity
to alienate power to caciques or *caudillos*, that they prefer centralization to decentralization, monism to pluralism, hierarchy to liberalism. All of this may be true. Certainly it is part of the story.
But it is wise to remember that there were Americans who wanted
George Washington to be crowned king. These alleged lovers of
republicanism were concerned to resolve similar sociopolitical
problems: how to ensure effective governance, how to avoid
tyranny, how to protect their interests. Republicanism was only
one solution, and one cannot be too sure whether, had Washington
indeed decided to be king, the road to republicanism in the United
States would have been as unobstructed as it proved to be.

Cultures are conditioned by circumstance. Thus the attractiveness of *caudillos* in Latin America was conditioned by the large-
scale violence of the immediate postindependence years. Under
conditions of anarchic instability, people are more willing to alienate power to a strongman protector. This is a rational calculation,
one that requires no reference to cultural antecedents. But why
was there so much violence in postindependence Latin America?
This we try to answer, in part, above; the cultural legacies of Spain
were doubtless an important cause. Thus culture becomes both
cause and effect. In making reference to it, then, we ought always
to try to identify its sources, whether in socioeconomic structures,
political institutions, or historical contingencies.

So culture is one part of the explanation, but let us look at the
intervening variables as well. Presidentialism has already been
discussed, as has its unhappy combination with proportional
representation (PR) electoral systems (see part I). This phenomenon has been almost ubiquitous in Latin America. Without going

into details again here, we reiterate that presidentialism and PR made it difficult for workable governing majorities to form in Latin America. Not only this, but Latin American governments did have a tendency (perhaps even a certain cultural propensity) to rewrite constitutions to give the executive more power in order to circumvent intransigent legislatures. To argue that this was nothing more than the self-interested attempts of charismatic leaders to extend their own offices trivializes the real debate and consideration that went into the ultimately fateful decisions to alienate so much power to chief executives. In Chile, the extension of decree powers to the president was accomplished by the right over the objections of the left, though in the end, it was the left that was able to exploit these powers. The attractions of centralized power were apparent to politicians from across the political spectrum, and not only to leaders but to many ordinary people who would suffer greatly under the abuses of Latin American hyperpresidentialism. Thus a constitutional flaw, interacting with cultural predispositions, has been partly responsible for the poor state of Latin American political institutions.

We may complement this political analysis with a more structural analysis. From this perspective, Latin American institutions were weak not solely or primarily because of their design but because of their weak social foundations. Thus democracy in Latin America has been nasty, brutish, and short because the strategic actors who are dedicated to republican structures and who actively participate in a civil society capable of limiting the hegemonic tendencies of the state have been fairly weak. Late industrialization in Latin America meant that a working class barely existed before the early twentieth century but, at the same time, the middle classes were mostly the creation of the state. Latin America possessed neither the vigorous independent bourgeoisie of North America nor the strong private professional classes that existed in Europe. Rather, what middle class there was in Latin America was utterly dependent on the state for its subsistence. It was thus in no position to form the bedrock of a thriving independent civil society.

Meanwhile the working classes in Latin America were too weak and isolated to channel their energies into reformist parties, and they were thus given to anarchism and radical attacks against the reigning order in the early twentieth century. One suspects that the very great gap between the wealthiest and poorest Latin Americans—not only economically but also ethnically in the Andean countries—made compromise between oligarchy and labor difficult at best. Attempts to incorporate the working classes into Latin American politics were severely destabilizing to many regimes, making corporatist control of labor a very attractive option. It is worth noting that the labor unrest of the early twentieth century paralleled the anarchy of the nineteenth century, in that many Latin American societies again turned to strongman rulers to help keep the fragments of society together. Hence the rise of Getúlio Vargas in Brazil and Juan Perón in Argentina.

An additional cultural point should be made. A long tradition unique to Latin America has argued for an extraconstitutional role for the military. Whereas North Americans came to believe that the constitution was the highest authority and that the separation of powers would insure that neither of the three branches of government could entirely usurp the power of the others, many Latin Americans came to rely on the military to maintain the proper balance between the various parts of government. This "escape clause" has significantly reduced the authority of Latin American constitutions. Very generous interpretations of the need for military intervention have been made, particularly by the military themselves, in order to maintain order. This does seem to have a cultural component, with the military assuming a political role throughout Latin American history, while it was fairly quickly marginalized in the United States.

Thus we point to several factors in explaining the failure of Latin American political institutions: first, poor design and implementation; second, cultural dispositions that both underlie and are the product of considerable violence and anarchy; finally, structural factors such as severe inequality coupled with weak and fragmented middle and working classes. In the sections that follow, we take a closer look at the factors underlying the weaknesses of political parties and civil society in Latin America as compared to the United States.

POLITICAL PARTIES

The party system of the United States is quite old. It has endured significant socioeconomic change, multiple wars, and severe crises. Most of the Latin American party systems are much younger; few parties can claim a legacy of more than fifty years. Still, several have long lineages, notably the parties of Chile, Colombia, and Uruguay. It is hard to escape the conclusion, however, that even party systems of substantial lineage in Latin America have contributed only marginally to stability. After all, Uruguay succumbed to dictatorship in the 1970s, and Colombia has been embroiled in seemingly endless violence for many years. Chile endured one of the harshest and longest military regimes on the continent. This is particularly striking because the patterns of political behavior in all three countries would seem to have established the conditions for democratization. Referring to nineteenth-century Uruguay and Colombia, Ruth Collier and David Collier write, "Neither side was able to fully defeat the other in the periods of civil war, creating the need for some form of accommodation that resulted in a long history of political pacts, coparticipation, and interparty coalitions that set an ultimate limit on fratricidal violence. . . . Such pacts would reappear in the accords later constructed between the two parties to deal with new forms of cleavage and violence in the mid-20th century."[1]

In theory, at least, these were optimal conditions for democracy. As argued in part I, democracy is most likely where major social antagonists find that they cannot destroy one another without obliterating society. Democracy thus represents a compromise permitting an end to violence and an accommodation serving the interests of all the relevant social actors. Furthermore, according to Robert Dahl's logic, societies that have institutionalized contestation with limited participation will ultimately have an easier time reaching full democracy by increasing participation than those societies in which participation is high but contestation is insignificant. The pitched battles between elite parties in Chile, and between more heterogeneous but still elite-dominated parties in Colombia and Uruguay, could have set the stage for an easy transition to full democracy. Yet in all three countries, democracy was, after a promising start, ultimately overtaken by instability, authoritarianism, and violence—just as in most of Latin America. In this section, we investigate the reasons why Latin American political parties have only rarely supported stable democratic regimes.

In considering Latin American political parties, one must begin by observing that the successful cleavage parties have been few and far between. As discussed in part I, cleavage parties are those based in long-standing structural traits—most commonly, class and religion. These contrast with the catchall party, organized primarily around the desire to win elections, a platform highly susceptible to change with the political winds, and a structure incorporating a wide range of social divisions.

A cursory review of Latin American parties reveals that, with the exception of Chile, there has been a dearth of organized cleavage parties throughout the region.[2] Countries that have had fairly long periods of democratic contestation, such as Uruguay, have parties that are quite old, but these are catchall, not cleavage, parties. Another country often cited as having had successful, significantly organized parties is Venezuela, but while Venezuelan parties have been linked to a labor or class cleavage, by comparison with European parties, these are still catchalls, or as they are more often referred to in Latin America, "populist" parties—not true cleavage parties.

The notion of cleavage parties is of more than academic interest, for those countries with parties that at some point were even weakly related to cleavages—particularly the secular/religious cleavage—have had more success with democracy. According to Kevin Middlebrook, there are really only three such countries in Latin America—Chile, Colombia, and Venezuela.[3] Of these, only Chile's party system has been similar to European systems in its degree of cleavage representation. Therefore, it is clear that the region lacks the kinds of parties typical of the most successful democracies—the class-based and religion-based parties.

It must be admitted, however, that in this regard, the Latin American polities are not so different from the United States, which has also lacked cleavage parties. Indeed, Lipset and Rokkan conspicuously ignored the North American case in their wide-ranging analysis because it did not fit the cleavage model. Thus, the lack of cleavage parties in Latin America might seem to help explain the relative failure of democracy there when compared to Europe. But it gives us little leverage in explaining that failure in comparison to the United States.

However, considering the reasons why catchall parties have had so much success in the United States brings differences with Latin America into clearer relief. It would be a mistake to argue that the United States has been a bastion of equality and homogeneity in any absolute sense. Nevertheless, as we argued in chapter 5, relative to Europe and Latin America, equality of opportunity in the United States and a generally homogeneous population well into the nineteenth century meant that the great cleavages of Europe—religion, urban/rural, class—were much less salient. They did exist of course, but they were of greatly diminished importance. As a result, divisions in the United States have more typically been ideological, rather than rooted in structural cleavages. And the American sense of ideology, at least in comparison to Europeans, is rather weak. Thus, as Robert Dahl pointed out some years ago, "Differences in [U.S.] political attitudes and actions are not highly related to differences in socioeconomic characteristics—region, status, occupation, etc." Furthermore, Dahl wrote, "differences in political attitudes and loyalties are not highly interrelated among themselves."[4] The relative economic homogeneity of American society historically—in contrast to the relatively distinct, cleavage-based subcultures of Europe—has led to weakly held and weakly integrated ideological beliefs.

There has been a paradoxical situation in the United States of too few and too many cleavages. As Dahl notes, the fractured ethnic and religious identities of the United States have made it difficult for parties to organize around class or any other single cleavage. At the same time, the facts that the suffrage was extended early and that the party system had already put down strong roots by the time a substantial working class emerged meant that "the vote," or democratization per se, did not become an important issue for the working class to rally around.[5] None of the major cleavages of Europe have been salient to the same degree in the United States. At the same time that ethnic identities in the United States have sometimes inhibited the development of class consciousness, they have not in and of themselves been strong enough or concentrated enough to be the foundation for distinct cleavages (with the partial exception of race).[6] Catchall parties have a certain rationale in countries that are fairly homogeneous in terms of class and/or ethnicity, where that which divides citizens is less salient than the ethos that unites them. Uruguay, whose great wealth, expansive middle-class, and cultural homogeneity were exceptional in Latin America, similarly depended for many decades on a catchall party system.

At the same time, an important aspect of party politics is whether conservative elite interests are protected in the existing system. Where these interests are safeguarded, democracy is likely to be more stable. Conservative parties offer one route to protection, though not the only one.[7] In the United States, it could be argued, a diffuse classical-"liberal" ethos infuses both political parties. Thus, because of the generalized support for an American libertarian ideology, conservative elite interests have been protected even without a strong cleavage-based conservative party. In Latin America, by contrast, while conservatives have not been well represented in conservative parties, neither have they managed to diffuse their ideology throughout Latin American society or the existing party systems.[8] Conservative interests may also be represented through ties between conservative civil society organizations and parties, whether these are explicitly conservative parties or not. This too has rarely occurred in Latin America, a point we discuss further below, in the section on civil society.

It must also be noted that, while there are no iron laws of party organization, plurality voting systems tend to promote two-party systems, and two-party systems tend to promote heterogeneous catchall parties. Since in societies with more than a single cleavage line it is not possible to represent all of them adequately in two parties, the result is that both parties try to represent a number of cleavages, and often both sides of the same cleavage. The United States is a classic example, with winner-take-all voting, an entrenched two-party system, and until very recently, quite heterogeneous catchall parties. Europe, in contrast, has tended toward proportional representation, multiparty systems, and strong cleavage parties. The American variety of presidentialism, however, exerts aggregative pressures on the party system because of the desire to control the single grand prize of politics. Only a large party with fairly widespread appeal can hope to capture the presidency. In parliamentary systems, the emphasis is on seats in the parliament, and even a small party with local appeal can exercise considerable power.

A superficial review of Latin America reveals that it has a unique mixture of social and political institutional features. On one hand, Latin American society generally has been very unequal, virtually feudal, with strong attention to status differentials—propitious conditions for class cleavage parties. It also has a great ethnic divide in the Andean countries between the descendents of Indians and those of the *criollos*—propitious for the development of ethnic/regional cleavage parties. There are exceptions—countries like Argentina and Uruguay have been much more homogeneous, though Argentina has had immigration levels similar to the United States. Finally, Catholicism's dominance in the region has made for religious homogeneity. The social institutions of Latin America suggest potential cleavages along class lines and along ethnic or center-periphery lines. They lend themselves less obviously to a religious cleavage, though an ideological church/state or clerical/anti-clerical divide would clearly be possible.

In terms of their political institutions, Latin Americans have made extensive use of European-style proportional representation, but they have coupled this with presidentialism. One might predict this mix of institutions to create incentives for both small parties and large aggregative parties. Small parties could never win the presidency but could exercise power at the parliamentary level. Large parties could win the presidency but would have trouble winning a majority in parliament.[9] Often, however, Latin American presidents have been given or have taken decree powers, allowing them to bypass the legislature. This type of incentive surely makes capturing the presidency a prize of immeasurable value and encourages the creation of larger, more aggregative or populist parties. Working for a decree-wielding president or presidential party yields more influence than membership in disciplined opposition parties when these operate in rubber-stamp or emasculated parliaments.

At a very superficial level, then, Latin America would appear to be ripe for class or ethnic cleavage parties but to have political institutions that operate to reduce the salience of cleavage parties. Our analysis has taken us only a very short way toward an explanation of party systems in Latin America. After all, how can we predict whether the social structure favoring cleavage parties is stronger or weaker than the political structure favoring catchall parties?

While the constellation of multiparty systems, proportional representation, and strong cleavage parties fits together nicely in the European case, it does not constitute a theory of parties. Lipset and Rokkan have tried to posit such a theory, but it relies heavily on the organization of interests by elites without much explanation of what predicts the likelihood of such organization. In other words, the Lipset-Rokkan theory details the sequences of cleavages that evolved in European countries and that formed the basis of the party systems there. This theory has been subsequently interpreted in two ways. Some scholars have assumed, incorrectly, that Lipset and Rokkan were arguing that the production of historically significant cleavages would inevitably result in their representation through party systems. If this were indeed true, the fact that Latin American parties have generally failed to articulate cleavage divides would have to be traced to a lack of significant cleavages in Latin American history, contrary to the evidence. More plausibly, it could be traced to a lack of broadly based cleavages. That is, perhaps the cleavages in Latin America have been like the cleavages among ethnic whites in America—the cleavages exist, but they result in groupings that are too fragmented, too small scale, and too weak to constitute the bases for political parties. On its face, this comparison is hard to fathom, given the significant class inequities in Latin America. We will further investigate this possibility below.

On the other hand, the second interpretation, truer to the Lipset-Rokkan argument, does not take us much further. This interpretation recognizes the important stress that "Cleavage Structures, Party Systems and Voter Alignments" put on the organization of

parties in civil society, the creation of isolated subcultures within
polities, and the role of elites in constructing subjective identities
rooted in objective conditions (see part I, chapter 4). According
to this interpretation, representation of cleavages is likely but
not inevitable. Leaders must come forth who actively choose to
organize, create subjective identities, and activate allegiances to
subcultures. If this interpretation is correct, then the absence of
cleavage parties in Latin America might be a result of leadership
decisions or lack of leadership rather than lack of cleavages.

This interpretation is also highly problematic. It seems unreasonable to condemn an entire region to one type of leadership. If
all the leaders in every case under similar circumstances make the
same choices, this seems to suggest that context or culture, rather
than leadership, is probably the controlling variable. After all, why
would so many leaders in Latin America make one choice and not
another?

Leadership, while an important variable, comes close to signaling a concession of defeat for social scientists. Leadership
alone does not help to explain very much. We are in search of
variables that can be seen over and across time, that explain more
than a single case, that have not only abstract but real, measura-
ble qualities. Leadership, at least without a more formal elaboration, is a deus ex machina in the context of good social science.

Nevertheless, the concept of leadership can be elaborated a bit
as a step toward a partial explanation of Latin American political
parties. In our earlier discussion of leadership's critical importance, we explored briefly the role of George Washington. But we
also noted, in attempting to make leadership a more concrete
and quantifiable concept, that Washington was a product of the
political culture of his time and that his act of leadership (relin-
quishing power) was important because it further cemented the
republican instincts of many of his compatriots while repudiat-
ing the monarchical tendencies of others. That is to say, Washington's leadership was important in the context of the culture

within which it was conceived and toward which he acted. Thus his leadership was an intervening variable between culture (itself both an independent and dependent variable) and regime type (our primary dependent variable here).

Albert Hirschman has also made some useful observations on the broader context into which leadership as a variable must fit. He takes as a starting point the assessment of "average beliefs, attitudes, and perceptions that prevail not only in the community at large, but also among its elites. One could then inquire whether and how leaders are liable to deviate from these averages and try to define leadership in terms of such deviations."[10] The problem with assuming that leadership should be defined in terms of deviations is that presumably, only some, very exceptional leaders would in fact deviate significantly from elite beliefs. Furthermore, since leadership is being looked at on a very gross level, the deviations that Hirschman would like to focus on are in all likelihood going to cancel each other out. In the aggregate, leader variations from cultural norms should regress toward "average beliefs, attitudes, and perceptions." It is only if one focuses on leadership in the exceptional cases that deviations from the average should appear in stark relief.

If we were going to adapt these kinds of arguments to present purposes, we would have to identify the ways in which Latin American cultural preconceptions inhibited and/or were reinforced by leaders' actions vis-à-vis the creation of catchall versus cleavage political parties. The question becomes, if political leadership on average in Latin America did not move to create cleavage parties, are there convincing cultural explanations for this? A related question, which we will only marginally address here, is, Can exceptional leadership be identified in the few cases in which successful cleavage parties were formed in Latin America, in spite of our expectations?

Leaders are driven not only by cultural mores but by structural factors as well. It is important to remember, however, that insofar as leadership has any unique explanatory value, it is in that sphere of life, however large or small, in which structural factors are not controlling. For if structural factors are determining, then leadership becomes irrelevant. Therefore, structural factors can be relevant to leadership only in a conditioning role. For example, the lack of a Protestant party in most Latin American countries is probably not due to leadership decisions, but to the lack of Protestants. It can safely be said that any leadership would have failed, for structural reasons, to create a Protestant party in Latin America. Thus leadership is an irrelevant variable in explaining the dependent outcome, paucity of Protestant parties. Alternatively, economic stratification is a structural factor that may play a conditioning, rather than a determining, role. Inequality may privilege the creation of class-based parties, but a patron-client economic structure may militate against an appeal to "objective" class interests. In such a situation, leadership may be constrained but still have room to maneuver. Therefore leadership becomes a potentially significant variable in explaining the dependent outcome: paucity of class parties.

Below we consider both cultural and structural factors that have contributed to the relative success of the catchall party in Latin America in comparison to the cleavage party. Our assumption is that one or both of the two possibilities described above must be true: either cleavages in Latin America have been too weak, too fragmented, too diffuse to form the basis for parties, or Latin American leadership has been culturally predisposed toward populism, or both.

To begin with culture: a great deal has already been said here about Latin American culture that has relevance to this question. This analysis will only be briefly reviewed here. Thomist political thought strongly emphasized the virtually unmitigated power of rulers and de-emphasized the need for institutional constraints. Organic-statist thought, meanwhile, envisioned each actor in society playing its assigned role in order to create harmony.

Roles were given (ascriptive), not fought over, and thus classes or other actors should not struggle for their own self-interest but should subordinate themselves to the greater good of society, embodied in the state and the executive.

The resilience of these concepts, and the parallel weakness of liberalism among Latin American elites, has meant that the idea of cleavage parties is basically anathema. Democratic competition not only implicitly denies that all citizens have the same interests in an organic system but also implies limited equality among players. The notion of stooping to form a competitive party to represent one's interests in competition with status inferiors has been totally foreign to Latin American elite sectors. It is quite true that conservatives in other countries have been reluctant to admit their social inferiors into the political arena, but Latin American elites have made their European brethren look pliable by comparison. This probably has both cultural and structural roots. Persistent, gross inequality has made it difficult for Latin American elites to change their anti-liberal cultural predispositions.

Combined with the Latin Catholic emphasis on hierarchy and authority, these traditions have been less propitious for the creation of parties organized around cleavages than for parties organized around charismatic leaders. Charismatic leaders can submerge conflicting interests, gloss over acute ideological clashes, and appeal to the national interest while maintaining studied neutrality on issues like equality. Nor were these traditions conducive to organization per se; well-organized parties are often able to put constraints on leaders, while personalistic parties, more loosely organized, follow the whims of their leadership. The postindependence legacy of *caudillo* rule and *caudillo* power grabs created a predisposition to support durable patrons rather than strong organizations. Latin American elites responded to the desire for strong, charismatic leaders unencumbered by powerful organizations dedicated to issue positions, even though such issues did exist.

What were these issues? In the nineteenth century, various factions struggled over the proper balance between church and state and the constitutional pros and cons of a federalized versus a centralized state. Many countries, including Colombia and Ecuador, had liberal or radical parties and conservative parties that had some weak relationship to their European counterparts but were basically clientelistic. Certainly the powers of the throne were not an issue, but regionalism and secularism were real topics of debate. In the Andean countries, regional struggles—dividing the export-oriented coast from the mountain areas—undergirded ethnic, constitutional, and economic feuds. Nevertheless, one gets the impression that these issues were often pretexts for naked power struggles. While substantive disputes were real, rarely did they result in programmatic parties or groups with the institutional strength to defend them. In Chile, of course, as J. Samuel Valenzuela has explained, the struggle over religion produced a very impressive political system, and ultimately democratic party politics.[11] But this was the exception.

In the twentieth century, Latin America, like Europe, faced an evolving worker/management cleavage. Modern party systems in Latin America show little evidence of cleavage alignments that predate the class cleavage. The rise of labor movements in Latin America led to political volatility, with most polities having difficulty incorporating labor into their party systems. The story of labor's incorporation, more or less successful, has been told by Collier and Collier in their weighty *Shaping the Political Arena*. Suffice it to say here that in five of the eight cases they examine, the incorporation of labor was a major factor in the breakdown of democracy.

Given the array of issues mentioned here—the Church's proper role, centralized versus federal systems, and labor versus management interests—it seems clear that Latin American elites had viable cleavages they could exploit for partisan purposes. And indeed, in some cases they did. Latin America has had traditional cleavage parties, and not in Chile alone. Socialists, communists, and Christian democrats have all made an appearance, as have more or less pure bourgeois liberal parties. But none of these parties has had the success of the many more pragmatic, catchall parties. And in some cases, even the putative cleavage parties have had very mixed constituencies.[12]

Special attention should be given to ethnic cleavages in Latin America, because they seem to have represented a double-edged sword. On one hand, as mentioned, they presented an opportunity to transform a structural cleavage into a viable party base. On the other hand, the vastness of the gulf between the descendents of Spaniards and indigenous peoples, the virulent racism and arrogance on the part of the former, and the sheer number of the latter made it very difficult to structure viable democratic cleavage parties around ethnicity. For most of the relatively small number of creoles and whites in countries like Peru, it was unthinkable to conceive of sharing power with darker-skinned natives. As Cynthia McClintock notes of the Peruvian case, "both arrogance and fear were factors in [elites'] decisions (even during nominally democratic governments) to severely restrict peasants' educational opportunities as well as peasants' rights to vote or join political organizations."[13]

It is a remarkable fact that observers of Latin American parties have had quite different perspectives regarding their typologies. Many years ago Frederico Gil attempted to categorize the parties that he found in Latin America. He identified several types, including the traditional cleavage parties, but he focused on the more predominant catchalls.[14] Gil identified at least two noncleavage party types—the *apristas* and the *peronistas*. The *apristas*—named for their model in Peru, APRA (Alianza Popular Revolucionaria Americana), but relevant to parties such as Acción Democrática (AD) in Venezuela and the Movimiento Nacional Revolucionario (MNR) in Bolivia—appeared to have their base in class and rural cleavages but ultimately moved toward cross-class coalitions with no single class predominating. As Gil noted in trying to explain the typical *aprista* voter base, these parties rely on the middle classes and intellectuals, the urban working class, the rural peasants, and the petty bourgeoisie. In Venezuela, for example, Acción Democrática moved to a broad cross-class alliance that was matched by its main opposition, COPEI (Comité de Organización Politica Electoral Independiente). Neither party could truly be labeled the party of the rich or the party of the poor—or of the working classes or the wealthy landowners or businessmen. As Robert H. Dix reported in 1989, a survey of AD and COPEI revealed that both parties were substantially heterogeneous, with "no less than 25 percent and no more than 45 percent for either party in every one of four social categories (upper, middle, working, and poor)."[15]

The second type of party Gil classified was the eponymous *peronista* party, named for Argentinian Juan Perón. These parties, with overtones of fascism, have been prime vehicles for the incorporation of labor in a more conservative direction than the *apristas*. They are terrific examples of the way that a charismatic leader has been able to dominate an organization to such an extent that he becomes more important than the program. Juan Perón and Getúlio Vargas in Brazil most clearly exemplified this pattern. Although there are some differences between *peronista* and *aprista* organizations, for Gil they are both types of catchall parties that have received broad class support. Workers supported both Perón and Vargas, but these leaders also appealed to the middle classes through their ability to control labor via corporatist forms.

More recently, scholars have challenged these characterizations of Latin American parties. Robert Kaufmann finds three ideal-type party systems in Latin America—machine, group based, and center dominant. He finds that the systems of Chile, Argentina, and Venezuela, while not cleavage parties, do engage in group-based mobilization around class in ways that are similar to, if significantly less extensive than, European systems.[16]

Kevin Middlebrook finds that the secular/religious divide has been the most important in Latin America, and he finds party systems partially structured around this cleavage in Chile, Colombia, and Venezuela. Kenneth Roberts divides party systems in Latin America into elitist and labor mobilizing. For Roberts, while few parties in Latin America have been based in cleavages to the same extent as in Europe, labor-mobilizing parties should still be considered cleavage parties, with their base in stratified social divisions. In Roberts's view, observers have underestimated the vitality of social cleavages in some Latin American nations. So he argues, contra Gil, that Argentina, Venezuela, and Peru have had cleavage parties. He also finds evidence of class cleavages in Bolivia, Brazil, Mexico, and of course, Chile. [17]

Each of these scholars argues against a catchall interpretation of Latin American parties and for a more nuanced view of the bases of conflict around which they organize. Kenneth Roberts makes the strongest case for considering many Latin American parties to be more cleavage based than generally assumed, so we consider his arguments in more detail here.

While Roberts is right to draw our attention to the fact that Latin American parties have had some relationship to structural cleavages, he protests too much. Roberts spends considerable time (1) trying to recast the meaning of cleavages and (2) generally portraying the prevalent definition of cleavage parties as too rigid and "exacting," pointing out that Latin America has been joined by the United States and Canada in having cleavageless parties. Yet he readily admits that Latin American parties simply do not meet the European standard of cleavage parties: "The cleavage structures of most Latin American party systems have had shallower roots in sociological distinctions of class and ethnicity." While trumpeting the undervalued role of organized labor in the labor-mobilizing states, Roberts is forced to concede that "populist coalitions often attracted elements of the urban and rural poor, middle class groups that benefited from growing public sector employment, and even industrialists who stood to gain from government protection. . . . Consequently, populist cleavages were well-defined politically, but somewhat amorphous sociologically and ideologically."[18]

It is hard to avoid the conclusion that Latin American parties truly have lacked structural cleavages. In our view, Roberts stretches the degree of cleavage strength in order to bolster his general argument (with which we agree) that whatever levels of cleavage basis there were for party systems in Latin America have been rapidly disintegrating in the neoliberal age. For such an argument to seem convincing, it helps to show that party systems had a fair degree of cleavage basis to begin with. In particular, Roberts argues that the neoliberal age has more strongly affected the cleavage-based parties than the "elitist" parties; since the elitist party systems did not have a cleavage basis to lose, neoliberalism has not corroded the degree to which their cleavages are manifested in the party system. Thus, neoliberalism has lead Latin American party systems toward convergence, so that none now has a substantial cleavage base.

Roberts's work is persuasive and his reasoning is cogent. In the end, however, while the labor-mobilizing party systems may have been highly structured around cleavages *relative to other Latin American nations,* they were quite weak when compared to European systems. Furthermore, Roberts finds evidence that APRA and AD both were weakening in their cleavage bases prior to the advent of neoliberalism, suggesting that even if some parties in Latin America have flirted with cleavage bases, these have been at best fleeting.

The basic tension that exercises Roberts is worth exploring further. The fact that some parties in Latin America were neither classical cleavage parties in the European sense nor, strictly speaking, catchall parties raises a serious classification problem. In Otto Kircheimer's now classic conception, catchall parties are distinct from parties of integration in their (1) ideological flexibility,

(2) efforts to encompass wide swaths of society rather than small sectors with unique interests, and (3) reliance on interest groups and individual voters in place of structured cleavages such as class and religion. Whereas cleavage parties aim to encapsulate the masses in a variegated set of institutions—schools, churches, recreational clubs—and leverage these institutions for the project of political socialization, catchall parties are primarily concerned with finding simple, popular messages that lead to electoral victory at any given time by attracting citizens from various backgrounds. Kircheimer saw catchall party competition in marketing terms: parties try to establish themselves as a brand and continually shift their product lines to appeal to consumers.[19]

How do parties such as AD, APRA, or the PJ (Partido Justicialista) in Argentina measure up to this conception of catchall? Nothing in either the theory or empirical study of catchall parties suggests that these parties need be without ideology or without any type of cleavage reference. The U.S. party system, considered by Kircheimer and nearly everyone else to be composed of catchall parties, has had both ideology and cleavage references. Both race and class have been utilized by party leaders to build electoral strategies. Franklin Roosevelt deliberately built ties to labor and to blacks during the 1930s, ties that have lasted for quite some time, though they have weakened. Nevertheless, the Democratic and Republican parties have been prototypical catchall parties with weak structural cleavage bases, flexible ideologies, and a reliance on popular messages and interest groups at election time. Thus the fact that AD, APRA, and the PJ have at different times enunciated ideologies and mobilized a structurally defined constituency (e.g., labor) does not preclude us from categorizing them as catchall.

Perhaps the fairest evaluation of these parties is to place them in a residual category, neither so catchall as North American parties nor so cleavage-based as European parties. They are significantly different from their North American counterparts in at least one important respect—they have actively sought to incorporate organizations like labor, not merely through ideological appeals but through mobilization of actual organizational linkages. In this sense, we agree with Roberts that dismissing their cleavage characteristics entirely is unreasonable. Yet we do not believe that these parties can be considered cleavage parties, and we stand by our contention that enduring cleavage parties have been few and far between in Latin America.

Thus far we have identified a number of cleavages in Latin America and a number of parties. We have demonstrated the disconnect between cleavages and parties that we asserted at the outset of this chapter. But we have failed so far to offer a convincing explanation for it.

We did, of course, discuss cultural explanations. But the cultural values we have drawn attention to—stress on hierarchy; alienation of power to charismatic leaders; lack of formal, institutionalized controls over leaders—cannot be said to have precluded cleavage parties, even if they militated against them. Surely cultural factors are not fixed in time, either, and are clearly related to economic structures; one must ask whether these factors have attenuated over time. Despite Latin America's cultural predispositions, cleavage parties were formed. Can their failure be attributed to cultural predispositions, or might it have something to do with the type and quality of cleavages?

All societies based on feudalistic ties between patrons and clients, as rural relations have been in Latin America, emphasize vertical relationships over horizontal relationships. That is, workers who are entangled in webs of clientelism tend to think in terms of what they owe and what is owed to them rather than in terms of class. Class consciousness has historically been a creation of urban manufacturing organization, in which many workers are in a concentrated area and all have obligations to a single management structure.[20] Labor relations in the countryside are diffuse, and peasants tend not to think in terms of class without substantial assistance from organizers located outside the patron-client system.

It follows that polities with very large rural sectors that are entrenched in feudal or semifeudal relations will not be likely to develop organized cleavage parties until the social structure changes. We have already observed that Latin America fits this description, that an extensive rural sector persisted for a very long time in Latin America and still does to some degree. In Europe, the development of the mass cleavage party did not really take off until the management/worker cleavage became salient and the socialists began to organize urban constituents. It is no exaggeration to suggest that the cleavage party is in part a product of industrialization and urbanization. Even the great religious cleavage parties, such as those of the Netherlands, did not become significant until the late 1800s, when the socioeconomic structure had begun to change.[21]

Latin America's "late late" industrialization not only has been delayed but has been qualitatively different from that of the advanced countries. First of all, Latin America has significantly industrialized over time and has always had a considerable degree of urbanization, but it has nevertheless had a weak working class. As Robert H. Dix notes,

> Whereas in the industrialized West those employed in the secondary sector, in industry and related occupations, succeeded agricultural and other primary sector employment as numerically predominant, in Latin America the tertiary or service sector has done so. Secondary sector employment has never predominated in Latin America, and presumably never will; as agricultural employment declines, the service sector has expanded more rapidly. . . . The more advanced countries of today's Latin America, still far from fully industrial, yet with the agricultural sector a rapidly diminishing proportion of the work force, have seen their service sectors reach proportions approaching those of the postindustrial West.[22]

Without this strong base of organization that was available to the early industrializers, labor parties have had a difficult time gaining steam. White-collar workers are harder to organize, and the fragmented nature of the labor market undermines solidarity among workers who do very different things for different managers and who are not socially isolated like the workers of the European past—a point Dix also brings to our attention. Thus the transformation of Latin American feudal production structures has begun to erode the old patron-client relations, but the type of industrialization that has occurred has been only slightly more conducive to organization along cleavage lines, particularly class, than the older structures.[23] This does not mean that there have been fewer strikes or less radicalism among Latin American labor, only that labor has faced limitations in forming a strong national political movement.

This problem was exacerbated by import substitution industrialization (ISI), a policy package followed by most Latin American nations for many years. ISI weakened the potential not only for an organized working class but for an organized bourgeoisie as well. We already know, from the work of Rueschemeyer, Stephens, and Stephens, that ISI perpetuated the weakness of the working class. In particular, the focus on capital-intensive industry—which, ironically, relied heavily on imported inputs—meant that the working class grew only incrementally during ISI. But beyond this, Albert O. Hirschman has offered some indirect insights into why ISI also might have negatively impacted the bourgeoisie from the perspective of democratization and the creation of cleavage parties.

Hirschman observes that the "late late" industrializers had class constellations distinct from the early and late industrializers. There were not only quantitative differences of size and thus organizational capacity between these groups of countries but also qualitative differences. For example, because the late late ISI industrializers were mimicking processes from advanced countries, there would be less trial and error, less experimentation, and thus a lesser development of critical entrepreneurial skills among the bourgeois classes in these states. "ISI thus brings in complex technology," Hirschman argues, "but without the sustained technological experimentation and concomitant training in innovation which are characteristic of the pioneer industrial countries."[24] The entrepreneurial class in Latin America would be less prone to take risks and thus less "entrepreneurial" in the sense in which this term is typically used.

Hirschman also observed that the creation of a "crisis" in the availability of imported goods tends to favor the creation of an entrepreneurial class dominated by outsiders and foreigners rather than natives. Former importers of foreign origins, as well as former exporters, lose their sources of revenue as import opportunities are closed off and raw materials are redirected to the domestic market. They therefore tend to have both the will and the skill to take advantage of new opportunities for industrial production. Thus the combination of late late industrialization with ISI yields a situation conducive to the creation of a weak, risk-averse, marginally entrepreneurial domestic bourgeoisie with neither the skill nor the confidence to lead a full-fledged industrial revolution. Instead, what industrialization there is tends to be dominated by a foreign or immigrant bourgeoisie.

This is important because ISI can work only if a process of "backward linkage" leads to economic development. Backward linkage means that the production of capital-intensive consumer goods that require imported inputs will eventually breed a domestic market for the production of these inputs, which will in turn lead to their production domestically. Backward linkage is the opposite of the textbook model of development followed by the advanced countries, especially Britain and Belgium, where light manufacturing leads to heavier manufacturing and so on, a process of forward linkage. The problem with relying on backward linkage is that the bourgeoisie that owns the means of production for the finished goods will not find it in their interests to have the needed inputs produced domestically, for the same reason that the goods they now produce were not being produced before: they were too expensive, and they were inferior to imports. They will see their own profit margins shrink if they are forced to depend on protected input-production markets.

As a result of all this, the bourgeoisie under ISI does not have a great interest in the promotion of backward linkage. Which is to say, given the conditions it is facing, that it does not have an overriding interest in widespread industrialization. Once these business owners become established, their interests lie in the protection of their own industries and in free trade in, or subsidies for, inputs. This, at least in theory, is different from the bourgeoisie under conditions of forward linkage. In this case, the creation of "higher" markets based on "lower" inputs is nearly always in the interests of the existing bourgeoisie, because it means expanded markets for their products.

This somewhat convoluted argument explains why the domestic bourgeoisie in Latin America has tended to be weak, divided, and easily co-opted by oligarchical interests, rather than representing, as in Europe, a powerful, often united force for industrialization at the expense of oligarchical aristocratic interests. In simpler terms, because the Latin American bourgeoisie was a creation of state policies, it was always a dependent partner, interested in the protection of its privileges rather than the creation of new wealth. It was not available to form a strong liberal or radical party, as the bourgeoisie in much of Europe—in a clear battle with the aristocracy—were wont to do.[25]

Hirschman himself does not make this argument. Indeed, he points out, rightly so, that it relies on the questionable theoretical assumption that the creation of backward-linked production would not be undertaken by the very same bourgeoisie that is already involved in higher-level production. If these entrepreneurs could in fact invest in and profit from this level of production, he argues, they would probably not resist extension of import controls to their own inputs.

It seems likely, however, by Hirschman's own logic, that the generally weak, dependent, and risk-averse domestic entrepreneurial class that is generated by ISI would not readily jump at the opportunity to create its own input markets. Those foreign entrepreneurs who might be more likely to make this leap would contribute little to the formation of a strong, independent domestic bourgeoisie—and thus would also contribute little to the push for democratization. Here one might interject a cultural argument too. After all, the tendency of ISI to undermine entrepreneurialism is only one in a long line of traditions dating back to the Spanish conquest that have done the same. The emphasis on state control and intervention in the economy has always reduced incentives to entrepreneurial activity in Latin America to levels below what they might have been. There is thus every reason to expect that the Latin American bourgeoisie would be less likely than the bourgeoisie of the early industrializers to take the risks necessary to foster backward linkage without guarantees from the state. And these they have rarely been strongly organized enough to demand.

In sum, the Latin American working classes and bourgeoisie have been weaker, more dependent, and more fragmented than their European counterparts. Since these classes formed the bases of the most successful cleavage parties in Europe, it seems probable that cleavage parties would have a hard time finding success in polities where they were debilitated. Furthermore, the classes that have been stronger than labor and capital are the peasants, white-collar workers, and state bureaucrats, none of which has shown the kind of organizational capacity necessary for the formation of strong cleavage parties. The weakness and fragmentation of classes in Latin America has not only made the organization of parties difficult but virtually necessitated the formation of cross-class alliances. Thus, organization around cleavages was counterproductive, since this would isolate and divide classes—too weak to stand alone—from potential allies. James Malloy has gone so far as to argue that populism has been a direct creation of the middle classes as a response to their weakness as a class:

> Elements of the middle class could not independently carry out basic structural transformation, and to buttress their position they had to seek allies in other social strata. Populism became the guise within which change-oriented segments of the middle class sought to construct multiclass coalitions powerful enough to gain control of the state and underwrite programs of structural transformation.[26]

It is also important to recognize that in Latin America the landed class has maintained its strength and political power for much longer than in Europe. The one class that was not generally weak, dependent, or fragmented was the landlord class. While the bourgeois industrial classes of Europe ultimately defeated the landed classes across the board, the industrialists of Latin America were often trumped by and dependent on the landed classes. In very few cases in modern history have the landed classes driven coalitions for democracy. Thus the relative strength of the landlord class in Latin America was not propitious for democracy. One important exception to this pattern was Costa Rica, where, James Mahoney has argued, a "reformist liberal" transformation of landholding patterns in the nineteenth century weakened the traditional landholding class and created a sizable middle-class farming sector.[27] The smaller "oligarchy" in Costa Rica was also more "commercialized" than "landed," leaving Costa Rica with both a larger independent middle class and a weaker landed class—both propitious for democracy. We make a similar argument regarding Chile.

In light of all this, has leadership been successfully sidelined as an important variable? It seems that structural and cultural factors, not leadership, determined the lack of cleavage parties in Latin America. Given the conditions of late late industrialization and subsequent attempts at ISI, would not any leadership have failed to create successful cleavage parties?

Certainly, the task was difficult. Yet there are two caveats. First, leadership can influence public policies that affect class structure. As Hirschman notes, leadership could have determined that creating backward linkage was a priority on its own and assisted the existing bourgeoisie by giving it the necessary guarantees to become involved in backward-linked production. Second, the success of some cleavage parties—for example, those of Chile—remains unexplained.

What of Chile? Avoiding detailed accounts of specific countries, we offer only a few specifics that could support a basically structuralist account of Chilean exceptionalism. J. Samuel Valenzuela has rightly argued that Chile poses a problem for Barrington Moore's analysis (discussed in chapter 5), primarily because the pro-democratic alliance in Chile originated in the landholding class. Valenzuela's (persuasive) explanation for this is that in Chile the dominant cleavage was religious/secular, not class. Conservative Catholic landholders pushed for democracy because they believed that the lower orders would fall in line to defend the prerogatives of the Church, as indeed they basically did.

Does this disprove the aphorism that landholding classes are always anti-democratic? This depends, of course, on the meaning of "landholding classes." We would argue that Chile does not represent an exception to Moore's argument in this regard, because the landholding class in Chile, as Valenzuela himself argues, was by the 1870s significantly fused with the bourgeoisie. This is reminiscent of, though different from, the British case, where agriculture and commercialism were fused to create an entrepreneurial landed class that transformed the old agricultural order into a new, protocapitalist one. The Chilean landholders, by Valenzuela's account, were commercial not in their landholding but rather in other economic spheres—mining, commerce, and industry. It was because of this that Chilean landholders did not have the kind of strong, vested interest in the organization of agricultural production that would make them likely to vigorously oppose democracy. In other words, large landholders in Chile were not engaged, at least as they pushed for democracy, in a feudal economy of the type that existed in Europe or in other parts of Latin America.

But if Chilean landholders did not have an overriding interest in the maintenance of feudal arrangements, then they would not be expected to play the role ascribed to them by Moore in his analysis. Indeed, in Britain commercial landholders laid the foundations for democracy by strengthening Parliament and destroying the peasant class. And in Chile, although landholders were not driven by their commercialism to support democracy, neither did their agricultural status cause them to actively oppose it. That Conservatives supported democracy in Chile, that they were motivated primarily by religious concerns rather than class interests, is testament to the fact that they were not typical landholders but rather were basically bourgeois. As Valenzuela puts it,

> If the large rural property owners in Chile did not depend on labor repression for their survival as a class, and if there was no significant challenge to landowner interests (in part given the cross-sectoral nature of the upper class's assets), then there was no need for landowners to coalesce politically into a landowner's party. Other political issues could push them in different directions. And indeed landowners could be found in all major non–working class parties of the time.[28]

Our point is that Chile differed from other Latin American states in that its landholding class was rather weak in the traditional role that the class played elsewhere. At the same time, this landholder bourgeoisie was stronger and was able to form a viable party system that was initially divided primarily by religion. As the quote above makes clear, however, a second, and ultimately more important, cleavage was already rearing its head: that between the landowner bourgeoisie and the working class. A relatively weak landholder class in the traditional sense, a relatively strong, landed bourgeoisie, and a relatively strong working class—these were ingredients that made democracy, and the formation of cleavage parties, more successful in Chile than elsewhere.

Which seems to leave little room for leadership as an important variable. Structural explanations, which in turn have geographical, historical, and cultural causes, can explain the basic weaknesses and strengths of cleavage parties in Latin America.

In conclusion, our argument is that the form Latin American political parties have taken is problematic because it has failed to allow for the adequate representation of cleavages through the political system. A party system that depends entirely on populist or catchall parties, such as the United States has had for many years, must have a relative degree of homogeneity—either ideologically or socioeconomically. Both the United States and Uruguay have had party systems in which the parties represent loose coalitions, which allow cleavages some representation but not of the direct sustained variety provided by the cleavage parties in Europe's more stratified societies.[29] Latin America has had the economic cleavages of Europe, but not the cleavage parties nor (Chile aside) any successful, organized parties of the left or right like those in Europe. As a result, when the occasional populist majority has been able to elect a government in Latin America through free elections, the lack of an organized party representing the interests of the right (or of widespread "liberal" tendencies) has meant, more often than not, that conservatives have turned to the military or to state repression as a way out. As Torcuato DiTella notes, "In many Latin American and Third World countries the diffuse conservative influences that operate in the more prosperous parts of the world do not exist. Free elections tend to produce popular majorities without an equivalent force on the other side. That is, results are similar to those feared by [John Stuart] Mill; hence the search for new methods of representation, like corporations, or simply the recourse to authoritarian solutions."[30]

Thus the failure of Latin American polities to sustain cleavage parties, itself rooted in structural and cultural problems, has contributed to the overall instability of Latin American democracies. As the case of Chile suggests, however, even where cleavage parties have had considerable success in Latin America, the political regime could not withstand the election of a leftist coalition. The stakes were too high. The Chilean breakdown has been explained in part by the excesses of Allende's leftist bloc, but it is also clear that the representation of cleavages as fierce as those in Chile—even greater in much of the rest of Latin America—created anguish on the part of conservatives that could not be dispelled by their organization in a party of the right. Likewise, the long persecution of semi-cleavage-based parties such as APRA in Peru suggest the same story: gross inequality in Peru meant that conservatives would not abide the election of, nor even electoral competition from, a remotely cleavage-based party of the left. It should be mentioned that, in their rejection of leftist party governments, conservatives in Latin America were often aided—sometimes through tacit approval and occasionally, as in Chile, through financial support—by the United States. Pursuing Cold War ends in Latin America, as in other parts of the world, the U.S. government was not above using anti-democratic means.

While we believe that Latin America's lack of cleavage parties has contributed to the instability of democracy there, we do not want to overemphasize this variable, which was probably not as significant as its broader structural and cultural antecedents. Furthermore, political parties are just one part of the broader institutional matrix we have identified as the Tocquevillian triad. As we argued earlier, parties work together with civil society to insure the stability of democracy. We thus turn now to civil society, a critical part of the institutional context in which political parties have operated in Latin America.

CIVIL SOCIETY

In part I of this book, we argued that to insure democratic success, civil society and political parties should function in creative tension with one another. Now we turn to civil society in Latin and North America and try to determine whether it has established this tension or not. In general, civil society in Latin America has not played the same role that it has in the United States. Below, we document this difference, try to explain it, and then attempt to understand the role civil society has played in our cases.

Historically, civil society in Latin America has been weaker than in North America. These trends continue today, as evidenced by World Values Survey data. Levels of membership in all kinds of voluntary associations are higher in the United States than in Latin America. The cumulative number of Latin Americans that claim to belong to sixteen different types of organizations is less than half the level in the United States.[31] In the survey whose results are reported in Table 13.1, respondents were asked whether they were active or inactive members in various types of associations in 1995. In most cases, the percentage of respondents claiming to participate in various organizations is significantly higher in the United States. (Unfortunately, results are available only for selected countries. For this reason, Table 14.1, containing data from Latinobarómetro, has also been included in the appendix to the book's concluding chapter. Although it includes all of the Latin American countries, Latinobarometro does not include the United States.)

This is not to imply that civil society organizations have failed to constitute important actors in Latin America. Civil society was a vital player on Latin America's political stage during much of the past century. In some countries, political parties have created,

TABLE 13.1.

Participation in Organizations in Selected Latin American Countries, the United States, and Sweden, 1995

					Percent reporting active/inactive membership				
	Active Church	Inactive Church	Active Sports	Inactive Sports	Active Arts	Inactive Arts	Active Union	Inactive Union
Argentina	14.64	19.18	8.16	7.78	9.82	4.82	1.76	3.99
Brazil	30.81	30.72	13.23	12.62	11.4	6.79	9.75	8.09
Peru	23.78	32.54	16.18	16.35	10.98	13.13	4.21	13.05
Chile	28.6	30.3	16.7	18.5	12.9	15.7	5.4	12.5
Mexico	39.27	30.26	24.3	21.06	21.36	17.35	9.87	16.56
Uruguay	14	21.4	8.4	10	12.2	6.9	4.5	6.5
Venezuela	20.95	23.87	16.85	12.49	10	12.27	5.2	9.22
Latin America*	24.58	26.9	14.83	14.11	12.67	10.99	5.81	9.99
United States	51.43	26.92	23.66	16.8	22.13	15.39	9.9	13.18
Sweden	7.73	20.91	26.46	17.74	12.49	9.61	12.78	62.24

	Active Party	Inactive Party	Active Enviro	Inactive Enviro	Active Profession	Inactive Profession	Active Charity	Inactive Charity	Active Other	Inactive Other
Argentina	3.15	6.95	2.59	3.61	5.1	2.97	6.3	3.99	4.17	1.48
Brazil	7.22	7.05	6.18	8.09	10.44	16.71	14.71	16.19	7.57	5.4
Peru	2.64	13.05	2.97	11.15	7.43	11.48	6.44	11.97	6.03	11.73
Chile	2.8	12.8	3.8	13.9	7	11.1	8.1	12.9	5.6	13.2
Mexico	9.14	14.11	9.41	14.71	11.32	12.25	9.34	10.79	8.41	10.13
Uruguay	6.1	10.1	4	9.1	3.8	4.8	3.7	5.8	3.3	4.3
Venezuela	3.85	9.97	5.52	9.28	8.37	7.87	7.19	9.95	6.53	8.28
Latin America*	4.99	10.58	4.92	9.98	7.64	9.6	7.97	10.23	5.94	7.79
United States	20.31	29.88	9.07	16.17	21.15	13.62	26.13	15.26	21.35	9.72
Sweden	4.66	10.11	2.23	10.73	5.15	10.8	6.54	15.46	18.43	16.06

SOURCE: *World Values Survey* (Ann Arbor, MI: Inter-university Consortium for Political and Social Research [ICPSR], 1995), www.icpsr.umich.edu.

*Figures are simple unweighted averages of values for countries above.

channeled, and manipulated civil society. Venezuelan and Chilean political parties, for example, followed a German Social Democratic model, paving their route to power by actually building and incorporating organizations of civil society. Thus civil society in these countries was broad and inclusive. But it was also characterized by "weakness and dependence."[32] By contrast, in Argentina, where political parties were weak, civil society organizations and personalistic leaders dominated the political scene. Argentina is a good example of a country with an active civil society but weakly institutionalized political parties that succumbed to authoritarianism—conditions associated with the classic case of Weimar Germany, discussed earlier in this book. As in Brazil and Peru, parties in Argentina have been personalistic rather than programmatic, and they were generally unsuccessful at mediating between the interests of civil society actors and the state.

Nevertheless, over the broad historical trajectories of Latin America and the United States, civil society has been more fiercely independent, more active and, simply more relevant to political outcomes in the United States. Political scientists' current focus on civil society has brought the important role played by voluntary organizations in opposing Latin American authoritarian regimes to the attention of even casual observers. Civil society has certainly performed very important functions in recent decades— not only confronting dictators but also representing the long-trampled rights of indigenous peoples, particularly in the Andean countries. From our longer-term historical perspective, however, more obvious is the weakness of Latin American civil society. The role of civil society in contemporary Latin America is vastly more significant than it has ever been in the past.

To date, there is very little research that one can draw upon to make quantitative historical comparisons of civil societies in different polities over time. Many projects to this end are under way, but even when they are completed, they will for the most part only measure civil society over the last generation or so. Furthermore, many recent studies of civil society are entangled with studies of democratization, which tend to emphasize those actors that directly confronted authoritarian regimes. It is no simple task to compare this type of "civil society" with that of countries that have been consistently democratic, where civil society has played a more subtle and less direct role in abetting democracy. How does one compare the role that unions have played, for example, in pushing for democracy in Franco's Spain or Pinochet's Chile with their role in the United States? Such a comparison begs more questions than it resolves.

Strictly quantitative comparisons have serious limitations. We included Table 12.1 to give readers an idea of the organizational tendencies of different nations. But as we argued in part I, civil society is primarily important in its ability to mediate between actors in society and the political system. Not only do these tables include groups (e.g., sports) that probably do not perform this function, but a simple quantitative assessment of the groups that probably do still tells us little about their actual relation to the political system. In the end, we are forced to rely on a smattering of monographic studies to gain some idea of the overall comparative strength of civil societies. We try to make a very general assessment of the weakness or strength of civil societies and the reasons for it and then, more important, to compare the roles and functions of civil societies.

To begin, civil society is determined by economic and cultural variables. In comparison with the United States, Latin America has had several such characteristics likely to dampen its civil societies. These are related to its production system, its cultural-religious tradition, and its failure to establish political order until the late nineteenth century.

As we pointed out in the preceding section on political parties, Latin America's semifeudal socioeconomic structures militated against the formation of autonomous associations. Where workers are entrenched in patron-client relationships, personalism and familism dominate, and the formation of horizontal associations (such as unions) are unlikely. Peasants tend to think in terms of their loyalties and debts, and they are generally isolated in small, inward-looking, holistic societies. This system was perhaps most refined in Brazil, though its elements could be found throughout the region. Philippe Schmitter has described the Brazilian case: "In return for his exercise of noblesse oblige and favoritism, the *patrao* [patron landholder] in this system expects unquestioning loyalty and voluntary compliance with his orders. The whole transaction involves warm, interpersonal ties; authorities and subordinates alike are treated with respect."[33] Even where this level of respect was not so great, peasants understood their world in terms of those above and below them and their personal inter-actions with them. Forming an association would have made little sense to them. This was, of course, very different from the United States (and Britain), where, even though many people rented their land, average citizens were able to participate in the wider polity and, eventually, the wider marketplace without reliance on the mediation of patrons. Outside the South, eco-nomic relations were always more protocapitalist than they were based in patron-client relations. Though many smallholders may have been only self-sufficient, as opposed to commercial, neither were they dependent on a particular large landholder for their subsistence.

It should be noted that another social structural variable asso-ciated with higher densities of civil society is urbanization. Civil society is generally stronger in urban locales, where populations live close together and associations are easier to form. Although Latin America has been semifeudal in comparison with the United States, it began with a fairly high degree of urbanization. It is quite difficult to find comparable data on urbanization from both the United States and Latin America going back to the eighteenth century. U.S. census data do provide urbanization statistics going

TABLE 13.2
*Urbanization in Latin America and the United States,
Late Eighteenth Century to 1920*

	Actual Year	Late 18th century Estimate	1800–30	1831–60	1861–90	1891–1920
Argentina	1778	24	17	11	14	24
Brazil	1777	8	6	5	7	7
Chile	1758–91	14	9	11	12	18
Colombia	1772	2	3	4	3	5
Mexico	1742	3	5	—	4	5
Peru	1791	13	—	—	7	7
Venezuela	1772	15	10	—	8	8
Latin America	—	11	8	8	8	11
United States						
Large cities	1790	3	4	6	8	10
Cities over 2,500	1790	5	7	15	29	45

SOURCES: Richard Morse, ed., *The Urban Development of Latin America, 1750–1920*
(Stanford: Stanford University Press, 1971); B. R. Mitchell, ed., *International Historical Statistics: The Americas, 1750–1993*, 4th ed., New York: Stockton Press, 1998);
U.S. Census Bureau, *Historical Statistics of the United States, 1790–1970*.
NOTE: Data for Latin American countries and regions are percentages of total
population that reside in the three or four largest cities.

back to 1790, but good Latin American data starts only in the
mid-twentieth century. Table 13.2 compares the urban populations living in the three or four biggest cities in Latin America
and the United States from the late eighteenth century to 1920.
Although this is not a very exact measure of urbanization, it is
the best data available on Latin America. The metric probably
understates urbanization in both regions. However, comparing
the large-cities metric for Latin America with the actual urbanization percentage in the United States makes the United States

look more urbanized than it should, because the U.S. percentage includes many more cities.

Both metrics (large cities and towns over twenty-five hundred) have been included for the United States. What this table and Figure 13.1 reveal is that as U.S. urbanization increases, the large-cities measure increasingly underestimates true urbanization. However, both measures do track a similar phenomenon: the curve of growth in urbanization is far steeper, but in the same general direction. Thus the large-cities measure does identify the trend's direction correctly, though it underestimates that trend. Since this measure also probably underestimates Latin American urbanization (though not as much), we can be fairly certain that Latin America was more urbanized than the United States at least until the 1830s, and perhaps through the 1850s. By the 1860s, it seems clear that the situation had reversed.

FIGURE 13.1
Comparison of U.S. Urbanization Measures,
Late Eighteenth Century to 1920

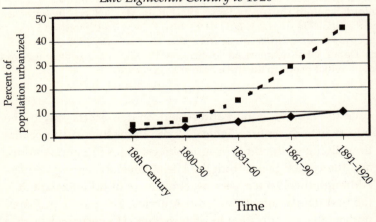

It would be nice to know a bit more about Latin American urbanization beyond the biggest cities. Standard definitions of urbanized areas have frequently treated any locale with over 2,000 or 2,500 people as urban. This is a far cry from assessing only the largest cities. Unfortunately, this data is simply not available for Latin America. However, a more restricted estimate of all areas with over 20,000 people is available from between 1850 and 1970 for both Latin America and the United States. Those data, reported in Table 13.3, suggest that while Latin America and the United States had quite similar levels of midrange to high-end urbanization in 1850, divergence proceeded apace from that time through the 1970s. These data are useful because it is particularly in larger towns that civil society should receive a boost from a more densely concentrated population and more accessible communications networks. Since the United States has had a higher concentration of population in large urban centers since somewhere between 1830 and 1860, it would be expected to have had a denser civil society as well. Urbanization does seem to be part of the solution to our dilemma.

Yet we would argue that urbanization really explains very little about the differential power and impact of civil society in the United States and Latin America. In the 1830s, Latin America was still at least as urbanized, if not more so, than the United States. But in 1831 Alexis de Tocqueville journeyed to the United States and famously observed the Americans' thriving civil society: "In no country in the world has the principle of association been more successfully used or applied to a greater multitude of objects than in America."[34] During the same period, there was little if any civil society in Latin America to speak of. Since civil society has historical and cultural roots in addition to structural roots, it seems likely that for reasons unrelated to urbanization per se, the United States has always had a stronger civil society than Latin America, and this has continued. Undoubtedly, urbanization has played some role. The large-cities measure for Latin America

TABLE 13.3

Percent of Total Population in Towns over 20,000 Persons, 1850–1970

	1850	1890	1900	1910	1920	1930	1940	1950	1960	1970
Argentina	12	19.3	24.9	28.4	37	38	41	50.9	54.9	63.3
Bolivia	4	3.4	6.6	9.2	9.4	13.1	18.7	19.6	18.3	24.3
Brazil	7	5.7	8.7	9.8	13	14	16	20.6	28.8	36.2
Chile	5.9	14.8	19.9	24.2	27.6	32	37	41.6	52.8	58
Colombia	3	5.8	6.2	7.3	8.9	10	14	21.4	31.4	41
Costa Rica	15	11.2	8.5	7.9	12.2	13.2	15.4	23.2	24	27
Ecuador	6	10.5	9.3	12	13.6	14	17	17.8	24.7	32
Mexico	7.9	7.4	9.2	10.8	12.6	15.6	18	24.1	28.7	34.7
Paraguay	4	6.5	13	17.7	18	12.9	15.7	na	22.8	25
Peru	5.9	6.5	6	5.4	5	9.6	12.9	17.1	26	32
Uruguay	13	26	na	26	27.8	37.6	36.8	43.3	56.2	60
Venezuela	7	8.4	8.5	9	11.7	19.4	28.5	31.9	48.3	56
Latin America	8	10	11	14	16	19	23	29	35	41
United States	8.8	22.1	25.9	30.8	42	47	47	51.1	58.5	64

SOURCE: Adapted from *Statistical Abstract of Latin America* 18 (1977), table 606a; data from Tatu Vanhanen, "Political and Social Structures, Part I: American Countries 1850–1973," *Research Reports* 38 (1975), appendix 4.

suggests that urbanization was basically flat in the nineteenth century, which corresponds with a period during which civil society there grew very little. But while greater urbanization is related to denser civil societies within both regions, it seems not to have much explanatory value in detailing the differences between Latin America as a whole and the United States.

Moving beyond socioeconomic structures, more explanatory leverage is gained by exploring the role of the Church in Latin America versus that of religion in North America. Early North American civil society was actively related to various Christian movements, a point noted by both Tocqueville and Max Weber. There were both philosophical and institutional reasons for this. First, according to Weber, the theology of the Protestants who came to North America preached the virtues of civic association. As Stephen Kalberg notes, "Weber identifies a world mastery, activity-oriented individualism and a demarcated civic sphere penetrated by a specific set of values as pivotal components in the American political culture, and locates their original source in ascetic Protestantism, particularly Reform Calvinism."[35] Institutionally, the lack of a strong state church in the United States opened the door to a highly competitive religious arena in which many sects vied for adherents. Even if many of the individual sects were not civic-minded or democratically organized, the net effect of religious competition was the democratization of Christianity.

It was probably in part due to the lack of status distinctions in the United States that church membership came to represent a form of identification, a badge of honor. Membership was chosen, not simply given. Sharp status distinctions in Latin America, in contrast, were coupled with a strong state-related Church and a very homogeneous Catholic base. Membership in the Church was taken for granted, so it ceased to be an important source of association or an important method of distinguishing among people. The Church was not only ubiquitous in Latin America but very different from the Protestant sects of North America.

The Church was very much an authoritarian institution. The sects of North America, by contrast, were often grassroots organizations with the smaller size and greater flexibility to allow acolytes to have an impact on their teachings and activities. Fundamentally, these sects often preached distrust of hierarchical institutions that mediated between believers and their God. Historian Nathan Hatch argues that American Christianity was infected by the values of the American Revolution in the early nineteenth century:

> In at least three respects the popular religious movements of the early republic articulated a profoundly democratic spirit. First, they denied the age-old distinction that set the clergy apart as a separate order of men, and they refused to defer to learned theologians and traditional orthodoxies. All were democratic or populist in the way they instinctively associated virtue with ordinary people rather than with elites, exalted the vernacular in word and song as the hallowed channel for communicating with and about God, and freely turned over the reigns of power. . . .
> Second, these movements empowered ordinary people by taking their deepest spiritual impulses at face value rather than subjecting them to the scrutiny of orthodox doctrine and the frowns of respectable clergymen. . . . [Third,] this upsurge of democratic hope, this passion for equality, led to a welter of diverse and competing forms, many of them structured in highly [internally] undemocratic ways. [36]

In other words, while the individual religious associations engineered by religious entrepreneurs were not necessarily democratic internally, the ease with which they could be formed by commoners, the wide-open religious marketplace, and the reliance on the approbation of those below rather than those above—all made American Christianity distinctly democratic. And this fervor, in turn, provided strong support for the creation of voluntary associations of all kinds. [37] Whereas the Catholic Church discouraged individual initiative, or the formation of nonfamilial associations, religious or otherwise, that might challenge the existing order or escape the grasp of the Church hierarchy, the Protestant sectarians thrived on the entrepreneurship of their members and encouraged association. It was only with the evolution of liberation theology after Vatican II that Catholicism would begin to mimic Protestant sectarianism in this way, with the creation of popular-based communities that in turn stimulated other charitable and activist associations. Though this process has been most evident, perhaps, in Brazil, it has also been important in the growth of indigenous movements in the Andean countries.[38]

It was not just Catholicism but the political philosophy of the postindependence leaders as well that discouraged associationalism in Latin America. Although many of these leaders were dedicated to republicanism, theirs was a form of republicanism that harked back to the ancients through the writing of Rousseau. In this conception, the ideal republic was one driven by militarism, a strong virtuous state, and the direct democratic mandate of the general will. Espoused by leaders like Simón Bolívar, this version of republicanism left little room for a democratic civil society, viewing associationalism rather as a type of invidious factionalism. Citizens learned democratic virtue through direct interactions with the state, not through the messy and divisive organizations of civil society.[39]

Finally, there is an important historical reason that civil society in North America would be stronger than that in Latin America, which relates to our discussion in part I. We argued that civil society had both top-down and bottom-up origins, and we emphasized the often neglected role of political institutions in forging civil society. The early establishment in the United States of order, boundaries, a demos, and a functioning democratic party system lent itself to the creation of associations. As Theda Skocpol and Morris Fiorina have argued, social mobilization was spurred by the creation of the American mass party in the early nineteenth century. As parties scrounged for support, they both relied on and strengthened associational networks. The fact is, therefore, that the late adoption of democracy and of more stable party systems in Latin America delayed incentives for the creation of durable civil societies. Furthermore, the lack of political order inhibited the creation of large organizations that relied on communication with far-flung parts of the country. Skocpol and Fiorina remind us that the U.S. government played an important role in stimulating associationalism by increasing the coverage of the mail and the frequency with which people received mail and newspapers. Latin America, engaged in disruptive conflict for most of the nineteenth century, had neither newspapers nor a state that could ensure a safe, reliable method of transporting them, such as was common in the United States by midcentury.[40]

There are therefore structural, cultural, and historical reasons to expect that civil society—the formation of voluntary, intermediate associations—in Latin America would be weaker and less prevalent than in North America. Thus, Schmitter reports that in Brazil by the early nineteenth century there were very few secondary associations and no press to speak of.[41] In Chile the Church was still actively suppressing independent associations and the press as late as the 1920s.[42] Workers' mutual aid societies were formed in Chile as early as the 1850s, but by 1870 there were still only thirteen.[43] By contrast, nineteenth-century observers of the United States found a flourishing civil society there. Tocqueville famously noted North Americans' propensity to join. Domingo Sarmiento, admiring the associational life of the United States, noted that "from here it is born that wherever ten Yankees whether poor, in tatters, or stupid are together; before cutting down a tree to build a dwelling, they get together to arrange the basis of association."[44]

To say that civil society in Latin America has been weaker than in the United States is to say very little, however, since the United States has traditionally had one of the most vibrant and diverse civil societies of any country in the world. Even a cursory comparison of the United States and Europe suggests that Americans are far more likely to join organizations than their counterparts in most advanced democracies, with the exception of highly corporatist Scandinavia and the Netherlands.[45] One must ask what a civil society is supposed to do, and whether civil society in Latin America has been significantly weak to the point that it has been precluded from performing its democratic function. Furthermore, as noted earlier, what matters is not only the strength or weakness of civil society but its orientation to the political system, as well. In many ways, Latin America's civil society has been problematic because Latin American political parties have been problematic. That is, it is not so much that Latin Americans have been atomized, without associations, as that their civil societies have either been dominated by the political system or independent but hostile toward and destabilizing to that system.

Where civil society is subordinated to political parties, the potential for political pact making and relatively tranquil political bartering is high; however, the locus of political participation is also narrowed.[46] Thus, political parties become the only organizations in society that structure political debate, and this debate is constituted by party leaders rather than following the impulses and demands of a vigorous, independent civil society. In contrast, where civil society exercises more independence, political parties are apt to compete for its support. Political contestation may occur in the wider society prior to its manifestation in political party platforms. Thus, in a system in which civil society is subordinate, the political system is more easily undermined, because centers of opposition are few in number and easily identifiable. The destruction of political parties in such a system severely weakens the articulation of political demands by all groups. In a more autonomous civil society, by contrast, the destruction of political parties means that the political regime must find new ways to accommodate the multiple, overlaying demands of a difficult-to-contain civil society. Thus such a polity is a bulwark to democracy and a defense against authoritarian control.

As was argued earlier in relation to the Weimar Republic, this conception of civil society must be carefully constructed. Civil society should be autonomous but should also have efficacious links to political parties and the state. Without these links, the constitution of new, nondemocratic parties (e.g., the Nazi party in Germany) that manage to create effective relationships with the organs of civil society can infect a democratic system and destroy it in rather short order. Civil society, therefore, must have a vested interest in the functioning of democratic politics without being overly dependent on any particular party organization to articulate its demands. [47]

Below we discuss three Latin American trends. The first, associated primarily with Venezuela and (historically) Chile, is that of the party-dominated civil society. The second, associated with Uruguay and Colombia, is the machine system, in which parties are strongly rooted in clientelism and civil society is more independent but weak. The third type, exemplified by Argentina and Bolivia, is that of the delinked or praetorian civil society, in which parties both fail to dominate civil society or to have any meaningful links with autonomous associations. Although there have been important historical differences among our cases, manifest in our trichotomous analysis, it seems that praetorianism has recently become the dominant trend in Latin American civil society–party relations.

Praetorianism merits a bit of explanation. It is a concept borrowed from Samuel Huntington, who used it in a more general sense to describe societies in which strategic actors resort to their own best defenses rather than relying on institutions to satisfy their interests. As he puts it, "The wealthy bribe; students riot; workers strike; mobs demonstrate; and the military coup. . . . The absence of effective political institutions in a praetorian society means that power is fragmented: it comes in many forms and in small quantities." [48] Huntington was concerned about the stability of political systems generally, not democracies in particular.

For our purposes here, *praetorianism* refers to the failure of actors to establish connections to democratic institutions, specifically political parties, that require compromise and coalition building. Instead, actors rely solely on force, aggression, direct control of the state or the military, strikes, and demonstrations. According to Huntington's original meaning, praetorianism stems from the weakness of political institutions, preeminently parties.

Before exploring these trends in more detail, it is important to recognize what we are, and are not, attempting to do. The notion of "civil society–political party relationships" applies primarily to democratic systems. That is, civil society and political parties should have effective links under democratic regimes. Under nondemocratic regimes the situation is different. Parties and civil society are often repressed or are nonexistent, and the primary task of these organizations, insofar as they are capable of carrying it out, often becomes the restoration of liberties, including the political liberties that constitute democracy. The forging of "efficacious links" is meaningless outside the context of a democratic system of party competition and rotation that allows for policy change. Of course, civil society under authoritarianism can still breed human and social capital and can still influence public policy. But it cannot serve the kind of mediating role that it ought to serve when political parties compete freely.

Therefore, our analysis here examines civil society primarily during periods of democratic rule, which for most of Latin America means focusing on the twentieth century, This analysis generally assesses the relationship between civil society and parties, not during periods of authoritarian rule or oligarchic semidemocracy, but only during periods when there has been party competition.

In considering the Latin American systems that have had subordinated civil societies, Venezuela is an archetypal case. Similar to Chile in terms of its vibrant but dependent civil society, Venezuela has also seen deterioration in both institutions. Venezuela's party system so deeply penetrated civil society by the 1970s that it "blocked informal channels of popular representation between elections."[49] The major parties have been weakened by both their failures to reform—in economic terms and in terms of ending their seeming collusion and cartelization—as well as by their successes—fostering decentralization and devolution of power to local leaders. Affiliation with them, therefore, has come to be viewed quite negatively. Not only Hugo Chavez but before him Rafael Caldera as well ran on an anti-party platform and won immense popularity. This was particularly significant in Caldera's case, because he was the founder of one of Venezuela's major parties, COPEI. The fall of the Venezuelan party system has led, however, not to a delinking of organizations of civil society from political parties but rather to the disintegration of both. As the party system declined over the course of the 1990s, Venezuela witnessed "the weakening and even disappearance of politically influential business groups and organized labor" at the national level and the simultaneous rise of local-level neighborhood associations.[50] The weakness of Venezuelan civil society outside the context of its party system is one reason that Chavez has had such smashing success in consolidating his control over industry and trade unions. National-level civil society has evolved in the last decade in Venezuela, but the point is that many of the more prominent organizations are very recent creations that have leapt into a vacuum.[51]

In Chile, civil society has shown two of the tendencies identified here as "Latin American." Historically, Chile was a perfect case study of a dominated civil society. As in Venezuela, political parties segmented social interactions and built organizations of civil society from the ground up. Thus civil society was invested with partisan significance and had limited independence from the party system. Remarkably, the fall of the democratic regime under Pinochet did not meet with any coherent response from civil society. A primary reason for this is that civil society in Chile was constituted, across much of the ideological spectrum, primarily through its dependent relationship to political parties. The perceived assault of the Allende government on the privileges of the right and center in Chilean politics meant opposition to Pinochet would immediately be centered on the left, of course. But by directly assaulting political parties in Chile, the Pinochet regime was able to effectively mute the demands of civil society. As Garretón notes, "The elimination of the party political arena and of the political system was not simply the elimination of a channel for demands . . . it meant the destruction of the principal mode by which social actors and subjects were constituted. . . . Social organizations like the union or student movements, for example, were national actors precisely because of their overlap with the political class and because of their relations with the state. Under the military regime, such organizations were deprived of those elements which made them nationally important political subjects."[52]

However, a closer inspection of the origins of the democratic breakdown in Chile suggests that by the late 1960s and early 1970s, an important segment of civil society had broken away from the party system altogether and begun to rely on more praetorian forms of politics. While Chile is often considered exceptional among Latin American states in terms of political stability, it is remarkable how similar to its neighbors it looked by the 1970s. As in much of the rest of Latin America, Chile never achieved success in incorporating its working classes or in socioeconomic leveling so as to moderate the revolutionary left. As a result, mobilization in the late 1960s, encouraged by the Frei administration and undertaken by the parties of the left and center, ultimately led to very high expectations of reform and the constitution of social organizations that were beyond the grasp of the political system.[53] Increasingly, these groups turned to violence, as did the forces of the right. As Arturo Valenzuela has argued, the distrust bred by the Christian Democratic party, and the mobilization of civil society without strong ties to the party system were primary factors leading to the breakdown of democracy in Chile.[54] We hypothesize that the praetorianism of civil society in the late 1960s and early 1970s was in part a reaction against parties' overdominance of civil society and the shortcomings of this arrangement. By suffocating civil society, political parties precluded healthy, negotiated relations between the two spheres, thus contributing to the emergence of movements that were completely disconnected from the party system.[55]

Unfortunately, the bulk of references to civil society–party relations refer primarily to only one part of civil society—that concentrated among the popular sectors, the center and left. The right is usually ignored. One reason for this is undoubtedly that the right tends to wield its influence outside the party system—through, for example, control of the economy's commanding heights and occasionally through right-wing paramilitary violence. However, scholars ignore the constitution of the right's civil society at their peril.[56] Where the right has no efficacious links to the party system, it is likely to turn from flexing its economic muscles alone to support of military interventionism. Alternatively, if it already has a tight grip over the state bureaucracy, the situation is less likely to turn to military authoritarianism—because it is already authoritarian. Very often in Latin America, the right has eschewed partisan politics and tried to take control of the state administration itself.[57] The right in Latin America has only rarely had efficacious links to the party system, and these have not received much attention.

We should point out here, therefore, while discussing Chile as a party-dominated case, that the Chilean right was only marginally constituted within the party system. Certainly, right-wing civil society was never dominated by the party system in Chile as center-left or popular civil society was. As Garretón notes, "The Right's civil society is much stronger than its party expression, and its social universe is poorly articulated in its partisan organizations. Much more important in this regard are conservative forces' autonomous economic base (entrepreneurs are genetically rightist), private primary and secondary schools and universities, and communications media."[58]

Beyond this, the right in Chile historically acted to control policy directly through its corporatist representation on governmental commissions. Thus the Chilean state had only limited autonomy from oligarchical interests, and the right exercised a form of direct control over society. Robert Kaufman notes of this brand of corporatism that "the groups are more likely to penetrate and colonize the state, rather than the other way around."[59] A broader view of Chile suggests that it had several strands of praetorianism—on both the right and the left—particularly by the 1960s and 1970s. In Venezuela, by contrast, civil society on the right has been generally weak, and right-wing forces have depended on clientelistic, personal ties to political parties. Although the Venezuelan party system has not created or controlled civil society on the right, it has dominated it—through what Michael Coppedge describes as a divide-and-conquer strategy that has undermined independent collective action on the right.[60] In Venezuela, then, parties have successfully dominated civil society as a whole.

Both Chile and Venezuela demonstrate the perils of polities in which civil society is weakly constituted outside the party system (though Chile in the late 1960s and early 1970s also began to manifest praetorian tendencies on both the left and right). In both polities, civil society has been unable to respond quickly to changes in the political environment, because it has not had enough autonomy from the party system. While civil society has developed in both countries over time, there is no question that the slow pace of this evolution has prevented civil society from playing a strong role in circumscribing authoritarian threats when these have risen.

Though Peru's history has been very different from that of Chile and Venezuela, Frances Hagopian argues that in the 1980s and 1990s, Peruvian social movements became too dependent on their ties to the political system. When the left, along with parties in general, came under fire from President Alberto Fujimori, these movements disintegrated quickly because they were not substantially autonomous in relation to the party and political system and because they had not developed sufficiently structured organizational capacity.[61] Like the historical cases of Chile and Venezuela, Peruvian civil society proved to be weakly constituted internally.

A second type of party–civil society complex is that of clientelist systems, or what Robert Kaufman has called "machine-based systems." The primary exemplars of this type are Colombia and Uruguay. In these polities, parties have endured, but both their organizations and those of civil society have been weak and fragmented in organizational structure. Party ties have been established on the basis of existing patterns of clientelism at the local level and of clientelistic ties between local elites and national power brokers. As in the party-dominant polities, these systems have powerful parties, but machine parties do not exert power through the penetration of civil society.[62] Rather, they preserve traditional, particularistic patronage relationships and ignore or inhibit the development of a pluralistic, independent civil society. In some ways, these are the systems most similar to that of the United States. They have long-established political traditions, catchall parties, and more diverse civil societies that have not been directly dominated by parties but have affected public policy. However, these systems have had much less pluralistic civil societies than the U.S. model, and political parties have based their power primarily in clientelistic ties rather than "efficacious links" with civil society.[63] This has allowed the party system to drift away from the demands of civil society, or to cartelize. Clientelistic politics makes it difficult for social groups to organize on the basis of general policy concerns and foment collective interests, since the party system inevitably tries to "buy off" dissatisfied groups through the use of state patronage. Thus these systems have had a "conservative" gloss, making reform difficult if not impossible.[64] Both the party-dominant and machine systems have also seen penetration into the state by the right—through corporatist control or state clientelism. Whereas both the left and right have had trouble establishing links to parties in machine systems, the right has had more success establishing direct relationships with the state, while the left has been continuously excluded.

The combination of clientelism with states that are only weakly independent of oligarchical interests has often forced social actors interested in reform toward praetorianism (a point that is also relevant to the party-dominant systems, particularly Chile). As Kaufman argues, "In Colombia and Uruguay, clientelism also keeps participation low, but in addition it weakens the center and, at times, produces pressures toward violent and destructive social behavior."[65] Violence has been endemic in Colombia, which witnessed a turn toward Chilean-style partisan mobilization followed by praetorianism in the 1940s and 1950s. After a brief period of stability and some meager attempts to reform the system, Colombian praetorianism rose again in the 1970s. Violence in Colombia has been directly related to the failures of the traditional parties to incorporate or establish any meaningful links to the left.

Uruguay faced violence from both the left (the Tupamaros) and the right in the 1960s, which played a significant role in the lead-up to the military coup.[66] The overwhelming power of organized interests in Uruguay in the mid- to late twentieth century suggests a move away from the traditional, clientelist pattern toward more clearly praetorian tendencies. As Martín Rama notes, the growing power of the public sector, unions, and ISI-created industrialists severely restricted the institutional autonomy of the state and the ability of parties to institute reform—in part leading to the coup.[67] Of late, however, the Uruguayan party system has shifted toward more ideological, less clientelistic

patterns of competition with the rise of the left coalition Frente
Amplio (Broad Front).

It will not have escaped the reader's notice that the party-
dominant systems and the machine systems, despite their flaws,
have had the longest periods of democratic rule in Latin America—outside Costa Rica, which is discussed below. All have had
durable party systems, and civil societies that intersected with
those party systems. While civil society has been weak, dominated, or often ignored, it has had to come to terms with a party
system. This has not been the case in the final class of party–civil
society relationships explored below. In this category we locate
systems in which parties have not been able to partner with civil
society and thereby manipulate, negotiate with, or compromise
successfully with it. These systems have been the least stable
democracies.

Before turning to the praetorian systems, we must briefly analyze the civil society–party nexus in Costa Rica, perhaps the most
distinctive trait of that small nation's successful democracy. Costa
Rica has a more or less two-party system that revolves around a
predominant social democratic–liberal party (the National Liberation Party, or PLN) and a conservative coalition (Unidad). What
is remarkable about Costa Rica, which has had uninterrupted
party competition for over a half century, is the very large number
of independent civil society groups that operate in creative tension
with the party system, many of which predated the creation of
the current party system. Indeed, the PLN was basically born out
of an independent policy think tank. The predominant PLN has
not tried to establish corporatist relations with major groups in
society, leaving them to operate independently. In fact, the establishment of a fairly advanced welfare state in Costa Rica has
accompanied the demobilization of traditional groups, such as
labor, and led to the mobilization instead of coalitions based on
interests in the maintenance of welfare state programs. This has
inspired the manifestation of cross-cutting, rather than additive,

cleavages in civil society, which has served to moderate the pressure brought to bear by civil society.[68] Furthermore, direct party–interest group ties have been inhibited by the extraordinary number of autonomous governing bodies in Costa Rica that limit the degree to which partisan meddling can affect policy. As a result, Costa Rican civil society has been far more independent of the party system than its Venezuelan or Chilean counterparts, but far more vigorous and programmatic (as opposed to clientelistic) than Uruguayan or Colombian civil society.

The nature of Costa Rican civil society, however, has changed in the wake of economic crises in the 1980s. Welfare state retrenchment in a society as poor as Costa Rica's is not as difficult as in the advanced states of Europe, because civil society does not have the same resources to fall back on in the fight to maintain service levels. Nor has the perennially weakened labor movement been able to rise to the occasion. Thus, as Carlos Sojo observes, "In the current situation, in the absence of mechanisms of mediation and representation, the only collective instruments of interest expression available are the strike, or other forms of civil disobedience, or street protest."[69] It would appear that Costa Rica is potentially headed for the kind of praetorianism that it has successfully evaded for over fifty years.

A final Latin American archetype of civil society–political party relations is that represented by Argentina and Bolivia, in which the parties have been only weakly related to civil society organizations and civil society has most often acted on its own without reference to parties. In these cases, by contrast with those analyzed above, civil society is strongly constituted outside the party system, and it is the parties that are the weak link. In Argentina, landowners traditionally worked through the Sociedad Rural Argentina (SRA), while workers united in the Confederación General de Trabajo (CGT).[70] Both of these found that acting on their own was more efficacious than building links to weak, inept parties.[71] Under Perón, attempts were made to incorporate labor into a corporatist regime in order to transform Argentina into a system with a more subordinated civil society. But this effort had limited success, representing more a triumph of personalism than incorporation. Peter Snow and Luigi Manzetti argue that

> the inclusion of corporatist elements in the Perónist movement's rhetoric, however, did not mean that Argentina became a corporatist state after 1946 . . . old values and political institutions survived without being wiped out by the incoming ones. Elitism, liberalism, *movimientismo*, corporatism and authoritarianism began to co-exist, but in a very uneasy manner. . . . Military coups, co-optation and/or repression, and armed revolution all became parts of an uncertain political game in which the lack of consensus on basic issues became the most distinctive feature of the Argentine political system.[72]

The latter point identifies a key characteristic of praetorianism—the failure to reach consensus on both the sources of authority and on a minimal notion of the common good. The failure of integrative institutions means that there is no organizational weight behind any vision of the common weal. Thus the pursuit of power by any means becomes acceptable, since power is the only good recognized by everyone as having virtue.

In Bolivia, as Ruth Collier puts it, "the main political actors have been the military and the workers."[73] We should probably add to these a variety of indigenous movements, at least one of which is based in racial antipathy, mainly among the Aymara Indians.[74] While Bolivia has made some progress in recent years in institutionalizing its party system, large-scale protest in 2000 suggests this has been limited. As Lawrence Whitehead has noted of the protest in Cochabamba, "The incident illustrated the extent to which not only the government but all the political parties were out of touch with popular sentiment, which regarded neither the Congress nor any other institutional forum for the expression and redress of grievances as fully legitimate."[75] In the Argentinian and Bolivian cases, then, civil society simply had no use for the party system, which was unable to represent its variegated interests. As a result, actors turned to their preferred means of expression—strikes, street protests, violence, and military intervention.

Collier argues that Bolivia and Argentina are the only cases with this level of praetorianism, but recent events seem to suggest similar tendencies across broad swaths of Latin America. In Ecuador the main actors are, as one scholar termed it, "colonels and Indians."[76] In January 2000 a coup coalition led by the junior military and an NGO formed around indigenous rights (CONAIE) seized power briefly before the senior military, under international pressure, restored civilian rule. Even so, CONAIE and its military sympathizers remain dominant actors in Ecuadorean politics, as evidenced by a new cycle of protest and violence about a year after the coup. In Colombia, of course, the most important and most tendentious actors in civil society act entirely outside the party system, in part because of the incredibly weak state. Left-wing guerillas and right-wing paramilitaries do battle with the state and the military, as well as with the broader society. This problem dates back to the National Front, when the party system first began to cartelize and popular movements, which had never been incorporated into the political system, began to explode in praetorian form. In Brazil large numbers of congressional representatives have no links to civil society through their parties or in any other manner, even though civil society in Brazil is quite active.[77] In the past decade, Venezuela has also joined the ranks of the praetorian societies, as its party system has imploded, several coups have been attempted, and as Larry Diamond puts it, "Venezuelan democracy [has] become more and more like the afflicted, delegative democracies of the region."[78] We have already noted that Uruguay seems to have passed through a praetorian phase, although it may have surmounted it. Indeed, it is possible that the pattern identified here primarily with Argentina and Bolivia has become one of the more pervasive tendencies in Latin America. If so, we view this development pessimistically, for, as Hagopian argues, "when citizens are represented largely by social movements or NGOs, they are detached from political institutions whose function it is to aggregate interests in a democratic society. This divorce may leave citizens unrepresented on such salient issues as monetary and trade policy, social security reform, and consumer protection. Although social movements and voluntary organizations can effectively *supplement* party networks of representation, there is no evidence that they work well as *substitutes* for them."[79]

Clearly, new social movements in Latin America, particularly those led by indigenous groups, are addressing centuries-old flaws in the constitution of Latin American nationalism and citizenship. Such movements have a role to play in creating more just and equitable societies in Latin America. But if they are to play this role well in the context of democratic political regimes, then they must forge effective links to political parties and the political regime. This is not only the responsibility of the new social movements. Often these movements have arisen because of the exclusionary nature of the party systems and the failures of political elites to address the interests and needs of marginal groups. Both political parties and political regimes, broadly defined, bear the responsibility in tandem with civil society to forge effective links among themselves.

The task will not be easy. Recent polling data suggest very weak confidence throughout Latin America in political parties or other institutions of national political integration. Among major institutions, political parties were viewed with the most skepticism, with only about 19 percent of Latin Americans expressing "a lot" or "some" confidence in parties, while the number edged up only slightly for the national legislature as a whole (about 23 percent).[80] While U.S. citizens are also skeptical of national institutions, Table 13.1 above reveals that about 50 percent of Americans identify themselves as active or inactive party members, far more than any of the Latin American countries for which data are available. Thus, even if Americans are skeptical of their political institutions, they are more likely to participate in them than their equally (or even more) dubious Latin American counterparts. This does not bode well for Latin America. If civil societies and political parties are to forge effective bonds in that region, they will have to overcome citizens' deep-rooted ambivalence.

CONCLUSION

IN PART III OF THE BOOK, WE SET OUT to answer the question, Why has the United States been so much more successful than Latin America in maintaining democracy? This question has taken us back through the centuries to the origins of the modern nation-states of North and Latin America. We started our response with an examination of the imperial legacies of the European colonial powers—England and Spain. This set the stage for an interpretation that relies heavily on historical-structural factors, including an evolving cultural matrix.

Critics of culturalist explanations generally claim that culturalists distort, exaggerate, and trivialize culture by characterizing it with broad strokes that ignore its more subtle nuances. But these critics are often guilty of depicting culturalist arguments with their own broad strokes. They accuse culturalists of making absolute judgments about cultures, when in fact their arguments are relative. They accuse culturalists of claiming to explain all of the variance in outcomes with culture, when in fact most culturalists argue for a multivariate approach. They accuse culturalists of putting forth a static notion of culture, yet they respond to culturalist theories either by creating equally static but different (e.g., more positive) characterizations of culture or, remarkably, by denying that culture has any importance at all. In these ways, among others, they distort and exaggerate the intentions behind culturalist arguments and further contribute to a distorted view of culture itself.

We do not maintain that the histories of the United States and Latin America were determined by their cultural heritages. Rather, we have tried to demonstrate here that cultural factors worked in tandem with historical contingencies, social structural conditions, and political institutions. It is quite impossible to disentangle culture entirely from these other variables.

The question is whether culture has any independent weight aside from other variables. Here the answer is a definitive yes. At a forum on culture at the American Enterprise Institute, Francis Fukuyama once argued that culture explained no more than about 20 percent of the variance of most things. While we are sympathetic to the idea behind this assertion, we would prefer to see culture not in terms of a chunk of variance, but rather in terms of a dynamic variable that impacts other variables in multifarious ways. This may add up to some number like 20 percent, but it would be hard to calculate. Nevertheless, numbers aside, one can certainly identify the impact of culture in particular circumstances. Let us prove the point by example.

We have argued that one of the critical distinctions between Latin and North America that laid the groundwork for their subsequent successes and failures with democracy stems from the nature of their independence wars. Clearly the nature of these wars, as with any war, was determined in part by the strength, will, and strategic competence of the opposing sides. Yet the origins and impact of these wars were also bound up with the culture of the antagonists.

In both regions, the struggle for independence was posited as a struggle to defend the rights of citizens of the respective empires. In both, colonists resented imperial attempts to usurp local power and control. Neither Britain nor Spain was able to effectively manage its empire without the assistance, or obeisance, of its colonials. When their subjects turned against them, neither imperial power had the physical or moral strength to quash the rebellion and chastise the rebels.

But the principles of citizenship in Britain and Spain were very different, and in this regard, cultural arguments become critical to explaining divergent outcomes. British North Americans took up arms to defend a long and distinguished tradition of relative decentralization, self-representation, and pluralism. It bears repeating that these values were in no sense the absolute property of the British, but the British partook of them to a much greater degree than the Iberians. These values were therefore instilled in North Americans to a greater degree than Latin Americans, and they fairly represented the institutional situation in both regions. Limited, decentralized republicanism characterized the colonies of North America prior to the Revolution. Limited, semicentralized authoritarianism characterized Latin America.

These institutional legacies, derived from the cultural heritages of the regions, informed each region's struggles for independence. British North Americans were culturally schooled in the virtues of representation and quickly seized the moral high ground in their struggle for autonomy. "No taxation without representation" was the irresistible battle cry of a movement that had history and culture on its side. The Americans were relatively united in their mission, having a clear sense of where authority and legitimacy lay—in the republican institutions of the emerging nation. The main task of the independence war was to eliminate the interventionist imperial state from the republican order, leaving power in the hands of the elected officials of the parliaments. This was not an egalitarian vision per se, but its republicanism without hesitation comprehended representation as a fundamental value.

Latin America had no such cultural or institutional legacy. Representation had only a weak pedigree in Latin history and thought, and Spanish America was organized on the basis of viceroyalties, direct representatives of the crown whose only check, the *audiencias*, was also responsible to the crown, not to the people of Latin America. Independence for Latin America was not inextricably linked with a legacy of self-representation. While many Latin Americans believed that power ought to be devolved on representative assemblies (*juntas*), others recognized only imperial authority. Even for those who agreed about the value of representation, the ultimate willingness of the crown to admit colonials into the imperial Cortes, at last conceding the value of representation, complicated the matter of determining whether the crown or the *juntas* were more legitimate. What seems clear is that Spanish America was not united with respect to any particular legitimating principles or authority. The centralized authoritarian Spanish empire disintegrated, but Latin Americans' cultural heritage made it difficult to establish republican institutions. Those that were attempted had neither historical precedence nor legitimacy. As a result, there was no authority in Latin America after the revolutions; rather, there was chaos, hostility, and destruction. The fact that this state of affairs endured for most of the nineteenth century could not have been predicted, but a lengthy period of disorder was foretold in the historical conditions and cultural traditions surrounding the Spanish conquest.

Culture does have independent weight in models predicting political outcomes. But culture eludes measurement. We have referred to an "evolving cultural matrix" rather than to cultural traits per se. This is because culture consists not of fixed traits but rather of dynamic shifting qualities that interact in varied ways with a society's other traits. Thus culture forms a matrix with other kinds of variables. In combination with poor economic performance, high levels of inequality, weak civil society, and fleeting non-cleavage-based political parties, the historical and cultural legacy of Latin America has played a critical role in determining the weakness of democracy there.

Given all the variegated evidence we have marshaled in defense of our argument, one might ask how Latin America has managed to have any democracy at all. This question, however, misunderstands the evidence we have presented and its relationship to democracy. Scholarly consensus now suggests that democracy itself is within reach of most societies. This is because the political life of nations is to a certain degree autonomous in relation to structural and cultural factors. Thus, if elites and citizens are committed to democracy, democracy is not out of the question. However, the correlates presented here generally insure the health and stability of democracy over the long term. Their absence explains what we have seen in Latin America—repeated attempts at democratization, relatively shorter or longer periods of democracy, and then breakdown.

Their limited presence also explains the more successful democracies in Latin America—Uruguay, Chile, Costa Rica. Chile and Uruguay have both been wealthier than most Latin American countries, and Uruguay and Costa Rica have both had substantial middle-class sectors and *relatively* egalitarian income distributions. Chile and Uruguay historically have had deep party systems, though only Chile's was really cleavage based until recently. Costa Rica's last half century of democracy has been marked by loosely cleavage-based party competition and an incredibly active civil society with efficacious links to the political system. The cultural legacies of Spanish rule in all three countries has been quite similar, although Costa Rica was generally less affected by the empire, the wars for independence, or the years of violent competition for state control after independence. A fiercely democratic political culture has been a distinct feature of Costa Rica. All three of these countries have also been far more socially homogeneous than either their Andean neighbors or Mexico, with ethnic cleavages playing a far smaller role in their politics.

Over time, Latin American society as a whole has become more conducive to democracy. In brief, it has become wealthier, less statist, less hierarchical, more open, more integrated, and more politically mature. Problems persist, however. The turn away from statism has, by most estimates, led to greater inequality and poverty in recent years, a negative trend for democracy. And political institutions have often been, in Larry Diamond's accurate phraseology, "hollow." Parties are still weak and even less cleavage based than before, politics is still personal, the military still plays an exaggerated political role, and the relationship between civil society and the party system remains problematic. As Diamond reveals, human rights abuses are still rampant in the region.[1] The awakening of long-marginalized indigenous people throughout the Andean countries portends long stretches of instability as these groups are incorporated into the polity. In all of these ways, Latin America remains a less hospitable home for democracy than the United States.

Not that everything is in order in the United States. Inequality here is high. After rising for many years, it began to fall slightly in the late 1990s, an encouraging sign. But with the recession of 2001–03, it is likely to climb higher again. The American system also faces legitimacy problems—particularly after the Election 2000 debacle.[2] And Americans, too, have to find ways to incorporate new social movements into the party system.

As we plod through the democratic century, problems of deepening, strengthening, and elaborating democracy remain. Perhaps the state of democracy in the world at large today may be likened to the civil rights movement in the United States after the 1970s: the easy work has been done; the hard work remains. Once it seemed that the hard work was to change the laws, but when this had been accomplished, civil rights leaders realized that actually institutionalizing new ways of thinking, ending private discrimination, and improving welfare were much more difficult tasks. Similarly, it once seemed that a world where the majority of nations would be democratic was a fantasy. But that work has been done. In the last twenty-five years, with an unrelenting pace, democracy has thrust forward throughout the world. Yet the hard work remains: consolidating, broadening, legitimizing.

In spite of the many differences between North and Latin America, these problems are rather similar in the two regions. Democracy is far more institutionalized in the advanced countries, of course. But North Americans too must find ways to reinvigorate our political system, represent the variegated interests of our people, limit demagoguery, and reduce inequality. We too must fortify our parties, work effectively with our civil societies, and extend our citizenry. From very different places, we arrive at broadly similar challenges. Onward and upward.

APPENDIX: LATINOBARÓMETRO CIVIL SOCIETY DATA

This appendix includes both more recent and more complete data than the World Values Survey data in Table 13.1. However, since these data were collected by Latinobarómetro, they do not include the United States. Some of the same questions asked by Latinobarómetro in 2000 were also asked by the Social Capital Community Benchmark Survey in the United States (2000), and we have included these in Table C.1 for comparative purposes. While the difference in participation rates in sports groups is not significant, the other differences hold up in the expected direction. It should be noted that the U.S. data on religious groups are the sums of answers to two questions: (1) "Are you a member of a local church, synagogue, or other religious or spiritual community?" (2) "Besides your local place of worship, answer YES if you have been involved in the past twelve months with any organization affiliated with religion, such as the Knights of Columbus, or B'nai Brith, or a Bible study group." This is more comparable to the Latinobarómetro question, which does not ask respondents to put aside their regular church membership when asking whether they participate in religious organizations.

TABLE C.1

Participation in Organizations, Latin America and the United States, 2000

	Percent active in organizations, by type								
	Religious	Communal	Artistic	Union	Ecology	Profession	Youth	Sport	Political
Argentina	17.5	3.5	3.7	1.3	1.7	3.8	2.3	8.2	4.7
Bolivia	39.5	17.8	6.7	9.4	3.8	12.2	19.4	33.3	5.3
Brazil	45.1	12.6	5.6	15.6	5.7	17.3	4	18	3.7
Colombia	45.7	13.1	5.9	6	4.4	12.5	8.3	23.2	4.6
Costa Rica	41.8	14.3	2.8	3.2	3.8	6.9	7.4	18.2	5.9
Chile	29.2	6.6	5.6	3.1	2.2	8.4	5.2	17.1	2.1
Ecuador	55.9	29.5	14.6	13.3	16.3	29.7	30.3	41.8	13.8
Mexico	24.4	5.5	3.3	2.2	2.1	3.3	4.6	13.8	4.4
Paraguay	55.3	14.8	4.3	1.7	2.2	7.6	10.6	24.9	8
Peru	36.6	16.2	5.4	3.2	3.1	12.9	8.9	26.8	3.9
Uruguay	13.2	3.7	3.6	2.8	1.2	4	2.5	9.2	7.4
Venezuela	41.5	18.8	4.8	4.1	7.2	11.6	15.7	27.5	6.7
Latin America*	36	11	5	8	4	12	6	18	4
United States†	82	—	17	12	—	25	22	21	9

SOURCE: Latinobarómetro (Santiago, 2000)

*Data are population-weighted averages of values for countries above.

†Data from Social Capital Benchmark Survey, 2000, available through the Roper Center, www.ropercenter.uconn.edu.

NOTES

INTRODUCTION

1. Adrian Karatnycky, "The 1999 Freedom House Survey: A Century of Progress," *Journal of Democracy* 11 (January 2000): 187–200.

2. Samuel Huntington, *The Third Wave: Democratization in the Late Twentieth Century* (Norman: University of Oklahoma Press, 1991), 13–26.

3. Adam Przeworski argues that Huntington's conception is misguided. See Przeworski, Michael E. Alvarez, José Antonio Cheibub, and Fernando Limongi, *Democracy and Development: Political Institutions and Well-Being in the World, 1950–1990* (Cambridge, UK: Cambridge University Press, 2000).

4. It should be noted in this regard that the current Bush administration's posture toward democracy is flavored much more by realpolitik than his immediate predecessors'. In particular, the administration has played an ambiguous role in recent events in Venezuela and, in Bolivia, has issued thinly veiled threats of suspended aid if elections resulted in a mandate for the left.

5. Cameron Duodu, "Dictators Beware," *New Internationalist* (September 2001).

6. Jon Jeter, "Opposition Gains in Zimbabwean Elections," *Washington Post*, June 27, 2000, A16.

7. Between 70 and 80 percent of the eligible population voted. Haleh Esfandiari, remarks at "A Symposium on the Iranian Elections: Implications for U.S. Foreign Policy," Woodrow Wilson International Center for Scholars, Washington, D.C., March 8, 2000.

8. Douglas Farah, "Ivory Coast Overthrows Military Ruler," *Washington Post*, October 26, 2000, A1.

9. A draft law to regulate the media in Belarus, under consideration in December 2001, "would ban any mentioning of the activities of unregistered political parties and nongovernmental organizations in the media" ("Belarus," *RFE/RL Media Matters*, December 10, 2001, http://www.rferl.org/mm/.

10. See International Helsinki Federation for Human Rights, *Report to the OSCE Implementation Meeting on Human Dimension Issues* (Warsaw, October 17–27, 2000).

11. Regional and municipal elections on October 29 proceeded with relative peace, but in the weeks leading up to these elections, violent interventions from various quarters were frequent. According to the *Economist*, well over half of the mayoral campaigns involved armed attacks of one sort or another. See "Colombia's Nervy Elections," *Economist*, October 28–November 3, 2000, 33.

12. "Unreforming," *Economist*, October 14–20, 2000, 55.

13. According to Transparency International, Nigeria ranks as the most corrupt country in the world. See Transparency International, *2000 Corruption Perceptions Index* (http://www.transparency.org).

14. Anthony Faiola, "Peruvian Insurgents Flee with Hostages," *Washington Post*, October 30, 2000, A21.

15. Leon Wieseltier, *New Republic*, October 23, 2001, 18.

16. Samuel Huntington, "Will More Countries Become Democratic?" *Political Science Quarterly* 99 (Summer 1984): 193–218.

17. Adam Przeworski, "Why Democracy Survives in Affluent Countries" (unpublished manuscript, 2000). Przeworski does *not* argue that democracy cannot survive in poor countries, but only that it will always survive in wealthy countries.

18. Seymour Martin Lipset, "Some Social Requisites of Democracy: Economic Development and Political Legitimacy," *American Political Science Review* 53 (1959): 69–105; and Lipset, *Political Man: The Social Basis of Politics,* 2nd ed. (Baltimore: Johns Hopkins Press, 1981; 1st ed., 1960).

19. Seymour Martin Lipset, "Conditions of the Democratic Order and Social Change: A Comparative Discussion," in S. N. Eisenstadt, ed., *Studies in Human Society: Democracy and Modernity,* vol. 4 (New York: E. J. Brill, 1992), 1.

20. Seymour Martin Lipset, *Political Man* (New York: Doubleday, 1960); Seymour Martin Lipset, Martin Trow, and James Coleman, *Union Democracy: The Inside Politics of the International Typographical Union* (New York: Free Press, 1959); Seymour Martin Lipset, "Some Social Requisites of Democracy, Economic Development and Political Legitimacy," *American Political Science Review* 53 (1959): 69–165; Lipset, Kyoung-Ryung Seong, and J. C. Torres, "A Comparative Analysis of the Social Requisites of Democracy," *International Science Journal* 45 (May 1993): 155–75; Lipset, "The Social Requisites of Democracy Revisited," *American Sociological Review* 59 (1994): 1–22.

21. The majority of this book was completed by 2001, and the research is current to 2000. Here and there, a few comments were added during editing that may reflect events as of 2001 or 2002. These have the awkward effect of making it unclear whether we were writing from the perspective of 2000 or 2002. I have therefore tried to keep these references to a minimum, but they have not been entirely eliminated (JML).

22. Theda Skocpol, *States and Social Revolutions* (Cambridge: Cambridge University Press, 1979), 21.

23. Amartya Sen, "Democracy as a Universal Value," *Journal of Democracy* 10 (July 1999): 3.

CHAPTER 1

1. See Adam Przeworski, "Minimalist Conception of Democracy: A Defense," in Ian Shapiro and Casiano Hacker-Cordon, eds., *Democracy's Value* (Cambridge, UK: Cambridge University Press, 1999).

2. Joseph Schumpeter, *Capitalism, Socialism and Democracy* (New York: Harper & Bros., 1947), 269.

3. Robert A. Dahl, *Polyarchy: Participation and Opposition* (New Haven: Yale University Press, 1971), 7.

4. Schumpeter made a similar point about the relationship between various freedoms and democracy, arguing that there was a relationship between them but that the relationship was not given a priori. See Schumpeter, *Capitalism, Socialism and Democracy*, 271–72.

5. This is an extreme, stylized example, used here to make a point. It should be clear, however, that even if the law stopped short of banning private advertising, the same basic issues would be at stake.

6. The democratic content of such a policy is debatable, particularly since, although voters claim to find personalistic attacks distasteful, they appear to base their assessments of candidates at least in part on their personal characteristics. Whether such characteristics are important or not should probably be left to the voters to decide, not a government body. For analysis of the "personal" side of voter assessments of candidates, see Arthur H. Miller, Martin Wattenberg, and Oksana Malanchuk, "Schematic Assessments of Presidential Candidates," *American Political Science Review* 80 (June 1986): 512–40. Prohibiting private advertising or funding may also do serious damage to the principle of contestation.

7. Ted Gurr, *Polity II: Political Structures and Regime Change, 1800–1986* (Boulder, CO: Center for Comparative Politics [producer], 1989. Ann Arbor, MI: Inter-University Consortium for Political and Social Research [distributor], Codebook) diskette, 38.

8. The fact that outcomes are uncertain does not mean that we have no idea what they will be but rather that we have only probabilistic knowledge of them.

9. Tocqueville himself believed that the poor, inherently a majority, would ultimately dominate the much smaller minority of the wealthy and force a transfer of wealth to themselves. There is a wide range of opinion as to why this seemingly inevitable result has not ensued. Marxists in the Gramscian tradition believe that the cultural hegemony of the ruling class breeds false consciousness of true interests among the working classes. As Robert Bocock describes Gramsci's notion of hegemony, "for Gramsci, hegemonic leadership fundamentally involved producing a world-view, a philosophy and moral outlook, which other subordinate and allied classes, and groups, in a society accepted" (Bocock, *Hegemony* [New York: Tavistock Publications, 1986], 46).

10. That is to say that democracy is a game in which the rules are sacrosanct. They are accepted by all as basically fair. This fairness derives from the fact that the outcome of the game can be determined not from the rules used but only from the effort put forth by various interests to exploit those rules. If the rules are not deemed to be fair, this is generally because they seem to favor some group over another. It should be noted that democracy is flexible with regard to outcomes but not process. Other regime types are much more flexible with regard to process, which is why they are generally not considered to be fair.

11. Among these was Proposition 187 (1994) in California, ending social services to illegal immigrants; Propositions 209 in California and I-200 (1999) in Washington state, ending affirmative action; and most recently, Initiative 695 (2000) in Washington state, essentially ending the power of the state legislature to raise taxes. The last example is a classic case: it enhances direct democracy but undermines representative democratic institutions. In so doing, it may not even be democratic, let alone good.

12. For an alternative view of the benefits of direct democracy in Switzerland, see Bruno S. Frey and Iris Bohnet, "Democracy by Competition: Referenda and Federalism in Switzerland," *Publius: The Journal of Federalism* (Spring 1993): 71–82. Frey and Bohnet argue that referenda break politician cartels and improve information access. Politicians (agents) have different interests than their principles in many cases, they argue, pointing to the fact that voters differed on the issue from their representatives in Parliament in 39 percent of the referenda between 1948 and 1990. Although the authors are correct to argue that elites may not be more competent to make choices in the public interest than voters, they fail to address the fact that professional politicians are supposed to know more about complex issues than voters, not simply because they are elites but because that is their job. In an increasingly complex world, voters cannot possibly be aware of all the issues before the state at any time; it is the politician's job, however, to be informed. Whether this holds in practice is, of course, another story.

13. Tedd Gurr, Keith Jaggers, and Will H. Moore, "Transformation of the Western State: The Growth of Democracy, Autocracy and State Power since 1800," *Studies in Comparative International Development* 25 (Spring 1990): 84.

14. Adam Przeworski, Michael Alvarez, Jose Antonio Cheibub, and Fernando Limongi, "What Makes Democracies Endure?" *Journal of Democracy* 7 (January 1996): 45. We discuss some limitations of this study below.

15. For a recent article that also takes an ambiguous position on referenda and other tools of direct democracy, see Monica Barczak, "Representation by Consultation? The Rise of Direct Democracy in Latin America," *Latin American Politics and Society* 43 (fall 2001): 37–60. Barczak writes, "*Consultas* and initiatives can be used in more pernicious ways. An authoritarian-minded president, for example, might see the referendum as a way to circumvent (and thereby weaken) the legislature. Citizens frustrated with weak political parties might see the initiative as a way of supplanting parties, ignoring the tougher task of strengthening them" (39).

16. In 1949 a minority socialist–led government held power in Japan. Subsequently, the Liberal Democrats (LDP) held power until 1993, when they were defeated by another socialist-led government. This in turn held power briefly before returning it to the LDP.

17. This is the approach taken by Dahl in *Polyarchy* (see pages 1–10).

18. This point is far from settled. It is not always true that democracies are more responsive than nondemocracies, though in general we tend to think they are. A counterexample is given by Gregory Luebbert, who argues, regarding the integration of the working class into modern politics, that "ironically, one indicator of the success of liberals in integrating the working class is that in some respects they actually had to do less for the material interests of workers than

did the leaders of authoritarian states. Peter Flora and Jens Alber have shown that social welfare measures were most highly developed before 1914 in those European societies that lacked parliamentary institutions and political rights for workers." See Gregory Luebbert, "Social Foundations of Political Order in Interwar Europe," *World Politics* 39 (July 1987): 454; Leubbert, *Liberalism, Fascism, or Social Democracy: Social Classes and the Political Origins of Regimes in Interwar Europe* (New York: Oxford University Press, 1991), 113–14.

19. Raymond Duncan Gastil, "The Comparative Study of Freedom: Experiences and Suggestions," *Studies in Comparative International Development*, 25 (Spring 1990): 33.

20. Michael Alvarez, José Antonio Cheibub, Fernando Limongi, and Adam Przeworski, "Classifying Political Regimes," *Studies in Comparative International Development* 31 (Summer 1996): 13.

21. Michael Coppedge and Wolfgang Reinicke, "Measuring Polyarchy," in Alex Inkeles, ed., *On Measuring Democracy* (New Brunswick, NJ: Transaction, 1991), 47.

22. Przeworski et al., "What Makes Democracies Endure?" Technically a prediction is different from a correlation. A prediction is an equation in the bivariate case that has the following form: $y = a + bx$, where y is the dependent variable, a is a constant, b the slope, and x is independent variable. The slope b tells us how to predict y from x. The correlation between y and x is a standardized form of b that tells us not how to predict y from x but what the strength of the relationship is in standard deviations. (The correlation is similar to the beta derived in bivariate regression). Thus, while b is unit dependent, the correlation r is not. A correlation of 0.87 means that a one-standard-deviation change in one scale amounts to a 0.87-standard-deviation change in the other scale. Without knowing the units of standard deviations, however, we cannot predict anything with this correlation. Furthermore, a prediction has a specific meaning in logistic regression, in which the dependent variable has only two possible outcomes. In this case, one can make a correct or incorrect prediction. In linear regression, very few predictions are "correct." The idea is to get as close as possible.

23. Keith Jaggers and Ted Gurr, "Tracking Democracy's Third Wave with the Polity III Data," *Journal of Peace Research* 32:4 (1995): 475.

24. For evidence of this bias found in a survey of studies, see David Collier and Robert Adcock, "Democracy and Dichotomies: A Pragmatic Approach to Choices about Concepts," *Annual Review of Political Science*, 2 (1999): 539.

25. Jaggers and Gurr, "Tracking Democracy's Third Wave," 475. The correlation between Gastil's political and civil rights indices is 0.92.

26. Dahl, *Polyarchy*, 21.

27. Mancur Olson, "Dictatorship, Democracy and Development," *American Political Science Review* 87 (September 1993): 567–76.

28. Continuing the example, Clinton's winning coalition would have been equal to approximately 100 million people, an extremely large group for whom to provide private goods.

29. Bruce Bueno de Mesquita, James D. Morrow, Randolph Siverson and Alistair Smith, "Political Competition and Economic Growth," *Journal of Democracy* 12 (January 2001): 58–72.

30. Dahl, *Polyarchy*, 28; R. J. Rummel, *Power Kills* (New Brunswick, NJ: Transaction, 1997).

31. Adam Przeworski, "Minimalist Conception of Democracy: A Defense," in Ian Shapiro and Casiano Hacker-Cordon, eds., *Democracy's Value* (Cambridge, UK: Cambridge University Press, 1999), 49. Soviet president Mikhail Gorbachev made a similar point regarding the role of an opposition in a multiparty system. He noted that under the Soviet single-party system, bureaucrats disobeyed him but no one told him. He called on the press to fill the role of an opposition party. See Mikhail Gorbachev, "Text of report delivered to plenary meeting of CPSU Central Committee," *Foreign Broadcast Information Service Daily Report: Soviet Union* (28 January), R2–R48; Gorbachev, "Text of report delivered to CPSU Central Committee at 19th All-Union CPSU Conference," *Foreign Broadcast Information Service Daily Report: Soviet Union* (28 June [Supp.]), 1–35.

32. Lipset, *Political Man.* This point was also made by Tocqueville in *Democracy in America*; see Seymour Martin Lipset, "The Indispensability of Political Parties," *Journal of Democracy* 11 (January 2000): 48–55, and our discussion of Lipset, Trow, and Coleman, *Union Democracy*, in chapter 4 of this book.

33. Lipset, Trow, and Coleman, *Union Democracy*, 15–16.

34. Theda Skocpol, *States and Social Revolutions* (Cambridge, UK: Cambridge University Press, 1979), 21.

CHAPTER 2

1. See chapter 6. Also see, for example, Peter A. Hall and David Soskice, "An Introduction to Varieties of Capitalism," in Peter A. Hall and David Soskice, eds., *Varieties of Capitalism: The Institutional Foundations of Comparative Advantage* (New York: Oxford University Press, 2001), 1–68.

2. Daniel J. Elazar, "Federalism and Consociational Regimes," *Publius* 15 (Spring 1985): 22.

3. Arend Lijphart, "Presidentialism and Majoritarian Democracy: Theoretical Observations," in Juan J. Linz and Arturo Valenzuela, eds., *The Failures of Presidential Democracy* (Baltimore: Johns Hopkins University Press, 1994), 91–105.

4. Przeworski et al., "What Makes Democracies Endure?" 45. Parliamentary regimes had a survival rate of seventy-one years, as compared to twenty for presidential systems.

5. Linz's most extensive indictment of presidentialism can be found in "Presidential or Parliamentary Democracy: Does It Make a Difference?" in Linz and Valenzuela, eds., *Failures of Presidential Democracy*, 3–90.

6. Presidentialism is still winner-take-all in one respect, regardless of gridlock: the losing candidate for president will generally play no role in the government. This is a legitimate disadvantage of presidentialism, though not, in our view, a fatal one. In states where the "opposition" is a group with a large following—rather than an individual—the exclusion of one individual from government should not be a disastrous outcome. This should be especially true if the presidential office is weak.

7. The French double-executive system is an anomaly. While the French do have a president and the president is the most powerful politician in the country under unified rule, the system avoids gridlock by reverting to an essentially parliamentary one under conditions of divided rule, or "cohabitation." The

president has certain reserved powers under such conditions, but these are reduced to foreign policy and the ability to delay, but not really impede, domestic policy. Under divided rule, the prime minister is the driving force behind legislation. See Jean V. Poulard, "The French Double Executive and the Experience of Cohabitation," *Political Science Quarterly* 105 (Summer 1990): 243–67.

8. Michael Coppedge, "Democratic in Spite of Presidentialism," in Linz and Valenzuela, eds., *Failures of Presidential Democracy*, 410.

9. David R. Mayhew, *Divided We Govern* (New Haven: Yale University Press, 1991). Intriguingly, it is also true that minority parliamentary governments, which might be expected to be dysfunctional for the same reason as divided presidential systems, are actually fairly successful. There is thus some reason to believe that the demands of governance prevent real gridlock from occurring in most circumstances. See Kaare Strom, *Minority Government and Majority Rule* (Cambridge, UK: Cambridge University Press, 1990).

10. Scott Mainwaring and Matthew Shugart, "Juan Linz, Presidentialism, and Democracy: A Critical Appraisal," *Comparative Politics* (July 1997): 453.

11. Scott Mainwaring makes similar arguments pertaining to the ill-fated combination of multipartism and presidentialism in his "Presidentialism, Multipartism and Democracy: The Difficult Combination," *Comparative Political Studies* 26 (July 1993): 198–228.

12. Fred W. Riggs, "The Survival of Presidentialism in America: Para-constitutional Practices," *International Political Science Review* 9 (October 1988): 260–61.

13. Mainwaring notes that stable democracies have tended to have very high proportions of the legislature controlled by the president's party, even when that party is in a minority.

14. Alfred Stepan and Cindy Skach, "Presidentialism and Parliamentarism in Comparative Perspective," in Linz and Valenzuela, eds., *Failures of Presidential Democracy*, 127.

15. In closed-list voting the party picks the candidates and assigns them a place on the party list, which the voters cannot change. Open lists allow for voters to change the ordering of the list. Single transferable vote systems allow voters to choose a candidate, rather than a party, and to transfer their vote to another candidate should their candidate not need the vote (because of either exceptionally good or poor performance).

16. Maurice Duverger, "Which is the Best Electoral System?" in Arend Lijphart and Bernard Grofman, eds., *Choosing an Electoral System: Issues and Alternatives* (New York: Praeger, 1984), 31–39.

17. George Tsebelis, "Decision Making in Political Systems: Veto Players in Presidentialism, Parliamentarism, Multicameralism and Multipartyism," *British Journal of Political Science*, 25 (July 1995): 289.

18. Ibid., 322–23.

19. Sarah A. Binder, "Going Nowhere: A Gridlocked Congress?" *Brookings Review* (Winter 2000): 19. The number of centrists is taken to imply a lack of coherence, meaning more legislators from both parties stray from the position of the party toward the center.

20. Amie Kreppel, "The Impact of Parties in Government on Legislative Output in Italy," *European Journal of Political Research* 31 (April 1997): 327–50.

21. Ibid., 337.

CHAPTER 3

1. Lipset, *Agrarian Socialism* (Berkeley: University of California Press, 1950; repr., New York: Doubleday, 1968), 245.

2. Ibid., 265.

3. Lipset, Trow, and Coleman, *Union Democracy*.

4. Such was certainly the implication of Robert Michels's book *Political Parties*, on which Lipset, Trow, and Coleman drew heavily in constructing *Union Democracy*. Michels purported to explain the unlikelihood of democracy in general by looking particularly at its status within a political party, the German Social Democratic Party (SPD). According to Michels, the probability of democracy succeeding could be deduced from looking at the internal workings of the party that most clearly preached its virtues and assessing how well it lived up to its own professed doctrine. The SPD did not, of course, perform very well. Lipset has acknowledged *Union Democracy*'s debt to Michels in his introduction to the 1962 edition of *Political Parties*, reprinted in 1999. See Michels, *Political Parties* (New Brunswick, NJ: Transaction, 1999), 15–39.

5. In drawing analogies between organizations and polities, we are not suggesting that there is necessarily any normative value to democracy within organizations nor that there is necessarily any relationship between the existence of democracy in organizations and the parallel existence in polities. To the contrary, we would argue, as Juan Linz has done, following Lipset, that "it is the pluralism *of* institutions, rather than the pluralism *in* institutions that supports a pluralistic society." That is, organizations contribute to democracy by their competition in the aggregate, not by their internal structure. See Juan Linz, "Change and Continuity in the Nature of Democracies," in Larry Diamond and Gary Marks, eds., *Reexamining Democracy* (Newbury Park, CA: Sage Publications, 1992), 194.

6. Not all successful parties are cleavage parties, but the majority are. In addition to the relevant passages in *Union Democracy*, an expansion of many of these ideas can be found in *Political Man,* chapter 12 ("The Political Process in Trade Unions"), 387–436.

7. Lipset, Trow, and Coleman, *Union Democracy*, 331.

8. Ibid., 308.

9. Ibid., 142.

10. Ibid., 241 (emphasis added).

11. Ibid., 259.

12. Ibid., 267.

13. Ibid., 79–80.

14. Ibid.; see 345–50 for a discussion of how voters are affected by propaganda.

15. Ibid.; see chapter 5, 83–105, for an elaboration of the occupational community's political function.

16. For an elaboration of the concepts of human and social capital, see chapter 4 of the present work, on civil society.

17. Lipset, Trow, and Coleman, *Union Democracy*, 180.

18. Ibid., 373–77.

19. Ibid., 148.

20. The methodological point about disentangling cause and effect was developed in Lipset, *Political Man*, 58–62. Lipset argued implicitly that dilemmas of multivariate causation could best be attacked by comparative empirical analysis.

21. Lipset made this point in terms of democracy's management of conflict and consensus; the triad is Tocquevillian because each unit manages conflict and simultaneously promotes consensus. See Lipset, *Political Man*, 7.

22. Lipset, Trow, and Coleman, *Union Democracy*, 11.

23. Judith Stepan-Norris, "The Making of Union Democracy," *Social Forces* (December 1997): 475–510. More recent research, incidentally, finds that the ITU no longer conforms to the model of a democratic organization. Kay Stratton argues that changing structural conditions within the craft, the economy, and the union—including a drop in membership, a decline in the occupational community, an increase in status differentials between leaders and workers—have led to a more oligarchical organization. This does not challenge Lipset, Trow, and Coleman's findings, because it posits that the lack of certain factors previously associated with democracy has meant a decline in democracy. However, more research would be needed to know why these changes occurred. See Kay Stratton, "Union Democracy in the International Typographical Union: Thirty Years Later," *Journal of Labor Research* 10 (Winter 1989): 119–34.

24. "Organizational weapon" refers to the superior organizing capabilities of communists, which, given their meager resources, are generally considered their greatest strength.

25. Actually, Stepan-Norris makes this point elsewhere, arguing that repression of Communists led them to develop a democratic ideology. See Stepan-Norris and Maurice Zeitlin, "The Insurgent Origins of Union Democracy," in Diamond and Marks, eds., *Reexamining Democracy*, 261. If repression leads to democratic norms, then democracy cannot be considered intrinsic to Communism. However, Stepan-Norris would then be correct to argue that Communists were no different than other factions in this respect, contradicting Lipset, Trow, and Coleman in *Union Democracy*, 248.

26. Stepan-Norris, "Making of *Union Democracy*," 495 (emphasis added).

27. This point was originally made by Lipset in *Political Man* (see chapter 12, "The Political Process in Trade Unions," esp. 395–99.

28. Alexis de Tocqueville, *Democracy in America* (New York: Knopf, 1997), 1:66–67.

29. Ibid., 1:67.

30. Indeed, some commentators have suggested that the weakness of civil society in Spain has actually been a boon to democracy, because it has limited the expression of fierce, ideological cleavages from the past that could tear Spanish civility asunder. For more on this perspective, see Peter McDonough, Doh C. Shin, and Jose Alvaro Moises, "The Churches and Political Mobilization in Brazil, Korea, and Spain," in Birol A. Yesilada, ed., *Comparative Political Parties and Party Elites* (Ann Arbor: University of Michigan Press, 1999), 197–237; and Omar G. Encarnacíon, "Tocqueville's Missionaries: Civil Society Advocacy and the Promotion of Democracy," *World Policy Journal* 17 (Spring 2000): 9–18, esp. 15.

31. For a brief review of the protracted struggle between central authority and the autonomous regions in Spain, see Alfred Montero, "Decentralizing Democracy: Spain and Brazil in Comparative Perspective," *Comparative Politics* 33 (January 2001): 149–69.

32. Omar Encarnación argues that federalism and corporatism balanced each other directly during and after the Spanish transition. See Omar Encarnacíon, "Federalism and the Paradox of Corporatism," *West European Politics* (April 1999): 90–129.

33. For an elaboration of the four essential characteristics of consociationalism, see Arend Lijphart, *Democracy in Plural Societies* (New Haven: Yale University Press, 1977), chapter 2.

34. Even though we agree that civil society in Spain is weak and that this weakness has actually been beneficial to Spanish democracy, we do not believe that this is an argument against having any civil society at all. Spanish democracy would be weaker if Spain had no civil society to speak of. See, for example, Kerstin Hamann, "Civil Society and the Democratic Transition in Spain," *Perspectives on Political Science* 27 (Summer 1998): 135–47. This distinguishes civil society from federalism, which many states completely eschew without deleterious consequences.

35. Giovanni Sartori, *Parties and Party Systems* (Cambridge, UK: Cambridge University Press, 1976), 42.

36. Ibid., 57.

37. For an analysis of how American political parties have expressed the interests of their electoral bases, see Seymour Martin Lipset, *Political Man*, 313–18. For an overview of what parties generally express in democracies around the world, see Seymour Martin Lipset, "The Indispensability of Political Parties," *Journal of Democracy* 11 (January 2000): 48–55.

38. A particularly obvious stage of this process occurred during the 2000 presidential primaries in the United States as the Republican leadership battled over how to interpret the great crossover appeal among Democrats of Republican insurgent John McCain's abortive presidential primary bid. Those who were most concerned to change the image of the Republican party understood that people who identify as Democratic because of particular issues that the Democratic party supports were willing to forgo party identification if someone from the other party prioritized their issues. This appeal was distinct from that of McCain among independents, who have no party affiliation.

39. The case of COPEI (Comité de Organización Politica Electoral Independiente), a major Venezuelan party, is also instructive. Originally a sectarian Catholic party, COPEI altered its appeal, form, and style in order to effectively compete with Acción Democrática, a mass-based, socially heterogeneous party. Because of the constraints of the Venezuelan party system, COPEI evolved into a very different kind of party. See Miriam Kornblith and Daniel Levine, "Venezuela: The Life and Times of the Party System," in Scott Mainwaring and Timothy Scully, eds. *Building Democratic Institutions: Party Systems in Latin America* (Stanford: Stanford University Press, 1995), 47.

40. Thomas R. Rochon, "Adaptation in the Dutch Party System: Social Change and Party Response," in Yesilada, ed., *Comparative Political Parties and Party Elites*, 97–122.

41. There are currently two distinct "Green party" constellations in the United States. These may be described as the moderate and the radical branches. The Green party that Ralph Nader ran with is the Association of State Green Parties. Its party platform can be viewed at www.gp.org. The "other" Green party is the Greens/Green Party USA, whose platform can be viewed through www.green-party.org. However, both parties affirm the point we are making, namely, that both platforms go beyond environmental concerns.

42. On Refah, see Birol A. Yesilada, "The Refah Party Phenomenon in Turkey," in Yesilada, ed., *Comparative Political Parties and Party Elites*, 123–50.

43. Richard Rose and Thomas Mackie, "Do Parties Persist or Fail?" in Kay Lawson and Peter Merkl, eds., *When Parties Fail* (Princeton: Princeton University Press, 1988), 533–58.

44. Seymour Martin Lipset and Stein Rokkan, "Cleavage Structures, Party Systems, and Voter Preferences," in Lipset and Rokkan, eds., *Party Systems and Voter Alignments: Cross-National Perspectives* (New York: Free Press, 1967), 1–64.

45. Robert Maynard Hutchins, ed., *Great Books of the Western World* (Chicago: Encyclopedia Britannica, 1952), 43:50.

46. Lipset, *Political Man*, 230.

47. Herbert Kitschelt, "The Formation of Party Systems in East Central Europe," *Politics and Society* 20 (March 1992): 16–17.

48. Ibid., 21.

49. Research on voter preferences in Russia in 1995 found that while a majority of the citizenry supported democracy, a majority also opposed market reform. This suggests too that a pro-reform/anti-reform divide cannot be presumed to subsume both political and economic reform. For the data on Russia, see Arthur Miller, William M. Reisinger, and Vicki L. Hesli, "Mass-Elite Linkage through Political Parties in Post-Soviet Russia," in Yesilada, ed., *Comparative Political Parties and Party Elites*, 287–310.

50. Alejandro Moreno has also attempted to map "cleavages" in post-Communist Europe as well as in post-authoritarian Latin America, but by *cleavages* he means political tendencies rather than social structural divisions. He argues that a major cleavage in new democracies is between pro-democracy and pro-authoritarian tendencies. This cleavage is similar to that identified by Kitschelt as libertarian-authoritarian but is conceptually distinct. Kitschelt assumes that the parties in East Central Europe will embrace democracy in its broadest forms. The cleavage between libertarians and authoritarians will be over how far to extend democratic processes into specific places—parties, nongovernmental institutions, etc.—as well as how centralized the national democracy should be. Moreno argues that initially, there will be disagreement in many states over the very legitimacy of democracy in the broadest national sense, that it will often take many years for broad acceptance of the system to emerge. He finds this cleavage to be salient in the former Soviet Union (FSU), particularly Russia, as well as the formerly authoritarian states Chile and Uruguay. But this cleavage has not developed in important East European cases such as Hungary, the Czech Republic, Slovenia, or Poland—where acceptance of democracy is nearly ubiquitous—and it has weakened as a cleavage in most of Latin America (Alejandro Moreno, *Political Cleavages* [Boulder, CO: Westview Press, 1999]).

51. Lipset, "The Indispensability of Political Parties," 52.

52. Arthur H. Miller, Gwyn Erb, William M. Reisinger, and Vicki L. Hesli, "Emerging Party Systems in Post-Soviet Societies: Fact or Fiction?" *Journal of Politics* 62 (May 2000): 455–90.

53. Argelina Cheibub Figueiredo and Fernando Limongi, "Presidential Power, Legislative Organization, and Party Behavior in Brazil," *Comparative Politics* (January 2000): 159–60.

54. Ibid., 164–65.

55. Scott Mainwaring, *Rethinking Party Systems in the Third Wave of Democratization* (Stanford: Stanford University Press, 1999), 337–41.

56. Stefano Bartolini and Peter Mair, *Identity, Competition and Electoral Availability* (Cambridge, UK: Cambridge University Press, 1990), 293.

57. For a schematic of these dichotomies and the resultant typology, see Lipset and Rokkan, "Cleavage Structures," 38.

58. Ibid., 46.

59. And in the United States, in fact, there has been a hidden religious divide between Democrats and Republicans, with the latter attracting primarily white Northern native-born Protestants and the former attracting non-Protestants and cultural pluralists. This divide was also manifest in the fight over Prohibition, with the Republicans supporting it against the Democrats, who represented wet Catholics, among others.

60. The correlation has been weakest in the United States but still exists there.

61. Ibid., 50 (emphasis in original).

62. Ibid., 51.

63. Guillermo O'Donnell and Philippe C. Schmitter, "Tentative Conclusions about Uncertain Democracies," in Guillermo O'Donnell, Philippe Schmitter, and Laurence Whitehead, eds., *Transitions from Authoritarian Rule: Prospects for Democracy* (Washington, D.C.: Woodrow Wilson International Center for Scholars, 1986), 41.

64. Terry Lynn Karl, "Petroleum and Political Pacts: The Transition to Democracy in Venezuela," in O'Donnell, Schmitter, and Whitehead, eds., *Transitions from Authoritarian Rule*, 217.

65. Lipset and Rokkan, "Cleavage Structures," 15.

66. John W. Veugelers, "A Challenge for Political Sociology: The Rise of Far Right Parties in Contemporary Western Europe," *Current Sociology* 47 (October 1999): 92.

67. In Venezuela, at least, Acción Democrática (AD) followed a pattern similar to that of the Social Democratic Party (SPD) in Germany but distinct from that of the British Labour Party. That is, AD helped create civil society: "Party activists were . . . present at the creation of organized civil society, including trade unions, peasant groups, teachers' organizations, and student and professional societies. Their efforts meant that these and similar groups were integrated into the party from the beginning." However, though well organized, AD and other Venezuelan parties have also had, contra SPD and Labour, socially heterogeneous, catch-all memberships. At the time of party organization in Venezuela, the suffrage was limited to 5 percent. See Kornblith and Levine, "Venezuela: The Life and Times of the Party System," 41.

68. Michael Coppedge, "Venezuela: Democratic despite Presidentialism," in Linz and Valenzuela, eds., *Failures of Presidential Democracy*, 402.

69. Veugelers, "Challenge for Political Sociology," 95.

70. Branch parties are heavily organized parties of integration, as opposed to parties of representation, a distinction made by Maurice Duverger some years ago in *Political Parties* (New York: Wiley, 1954). Parties of integration attempt to influence their constituents by providing them with extensive information, networks, and activities, and isolating them from cross-pressures. Parties of representation tend to present notables for election and spend little time organizing constituents. Rather, they attract constituents by the platforms and personalities they present.

71. Alan Ware, *Political Parties and Party Systems* (Oxford, UK: Oxford University Press, 1996), 95.

72. See Lipset and Rokkan, "Cleavage Structures," 27.

73. Richard Katz and Peter Mair, "Party Organizations: From Civil Society to the State," in Richard Katz and Peter Mair, eds., *How Parties Organize* (London: Sage Publications, 1994), 7–8.

74. However, Venezuela's party system has been distinct from European systems in that it has been organized more along catch-all than ideological lines.

75. Kornblith and Levine, "Venezuela: The Life and Times of the Party System," 70.

76. Giovanni Sartori, "Video-Power," *Government and Opposition* 24 (Winter 1989): 39–53.

77. Juan Linz, "Change and Continuity in the Nature of Democracies," in Diamond and Marks, eds., *Reexamining Democracy*, 182–207.

78. De Lima notes that "Brazil is a country that 'jumped' from a pre-Gutenbergian condition (very low levels of literacy and print media circulation) to a condition in which the most-advanced technical sophistication of images predominates. There is little or no knowledge about the cognitive effects of this media 'jump.'" See Venicio A. DeLima, "Brazilian Television in the 1989 Election: Constructing a President," in Thomas Skidmore, ed., *Television, Politics, and the Transition to Democracy in Latin America* (Washington, D.C.: Woodrow Wilson Center Press, 1993), 113.

79. Curt Suplee, "The Speed of Light Is Exceeded in Lab," *Washington Post*, July 20, 2000, A1.

80. It would appear that computer capabilities can develop faster than this time frame for technological developments, canonized in Moore's Law, allows.

81. Joseph Straubhaar, Organ Olsen, and Maria Cavaliari Nunes, "The Brazilian Case: Influencing the Voter," in Skidmore, ed., *Television, Politics, and the Transition to Democracy in Latin America*, 118–36, esp. 124.

82. See Robert Putnam, *Bowling Alone* (New York: Simon & Schuster, 2000), 221–45. Whether television actually causes civic disengagement or not, it is clear that before there was television, people tended to spend more time together for entertainment. Now they don't have to, and this cannot but be part of the explanation for why people appear to interact less in formal groups. Lipset and William Schneider came to similar conclusions some years earlier in *The Confidence Gap: Business, Labor, and Government in the Public Mind* (New York: Free Press, 1983).

83. Putnam, *Bowling Alone*, 228.

84. Ibid., 219.

85. Eric Uslaner, "Social Capital, Television, and the 'Mean World': Trust, Optimism, and Civic Participation," *Political Psychology* 19 (September 1998): 441–67, esp. 459. Optimism and trust are positively associated with membership in voluntary organizations.

86. Straubhaar, Olsen, and Cavaliari Nunes, "The Brazilian Case," 118–36. Voting research suggests that although citizens tend to pay attention to political speeches and papers they agree with, when they are exposed to alternative views, this competing information tends to render them inactive and apathetic. Thus the effects of media coverage depend in part on whether viewers can successfully insulate themselves from cross-pressures.

87. "Tackling the Chaos in Brazil's Prisons," *The Economist*, February 24, 2001, 6, 37.

88. Peter McDonough, Doh C. Shin, and Jose Alvaro Moises, "The Churches and Political Mobilization in Brazil, Korea, and Spain," in Yesilada, ed., *Comparative Political Parties and Party Elites*, 197–237. Spain is exceptional in this regard. Religious affiliation does not strengthen political participation or civic activism in Spain.

89. Ronald Inglehart reports that "we do find indications of a religious resurgence in Latin America, Africa and Eastern Europe—but a marked decline in most advanced industrial societies" (Inglehart, *Modernization and Postmodernization* [Princeton: Princeton University Press, 1997], 284).

CHAPTER 4

1. See Seymour Martin Lipset, "Democracy in Private Government," *British Journal of Sociology* (March 1952): 47–63. Other works that reported findings similar to Lipset's include Immanuel Wallerstein, *The Road to Independence: Ghana and the Ivory Coast* (Paris: Mouton & Co., 1964). Wallerstein notes: "Lipset hypothesized the need for a multitude of independent secondary organizations in a society as a structural basis for the possibility of a democratic society. . . . We find that this analysis may be largely applied to West African society today, that voluntary organizations have been or potentially might be used to serve these functions in Ghana and the Ivory Coast" (114).

2. See, among other works, William Kornhauser, *The Politics of Mass Society* (Glencoe, IL: The Free Press, 1959); Sigmund Neumann, *Die Politischen Parteien der Weimarer Republik* (Stuttgart, 1965), and *Permanent Revolution* (New York: Harper & Brothers, 1942). Kornhauser's book was written for a project headed by Lipset.

3. Coleman's brilliant description of social capital can be found in "Social Capital in the Creation of Human Capital," *American Journal of Sociology* 94 (supplement 1988): S95–S120.

4. Immanuel Wallerstein, while a student of Lipset, built on the ITU study in demonstrating that voluntary associations taught their members how to interact with others in modern urban(e) settings, taking the place of formal education in developing societies, where many migrants were moving from country to town and where educational systems were weak. See Wallerstein, *Road to Independence*, 104–8.

5. Tocqueville, *Democracy in America*, 2:116.

6. Although political parties may be considered part and parcel of civil society, we believe that there are important theoretical and empirical reasons for distinguishing political parties from the broader civil society. These reasons should become clearer below.

7. James Coleman, *Foundations of Social Theory* (Cambridge, MA: Harvard University Press, 1990), 302.

8. Although, as we will see, a large majority of people must know each other for norms to develop in the first place.

9. Coleman, *Foundations of Social Theory*, 318–20.

10. See Margaret Levi, "Social and Unsocial Capital: A Review Essay of Robert Putnam's *Making Democracy Work*," *Politics and Society* 24 (March 1996): 45–55.

11. For some relevant work on corruption, see Seymour Martin Lipset and Gabriel Lenz, "Corruption, Culture and Markets," in Lawrence Harrison and Samuel Huntington, eds., *Culture Matters* (New York: Basic Books, 2000), 112–24.

12. See Michael Woolcock, "Social Capital and Economic Development: Toward a Theoretical Synthesis and Policy Framework," *Theory and Society* 27 (April 1998): 167–72.

13. This may still be a very important concept for democracy. Coleman himself tells of the formation of protest groups in Korea out of study groups that are in turn formed out of small communities or church groups (see Coleman, *Foundations of Social Theory*, 303). Likewise, it was this kind of interconnection among groups that Lipset et al. used to explain democracy in the ITU in *Union Democracy*, as detailed in chapter 2.

14. Robert Putnam, *Making Democracy Work* (Princeton: Princeton University Press, 1993), 173–74.

15. Putnam's theoretical arsenal seems to rely heavily on the kinds of sanctions available to communities that are relatively closed. This is of little help in explaining society-level interactions with unfamiliar citizens.

16. Levi, "Social and Unsocial Capital," 47–48.

17. Some evidence of the value of projections comes from a study of cooperators and defectors by Orbell and Dawes that found that cooperators were more likely to participate in games than defectors, because they were more likely to expect cooperation than defectors; that is, they projected their cooperative nature onto others (John M. Orbell and Robyn M. Dawes, "Social Welfare, Cooperators' Advantage, and the Option of Not Playing the Game," *American Sociological Review* 58 (December 1993): 787–800.

18. Indeed, the relationship between our beliefs in general about people and our actions is not well understood. The assumption that beliefs learned in one setting will transfer to other settings is not well founded. Particular beliefs formed within a group may be based on an us/them distinction—trust within the group but not of those outside it. These particular beliefs are unlikely to translate into general ones, nor do general beliefs often translate into particularized actions. Orbell, Dawes, and Schwartz-Shea report that, although both men and women believe that women are more likely to cooperate in general, neither sex, when confronted with actual people in an experimental design, actually judged that the women in the experiment would be more likely to

cooperate. Thus general beliefs manifestly did not translate into particular beliefs or actions. See John Orbell, Robyn Dawes, and Peregrine Schwartz-Shea, "Trust, Social Categories, and Individuals: The Case of Gender," *Motivation and Emotion* 18:2 (1994): 109–28.

19. Russell Hardin, "Do We Want Trust in Government?" in Mark E. Warren, ed., *Democracy and Trust* (Cambridge, UK: Cambridge University Press, 1999), 26.

20. Toshio Yamagishi and Midori Yamagishi, "Trust and Commitment in the United States and Japan," *Motivation and Emotion* 18:2 (1994): 136. This definition of trust implies that it is proportionately more important in situations where there is less social capital. That is, social capital reduces the need for trust, because it provides more "available information," reducing the risk involved in transactions. Yamagishi and Yamagishi distinguish between knowledge-based trust and general trust, the former being more applicable to conditions of social capital—where people and reputations are known—and the latter more applicable to conditions of social uncertainty. Evidence that these are in fact distinctive types of trust comes from the very low correlation they find between them in their samples of U.S. and Japanese general populations and students. (The highest r is 0.22, the lowest, 0.00. See 153).

21. We consider this a form of trust, not simply an expectation, because it is in the interests of both winners and losers that the democratic system be maintained; this is true because the state of being a winner or loser is subject to frequent change in a democracy.

22. Levi, "Unsocial Capital," 51.

23. Edward Muller and Mitchell Seligson, for example, found in a survey of twenty-five countries that long-term continuous democracy spurred greater levels of interpersonal trust. See "Civic Culture and Democracy," *American Political Science Review* 88 (September 1994): 645.

24. John A. Booth and Patricia Bayer Richard, "Civil Society and Political Context in Central America," *American Behavioral Scientist* 42 (September 1998): 33–46.

25. Ibid., 39.

26. Uslaner, "Social Capital, Television, and the 'Mean World,'" 459.

27. See Dietland Stolle, "Bowling Together, Bowling Alone: The Development of Generalized Trust in Voluntary Associations," *Political Psychology* 19 (September 1998): 497–525. In contrast, J. Brehm and W. Rahn find a significant effect of associationalism on trust in the United States. However, their evidence suggests a mixed model, with bottom-up trust rivaled by an even more pronounced effect of top-down trust as measured by a "confidence in institutions" metric. The standardized coefficients suggest that confidence in institutions has four times the effect of civic engagement. See Brehm and Rahn, "Individual-Level Evidence for the Causes and Consequences of Social Capital," *American Journal of Political Science* 41 (July 1997): 999–1023.

28. Ronald Inglehart, "Trust, Well-Being and Democracy," in Warren, ed., *Democracy and Trust*, 94, 111. In Inglehart's parsimonious model, three variables explain 86 percent of the variance in stability of democracy: subjective well-being, trust, and gross domestic product (GDP) per capita.

29. About 31 percent of the variance in interpersonal trust is explained by "years of continuous democracy." Conversely, the effect of interpersonal trust

on democracy is small and statistically insignificant (Muller and Seligson, "Civic Culture and Democracy," 642, 645).

30. Orlando Patterson, "Liberty against the Democratic State," in Warren, ed., *Democracy and Trust,* 191. As Patterson notes, minority status per se cannot explain trust, because Jews have consistently been among the most trusting Americans and have really bucked the trend toward decline, remaining trusting over time.

31. Theda Skocpol has argued that both top-down and bottom-up explanations of civil society formation explain the high levels of associationalism in the early United States. See "A Nation of Organizers: The Institutional Origins of Civic Voluntarism in the United States," *American Political Science Review* 94 (September 2000): 527–46.

32. This theory can be traced to Edward Banfield's classic study of Italy, *The Moral Basis of a Backward Society* (New York: Free Press, 1958).

33. Inglehart, "Trust, Well-Being and Democracy," 94 (see table).

34. Uslaner, "Social Capital, Television, and the 'Mean World,'" 452. Obviously, intranational studies of this sort control for polity-level effects, which means that even given a particular level of democracy, income and education have an impact on the level of trust.

35. Orlando Patterson, "Liberty against the Democratic State," 188.

36. This data is available through the Roper Center at www.ropercenter. uconn.edu (study #USMISC2000-SOCCA). The study was designed by the Saguaro Seminar at Harvard University. For the full regression, see the appendix to this chapter.

37. Patterson, "Liberty against the Democratic State," 186.

38. It should be noted in this regard that the scholarly debate over the effects of television remain inconclusive precisely because of the socialization argument. While Uslaner finds that baby boomers have eliminated the socialization effects of television in the most recent period, his larger argument is that optimism or pessimism, not television, conditions trust and participation. It is not possible, however, to control for the childhood effects of television on the socialization process—that is, on the evolution of optimistic or pessimistic outlooks today.

39. See Peter B. Evans, Dietrich Rueschmeyer, and Theda Skocpol, eds., *Bringing the State Back In* (New York: Cambridge University Press, 1985).

40. An interesting case study that relates more to political culture than to trust but raises the issue of elite-mass interactions is Honduras. As reported by Muller and Seligson, support among the (urban) public for gradual reform was about 85 percent at the time of their study (Muller and Seligson, "Civic Culture and Democracy," 647). This was the highest level among all countries in their sample, even though Honduras had the highest levels of income inequality as well. Why? Culture? Socialization? State action? None are particularly convincing.

41. Kornhauser, *The Politics of Mass Society.*

42. Dietland Stolle and Thomas Rochon, "Are All Associations Alike?" *American Behavioral Scientist* 42 (September 1998): 47–65.

43. Stolle and Rochon themselves define *social capital* as political action by individual members. But this is human capital as we have described it. While

we generally dissent from the uses to which these authors put the term *social capital,* the data speak for themselves. The average impact on political action (human capital) of belonging to an association is an increase of 73.4 percent. The impact on the next most affected variable, a social capital measure, is 30.7 percent.

44. Booth and Richard, "Civil Society and Political Context," 49. Almond and Verba demonstrated that although all associations have an impact on political attitudes, "political organizations yield a larger political 'dividend' than do nonpolitical organizations" (see Gabriel A. Almond and Sidney Verba, *The Civic Culture: Political Attitudes and Democracy in Five Nations* (Princeton: Princeton University Press, 1963), 265). A dissent from our disparaging treatment of recreational groups can be found in Eric M. Uslaner, "Democracy and Social Capital," in Warren, ed., *Democracy and Trust,* 121–50. Uslaner argues that the kinds of norms governing competition and cooperation on the field are very similar to the norms of democratic competition and that the affinity between recreational groups and political participation is more, not less, pronounced. Wallerstein noted some years ago that in many African countries, sports clubs were often composed of the highly educated because European sports like soccer were introduced into elite schools first during the colonial period. Thus the Rhodes-style scholar-athlete was an important figure in Africa, and sports clubs were important arenas of elite interaction where politically relevant social capital was fostered. See Wallerstein, *The Road to Independence,* 90.

45. Booth and Richard, "Civil Society and Political Context," 33–46; Booth and Richard, "Civil Society, Political Capital and Democratization in Central America," *Journal of Politics* 60 (August 1998): 780–800.

46. Booth and Richard, "Civil Society, Political Capital and Democratization," 791.

47. See Uslaner, "Democracy and Social Capital," 127–28.

48. James L. Gibson, "Social Networks, Civil Society and the Prospects for Consolidating Russia's Democratic Transition," *American Journal of Political Science* 45 (January 2001): 64.

49. Booth and Richard, "Civil Society, Political Capital and Democratization," 790. In their regression analysis, civil society accounts for less than 1 percent of the variance in levels of interpersonal trust.

50. Other scholars associated with mass theory include Hannah Arendt, Sigmund Neumann, and Emil Lederer. For a critical assessment of each of these theorists vis-à-vis Weimar Germany, see Bernt Hagtvet, "The Theory of Mass Society and the Collapse of the Weimar Republic: A Re-examination," in Stein Ugelvik, Bernt Hagtvet, and Jan Peter Myklebust, eds., *Who Were the Fascists?* (Bergen, Norway: Universitetsforlaget, 1980), 66–117.

51. William Kornhauser, *The Politics of Mass Society,* 32.

52. Ibid., 44.

53. Ibid., 100.

54. For related work on the concept of elite-mass interactions in the specific realm of political parties, see Samuel J. Eldersveld, *Political Parties: A Behavioral Analysis* (Chicago: Rand McNally, 1964).

55. To clarify, Kornhauser's conception actually depends on a minimum of associationalism. Indeed, some organization—such as the Nazi party—that can

channel information between masses and elites is essential to the existence of totalitarianism. However, Kornhauser contended that a mass society creates the *conditions for totalitarianism;* the Nazi party could succeed in circumstances of mass deprivation because of the failures of and decline of associations in Weimar.

56. Kornhauser, *The Politics of Mass Society.*

57. Sheri Berman, "Civil Society and the Collapse of the Weimar Republic," *World Politics* 49 (April 1997): 401–29.

58. Hagtvet, "The Theory of Mass Society and the Collapse of the Weimar Republic," 104 (emphasis in original).

59. Confirmation of this point comes from the political histories of neighboring Canadian provinces Alberta and Saskatchewan. Very similar economic and political conditions existed in both provinces. A high degree of participation in secondary associations facilitated the rise of populist movements in both. But in Alberta the populist movement that came to power became exclusionary and anti-Semitic; in Saskatchewan it was an inclusionary social democratic movement. See Lipset, *Agrarian Socialism.*

60. Berman, "Civil Society and the Collapse of the Weimar Republic," 424.

61. Not coincidentally, the distinction between the party and the bureaucracy is ambiguous in one-party states such as, until 2000, Mexico. Where the party and the state are as entangled as the PRI and the Mexican state have been historically, the potential for state domination of civil society through the party is high, and the result is often a kind of corporatism that is highly detrimental to democracy.

62. Thomas Ertman, "Democracy and Dictatorship in Interwar Western Europe Revisited," *World Politics* 50 (April 1998): 499.

63. Marina Ottaway and Theresa Chung, "Toward a New Paradigm," *Journal of Democracy* 10 (October 1999): 106–9.

64. John D. Holm, Patrick Molutsi, and Gloria Somolekae, "The Development of Civil Society in a Democratic State: The Botswana Model," *African Studies Review* 39 (September 1996): 56.

65. See Putnam, *Making Democracy Work.*

66. Michael W. Foley and Bob Edwards, "The Paradox of Civil Society," *Journal of Democracy* 7 (July 1996): 40.

67. Quality is also determined by the organizational nature and strategic purpose of the associations that constitute civil society.

CHAPTER 5

1. Well, virtually. Edward Muller has suggested in different studies that the relationship between GDP per capita and democracy is spurious, because GDP per capita is just a proxy for income inequality. See Muller and Seligson, "Civic Culture and Democracy: The Question of Causal Relationships," and Muller, "Economic Determinants of Democracy," *American Sociological Review* 60 (December 1995): 966.

2. Seymour Martin Lipset, "Some Social Requisites of Democracy," *American Political Science Review* 53 (1959): 56. Larry Diamond has exhaustively reviewed the pre-1992 literature on this topic in "Economic Development and Democracy Reconsidered," and found the relationship to be robust. The essay is in Diamond and Marks, eds., *Reexamining Democracy,* 93–139.

3. Przeworski et al., "What Makes Democracies Endure?" 41. The other two studies from 1996 are Robert J. Barro, "Determinants of Economic Growth," National Bureau of Economic Research working paper 5698, August 1996; and John B. Londregan and Keith T. Poole, "Does High Income Promote Democracy?" *World Politics*, 49 (October 1996). Also see Henry Rowen, "The Tide Underneath the 'Third Wave,'" which was actually published earlier, in *Journal of Democracy* 6 (1995): 52–64.

4. The exact threshold is open to debate, though the basic differences in figures result from using different measures to calculate GDP per capita.

5. Robert J. Barro, *Determinants of Economic Growth: A Cross-Country Empirical Study* (Cambridge, MA: MIT Press, 1997), 52.

6. The standardized coefficient is followed by the standard error in parentheses.

7. Gastil's index does not start until 1972, so Bollen's is used prior to this.

8. It is reasonable because, theoretically, there should be some time lag between the achievement of an income level and resultant democratization. It is arbitrary because we have no idea how long the lag is. But it is problematic because we should anticipate that trends in the variable may be as important as thresholds.

9. Furthermore, in an expanded model, Barro included an additional variable for prior democracy at ten years previous. This variable proved small and insignificant. This means that the key explanatory variable in the base model is of use in explaining the dependent variable only within a short interval. Does this imply that behaviors are learned and unlearned in a very short time? Or that experience with democracy tends to have as much of a solidifying as an undermining effect on democracy's chances?

10. Londregan and Poole, "Does High Income Promote Democracy?" 20.

11. Other studies have shown that the effects are much more apparent in Europe. Burkhart and Lewis-Beck found that countries in the "core" (using world systems theory terminology) were more affected by economic development than countries in the periphery, though the differences were not huge. The core countries are primarily Europe and the English-speaking settler colonies (plus Japan). See Ross Burkhart and Michael Lewis-Beck, "Comparative Democracy: The Economic Development Thesis," *American Political Science Review* 88 (December 1994): 903–10. Henry S. Rowen also found that the effects were weaker but still significant when Europe was excluded from the analysis. Rowen's 1996 cross-national survey of the relationship between income and freedom, using the Freedom House score of civil liberties and political rights, found that "the more [economic] means people acquire, the more likely they are to want a say in making the rules under which they live; the upshot is a wider domain of political freedom." Of the twenty-eight nations with annual per-capita GDPs exceeding $8,000 in 1992, only Singapore was "less than wholly free." See Rowen, "The Tide underneath the Third Wave," in Larry Diamond and Marc Plattner, eds., *The Global Resurgence of Democracy* (Baltimore: Johns Hopkins University Press, 1996), 307–19, esp. 308.

12. Current growth is negative, but the error is large in relation to the coefficient: –0.23 (0.16). Lagged growth is positive, but the error term is bigger than the coefficient: 0.003 (0.156). This contrasts with Przeworski et al.'s 1996 study

of economic growth rates, which found that democracies were more than twice as likely to survive when growth was positive than negative. The evidence on growth seems inconclusive.

It is also interesting that Linz's parliamentary effect is held not to be very large, though it is significant. A country with a coefficient of 0 would move to 1.45 with a parliamentary system. Londregan and Poole point out that, on the Gurr scale, a parliamentary system is automatically more democratic according to the classification rules. But this is in fact incorrect. The Gurr scale awards more points to presidential systems and *less* to parliamentary ones because presidents are weaker executives than prime ministers. The 1.45 jump is therefore more, not less, impressive and suggests there are benefits to a parliamentary system. See Londregan and Poole, "Does High Income Promote Democracy?" 19–20.

13. Londregan and Poole, "Does High Income Promote Democracy?" 22–23.

14. Different GDP-per-capita lags could be used in tandem with growth rates to see if there is a dynamic relationship between these variables as well.

15. Przeworski et al., "What Makes Democracies Endure?" 41. In fact, Przeworski argues elsewhere that income is not related to the transition to democracy at all. See Przeworski and Fernando Limongi, "Modernization: Theories and Facts," *World Politics* 49:2 (1997): 155–83.

16. Again, this reflects the fundamental difference in perspective between Przeworski and his collaborators on one hand and Lipset and others on the other: Przeworski does not believe that democratization produces democracy, but rather, if anything, the reverse. There is therefore no overriding purpose to studying democratization. In our opposing view, of course, this is an assumption that should be judged empirically.

17. We are indebted to Larry Diamond for pointing this out.

18. It is too early to say whether this result will hold. If it does, this "new historical period" could be one in which strong international pressures do turn out to play a more significant role than in the past.

19. Calculations are based on information contained in the World Bank, *World Development Report 1992* (Oxford, UK: Oxford University Press, 1992), and *World Development Report 2000–2001* (New York: Oxford University Press, 2000); Freedom House, *Freedom in the World* (Piscataway, NJ: Transaction, 1991, 1992, 2001); and Aili Piano and Arch Puddington, "Gains Offset Losses," *Journal of Democracy* 12 (January 2001): 90–91.

20. Seymour Martin Lipset, "Some Social Requisites of Democracy: Economic Development and Political Legitimacy," *American Political Science Review* 53 (March 1959), 75.

21. Rowen had to omit the Hindu civilization because there were not enough countries to permit statistical analysis.

22. Rowen, "The Tide," 311.

23. Lipset originally argued in *Political Man* that increased literacy, material security, and a burgeoning middle class were all products of a modernization process that resulted in greater support for democracy. See chapter 2 of *Political Man*.

24. Przeworski and Limongi, "Modernization: Theories and Facts."

25. Przeworski and Limongi seem to think that this case distribution bolsters their argument, since it demonstrates that few authoritarian governments

actually do develop, which in turn suggests that most development takes place under democracies.

26. Przeworski and Limongi, "Modernization," 163.

27. The rational choice school uses economic models and the key assumption of economists—that individuals and groups are self-interested utility maximizers—to predict political outcomes.

28. Actually, in an unpublished manuscript, Przeworski does pay attention to the distribution of income, but mainly insofar as it alters thresholds for the theory. The main argument still rests primarily on level of GDP per capita. See Adam Przeworski, "Democracy as an Equilibrium" (Department of Politics, New York University, 2001).

29. Barro, *Determinants of Economic Growth*, 66.

30. Londregan and Poole, "Does High Income Promote Democracy?"

31. Barro, *Determinants of Economic Growth*, 63.

32. It is not possible to completely separate economy and culture; in this regard, it is worth noting that European capitalism was associated with a post-feudal social structure, monarchy, powerful churches, and so forth. These together shaped the experience of capitalism in Europe.

33. It should be noted, though we will not discuss it here, that European countries are also quite varied in their histories of feudalism, perhaps partly reflected in their differential patterns of capitalism.

34. These ideas are developed in Milton Friedman, *Capitalism and Freedom* (Chicago: University of Chicago Press, 1962), esp. 10; and Friedrich A. Hayek, *The Road to Serfdom* (1944; repr., Chicago: University of Chicago Press, 1994).

35. See Goran Therborn, "The Rule of Capital and the Rise of Democracy," *New Left Review* 103 (May–June 1977), and Dietrich Rueschemeyer, Evelyne Huber Stephens, and John D. Stephens, *Capitalist Development and Democracy* (Chicago: University of Chicago Press, 1992).

36. Huber, Rueschemeyer, and Stephens, "The Impact of Economic Development on Democracy," *Journal of Economic Perspectives*, 7 (Summer 1993): 74–75.

37. Other recent critiques of an overemphasis on the role of the working class include Thomas Ertman's incisive review of the literature in "Democracy and Dictatorship in Interwar Europe Revisited" *World Politics* 50 (April 1998): 475–505; and Ruth B. Collier, *Paths toward Democracy* (Cambridge, UK: Cambridge University Press, 1999).

38. From a cultural or intellectual point of view, the bourgeoisie, while in practice sometimes limiting democracy's applicability, still contributed in important ways to the development of modern democracy. Bourgeois democracy was in an important sense meritocratic. While social mobility was low, it was nevertheless true that bourgeois democracy did not exclude any individual male in principle who could, for example, meet some minimum income threshold. The aristocratic version of contestation, however, was rooted in ascription. The gradual shift from ascription to achievement that was influenced by the bourgeoisie has to be seen as a boon to democracy and one that ultimately derives from liberalism.

39. There is wide agreement on this point across the political spectrum. Samuel Bowles and Herbert Gintis—who argue, contrary to us, that democracy

and capitalism are inherently contradictory—still note: "The road from the eighteenth-century Rights of Man, which excluded not only women but most people of color as well, to the late twentieth-century civil rights movements, feminism, and the right to a job has been a torturous one, but the route was prefigured in the discourses of eighteenth-century liberalism" (Bowles and Gintis, *Democracy and Capitalism* [New York: Basic Books, 1986], 3–4). Even Goran Therborn, writing from a Marxist perspective that negates political culture, concludes that capitalism is structurally inclined to create a disunified capitalist class, political contestation, and thus a door through which an organized working class may struggle to fit. Indeed, the tendency of capitalism to create contestation is a central part of Therborn's overall argument explaining the positive relationship between democracy and capitalism (Therborn, "The Rule of Capital and the Rise of Democracy," esp. 32–33). The relative benefits of following a path from contestation to participation, rather than the other way around, are affirmed by Michael Bratton and Nicolas van de Walle's work on Africa. See Bratton and van de Walle, *Democratic Experiments in Africa* (Cambridge, UK: Cambridge University Press, 1997), esp. 273.

40. Gregory Luebbert, "Social Foundations of Political Order in Interwar Europe," 456. This does not mean that all countries with weak liberal parties became fascist; the "social democracies" of Scandinavia maintained democracy in the interwar period. What we can say is that the earliest democratizing countries (prior to World War I) were those where the liberals were a strong force. Furthermore, the importance of the bourgeois liberals can be extended to the social democracies in the sense that in many of these states, liberals mobilized the agrarian proletariat and thus (indirectly) paved the way for social democracy by closing off this option for social democratic parties. Where this option was left open, the result was fascism. Clearly, however, the bourgeoisie was not a uniform defender of democracy, as the cases of Finland, Austria, and Hungary make clear.

41. Barrington Moore, *Social Origins of Dictatorship and Democracy: Lord and Peasant in the Making of the Modern World* (Boston: Beacon Press, 1966), 30.

42. See Lipset, Trow, and Coleman, *Union Democracy* on this point.

43. See Juan Linz, "The Breakdown of Democracy in Spain," in Linz and Stepan, eds., *Breakdown of Democratic Regimes*, 142–215 (quote on 179).

44. Seymour Martin Lipset, *Political Man*, chapter 4, esp. 89–90.

45. See Rueschemeyer, Stephens, and Stephens, *Capitalist Development and Democracy*.

46. Skocpol's review of Moore originally appeared in *Politics and Society* in 1973, but is now the first chapter of her book, *Social Revolutions in the Modern World* (Cambridge, UK: Cambridge University Press, 1994), 25–54.

47. Skocpol, *Social Revolutions in the Modern World*, 154.

48. For a masterful interpretation of Chilean democratization and a critique of Moore and his followers, see J. Samuel Valenzuela, "Class Relations and Democratization: A Reassessment of Barrington Moore's Model," in Miguel Angel Centeno and Fernando Lopez-Alves, eds., *The Other Mirror: Grand Theory through the Lens of Latin America* (Princeton: Princeton University Press, 2000), 240–86.

49. The struggle for power among strong groups led to the creation of systems allowing for coexistence, among them a more liberal political system. As Lipset has written, "universal suffrage and freedom of organization and opposition developed in many countries either as concessions to the established strength of the lower classes, or as means of controlling them—a tactic advocated and used by such sophisticated conservatives as Disraeli and Bismarck" (Lipset, *Political Man*, 123).

50. Moore, *The Social Origins of Dictatorship and Democracy*, 420.

51. C. Wright Mills has described early American society with a Jeffersonian flourish:

> The most important single fact about the society of small entrepreneurs was that a substantial proportion of the people owned the property with which they worked. Here the middle class was so broad a stratum and of such economic weight that even by the standards of the statistician the society as a whole was a middle-class society: perhaps four-fifths of the free people who worked owned property. . . . [T]his world did in reality contain propertyless people, but there was so much movement in and out of the petty-bourgeois level of farmers that it appeared that they need not remain propertyless for long. . . . In owning land, the small entrepreneur owned the sphere of his own work, and because he owned it, he was independent.
>
> (Mills, *White Collar* [New York: Oxford University Press, 1953], 7–9).

52. It was this fact that brought Marx to the conclusion that socialism in the United States would first appear in the guise of a pro-capitalist movement, with the mythic ideal of the self-sufficient capitalist farmer at its core. See Michael Harrington's discussion of Marx's thoughts on the United States in Harrington, *Socialism* (New York: Bantam Books, 1972), esp. 131–61.

53. Rueschemeyer, Stephens, and Stephens emphasize the importance of relatively egalitarian land distribution in these countries (*Capitalist Development and Democracy*, 140).

54. This point was made by a former president of Argentina and acute observer of both Latin and North America, Domingo Sarmiento, who believed that the inegalitarian pattern of land distribution in Latin America as compared to North America was a major factor that explained the politicoeconomic differences between the two regions. See Domingo F. Sarmiento, *Estados Unidos* (Buenos Aires: Colección Buen Aire, Emecé Editores, 1942).

55. Carlos Waisman, "Capitalism, the Market and Democracy," in Diamond and Marks, eds., *Reexamining Democracy*, 140–55.

56. Lipset originally argued that if too severe, income inequality could have negative psychological consequences for democracy:

> The poorer a country and the lower the absolute standard of living of the lower classes, the greater the pressure on the upper strata to treat the lower as vulgar, innately inferior, a lower caste beyond the pale of human society . . . consequently, the upper strata in such a situation tend to regard political rights for the lower strata, particularly the right to share power, as essentially absurd and immoral. The upper strata not only resist democracy

themselves; their often arrogant political behavior serves to intensify extremist reactions on the part of the lower classes.

(Political Man, 51).

57. Actually, Przeworski argues, from a very different perspective, that income inequality may affect the degree to which rational actors accept electoral results. Because the poor in relatively egalitarian societies have more to lose, they are more likely to accept electoral results that are contrary to their interests (than to take up arms against democracy). This argument, however, does not really eliminate the theoretical debate over whether it is access to some minimum income or inequality per se that really matters. On one hand, the poor in a very rich country could probably stand to see the incomes of the wealthy increase without their own incomes falling and would still have an incentive to participate in democracy. On the other hand, what often matters are perceptions, and income inequality can make people *feel* poorer even when they are not. Przeworski's most sophisticated rational choice analysis of democracy is in "Why Democracy Survives in Affluent Societies"; the discussion of income inequality is on 17–19.

58. This is an empirical question, though not necessarily a simple one to investigate. The argument about income inequality stems from the minimalist definition of democracy—in particular, contested elections. Contestation that is unduly influenced by economically powerful interests in society may well be inadequate. One can imagine a contested election between two oligarchs who differ on abortion rights but have no substantive programs for the poor nor advocate lowering taxes on the wealthy. The election is contested on the social dimension but not adequately on the economic dimension. The same would be true if the positions were reversed—two candidates who differ on abortion but agree that the wealthy should be taxed exorbitantly and all the revenue redistributed to the poor.

59. See Lipset, Trow, and Coleman, *Union Democracy.*

60. This was well understood by Marx, who believed that the seeds of the proletarian revolution were planted by the organization of the bourgeois capitalist system. It was capitalism that created the working class: "Large-scale industry concentrates in one place a crowd of people unknown to one another. . . . Economic conditions had first transformed the mass of the people of the country into workers. The domination of capital has created for this mass a common situation, common interests. This mass is already a class as against capital, but not yet for itself. In this struggle, of which we have noted only a few phases, this mass becomes united, and constitutes itself as a class for itself" (quoted in Seymour Martin Lipset and Reinhard Bendix, "Karl Marx's Theory of Social Classes," in Seymour Martin Lipset and Reinhard Bendix, eds., *Class, Status and Power* (New York: Free Press, 1953), 31.

61. Francis Fukuyama, *The End of History and the Last Man* (New York: Free Press, 1992).

62. Lipset, *Political Man,* chapter 2.

63. Kenneth Bollen, "Political Democracy and the Timing of Development," *American Sociological Review* 44 (August 1979): 572–87.

64. We have some reservations about Vanhanen's operationalization of variables, however, particularly the index of democracy, which is measured in

part by the voter participation rate. See Tatu Vanhanen, *Prospects of Democracy* (London: Routledge, 1997), esp. 67–98.

65. Larry Diamond, "Economic Development and Democracy Reconsidered," in Diamond and Marks, eds., *Reexamining Democracy*, 107.

66. See for example, Edward N. Muller, "Economic Determinants of Democracy," 966. Muller and Seligson also report a negative correlation between income inequality and democracy for a smaller sample in "Civic Culture and Democracy." The latter study—though convincing, if of limited generalizability—is problematic in that it finds a negative, statistically insignificant relationship between GDP per capita and democracy, which, as noted above, is refuted by most other studies. Muller's work has been challenged by Kenneth Bollen and Robert Jackson in "Income Inequality and Democratization Revisited: Comment on Muller," *American Sociological Review* 6 (December 1995): 987.

67. World Bank, *World Development Report 2000–2001* (New York: Oxford University Press, 2000), 285.

68. Rowen, "The Tide," 312. Rowen asserts that increasing the level of education will spread the proliferation of democracy and that it is a better predictor than income. In projecting democracy in the year 2020, Rowen looks at education growth of 6.6 percent and income at 3 percent and says that the combined total will increase the number of "free" countries from sixty-one in 1990 to seventy-five in 2020. Freedom House defines *free* more stringently than as consisting only of electoral democracy.

69. Alex Inkeles and David H. Smith, *Becoming Modern: Individual Change in Six Developing Countries* (Cambridge, MA: Harvard University Press, 1974), 133.

70. Francis Fukuyama, *The End of History and the Last Man*; and "Capitalism and Democracy: The Missing Link," *Journal of Democracy* 3 (July 1992).

71. Larry Diamond, *Developing Democracy* (Baltimore: Johns Hopkins University Press, 1999), 199.

72. Russell Farnen and Jos Meloen, *Democracy, Authoritarianism and Education: A Cross-National Empirical Survey* (New York: St. Martin's Press, 2000), esp. chapter 9; quote on 137.

73. Norman H. Nie, Jane Junn, and Kenneth Stehlik-Barry, *Education and Democratic Citizenship in America* (Chicago: University of Chicago Press, 1996).

CHAPTER 6

1. Lipset, *Political Man*, 50.

2. Huntington, *The Third Wave*, 17–21; Juan J. Linz, "Crisis, Breakdown, and Reequilibration," in Juan Linz and Alfred Stepan, eds., *The Breakdown of Democratic Regimes: Crisis, Breakdown and Reequilibrium* (Baltimore: Johns Hopkins University Press, 1978), 3–124.

3. Huntington, *The Third Wave*.

4. Piano and Puddington, "Gains Offset Losses," 89.

5. Lipset, Trow, and Coleman, *Union Democracy*.

6. Muller, "Economic Determinants," 976–77; Barro found that this relationship was not statistically significant, but he suggests that it may be mediated through effects on other variables, such as standard of living. See Barro, *Determinants of Economic Growth*, 70, 75–76.

7. Myron Weiner, "Empirical Democratic Theory," in Myron Weiner and Ergun Ozbunden, eds., *Competitive Elections in Developing Countries* (Durham, NC: Duke University Press, 1987), 20. Also see Barro, *Determinants of Growth,* and Lipset, Seong, and Torres, "A Comparative Analysis of the Social Requisites of Democracy."

8. Weiner, "Empirical Democratic Theory," 20.

9. Dahl, *Polyarchy,* 36–40.

10. Myron Weiner, "Institution Building in South Asia," in Robert A. Scalapino, Seizaburo Sato, and Jusuf Wanandi, eds., *Asian Political Institutionalization* (Berkeley: Institute of East Asian Studies, University of California, 1986). Pakistan was also poorer and predominantly Muslim in comparison with India.

11. Carl Stone, *Class, State and Democracy in Jamaica* (New York: Praeger, 1986), 22. It must be noted, however, that Jamaica is in many ways a less than exemplary model of a formerly colonial democracy. Gang-related violence is interwoven with political competition in ways that may undermine the fairness of electoral activity. See, for example, "Burning," *The Economist,* July 12, 2001.

12. Larry Diamond, "Introduction," in Diamond, Juan Linz, and Seymour Martin Lipset, eds., *Democracy in Developing Countries: Africa* (Boulder, CO: Lynne Rienner Publishers, 1988), 9. This section on Africa owes much to Larry Diamond's work. For more on the deleterious divide-and-rule tactics of the British in Africa, see Diamond, "Nigeria: Pluralism, Statism, and the Struggle for Democracy," in Diamond, Linz, and Lipset, eds., *Democracy in Developing Countries: Africa,* 33–91; and Diamond, *Class, Ethnicity and Democracy in Nigeria: The Failure of the First Republic* (Basingstoke, UK: Macmillan, 1988).

13. William Tordoff, *Government and Politics in Africa* (Bloomington: Indiana University Press, 1984), 69–70.

14. Bratton and van de Walle, *Democratic Experiments in Africa,* esp. 172–75.

15. Samuel Huntington, *Political Order in Changing Societies* (New Haven: Yale University Press, 1968).

16. Simon Kuznets, *Modern Economic Growth: Rate Structure and Spread* (New Haven: Yale University Press, 1966), 64–65.

17. Lipset, *Political Man;* see also Lipset, "Socialism—Left and Right, East and West," *Confluence* 7 (Summer 1958): 173–92; Val Lorwin, "Working Class Politics and Economic Development in Western Europe," *American Historical Review* 63 (January 1958): 338–51, esp. 350; Mancur Olson, Jr., "Rapid Growth as a Destabilizing Force," *Journal of Economic History* 23 (December 1963): 529–52.

18. Colin Clark, *The Conditions of Economic Progress* (London: Macmillan, 1951), 421.

19. See Ossip Flechtheim, *Die KPD in der Weimarer Republik* (Offenbach am Main, Germany: Bollwerk-Verlag Karl Drott, 1948), 213–14.

20. Summary of the main thesis of Edward Bull, "Die Entwicklung der Arbeiterbewegung in den drei skandiavshen Landern," *Archiv fur die Geschichte der Sozialimus und der Arbeiterbewegung* 10 (1922), in Stein Rokkan and Henry Valen, "Parties, Elections and Behavior in the Northern Countries: A Review of Recent Research," in Otto Stammer, ed., *Politische Forschung* (Köln: Westdeutscher Verlag, 1960), 110; see also Walter Galenson, "Scandinavia," in Galenson, ed., *Comparative Labor Movements* (New York: Prentice-Hall, 1952).

21. Przeworski et al., "What Makes Democracies Endure?" 42. The evidence on growth is not conclusive. Londregan and Poole's 1996 study, "Does High Income Promote Democracy?" (see our discussion in chapter 5) found no statistically significant effect of growth on democracy. Even if we accepted this study, however, it would seem that the negative consequences of growth in the current era are hard to find.

22. Bollen, "Political Democracy and the Timing of Development," 572–87.

CHAPTER 7

1. Lee Kuan Yew, "Is Confucianism Dead?" in "The New Asia," special issue, *Newsweek*, August 2000, 49. Lee writes, in a dizzying display of having one's cake and eating it too, "There is no reason to abandon our values. Confucianism must adjust and change with changing structures of the economy and society," and, in the same article, "The process of opening up may make our society more unruly. The gravest challenge will be to protect the values we cherish. We can allow a bohemian quarter where creative people do their thing, but our whole city does not need to be that way." Lee appears to recognize that the new economy may require political changes that the old economy did not. Yet he still seems to think these nefarious "values" can be quarantined while Asian values persist unscathed in the larger polity.

2. Barro, *Determinants of Economic Growth*, 77; Rowen, "The Tide," 311.

3. For more on this point, see Larry Diamond, "The Globalization of Democracy: Trends, Types, Causes and Prospects," in R. Slater, B. Schutz, and S. Dorr, eds., *Global Transformation and the Third World* (Boulder, CO: Lynne Rienner Publishers, 1992), 31–70.

4. Almond and Verba, *The Civic Culture*, 16–20. We discuss the civic culture in greater detail in the section of this chapter entitled "Excursis on the Democratic Culture."

5. Pierre Trudeau, "Some Obstacles to Democracy in Quebec," in M. Wade, ed., *Canadian Dualism* (Toronto, Ontario: University of Toronto Press, 1960), 240.

6. Mohamed Elhachmi Hamdi, "The Limits of the Western Model," *Journal of Democracy* (April 1996): 84.

7. A quote from a Taliban representative makes the point. In March 2001 the Taliban ordered the destruction of historic statues of the Buddha in Afghanistan, despite worldwide repudiation of these acts. In response to this criticism, the Taliban's information minister said, "The decision on the Buddhas was made according to Islamic rules. It was not done to insult any particular religion, but once an Islamic order is made it cannot be changed." That is, there is no room for negotiation within the Taliban version of Islam; thus, one principle anchor of democratic praxis is eliminated (statement reported in Pamela Constable, "Buddha's Rubble Marks a Turn for Taliban," *Washington Post*, March 20, 2001, A1).

8. Shmuel N. Eisenstadt, "The Protestant Ethic Theses in the Framework of Sociological Theory and Weber's Work," in Eisenstadt, ed., *The Protestant Ethic and Modernization: A Comparative View* (New York: Basic Books, 1968), 3–45.

9. Amartya Sen, "Democracy as a Universal Human Value," *Journal of Democracy* 10 (July 1999): 16.

10. Sen has expanded his critique of Asian values and defense of democracy on instrumental and constructive, as well as intrinsic, grounds, in *Development as Freedom* (New York: Alfred A. Knopf, 1999), esp. chapters 6 and 10; quote on 248.

11. Some would argue that it still has not. Surely, however, it has made strides in that direction.

12. Abdou Filali-Ansary, "Muslims and Democracy," *Journal of Democracy* 10 (July 1999): 30. This view is echoed by Alain Touraine, who writes, "The constantly repeated assertion that religions or certain religions—especially Islam—reject the separation of temporal and spiritual powers as a matter of principle is based on the unacceptable view that history is nothing more than a field for the realization of social, cultural, or political projects that have a metahistorical essence. We would do well to take a more cautious view and look at the historical conditions that allow the social order to be regarded as sacred, or, conversely, that allow the spiritual and the temporal to achieve a degree of relative autonomy" (Alain Touraine, *What Is Democracy?* trans. David Macey [Boulder, CO: Westview Press, 1997], 171).

13. Huntington, *The Third Wave*, 76.

14. Ibid., 77.

15. George Weigel, "Catholicism and Democracy: The Other Twentieth-Century Revolution," in Brad Roberts, ed., *New Democracies: Global Change and U.S. Policy* (Cambridge, MA: MIT Press, 1990), 17–37. The following outline is culled from Weigel's insightful essay—particularly 19–27, and to him we are indebted.

16. Thomas F. O'Dea, *Catholic Crisis* (Boston: Beacon Press, 1968), 112.

17. Ibid., 6.

18. Ibid., 25–27. This theological shift also paved the way for a revised relationship between Catholics and Jews. Under the leadership of Pope John Paul II, the Church accepted the continuity of the Covenant with the Jews.

19. Lipset made a similar point about the transformation of the labor movement's dogma over time: "The fact that the movement's ideology is democratic does not mean that its supporters actually understand the implications. The evidence seems to indicate that understanding of and adherence to these norms are highest among leaders and lowest among followers" (Lipset, *Political Man*, 123).

20. As an aside, it may be noted that Antonio Gramsci also recognized the multiple, independent, but intersecting layers that inhere in religious cultures. He wrote: "Every religion, even Catholicism . . . is in reality a multiplicity of distinct and often contradictory religions: there is one Catholicism for the peasants, one for women, and one for the intellectuals which is itself variegated and disconnected" (Gramsci quoted in Bocock, *Hegemony*, 88).

21. We would posit that values have indeed shifted in Quebec, the Netherlands, and Ireland, for example.

22. O'Dea, *Catholic Crisis*, 141.

23. Luis Pásara, "The Leftist Angels," in Alexander Wilde and Scott Mainwaring, eds., *The Progressive Church in Latin America* (Notre Dame, IN: University of Notre Dame, 1989), 279.

24. David Levine, *Popular Voices in Latin American Catholicism* (Princeton: Princeton University Press, 1992), 40.

25. Fukuyama, "Confucianism and Democracy," *Journal of Democracy* 6 (April 1995): 32.

26. Robert Bellah, *Tokugawa Religion: The Values of Pre-Industrial Japan* (Glencoe, IL: Free Press, 1957).

27. Robin Wright, "Two Visions of Reformation," *Journal of Democracy* 7 (April 1996): 65.

28. We realize that we are not being particularly careful to distinguish between religion and culture. Clearly religion is a subordinate category of culture but in many cases represents an entire culture unto itself. The literature tends to see defining characteristics of religions as defining characteristics of cultures as well (Weber's thesis clearly mixed the two). Of particular interest to Islam is the claim, put forward by Filali-Ansary ("Muslims and Democracy"), that there has never been a distinction comparable to that between "Christendom" and "Christianity" within Islam. In this sense, the culture of Islam and the religion have been considered equal, and this, however untrue in the past, serves to justify the claims of fundamentalist constituencies in modern Islamic societies.

29. Ibid., 75.

30. Quoted in Fareed Zakaria, "A Conversation with Lee Kuan Yew," *Foreign Affairs* (March–April 1994): 118.

31. Adam Przeworski, "Culture and Democracy," *World Culture Report: Culture, Creativity and Markets* (Paris: UNESCO, 1998), 127.

32. In fact, it is unclear whether Przeworski feels that Mill's position reflects his own or is still too "cultural." Przeworski seems not to believe in the importance of any values but then uses Mill to deflect those who do. This contradiction—"values are irrelevant" versus "values are relevant but subject to complete metamorphosis"—is left unresolved.

33. See Inglehart, *Modernization and Postmodernization*, 372–79.

34. Almond and Verba, *The Civic Culture*, 16–20.

35. Ibid., 30.

36. Ibid., 230–31.

37. Ibid., 114.

38. Ibid. See, for example, 164–65 regarding subjective competence.

39. Many of these criticisms can be found in the edited volume by Almond and Verba, *The Civic Culture Revisited* (Newbury Park: Sage Publications, 1989). In particular, the criticisms we mention here are captured in the chapters by Carole Pateman and Jerzy Wiatr.

40. Carole Pateman, "The Civic Culture: A Philosophic Critique," in Almond and Verba, eds. *Civic Culture Revisited*, 65.

41. James Gibson, "The Political Consequences of Intolerance: Cultural Conformity and Political Freedom," *American Political Science Review* 86 (June 1992): 340.

42. However, Almond and Verba tie their concept of moderation to a specific function in democracies; it is a pragmatic response to the need to balance parochialism and participation. This is quite different from the idea of moderation as a policy response to competing interests.

43. Przeworski, "Why Democracy Survives in Affluent Countries," 22. The evidence for this causal relationship is, according to a footnote in the manu-

script, that the rate of death for democracies falls as they get older. While this might seem to support a cultural view, it does not, according to Przeworski, because, if per-capita wealth is controlled for, the rate of death is constant over the life of the democracy. This is a curious defense of an argument that relies on economic thresholds. Above some point, one would really not expect the increase in life expectancy to be related to increases in GDP anymore. Even if GDP does not increase, it is in no one's interest to undermine democracy. Yet it appears that increases in wealth do continue to have an impact above the threshold. Does it become more and more rational to be a democrat the wealthier one gets?

44. The problem is particularly acute for dilemmas of collective action, among which we have included democracy. See chapter 8, on legitimacy. Many interactions in society can be modeled as modified prisoner's dilemmas. But the modification is important. Rather than knowing nothing about what the other player will do, we have a number of reasons to assume that the other player will act in a particular way. These assumptions can and do change, and this is ultimately where the significance of concepts like culture and legitimacy lie.

45. This is the major difference in the analysis of iterated behaviors, but another difference arises in one-shot games, in which cultural behaviors cannot converge toward rational behaviors over time. Many political situations are not iterated or, at the very least, allow for no reasonable expectation of iteration. In these cases, culturalists and rationalists may disagree over whether culture or self-interest is determinant of behaviors. Furthermore, because actions executed in the "meantime" or "short run" may have a critical impact on the long run (by taking societies down different roads to different critical junctures), culturalists and rational-choice scholars may come to quite different conclusions even about the long run.

46. Robert H. Bates, Rui J. P. De Figueiredo, Jr., and Barry Weingast, "The Politics of Interpretation: Rationality, Culture, and Transition," 26 (June 1998): 221–56.

47. Dennis Chong, "Rational Choice Theory's Mysterious Rivals," in Jeffrey Friedman, ed., *The Rational Choice Controversy* (New Haven: Yale University Press, 1996), 37–57. Bates et al. and Chong emphasize the endogeneity of value preferences and the usefulness of rational choice in this process of determination.

CHAPTER 8

1. Lipset, *Political Man*, chapter 3.

2. Diamond, *Developing Democracy*, 68. Actually, two-thirds is a liberal minimum; Diamond prefers 70 to 75 percent.

3. See Diamond, *Developing Democracy*, chapter 5.

4. Juan Linz and Alfred Stepan, *Problems of Democratic Transition and Consolidation* (Baltimore: Johns Hopkins University Press, 1996), 129.

5. Ibid., 144. Linz and Stepan find, for example, that though 61 percent in Spain and 57 percent in Portugal said that the Franco and Salazar regimes respectively were good or partially good, 70 percent in Spain and 61 percent in Portugal also said that democracy was the preferred regime type to all others. This data is from 1985.

6. The prisoners' dilemma is actually a specific case of a more general phenomenon known in economics as moral hazard. Moral hazard is the attempt by individuals to externalize the costs of collective goods while extracting the benefits. In the prisoners' dilemma, the prisoners want the benefits that come from cooperation, but they do not want to pay the costs. Their optimal outcome is the one in which the other player cooperates and they derive all the benefits themselves. Since neither prisoner is willing to risk cooperation under these conditions, the collective good ("light sentences") is not produced.

7. The formal prisoners' dilemma model applies to any case in which the individual prisoner A's preferences have the order $T > R > P > S$. T is the outcome where A defects and prisoner B cooperates. R is the outcome where both A and B cooperate. In outcome P both defect. And in S, A cooperates and B defects.

8. Quoted in Juan Linz, "Crisis, Breakdown, and Reequilibration," in Linz and Stepan, eds., *The Breakdown of Democratic Regimes*, 23.

9. Ibid., 55. Linz modifies Hirschman's theory of loyalty to firms in applying it to political institutions.

10. See H. H. Gerth and C. Wright Mills, eds., *From Max Weber: Essays in Sociology* (New York: Oxford University Press, 1946), 78–79. Lipset has elaborated on these types of legitimacy in *Political Man*, chapter 3.

11. Juan Linz, "Crisis, Breakdown, and Reequilibration," 47.

12. It is probably also fair to say that neither elites nor masses can have as profound an impact alone as they can have when they ally with each other.

13. Joseph Schumpeter made a similar point about capitalism, which he considered to be a superior economic system. He expected that it would fail, however, not because of any intrinsic defects but because intellectuals would nibble away at its legitimacy. See Schumpeter, *Capitalism, Socialism and Democracy*.

14. Lipset, *Political Man*, 65.

15. John Holm, "Botswana: A Paternalistic Democracy," in Diamond, Linz, and Lipset, eds., *Democracy in Developing Countries: Africa*, 195.

16. L. D. Ngcongco, "Tswana Political Tradition: How Democratic?" in John Holm and Patrick Molutsi, eds., *Democracy in Botswana* (Athens: Ohio University Press, 1989), 45–46.

17. One problem with the use of the *kgotla* in other contexts is that Botswana is, certainly by African standards, a relatively homogenous society in which there can be widespread agreement about the value of a particular tradition. In ethnically divided societies, this is a much more intractable problem since there is no a priori consensus about what constitutes "tradition."

18. A more modern example comes from Spain. The revised Spanish monarchy played a major role in halting the military coup against the republic in 1981. The king was able to retain the loyalty of the military, and his actions were widely viewed as legitimating the republic.

19. Lipset has previously argued that it was also the uniquely achievement-oriented values of the United States that facilitated the acceptance of the new regime:

> If the basic value pattern of the society includes a strong emphasis on ascription, new governments will find it difficult to rule by any means except force. Only where the value pattern stresses achievement will the political system,

like other institutions and positions, be evaluated by achievement criteria. Thus the success of the American Republic in establishing a post-revolutionary democratic legitimacy may be related to the strength of achievement values in the society.

(Lipset, *The First New Nation* [New York: W. W. Norton, 1963], 245).

20. Bruce Ackerman, *The Future of Liberal Revolution* (New Haven: Yale University Press, 1992), chapter 4.

21. Karuti Kanyinga, "Contestation over Political Space: The State and the Demobilisation of Opposition Politics in Kenya," in Adebayo O. Oluksohi, ed., *The Politics of Opposition in Contemporary Africa* (Uppsala, Sweden: Nordiska Afrikainstitutet, 1998), 39–90.

22. The island of Zanzibar is exceptional in this respect.

23. Goran Hyden, "Top-Down Democratization in Tanzania," *Journal of Democracy* 10 (October 1999): 142–55. One should also note, however, that democracy in Tanzania has been enormously benefited by Nyerere's own determination to step down from power and to support the transition to multipartyism.

24. Lipset, *Political Man*, 77–92; Linz and Stepan, *Problems of Democratic Transition*, 76–81.

25. We are grateful to Cynthia McClintock for pointing out our omission of this phenomenon in an earlier draft.

26. The development of legitimacy, like trust, social capital, or "moral sentiment," is taken to have evolved out of social experience but is then transferable to other situations without the necessity of a long period of experience. In broad historical terms, "legitimacy" may have been the outcome of protracted struggles leading to P outcomes. But in modern times, legitimacy may be as much the cause as the effect of particular outcomes. The same case has been made pertaining to ethics: "Moral sentiments originate in ongoing relationships where they help players resist the temptation to cheat so that they might secure the benefits of more farsighted behavior." See Michael W. Macy and John Skvoretz, "The Evolution of Trust and Cooperation between Strangers: A Computational Model," *American Sociological Review* 63 (October 1998): 640.

CHAPTER 9

1. See, for example, Samuel Huntington and Joan M. Nelson, *No Easy Choice: Political Participation in Developing Countries* (Cambridge, MA: Harvard University Press, 1976), 76. The authors argue that meaningful land reform requires an authoritarian regime: "What is needed for reform in these circumstances is the limitation of participation and the centralization of power in an autocratic ruler." Also see Mancur Olson, *The Rise and Decline of Nations* (New Haven: Yale University Press, 1982).

2. Though he did not go this far, Mancur Olson's more contemporary work emphasized democracy's economic advantages. These were purported to result from the lower rate of rent-seeking taxation that would be sought by majorities than by autocrats. Since majorities themselves play a greater role in the production of national income, they lose much more, and more quickly, from high taxation than autocrats, whose sole source of income is taxation. The assumption is that lower taxes lead to higher investment. Olson also argued that

democracies do a better job of protecting property rights. See "Dictatorship, Democracy and Development."

3. Nor is the empirical evidence overwhelming. For the most part, the literature shows only a muddled effect of regime type on economic development. Przeworski and others, in a new study, find no impact of regime type on GDP, but democracy has a positive effect on GDP per capita. The source of this appears to be the effects of regime type on population growth, rather than on economic activity per se. See Przeworski, Alvarez, Cheibub, and Limongi, *Democracy and Development*.

4. Amartya Sen has shown that some states in India that have undertaken public discussion of fertility have been able to bring population growth rates down to levels lower than the authoritarian Chinese, thus improving prospects for development (Sen, *Development as Freedom*, 153–54). Anders Aslund, studying Eastern Europe and the FSU, has found that support for tough, modernizing economic reforms was generally strongest in the more democratic, not the more authoritarian, states. See Aslund, *Building Capitalism* (Cambridge, UK: Cambridge University Press, 2002), esp. 377–78.

5. This view is noncommittal on the role of the state. There is clearly some point at which the state becomes so large that it inhibits economic freedom. What this view recognizes is that the state is an important actor in the process of development and democracy and that it can be both a means to freedom and an obstacle.

6. Touraine, *What Is Democracy?* 158.

7. Sen, *Development as Freedom*, 178–88.

8. Thomas D. Zweifel and Patricio Navia, "Democracy, Dictatorship, and Infant Mortality," *Journal of Democracy* 11 (April 2000): 99–114.

9. The Asian tigers and most of the developed world cast doubt on the idea that democracy can be a quid pro quo for development. They also suggest, when looked at in the context of India, that one's definition of development is central to the contention. Dictatorships, if they are benevolent and dedicated to purely economic development, may get better results faster. The case for democracy rests not so much on denying this point as on suggesting that the "if" involved is rather too big. Furthermore, the case is built on Touraine's argument that development is not only economic but also political.

10. This point was originally made by Robert Dahl in his classic text, *Polyarchy: Participation and Opposition* (New Haven: Yale University Press, 1971), 28.

11. R. J. Rummel, *Power Kills: Democracy as a Method of Nonviolence* (New Brunswick, NJ: Transaction, 1997). Rummel's data are for the second half of the twentieth century, but an earlier study by J. David Singer and Melvin Small found essentially the same results between 1816 and 1965 (Singer and Small, *The Wages of War, 1816–1965: A Statistical Handbook* [New York: John Wiley & Sons, 1972], 227). Rummel also devotes a chapter in *Power Kills* (chapter 5) to the issue of domestic peace, in which he concurs with Dahl.

12. Brandon C. Prins, "Democratic Politics and Dispute Escalation: Examining the Effects of Regime Type on Conflict Reciprocation, 1816–1992" (paper presented at the annual meeting of the American Political Science Association, Washington, D.C., August 2000), 19.

13. Sarah McLaughlin Mitchell and Brandon C. Prins, "Beyond Territorial Contiguity: Issues at Stake in Democratic Militarized Interstate Disputes," *International Studies Quarterly* 43 (March 1999): 169–83.

14. International Helsinki Federation for Human Rights, *Report to the OSCE Implementation Meeting on Human Dimension Issues* (Warsaw, October 17–27, 2000).

CHAPTER 10

1. Douglass North, William Summerhill, and Barry Weingast, "Order, Disorder and Economic Change," in Bruce Bueno de Mesquita and Hilton Root, eds., *Governing for Prosperity* (New Haven: Yale University Press, 2000), 18.

2. Weber argued, in an anticipation of path-dependency theory, that if history is viewed in terms of the rolling of dice, each historical outcome biases the dice in a particular direction, though they were not loaded at the beginning. For every seven that is rolled, the probability of rolling a seven increases. Thus particular critical events in a society's history "load the dice" in a particular way. See Weber, *The Methodology of the Social Sciences* (Glencoe, IL: The Free Press, 1949), 182–85; also Lipset, *American Exceptionalism: A Double-Edged Sword* (New York: W. W. Norton, 1996), 23–24.

3. Rueschemeyer, Stephens, and Stephens, *Capitalist Development and Democracy*, 227.

4. Ruth Berins Collier and David Collier, *Shaping the Political Arena* (Princeton: Princeton University Press, 1991).

5. Seymour Martin Lipset, *Continental Divide: The Values and Institutions of the United States and Canada* (New York: Routledge, 1991).

6. Mainwaring and Scully, eds., *Building Democratic Institutions: Party Systems in Latin America*; Larry Diamond, Jonathan Hartlyn, Juan Linz, and Seymour Martin Lipset, eds., *Democracy in Developing Countries: Latin America* (1st ed., Boulder, CO: Lynne Rienner Publishers, 1989; 2nd ed., 1999); Ronald McDonald and J. Mark Ruhl, *Party Politics and Elections in Latin America* (Boulder, CO: Westview Press, 1989); Howard J. Wiarda and Harvey F. Kline, eds., *Latin American Politics and Development*, 2nd ed. (Boulder, CO: Westview Press, 1985); and Freedom House, *Freedom in the World, 2000-2001* (Piscataway, NJ: Transaction, 2001). In addition, the footnotes at the end of many of the summaries reference texts of importance to that particular case.

7. Scott Mainwaring, *Rethinking Parties in the Third Wave of Democratization: The Case of Brazil* (Stanford: Stanford University Press, 1999); Argelina Cheibub Figueiredo and Fernando Limongi, "Presidential Power, Legislative Organization, and Party Behavior in Brazil," *Comparative Politics* (January 2000): 151–70; and Thomas Skidmore, *Politics in Brazil, 1930–1965: An Experiment in Democracy* (New York: Oxford University Press, 1967).

8. Arturo Valenzuela, "The Breakdown of Democratic Regimes: Chile," in Linz and Stepan, eds., *The Breakdown of Democratic Regimes*, part 4; Pamela Constable and Arturo Valenzuela, *A Nation of Enemies: Chile under Pinochet* (New York: W. W. Norton, 1991); Simon Collier and William F. Sater, *A History of Chile, 1808–1994* (New York: Cambridge University Press, 1996); Pilar Vergara, *Auge y Caida del Neoliberalismo en Chile* (Santiago: FLACSO, 1985).

9. James Mahoney, "Radical, Reformist and Aborted Liberalism: Origins of National Regimes in Central America," *Journal of Latin American Studies* (May 2001): 221–56; Orlando Salazar Mora and Jorge Mario Salazar Mora, *Los Partidos Politicos en Costa Rica* (San José: Editorial Universidad Estatal a Distancia, 1991); Carlos Sojo, "Costa Rica: Invulnerable Gobernabilidad," *Espacios*, no. 3 (1995).

10. Catherine Conaghan, "Politicians against Parties: Discord and Disconnection in Ecuador's Party System," in Mainwaring and Scully, eds. *Building Democratic Institutions*, 436.

11. David Schodt, *Ecuador: An Andean Enigma* (Boulder, CO: Westview Press, 1987).

12. Daniel Cosio Villegas et al., *Historia Minima de Mexico* (Mexico City: Fondo de Cultura Economica, 1994).

13. Carlos A. Miranda, *The Stroessner Era* (Boulder, CO: Westview Press, 1990).

14. Rama finds that, rather than economic policy, the institutional capacity of the state to implement policies detrimental to some social actors explains success and failure in Uruguayan economic history. His lucid piece is "Crecimiento y estancamiento económico en Uruguay," in Magnus Blomstrom and Patricio Meller, eds., *Trayectorias Divergentes: Comparacion de un Siglo de Desarollo Económico Latinoamericano y Escandinavo* (Santiago: Cieplan-Hachette, 1991), 115–44.

15. Charles G. Gillespie, *The Breakdown of Democracy in Uruguay: Alternative Political Models*, working paper 143 (Washington, D.C.: Latin American Program, The Wilson Center, 1984).

16. Cartelization is a process whereby parties that should be competing for resources end up working together to extract resources from the state and protect their power and privileges. This generally occurs as party systems age and the political environment stabilizes. "In this sense, it is perhaps more accurate to speak of the emergence of cartel parties, since this development depends on collusion and cooperation between ostensible competitors, and on agreements which, of necessity, require the consent and cooperation of all, or almost all, relevant participants." See Richard Katz and Peter Mair, "Changing Models of Party Organization and Party Democracy: the Emergence of the Cartel Party," *Party Politics* 1:1 (1995): 5–28; reprinted in Steven B. Wolinetz, ed., *Political Parties* (Brookfield: Ashgate, 1998), 473–96, quote on 485.

17. John D. Martz, *Acción Democratica: Evolution of a Modern Political Party in Venezuela* (Princeton: Princeton University Press, 1966); Moses Naím, "The Real Story behind Venezuela's Woes," *Journal of Democracy* (April 2001): 17–31; and Javier Corrales, "Reform-Lagging States and the Question of Devaluation: Venezuela's Response to the Exogenous Shocks of 1997–98," in Carol Wise and Riordan Roett, eds., *Exchange Rate Politics in Latin America* (Washington, D.C.: Brookings Institution Press, 2000).

18. We did not amend the chart to include this additional information because it would be hard to remain consistent with the original criteria used by Rueschemeyer, Stephens, and Stephens.

19. Keith Jaggers and Ted Robert Gurr, *Polity III: Regime Type and Political Authority, 1800–1994*, 2nd version (Ann Arbor, MI: Inter-university Consortium for Political and Social Research [ICPSR], 1996), diskette.

CHAPTER 11

1. Richard M. Morse, "The Heritage of Latin America," in Howard J. Wiarda, ed., *Politics and Social Change in Latin America: The Distinct Tradition* (Amherst: University of Massachusetts Press, 1974), 100.

2. Ricardo Lasso Guevara, *Los Estados Unidos del Norte y Los Des-Unidos del Sur: Paralelismo Histórico y Lecciones en Teoría Política* (Miami: International Press of Miami, 1990), 11 (translated by the authors).

3. Ibid., 92–95.

4. Timothy E. Anna, *Spain and the Loss of America* (Lincoln: University of Nebraska Press, 1983), 4–5.

5. Ibid., 6.

6. Kenneth Paul Erickson, "Brazil: Corporatism in Theory and Practice," in Wiarda and Kline, eds., *Latin American Politics*, 145.

7. Alan MacFarlane, *The Origins of English Individualism: The Family, Prosperity and Social Transition* (Oxford, UK: Basil Blackwell, 1978), 123.

8. Ibid., 154.

9. Ibid., 163.

10. Lasso Guevara, *Los Estados Unidos del Norte*, 73–74.

11. Douglass North and Robert Thomas, *Rise of the Western World: A New Economic History* (Cambridge, UK: Cambridge University Press, 1973), 149.

12. Gordon Wood, *The Radicalism of the American Revolution* (New York: Knopf, 1992), 98–99.

13. Octavio Paz, *The Labyrinth of Solitude* (New York: Grove Press, 1985), 359–60.

14. Ibid., 361.

15. Salvador de Madariaga, "Englishmen, Frenchmen and Spaniards" (New York: Hill & Wang, 1969).

16. Daniel Friedenburg, *Life, Liberty and the Pursuit of Land: The Plunder of Early America* (Buffalo: Prometheus Books, 1992), 33.

17. Max Savelle, *Europe and the World in the Age of Expansion*, vol. 5, *Empires to Nations: Expansion in America, 1713–1824* (St. Paul: University of Minnesota Press, 1974), 25.

18. Mario Góngora, *Studies in the Colonial History of Spanish America*, trans. Richard Southern (Cambridge, UK: Cambridge University Press, 1975), 82–83.

19. Morse, "Heritage of Latin America," 95–96.

20. Stephen Clissold, *Latin America: New World, Third World* (London: Pall Mall, 1972), 51.

21. Morse, "Heritage of Latin America", 35.

22. James Scobie, *Argentina: A City and a Nation* (New York: Oxford University Press, 1964), 62.

23. Morse, "Heritage of Latin America," 35–36.

24. North, Summerhill, and Weingast, "Order, Disorder, and Economic Change," 44–45.

25. Wood, *Radicalism*.

26. Ibid., 7.

27. Jack Greene, "The American Revolution," *American Historical Review* 105 (February 2000): 93–102.

28. Wood, *Radicalism*, 12–16.

29. Frank Safford, "Politics, Ideology and Society in Post-independence Spanish America," in Leslie Bethell, ed., *Cambridge History of Latin America* (Cambridge, UK: Cambridge University Press, 1985), 3:360.

30. Charismatic legitimacy is contrasted with other types of legitimacy in chapter 8.

31. Jaime E. Rodriguez O., "The Emancipation of America," *American Historical Review* 105 (February 2000): 143.

32. Ibid., 145.

33. See for example, R. R. Palmer, *The Age of the Democratic Revolution: A Political History of Europe and America, 1760–1800* (Princeton: Princeton University Press, 1959).

34. Arthur Whitaker, "The Americas in the Atlantic Triangle," in Lewis Hanke, ed., *Do the Americas Have a Common History? A Critique of the Bolton Theory* (New York: Knopf, 1964), 150–51.

35. Timothy E. Anna, *The Fall of the Royal Government in Mexico City* (Lincoln: University of Nebraska Press, 1978), xvi.

36. Ibid., 204.

37. Ibid., 225.

38. Howard J. Wiarda and Harvey F. Kline, "The Latin American Tradition and Process of Development," in Wiarda and Kline, *Latin American Politics*, 30.

39. Octavio Paz, *The Labyrinth of Solitude: Life and Thought in Mexico,* trans. Lysander Kemp (New York: Grove Press, 1961), 122.

40. Simón Bolívar, "Carta de Jamaica," in Manuel Perez Vila, ed., *Doctrina del Libertador* (Venezuela: Editorial Arte, 1976), 67 (translated by the authors).

41. Simón Bolívar, "El Discurso de Angostura," in Vila, ed., *Doctrina del Libertador,* 108 (translated by the authors.

42. Simón Bolívar, "Carta al general Daniel Florencio O'Leary Guayaquil, 13 de setiembre de 1829," in Vila, ed., *Doctrina del Libertador,* 302 (translated by author).

43. Douglass C. North, *Institutions, Institutional Change and Economic Performance* (New York: Cambridge University Press, 1990), 103.

44. Timothy E. Anna, "The Last Viceroys of New Spain and Peru: An Appraisal," *American Historical Review* 81 (February 1976): 63.

45. North, Summerhill, and Weingast write: "Creoles gaining power after independence inherited a centralized political system without inheriting critical elements of the formal and informal constraints protecting corporate groups and other elites…The absence of constraints meant a potentially unconstrained executive and administrative apparatus" ("Order, Disorder and Economic Change," 46).

46. Carlos Rangel, *The Latin Americans: Their Love-Hate Relationship with the United States* (New Brunswick, NJ: Transaction, 1987), 74.

47. Wiarda and Kline, "Latin American Tradition," 33.

48. Leslie Bethell, "The Independence of Brazil," in Bethell, ed., *Cambridge History of Latin America,* 3:196.

49. Seymour Martin Lipset, "George Washington and the Founding of Democracy," *Journal of Democracy* 9 (October 1998): 24–38.

50. Wood, *Radicalism,* 206.

51. North, Summerhill, and Weingast, "Order, Disorder, and Economic Change," esp. 47.

52. Tocqueville, *Democracy in America*, 1:319–20.

53. Domingo F. Sarmiento, "Travels in the United States in 1847," in Allison Williams Bunkley, ed., *A Sarmiento Anthology*, trans. Stuart Edgar Grummon (Port Washington, NY: Kennikat Press, 1972), 196.

54. Sarmiento, *Estados Unidos*, 90 (translated by the authors).

55. Lipset, *American Exceptionalism*, 19.

56. World Values Survey data (Ann Arbor, MI: ICPSR, 1995) www.icpsr. umich.edu. Countries for which data are available include Argentina, Brazil, Peru, Chile, Colombia, Uruguay, Venezuela, and the United States. Analysis by authors. All differences are statistically significant (n for all countries is between 1,000 and 6,000).

57. M. Blomstrom and D. Meller, *Trayectorias Divergentes: Cien Años de Desarollo en Latinoamerica y Escandinavo* (Santiago: CIEPLAN, 1991). Blomstrom and Meller find that the lack of technical education is a major factor explaining the later development of Latin American countries when compared to their Scandinavian counterparts.

58. Seymour Martin Lipset, "Values, Education and Entrepreneurship," in Lipset and Aldo Solari, eds., *Elites in Latin America* (New York: Oxford University Press, 1967), 20.

59. Ibid., 22.

60. Ibid., 29.

61. Atilio A. Borón, "Ruling without a Party: Argentine Dominant Classes in the Twentieth Century," in Kevin J. Middlebrook, ed., *Conservative Parties, the Right, and Democracy in Latin America* (Baltimore: Johns Hopkins University Press, 2000), 146. Also see Borón, "Becoming Democrats? Some Skeptical Considerations on the Right in Latin America," in Douglas Chalmers, Mario do Carmo Campello de Souza, and Borón, eds., *The Right and Democracy in Latin America* (New York: Praeger, 1992), 68–95.

62. Lipset has argued in *Political Man* that gross inequality inhibits the development of liberal values of equality and tolerance.

CHAPTER 12

1. Lipset, *Political Man*, 35.

2. We use data from the Penn World Tables, Version 5.6, a project of the University of Pennsylvania's Center for International Comparisons. These data are relevant only insofar as they provide us a standard set of numbers, so that we avoid comparing numbers from reports that use different methods of accounting or estimating.

3. This is the median of the aggregated data, not an actual median income within any country.

4. Colombia is problematic. Its central government is democratic but has control over only part of the country. The rest is controlled by paramilitary groups and guerillas.

5. The reader will note that these figures actually represent a decline for Venezuela, reflecting a combination of actual decline with the effects of different accounting principles.

6. Mitchell Seligson, "Political Culture and Democratization in Latin America," in Roderic Ai Camp, ed., *Democracy in Latin America: Patterns and Cycles* (Wilmington, DE: Jaguar Books, 1996), 67–90.

7. Clissold, *Latin America: New World, Third World*, 43.

8. Góngora, *Colonial History of Spanish America*, 132.

9. Ibid., 134.

10. Ibid., 143.

11. Ibid., 149.

12. Ibid., 56.

13. Wiarda and Kline, "Latin American Tradition," 9.

14. Morse, "Heritage of Latin America," 45.

15. Russell H. Fitzgibbon and Julio A. Fernandez, *Latin America: Political Culture and Development* (Englewood Cliffs, NJ: Prentice Hall, 1981), 6.

16. Carlos Rangel, *The Latin Americans: Their Love-Hate Relationship with the United States* (New Brunswick, NJ: Transaction, 1987), 185. A cacique is a person who dominates the political affairs of a village or region. Previously, caciques were the chiefs of native American tribes.

17. Ibid., 190–91.

18. Clissold, *Latin America: New World, Third World*, 230–31.

19. Scobie, *Argentina: A City and a Nation*, 25.

20. Ibid., 45.

21. Ibid., 48.

22. Edmund Stephen Urbanski, *Hispanic America and Its Civilizations* (Norman: University of Oklahoma Press, 1978), 114–15. The American South was exceptional in this regard, though Urbanski sees North American slavery as a minor chord in the North American cultural complex when compared to Latin American conquest.

23. Paul W. Gates, *History of Public Land Law Development* (Washington, D.C.: Public Land Law Review Commission, 1968), 67.

24. Hernando de Soto, *The Mystery of Capital: Why Capitalism Triumphs in the West and Fails Everywhere Else* (New York: Basic Books, 2000), 119–20.

25. Gates, *History of Public Land Law Development*, 59–72.

26. Adam Smith, *An Inquiry into the Nature and Causes of the Wealth of Nations*, ed. Edwin Cannan (1776; New York: Random House, 1994), 617.

27. Ibid., 620.

28. Ibid., 617.

29. Ibid., 618.

30. Lee Soltow, "Land Equality on the Frontier: Distribution of Land in East Tennessee at the Beginning of the Nineteenth Century," *Social Science History* 5:3 (1981): 279.

31. Lee Soltow, *Distribution of Wealth and Income in the United States in 1798* (Pittsburgh: University of Pittsburgh, 1989), 42; and "Kentucky Wealth at the End of the Eighteenth Century," *Journal of Economic History* 43 (September 1983): 617–33.

32. See, among others, Steven Sarson, "Landlessness and Tenancy in Early National Prince George's County, Maryland," *William and Mary Quarterly*, 3rd ser., 57 (July 2000): 577.

33. Soltow, "Kentucky Wealth," 633.

34. Robert E. Brown, *Middle-Class Democracy and the Revolution in Massachusetts, 1691–1780* (Ithaca: Cornell University Press, 1955), 16.

35. Vanhanen, *Prospects of Democracy*, 47.

36. Mitchell Seligson has noted the weaknesses in this data set, though he considers it to be the most reliable extant data. See Seligson, "Tatu Vanhanen's Thesis and the Prospects of Democracy in Latin America," in Vanhanen, *Prospects of Democracy*, 277–83.

37. Ernest Feder, *The Rape of the Peasantry: Latin America's Landholding System* (Garden City, NY: Doubleday Anchor Books, 1971), 17.

38. Wood, *Radicalism*, 138.

39. Ronald J. Clark, "Bolivia," in *The Land Tenure Center Annual Report, 1968* (Madison: University of Wisconsin Press, 1968), 7.

40. José Luis de Imaz, *Los Que Mandan* (Buenos Aires: Editorial Universitario de Buenos Aires, 1964), 160, quoted in Lipset, "Values, Education and Entrepreneurship," 9.

41. Herman Felstehausen, "Colombia," in *Land Tenure Center Annual Report, 1968*, 36.

42. Feder, *Rape of the Peasantry*, 9.

43. Lasso Guevara, *Los Estados Unidos del Norte*, 108 (translated by the authors).

44. Savelle, *Empires to Nations*, 69–98.

45. The history of this seemingly absurd proviso is discussed in Scobie, *Argentina: A City and a Nation*, chapter 2.

46. Smith, *Wealth of Nations*, 621.

47. Savelle, *Empires to Nations*, 98.

48. Smith, *Wealth of Nations*, 623.

49. Ibid., 627.

50. Ibid., 620.

51. Ibid., 618.

52. Claudio Véliz, *The New World of the Gothic Fox: Culture and Economy in English and Spanish America* (Berkeley: University of California Press, 1994), 34.

53. Ralph Lee Woodward, Jr., "The Merchants and Economic Development in the Americas, 1750–1850: A Preliminary Study," *Journal of Inter-American Studies* 10 (January 1968): 136–37.

54. Ibid., 145.

55. North, Summerhill, and Weingast, "Order, Disorder, and Economic Change," 40.

56. ISI was a strategy whose logic dictated that developing countries needed to industrialize by pursuing capital-intensive development modeled on the advanced countries' existing economies. In order to accomplish this, high protective tariffs on manufactured goods were needed to nurse infant domestic manufacturing. ISI was an inward looking strategy that ultimately privileged production for domestic markets over the creation of an internationally competitive export sector, though this was not its original intent. It therefore eschewed the alternative logic of comparative advantage.

57. See Larry Diamond, Jonathan Hartlyn, and Juan J. Linz, "Introduction: Politics, Society and Democracy in Latin America," in Diamond, Hartlyn, Linz, and Lipset, eds., *Democracy in Developing Countries: Latin America*, 2nd ed., 16–17.

Also see, in the same volume, Arturo Valenzuela, "Chile: Origins and Consolidation of a Latin American Democracy," 131–90.

58. Rueschemeyer, Stephens, and Stephens, *Capitalist Development and Democracy*, 180.

59. We discuss structural factors in more detail in the following chapter in a section on political parties.

CHAPTER 13

1. Collier and Collier, *Shaping the Political Arena*, 125.

2. According to Kenneth Roberts, the trend away from class-cleaved parties has actually worsened in recent years. See Roberts, "Social Inequalities without Class Cleavages in Latin America's Neoliberal Era," *Studies in Comparative International Development* (Winter 2002).

3. Kevin J. Middlebrook, "Introduction: Conservative Parties, Elite Representation, and Democracy in Latin America," in Middlebrook, ed., *Conservative Parties*, 1–50.

4. Robert A. Dahl, "The American Oppositions: Affirmation and Denial," in Robert A. Dahl, ed., *Political Oppositions in Western Democracies* (New Haven: Yale University Press, 1966), 53–54.

5. Seymour Martin Lipset and Gary Marks, *It Didn't Happen Here: Why Socialism Failed in the United States* (New York: W. W. Norton, 2000), 58–63.

6. Some would argue that race has been the great cleavage of the United States and that it is precisely because of race that other ethnic cleavages failed to solidify into political parties. That is, the black-white divide prevented ethnic whites from focusing too intently on the differences between, for example, Italians and Irish. The unified black vote in America, though anomalous, is evidence of a racial cleavage conceived of politically, but because blacks are a minority, a black party has never been a realistic vision, at least not in a plurality system like that of the United States.

7. This point is made by Michael Coppedge, "Venezuelan Parties and the Representation of Elite Interests," in Middlebrook, ed., *Conservative Parties*, 110–38.

8. See Torcuato DiTella, *Latin American Politics* (Austin: University of Texas Press, 1990).

9. Large parties are always in danger of fragmenting over compromises because small breakaway parties have a much greater chance of gaining seats in a parliamentary system than they do under presidentialism.

10. Albert O. Hirschman, "Underdevelopment, Obstacles to the Perception of Change, and Leadership," *Daedalus* 97 (Summer 1968): 933.

11. Valenzuela, "Class Relations and Democratization."

12. Torcuato DiTella writes of the Argentinian left: "In the political parties (Socialist and Communist), the cooperatives, and cultural and press activities, there was a sizable middle-class element. . . . This latter component was probably stronger than in the European cases because of a lower level of industrialization and the greater difficulty of reaching the lower stratum of workers, as well as because of more insecure political conditions" (DiTella, *Latin American Politics*, 104).That is, the class structure of Latin America made it harder than in Europe to base a strong party exclusively on the working class.

13. Cynthia McClintock, "Peru: Precarious Regimes, Authoritarian and Democratic," in Diamond, Hartlyn, Linz, and Lipset, eds., *Democracy in Developing Countries: Latin America,* 2nd ed., 341.

14. Frederico G. Gil, "Responsible Parties in Latin America," *Journal of Politics* 15 (August 1953): 333–48.

15. Robert H. Dix, "Cleavage Structures and Party Systems in Latin America," *Comparative Politics* 22:1 (1989): 28.

16. Robert Kaufman, "Corporatism, Clientelism and Partisan Conflict: A Study of Seven Latin American Countries," in James Malloy, ed., *Authoritarianism and Corporatism in Latin America* (Pittsburgh: University of Pittsburgh Press, 1977).

17. Roberts, "Social Inequalities without Class Cleavages," 12.

18. Ibid., n. 11.

19. Otto Kircheimer, "The Transformation of the Western European Party Systems," in Joseph LaPalombara and Myron Weiner, eds., *Political Parties and Political Development* (Princeton: Princeton University Press, 1966).

20. This is the view of an influential line of thinkers since at least Karl Marx. See for example, Seymour Martin Lipset and Reinhard Bendix, "Karl Marx's Theory of Social Classes," in Lipset and Bendix, eds., *Class, Status and Power* (New York: Free Press, 1953), 26–35; Rueschemeyer, Stephens, and Stephens, *Capitalist Development and Democracy;* Leubbert, *Liberalism, Fascism or Social Democracy.*

21. According to Ruth B. Collier, the first mass party in the Netherlands was the Anti-Revolutionary Party, organized in 1878 (*Paths toward Democracy,* 93).

22. Dix, "Cleavage Structures and Party Systems," 31–32.

23. This argument is implicitly similar to the argument of the postmaterialists, who find that the advanced industrial countries of today have class structures that are no longer conducive to organization around the old cleavages. Thus new cleavages have formed, among them the postmaterialist/materialist cleavage, which is rooted in political attitudes rather than social position. See Inglehart, *Postmodernization and Modernization.*

24. Albert O. Hirschman, "The Political Economy of Import-Substituting Industrialization in Latin America," *Quarterly Journal of Economics* 82 (February 1968): 8.

25. Where the liberal or radical party in Europe was weak, this was often because the middle and bourgeois classes were divided over another cleavage, often religion.

26. James Malloy, "Authoritarianism and Corporatism in Latin America: The Modal Pattern," in Malloy, ed., *Authoritarianism and Corporatism in Latin America,* 9.

27. Mahoney, "Radical, Reformist, and Aborted Liberalism," 2001.

28. Valenzuela, "Class Relations and Democratization," 265.

29. Interestingly, in recent years the catchall aspects of parties has begun to change in both the United States and Uruguay. In Uruguay the genesis of a leftist coalition, the Frente Amplio (Broad Front), has injected ideological, cleavage-based divisions into the party system. In the United States, the Republican and Democratic parties have both become "purer" in the sense that more leftist tendencies are concentrated in the Democratic party and more

rightist tendencies are concentrated in the Republican party. Interestingly, class seems to have played only a minor role in this shift. A religiosity/secularism cleavage, however, emerged as a fairly salient division quite clearly in the 2000 presidential election.

30. DiTella, *Latin American Politics*, 64.

31. Inglehart, *Modernization and Postmodernization*, 190.

32. Manuel Antonio Garretón, "The Political Evolution of the Chilean Military Regime," in Guillermo O'Donnell, Philippe C. Schmitter, and Laurence Whitehead, eds., *Transitions from Authoritarian Rule: Prospects for Democracy* (Baltimore: Johns Hopkins University Press, 1986), 96.

33. Philippe Schmitter, *Interest Conflict and Political Change in Brazil* (Stanford: Stanford University Press, 1971), 56.

34. Tocqueville, *Democracy in America*, 1:191.

35. Stephen Kalberg, "Tocqueville and Weber on the Sociological Origins of Citizenship: The Political Culture of American Democracy," in Ralph Schroeder, ed., *Max Weber, Democracy and Modernization* (New York: St. Martin's Press, 1998), 109.

36. Nathan O. Hatch, *The Democratization of American Christianity* (New Haven: Yale University Press, 1989), 9–10.

37. As Hatch observes, the genesis of new Christian groups put pressure on the older denominations to "modernize," as one would expect in any open market. In Latin America, by contrast, it is probably fair to say that much of the pressure on the Catholic Church came not from within Catholicism but from without, with the sudden appeal of Protestant Pentecostal groups in Latin America. As the Church began to lose its monopoly, it too was forced to contend with market forces. The point for present purposes is that it took almost two centuries for the pressures on the Catholic Church to reach the level they had reached in North America by the first decades after the American Revolution.

38. See, for example, Edward L. Cleary, "From Theology of Liberation to Enculturation: Emergence of Indigenous Religious Centers and Movements in Peru and Bolivia" (paper presented at the Latin American Studies Association, Washington, D.C., 2001).

39. See Luis Castro Leiva and Anthony Pagden, "Civil Society and the Fate of the Modern Republics of Latin America," in Sudipta Kaviraj and Sunil Khilnani, eds., *Civil Society: History and Possibilities* (Cambridge, UK: Cambridge University Press, 2001), 179–203.

40. Theda Skocpol and Morris Fiorina, "Making Sense of the Civic Engagement Debate," in Skocpol and Fiorina, eds., *Civic Engagement in American Democracy* (Washington, D.C.: Brookings Institution Press, 1999), 43–46.

41. Hatch, *Democratization of American Christianity*, 60.

42. Ben G. Burnett, *Political Groups in Chile* (Austin: University of Texas Press, 1970), 61.

43. Ibid., 102.

44. Sarmiento, *Estados Unidos*, 91.

45. The United States has a generally higher level of associationalism than every country in Eastern and Western Europe, as well as Japan. The only coun-

tries that have a significantly higher level are Iceland and the Netherlands. See Inglehart, *Modernization and Postmodernization*, 190.

46. Terry Lynn Karl, the foremost student of political pact making, has observed of pacts that they are "aimed at restricting the scope of representation in order to reassure traditional dominant classes" and that they are essentially "anti-democratic mechanisms." From our perspective, while pacts can be extremely important in democratic transitions, party dominance of civil society has some negative implications for long-term democratic stability. See Karl, "Dilemmas of Democratization in Latin America," *Comparative Politics* 23 (October 1990): 1–21.

47. Nor should civil society be overly dependent on control of the state, a point that has relevance for states that frequently alternate between democratic and nondemocratic party competition. Where the state is controlled outright by oligarchic groups, this is really another form of praetorianism, in which democratic competition and persuasion are eschewed in favor of bureaucratic repression.

48. Huntington, *Political Order in Changing Societies*, 196.

49. Coppedge, "Venezuelan Parties," 132.

50. Moses Naim, "The Real Story behind Venezuela's Woes," *Journal of Democracy* 12 (April 2001): 23.

51. A discussion of some of these new groups, including Queremos Eligir, can be found in Juan Carlos Navarro, "Venezuela's New Political Actors," in Louis W. Goodman, Johanna Forman, Moises Naim, Joseph Tulchin, and Gary Bland, eds., *Lessons of the Venezuelan Experience* (Washington, D.C.: Woodrow Wilson Center Press, 1995), 115–35.

52. Garretón, "Political Evolution of the Chilean Military Regime," 118.

53. For a discussion of how Chilean civil society organizations used the worldviews and cognitive tools provided to them by political parties to free themselves from the grip of those parties, see Edward Greaves, "Political Parties and the Rise and Decline of Popular Civil Society (II): The Emergence of a Subaltern Counterpublic in Chile, 1950–73" (paper presented at the Latin American Studies Association meeting, Washington, D.C., 2001).

54. Valenzuela, "Breakdown of Democratic Regimes: Chile," part IV, esp. 69.

55. Chile had demonstrated similar tendencies in the late predemocratic era. At that time civil society was repressed by an oligarchy-dominated state. Since the working classes could not vote, they made their preferences known through civil disobedience and violence—actions that did succeed in altering the course of national elections. See Collier and Collier, *Shaping the Political Arena*, 112–13.

56. Several scholars have argued that in Europe, democracy survived in particular where bourgeois civil society was linked to the political party system. We discuss this in part I. See Ertmann, "Democracy and Dictatorship in Interwar Western Europe Revisited," and Berman, "Civil Society and the Collapse of the Weimar Republic."

57. Edward Gibson argues that the propensity of the right to establish efficacious links to a party is determined in great measure by the degree of control

the right exercises over the state itself. See Gibson, "Conservative Electoral Movements and Democratic Politics: Core Constituencies, Coalition Building, and the Latin American Electoral Right," in Chalmers, Campello de Souza, and Boron, eds., *The Right and Democracy in Latin America*, 31–33.

58. See Manuel Antonio Garretón, "Atavism and Democratic Ambiguity in the Chilean Right," in Middlebrook, ed., *Conservative Parties and Democracy*, 55.

59. Kaufman, "Corporatism, Clientelism, and Partisan Conflict," 126.

60. Coppedge, "Venezuelan Parties," 124.

61. Frances Hagopian, "Democracy and Political Representation in Latin America in the 1990s: Pause, Reorganization, or Decline?" in Felipe Aguero and Jeffrey Stark, eds., *Fault Lines of Democracy in Post-Transition Latin America* (Miami: North-South Center Press, 1998), 124–25.

62. Kaufman, "Corporatism, Clientelism, and Partisan Conflict," 128–30.

63. Robert Archer argues that Colombia is a partial exception to this generalization because there was some linkage with elite civil society. This did not reach the mass level as it did in Chile or Venezuela, however. See Archer, "Party Strength and Weakness in Colombia's Besieged Democracy," in Mainwaring and Scully, eds., *Building Democratic Institutions*, 174–75.

64. By *conservative* here we mean not ideological conservatism but rather "resistant to change."

65. Kaufman, "Corporatism, Clientelism, and Partisan Conflict," 134.

66. Luis González, "Continuity and Change in the Uruguayan Party System," in Mainwaring and Scully, eds., *Building Democratic Institutions*, 151.

67. Rama, "Crecimiento y estancamiento en Uruguay."

68. John A. Booth, "Costa Rica: The Roots of Democratic Stability," in Diamond, Linz, and Lipset, eds., *Democracy in Developing Countries: Latin America*, 2nd ed., 407–10.

69. Carlos Sojo, "Costa Rica: Invulnerable Gobernabilidad," *Espacios*, no. 3 (1995) (translation by the authors).

70. James McGuire, "Political Parties and Democracy in Argentina," in Mainwaring and Scully, eds., *Building Democratic Institutions*, 202.

71. Samuel Huntington observed the following about increasing the scope of political participation in Argentina: "In praetorian societies, . . . the participation of new groups exacerbates rather than reduces tensions. It multiplies the resources and methods employed in political action and thus contributes to the disintegration of the polity. New groups are mobilized but not assimilated. The expansion of political participation in Great Britain made Disraeli's two nations into one. The expansion of participation in Argentina made the same two nations into mortal enemies" (Huntington, *Political Order in Changing Societies*, 198).

72. Peter G. Snow and Luigi Manzetti, *Political Forces in Argentina*, 3rd ed. (Westport, CT: Praeger, 1993), 84–85.

73. Collier, *Paths toward Democracy*, 143.

74. Some of these movements are discussed briefly in Edwin G. Corr and Lupe Andrade, "The Challenges to Democratization in Bolivia" (paper presented at the Latin American Studies Association meeting, Washington, D.C., 2001).

75. Lawrence Whitehead, "Bolivia and the Viability of Democracy," *Journal of Democracy* 12 (April 2001): 12.

76. Jose Antonio Lucero, "Crisis and Contention in Ecuador," *Journal of Democracy* 12 (April 2001): 59–73.

77. Hagopian, "Democracy and Political Representation," 125. See also Omar G. Encarnacíon, "Tocqueville's Missionaries: Civil Society Advocacy and the Promotion of Democracy," *World Policy Journal* 17 (Spring 2000): 9–18.

78. Diamond, *Developing Democracy*, 39.

79. Hagopian, "Democracy and Political Representation," 126.

80. "An Alarm Call for Latin America's Democrats," *The Economist*, July 26, 2001. Data from Latinobarómetro, a polling outfit based in Santiago, Chile.

CONCLUSION

1. Larry Diamond, *Developing Democracy* (Baltimore: Johns Hopkins University, 1999), especially 31–49.

2. Actually, polling data suggest that George W. Bush's legitimacy is quite high and has been since his election, in spite of our electoral system's poor performance in 2000. See the collection of poll data compiled by Karlyn Bowman and available through the American Enterprise Institute Web site, at http://www.aei.org/ps/psbowman6.pdf.

INDEX

Acción Democrática (AD) (Venezuela), 276, 277, 363, 364, 366, 367, 428n.67
Ackerman, Bruce, 218
Activism, and democratic culture, 199
Africa, 7, 173, 176, 177, 178, 216, 219–21, 236
African Americans, 107, 112, 113, 114, 367, 458n.6
African National Congress (ANC), 219
Agrarian Socialism (Lipset), 51–52, 92
Agriculture, 324, 325, 326, 341; in Latin America, 318, 319, 329–30, 335, 369; in North America, 244, 245, 329
Alfonsín, Raul, 251
Allende, Salvador, 6, 44, 258, 378, 397
Almond, Gabriel, 94, 117, 185, 198–204
American Creed, 307
American Revolution, 289, 292–97, 304, 305, 390
Anarchosyndicalists, 156
Anarchy, 350, 351
Angola, 178
Anna, Timothy E., 282–83, 298, 301
Anti-colonial movements, 73
Anti-statism, 170
Apristas (APRA; Alianza Popular Revolucionaria Americana) (Peru), 271, 272, 363, 364, 366, 367, 378
Arendt, Hannah, 124
Argentina, 181, 244, 248–51, 291, 296, 302, 313, 350, 356; capitalism in, 337; civil society in, 380, 382, 394, 403–405; democratic and authoritarian rule in, 279; economic development in, 312–15, 319; family farm index, 325; labor force in agriculture, 326; land distribution in, 328, 330; participation in organizations, 414; political parties of, 249–51, 364, 365, 367, 382; poverty in, 345, 346; trade, 332; urbanization of, 385, 388; working class in, 342

Aristocracy, 121–22, 164; British, 285; Latin American, 308, 318, 320
Aristotle, 12, 164
Asia, 176, 184, 187, 195, 196, 236
Asian Americans, 113, 114, 195
Association of Catholic Trade Unionists (ACTU), 59
Audiencias, Spanish, 290, 411
Australia, 173
Authoritarianism, 12, 70, 71, 72, 183, 188, 222; in Argentina, 382; in Asia, 187; in Chile, 256, 257; civil society and, 125, 395; in Colombia, 260; economic development and, 141–42, 149, 229; and education, 167; in Latin America, 156, 245, 246, 279, 298, 410, 411; legitimacy and, 211, 214, 220; in Paraguay, 268, 269; party systems emerging from, 73; in Spanish political culture, 282; voluntary associations and, 93; of working class, 156
Authority, Anna's concept of, 298
Autocracies, 33
Autonomy, 161, 289, 291, 294–95
Aymara Indians, 404

Backward-linked production, 371–72, 373, 375
Bangladesh, 60
Banzer, Hugo, 253, 254
Barro, Robert, 140, 143–44, 148, 151

Bartolini, Stefano, 75
Bates, Robert, 206
Batlle y Ordoñez, José, 274
Belarus, 8
Belaunde, Fernando, 271, 272
Belgian colonies, 174, 178
Belgium, 180
Bellah, Robert, 195
Betancourt, Romulo, 276
Binder, Sarah, 48–49
Blacks. *See* African Americans
Bolívar, Simón, 300, 391
Bolivia, 89, 313; capitalism in, 336, 337; civil society in, 394, 403, 404, 405; democratic and authoritarian rule in, 279; economic development in, 315; family farm index, 325; income inequality in, 343; indigenous people of, 288, 305; labor force in agriculture, 326; land distribution in, 327, 328, 330; participation in organizations, 414; political parties of, 252–54; 363, 365; poverty in, 345; urbanization of, 388
Bollen, Kenneth, 31, 165, 182
Booth, John A., 105, 117
Borón, Atilio A., 310
Botswana, 27, 36, 128, 176, 216–17, 234
Bourgeois class, 153–56, 164, 338, 438n.38; in Chile, 376, 377; industrialization and, 371–72; political parties and, 364, 370, 371
Brazil, 74, 87–90, 179, 181, 222, 254–56, 283, 289, 298, 302, 303, 313, 350; capitalism in, 337; civil society in, 380, 384, 392, 405; democratic and authoritarian rule in, 279; economic development in, 315; family farm index, 325; income inequality in, 343; labor force in agriculture, 326; land distribution in, 328; market system of, 334; participation in organizations, 414; political parties of, 364, 365, 382; poverty in, 345; religion in, 193, 391; urbanization of, 385, 388; working class in, 342
Brown, Robert, 323
Buddhism, 187
Bueno de Mesquita, Bruce, 33, 34
Bull, Edward, 180
Bureaucracy, state, 157–58; English, 285; Spanish, 333
Burundi, 178

Bush, George H. W., 33
Bustamante, José Luis, 271

Cabildos, Spanish colonial, 290–91
Cabinet ministers, experience of, 46–47
Caldera, Rafael, 396
Calderón, Rafael, 261–62, 278
Calles, Plutarco, 266
Calvinism, 195, 389
Cambodia, 24
Campaign finance reform bill, 22
Canada, 160, 186, 242, 248; democracy in, 280; economic development in, 315; family farm index, 325; income inequality in, 343; land distribution in, 314, 328; political parties in, 365; poverty in, 345; volunteer organizations in, 92; working class in, 342
Capital–intensive industry, 370, 371
Capitalism, 150, 152–64, 161–62, 231–32, 237, 329–40, 439n.39; Confucian values and, 195; Protestantism and, 194
Capitalism, Socialism and Democracy (Schumpeter), 19
Cárdenas, Cuauhtémoc, 267
Cárdenas, Lázaro, 267
Cardoso, Fernando Enrique, 256
Caribbean, 176
Cartelization, 452n.16
Carter, Jimmy, 6
Catchall political parties, 352–60, 363–67, 377, 400, 459n.29
Catholicism, 76, 158, 184–94, 232, 245, 309; and indigenous people, 287; and land management, 322; in Latin America, 356, 389–92; vision of society in, 284, 286, 361
Caudillos, Latin American, 292, 296, 299, 302, 348, 361
Cell phones, 86, 89
Center-left social democratic parties, 72–73
Central America, 106, 117, 247
Centralized control: in Latin America, 349, 362; in Spanish political culture, 244, 282, 300–301, 411
Charismatic legitimacy, 215, 219, 221, 296, 349, 361, 364
Chavez, Hugo, 7–8, 278, 396
Cheibub Figueiredo, Argelina, 74, 146
Chen Shui-bian, 236
Children, 205

Chile, 6, 44, 80, 155, 158, 231, 244, 246, 256–59, 296, 302, 313, 412; capitalism in, 336, 337; civil society in, 380, 381, 382, 392, 394, 396–99; democratic and authoritarian rule in, 279; economic development in, 314, 315; family farm index, 325; income inequality in, 343; labor force in agriculture, 326; labor unions in, 383; land distribution in, 328; landed class in, 374, 375, 376; market system of, 334; participation in organizations, 414; political parties of, 351, 352, 353, 362, 364, 365, 396, 397; poverty in, 345, 346; presidential power in, 349; social cleavage in, 375–78; urbanization of, 385, 388; violence in, 397; working class in, 342

China, 34, 160

Chong, Dennis, 206

Christian Democratic party (Chile), 397

Christianity, 196. *See also* Catholicism; Protestantism

Church and state issues, 76, 189, 190, 302, 362

Church-related parties. *See* Confessional parties

Civic culture, 185, 199–204

Civic Culture, The (Almond and Verba), 94, 117, 198–202

Civilization, Huntington's notion of, 148

Civil rights and liberties, 190, 202–203, 413; legitimacy and, 210

Civil society, 27, 36, 56, 58, 63, 92–95, 347; autonomous, 393–94; diffusion of wealth and, 152; in Latin America, 379–407; and mediation, 119–30; in North America, 379–82, 391, 392; participation in organizations, 414; and political parties, 64, 80, 91, 125–30, 234–37, 379, 382, 392–407, 413; and religion, 389–92; social capital and, 96–102, 116–19; and trust, 102–16; in United States, 382; and urbanization, 384–89

Civil wars, 293, 295, 296, 301–302

Clark, Ronald, 330

Class differences: democracy and, 12; industrialization and, 370–71; and instability, 54; and political parties, 69–70, 76–77, 235, 352, 353, 354, 356, 363, 364, 367, 373; trust and, 108; urbanization and, 368

Cleavage structures: Moreno's notion of, 427n.50. *See also* Social cleavages

"Cleavage Structures, Party Systems and Voter Alignments" (Lipset and Rokkan), 76, 357

Clientelism, 362, 368, 394, 399, 400, 401

Clinton, Bill, 33

Clissold, Stephen, 290, 319

Closed community, 96

Closed-list voting, 47, 423n.15

Coalitions, 33, 68, 218; in Costa Rica, 402; and ethnic conflict, 220

Cold War, 5–6, 13

Coleman, James, 52–58, 92, 93, 96, 98, 99, 120, 121, 173

Collective action, legitimacy and, 211–15

Collegial executive system, 274

Collier, David, 247, 342, 351, 362

Collier, Ruth Berins, 155, 247, 342, 351, 362, 404, 405

Collor, Fernando, 88, 89

Colombia, 8, 30, 236, 259–60; capitalism in, 337; civil society in, 394, 400, 401, 405; democratic and authoritarian rule in, 279; economic development in, 315; family farm index, 325; income inequality in, 343; labor force in agriculture, 326; land distribution in, 328, 330; participation in organizations, 414; political parties of, 351, 352, 353, 362, 365; poverty in, 345; urbanization of, 385, 388; violence in, 30, 259, 260, 351, 401, 405; working class in, 342

Colonies. *See* Belgian colonies; Decolonization; Dutch colonies; French colonies; Great Britain, colonization and colonial legacy of; Portuguese colonies; Spanish colonies

Commercial systems. *See* Market systems

Communication: high-tech, 86–87; and political parties, 64–65, 80

Communists, 156, 216; holdover parties, 72; in labor unions, 59–60

Communitarianism, 198

Community, social capital and, 96, 97

Community participation, 117–18. *See also* Voluntary associations

Competition, democratic, 361

Competition, economic, 14, 164, 231–32; of British colonies, 332, 334

Compromise, 85, 86, 90, 116, 119, 128, 129, 204, 232, 352

Conaghan, Catherine, 265

Confessional parties, 65, 66, 67, 79, 235, 352, 353, 354, 356
Confidants, and trust, 111, 114
Confucianism, 186, 187, 195
Congo, 8, 178
Congress, U.S., 39
Congress party (India), 73, 175
Conquistadors, 290, 319–20
Consciousness, democratic culture and, 199–200
Conservatives, 158, 354–55; in Chile, 257, 376, 378; in Colombia, 259; in Ecuador, 263, 264, 265; in Latin America, 310, 361, 362; in Mexico, 266
Consociationalism, 63; in Colombia, 259
Constituency voting, 47
Constitutional legitimacy, 218–19
Constitutions: Latin American, 299, 300, 349, 350; U.S., 215, 218, 300
Consulados, 334
Consumption, levels of, and democracy, 150
Contestation, political, 154, 155, 182, 352
Continental Divide (Lipset), 37
Convergence toward democracy, 142, 187
Cooperative Commonwealth Federation (CCF) (Canada), 51, 92
COPEI (Comité de Organización Política Electoral Independiente) (Venezuela), 277, 278, 364, 396, 426n.39
Coppedge, Michael, 30, 31, 43, 80, 399
Corporations, concentration of power in, 161
Corporatism, 245, 283; in Latin America, 250, 350, 364, 399, 401, 404
Corruption, 97, 98
Cortes, Spanish, 296, 297, 411
Costa Rica, 36, 248, 261–63, 302–3, 412; capitalism in, 336, 337; civil society in, 402–403; economic development in, 315; family farm index, 325; income inequality in, 343; labor force in agriculture, 326; land distribution in, 328; landholding pattern of, 324, 327, 374; participation in organizations, 414; political parties of, 402, 412; poverty in, 345, 346; urbanization of, 388
Council of the Indies, Spanish, 289, 290
Creoles (*criollos*), Latin American, 291, 356
Culture, 12–13, 35, 149, 151, 170, 171, 183, 184–88, 198–204, 207–208, 232–33, 408–409, 411; gradualism and, 172; in Latin America, and democratization of,

15, 348, 350, 351, 409–14; Latin America and North America compared, 305–11, 409–10, 414; and political parties, 359, 360, 368; and rational choice, 204–207; stability and change, 194–98
Czechoslovakia, 73
Czech Republic, 10

Dahl, Robert, 20–21, 25, 32, 34, 154, 174, 182, 352, 354
Darwinism, 188
Decentralization, 61, 62, 63; in British political culture, 244, 245, 410; of Catholic Church, 193; Latin American problems with, 300–301; of North American settlement, 320
Decolonization, 173–79, 219; ethnic conflict and, 220–21
De Figueiredo, Rui J. P., Jr., 206
Democracy: capitalism and, 152–64; civil society and, 94–95, 124–30; and class differences, 12; consequences of, 227–30; correlates of, 35–37, 230; definitions of, 19–24, 31–32; in Europe, 126–27; and factionalism, 61, 62; justifications for, 32–35; in labor unions, 52, 59–60; levels of, 145; longevity of, 146; and mass society, 121; measurements of, 31; moral value of, 24–27; multivariate analysis of, 11, 36, 230–31; and nongovernmental organizations, 127–28; operational definition of, 27–31; opposition in, 54–55; as political concept, 10–11; political culture of, 195; political parties and, 54–55, 64–82, 91; religion and, 390; rise of, and cleavage formation, 76, 78, 79; social capital and, 99; social conditions and, 50–51; status in, 58–59, 61–62; trust and, 102–103, 105, 106, 107, 115, 116, 118; variables associated with, 143–46; violence and, 34–35. *See also specific correlates and variables associated with, such as* Culture; Economic development; *and* Education
Democracy in America (Tocqueville), 93, 121
Democratic party (U.S.), 64, 367
"Democratic stratum," 160, 162
Democratization, 3–5, 10, 81, 92, 237, 238; and civil society, 383; culture as obstacle to, 207; in Europe, 126–27; gradualism and, 172–83; of Latin America, 245–47, 412

Democrats 66 (Dutch political party), 66
Denmark, 180, 338, 340
Dependency, of freed peasants, 318
Dependency theory, 141
Developing countries, 183; capitalism in, 152; economic growth in, 179; and non-governmental organizations, 127–28, 141
Development, 228–29. *See also* Economic development; Political development
Diamond, Larry, 165, 167, 176, 177, 210, 405, 413
Díaz, Porfirio, 266, 302
Dictatorships, 35; in Argentina, 249; in Chile, 257; and economic growth, 227; in Paraguay, 269, 270; and secondary organizations, 55; in Uruguay, 274; in Venezuela, 276
Discrimination, trust and, 107, 112–13
DiTella, Torcuato, 377
Dix, Robert H., 364, 369, 370
Domestic factors, and democracy, 231
Dominant party systems, 28
Dutch colonies, 174

East Central Europe, party systems in, 70, 71
East Germany, 73
Economic development, 11, 12, 23–24, 35, 36, 139–59, 159–66, 169, 181, 227–33; of British and Spanish colonies, 244, 245; cultural values and, 308–10; education and, 166–68; in Latin America, 246, 308–309, 312–27; legitimacy and, 171, 221; level and timing of, 182; and political parties, 77, 360; and taxation, 33; and trust, 108, 115; in United States, 312, 313, 315. *See also* Capitalism; Land distribution and management; Income; Market systems; Poverty
Ecuador, 8, 173, 222, 263–65, 313; capitalism in, 336, 337; civil society in, 405; democratic and authoritarian rule in, 279; economic development in, 315; family farm index, 325; income inequality in, 343; indigenous people of, 288, 305, 405; labor force in agriculture, 326; land distribution in, 327, 328, 331; participation in organizations, 414; political parties of, 362; poverty in, 345; urbanization of, 388
Education, 108, 143, 150, 156, 165, 166–68, 308

Edwards, Bob, 128
Egalitarianism, 36, 294, 295, 307, 309
Eisenstadt, Shmuel, 186–87
Elazar, Daniel J., 39
Elections: competitiveness of, 20, 21, 22, 27–30, 32; inclusiveness of, 20, 21, 22; violence and, 34
Electoral systems, 38, 39, 234; and political parties, 47
Elite classes, 201–205, 233; in Argentina, 249; and authoritarianism, 141; in Bolivia, 252; and Catholicism, 190–93; in Ecuador, 265; education of, in Latin America, 308; in Latin America, 361, 362, 363; legitimacy and, 215–16, 219; and mass interactions, 117; and mass society, 121–23; political contestation in, 154; and political parties, 354–55, 357, 358, 365, 366; and trust, 115
Encomienda system, 282, 315–16, 317
Engels, Friedrich, 160
England. *See* Great Britain; United Kingdom
Enlightenment, 310
Entrepreneurial class, 371, 373, 375, 399
Equilibrium culture, Przeworski's notion of, 205–206
Ertman, Thomas, 126–27
Ethnicities: in British colonies, 176–78; legitimacy and, 219–21; and political parties, 66, 353, 356, 363. *See also* Indigenous population
Europe, 150–57, 237; bourgeoisie in, 372; capitalism in, 338, 339, 340; civil society in, 126; landholding in, 322; legitimacy of democracy in, 210–211; parliamentary systems in, 44; party systems in, 75, 76, 77, 81, 355, 357, 369
Executive systems, 41–49. *See also* Parliamentary systems; Presidential systems
Export economy, growth of, 339

Factionalism, 61, 62; political parties and, 69
Falkland Islands War, 251
Families, size of, 205
Farnen, Russell, 167
Fascism, 155, 216; in Paraguay, 269; of *peronistas*, 364
Febres Cordero, Léon, 264

Feder, Ernest, 330
Federalism, 39, 55–58, 60, 61, 62, 234, 347, 362
Federalist, The (Madison), 69
Fernandez, Julio, 318
Feudal society, 155, 156, 320, 368–69, 370
Figueres, José, 262
Filali–Ansary, Abdou, 187
Fiorina, Morris, 391, 392
Fitzgibbon, Russell, 318
Foley, Michael, 128
Former Soviet Union (FSU), 173, 237
Forward–linked production, 371, 372
Fox, Vicente, 9, 267, 278
France, 46, 155, 217, 222, 422n.7; capitalism in, 338, 340; economic development in, 315; family farm index, 325; income inequality in, 343; land distribution in, 328; poverty in, 345; working class in, 342
Freedom House, 3, 143, 166, 173
Free markets, 139, 161, 162
Free press, 21
Free speech, 20, 21, 22
Free trade, 302
Freezing hypothesis, of Lipset and Rokkan, 77
Frei Montalva, Eduardo, 397
French colonies, 174, 178
French Revolution, 188, 293
Friedenberg, Daniel, 288
Friedman, Milton, 153
Frontiersmen, North American, 320
Front National (France), 80
Fujimori, Alberto, 7, 9, 272, 273, 400
Fukuyama, Francis, 195, 409

García, Alan, 272
Garretón, Manuel Antonio, 397, 398
Gastil freedom index, 31, 143
Georgia, 173
Germany, 106, 117, 155, 156, 209, 217, 222, 382, 394, 424n.4; anti-system parties in, 46; Great Depression in, 206; Marxist movement in, 179; mass society in, 124, 125; voluntary associations in, 126–27
Ghana (Gold Coast), 177
Ghannouchi, Rachid al-, 196
Gibson, James, 118, 202
Gil, Frederico, 363, 364
Gomez, Juan Vicente, 276

Góngora, Mario, 290, 316, 317
"Good society, the," 24–25
Goulart, Joao, 255
Government: and nongovernmental organizations, 127–28; and political culture, 200; trust and, 105, 109–15
Government of India Act of 1935, 175
Gradualism, 170–83, 204
Gramsci, Antonio, 24, 419n.9, 445n.20
Great Britain, 155–56, 180, 200; civil society in, 384; colonization and colonial legacy of, 173–78, 220–21, 242–45, 286–89, 292–97, 301, 321, 409–10; economic regulation of colonies by, 332, 333; and indigenous people, 287; industrialization of, 243; landed class in, 375, 376; political history of, 284–86
Great Depression, 206; in Argentina, 250
Greece, 210
Greene, Jack, 294, 295
Green party (U.S.), 67, 427n.41
Gridlock, in legislative enactment, 41–45
Gross domestic product (GDP) per capita, 139, 140, 143, 145, 149, 150, 312–15
Gross national product (GNP) per capaita, 108
Guevara, Lasso, 331
Guinea-Bissau, 178
Gurr, Ted, 22, 25, 31, 145, 280

Hacienda system, 317–18
Hagopian, Frances, 399, 406
Hagtvet, Brent, 125
Haiti, 236
Hamdi, Mohamed Elhachmi, 186
Happiness, 113
Hardin, Russell, 101
Hatch, Nathan, 390
Havel, Vaclav, 10
Haya de la Torre, Victor Raúl, 271
Hayek, Friedrich, 153
Heuristics, 205; and social capital, 100, 101, 115–16
Hidalgo rebellion, Mexico, 298
Hinduism, 186
Hirschman, Albert O., 215, 359, 370–73, 375
Hispanic Americans, 112, 114–15
Historical sequencing, 182–83
History of the Russian Revolution (Trotsky), 179
Holm, John, 216

Homestead Act of 1862, 321
Homogeneity, and democratic political systems, 53–54
Hong Kong, 196
House of Representatives, U.S., length of service in, 59
Huber, Evelyne. *See* Stephens, Evelyne Huber
Human capital, 93, 94, 100, 101, 236; and associational activity, 117; in colonies, 292; diffusion of wealth and, 152; voluntary associations and, 121
Human Development Index (HDI), 344, 345
Hungary, 72, 167
Huntington, Samuel, 4–5, 10, 148, 172, 188, 227, 394, 395

Ibarra, José Maria Velasco, 264, 265
Ideology, in political parties, 53
Immigration, 25; to Argentina, 249; to Costa Rica, 263; and Latin American culture, 308
Import substitution industrialization (ISI), 141, 142, 335, 339, 370–73, 457n.56; in Uruguay, 274, 401
Income: education and, 166–68; inequalities in distribution of, 59, 139, 159–66, 341–43, 412; Latin America and United States compared, 312, 313, 314; levels of, 140, 145, 146, 148, 149; trust and, 108
India, 36, 73, 156, 173, 174–75, 186–87, 311
Indigenous population: of Bolivia, 252, 305, 404; civil society and, 382; of Ecuador, 263–64, 265, 305, 405; under *encomienda* system, 316; under hacienda system, 317–18; of Latin America, 282, 287, 288, 305, 356, 363, 406, 413; of Mexico, 268; of North America, 287–88; of Peru, 271, 305
Individualism, 154, 189, 245, 307, 389; in England, 284
Indonesia, 184, 236
Industrialization, 141, 142, 156, 179–83, 243; of Argentina, 249; of Brazil, 255, 256; of Chile, 257; of Costa Rica, 263; cultural values and, 309; in Latin America, 334–35, 339, 340, 349, 369–72; and political parties, 369
Industrial Revolution, 76
Infant mortality, 229
Information, 56, 124; access to, 84, 86, 87; and elite-nonelite interaction, 122–24; political parties and, 64–65

Inglehart, Ronald, 106, 107, 108
Inkeles, Alex, 166–67
Instability. *See* Stability
Institutions, 21, 26, 27, 35, 38, 39, 40, 58, 130–31; changes in, and implementation of democracy, 194–95; faction-inducing, 62; importance of, 74, 75; Latin American, 246, 347–51; and trust, 103–106, 109, 111. *See also* Political parties
Integration, and intracommunity ties, 97, 98
Intellectuals, 364
Interest groups, 67, 236
International factors, and democratization, 13–14, 231
International Helsinki Federation for Human Rights, 237
International Typographical Union (ITU), 52–59, 60, 124, 425n.23
Internet, 80, 84, 86
Iran, 7, 9
Ireland, 173
Islam, 67, 148, 149, 184–88, 195–96, 204, 232, 233, 237, 444n.7
Israel, 43, 68
Italy, 43, 49, 73, 155, 156, 222; voluntary associations in, 127
Ivory Coast (Côte d'Ivoire), 7, 9, 173, 214

Jamaica, 175–76
Japan, 27, 29, 97, 156, 195, 217, 310, 315, 328, 343, 345
Jefferson, Thomas, 159
Juárez, Benito, 266
Junn, Jane, 167
Juntas, Spanish colonial, 296, 411

Kalberg, Stephen, 389
Karl, Terry Lynn, 78
Katz, Richard, 82
Kaufman, Robert, 364, 399, 400, 401
Kennedy, John F., 213
Kentucky, landholding in, 323
Kenya, 220
Kenyatta, Jomo, 220
Kircheimer, Otto, 366–67
Kirgiz Republic, 173
Kitschelt, Herbert, 70–71
Kline, Harvey F., 302, 317
Korea, 90, 196
Kornhauser, William, 93, 116, 120–24, 127, 235

Kostunica, Vojislav, 7, 9
Kreppel, Amie, 49
Kyrgystan, 8

Labor movements, 157, 180, 383; in agriculture, 326; in Argentina, 250, 404; and authoritarianism, 141–42; in Brazil, 250; and capitalism, 164; in Colombia, 259; Communists in, 59–60; in Costa Rica, 261, 262; International Typographical Union, 52–59; in Latin America, 350, 362, 364, 365, 366, 368; of Latin American Indians, 316, 317, 318; and political parties, 367, 369–70; United Automobile Workers, 59–62
Lagos, Ricardo, 6, 259
Laissez–faire, 307
Land distribution and management: in Bolivia, 252, 253; in Latin America, 314–31, 341, 374; in North America, 309, 314, 315, 319–24, 326–29
Landes, David, 149
Landholding classes: in Argentina, 249, 250, 403; in Brazil, 384; in Chile, 375, 376, 377; in Costa Rica, 261; in Latin America, 374
Lasso Guevara, Ricardo, 281, 282, 285
Latifundismo system, 318–19, 327
Latin America, 15, 37, 176, 179, 184, 232, 236, 247; authoritarianism in, 156, 279; capitalism in, 335–40; civil society in, 379–407; class-based cleavages in, 54; colonization and colonial legacy in, 244–45, 281, 286–93, 295–99, 348, 361; constitutions of, 299; cultural values and development in, 305–11, 409–15; democratization of, 246, 279, 280, 341; economic development in, 246, 308–309, 312–26; education in, 308; family farm index, 324, 325; income inequality in, 341–43; independence and state consolidation in, 293; industrialization of, 181, 334–35; institutions of, 347–51; labor force in agriculture, 326; land distribution and management in, 314–31, 341; market systems of, 329–34; military's role in, 350; North American development compared with, 241–43; participation in organizations in, 414; political parties in, 347, 351–79, 392–407, 412, 413; postindependence problems of, 299–305; poverty

in, 344, 345, 346; presidential systems in, 40, 42, 44, 45, 234; private ownership in, 161; religious changes in, 191–94, 232; representation in, 297; right–wing movements in, 6; stability and legitimacy in, 217–18, 222, 278–80, 296; urbanization of, 384–89; violence in, 348, 351, 352; voter alignment in, 71; wars of independence in, 300–305; working classes in, 339, 342. *See also* Indigenous population; *and specific countries*
Law, respect for, 202–4, 198, 200; and legitimacy, 218
Leadership, 1, 58–59, 94–95, 358–61, 374–75
Lee Kuan Yew, 184, 196, 207
Left-wing movements, 6, 401; in Chile, 378, 397; in Colombia, 405; industrialization and growth of, 179–80; in post-Communist states, 72; in Uruguay, 401, 402
Legislatures: and executive systems, 41, 42, 43; fixed terms of, 45; and multiparty coalitions, 48–49; and plurality systems, 44–45; and proportional representation, 44
Legitimacy, 54–55, 171, 209–11, 234; in Brazil, 303; ethnicity and, 219–21; Latin American problems with, 246, 295–99, 305; and prisoners' dilemma, 211–14, 224–26; sources and variants of, 215–19, 221–24
Le Pen, Jean Marie, 80
Less developed countries. *See* Developing countries
Levi, Margaret, 100, 105
Levine, David, 193
Liberal capitalism, 161–62
Liberalism, 153, 154, 155, 158, 159, 187, 188, 189, 245; in Chile, 257; in Colombia, 259; in Costa Rica, 262; and development, 228; in Ecuador, 263, 264, 265; in India, 311; in Latin America, 310, 311, 361, 362; in Mexico, 266; in Paraguay, 269, 270; in Spain, 311; in United States, 355; in Venezuela, 276
Liberation theology, 192, 193, 194, 232, 391
Libertarianism, 70, 71, 72
Liberties, democracy and, 21, 32, 157, 307
Life expectancy, democracy and, 143
Lijphart, Arend, 41, 63
Limongi, Fernando, 74, 146, 149

Linkage, extracommunity, 97, 98, 99
Linz, Juan, 26, 41, 42, 45, 46, 84, 156, 172, 210–11, 213, 215
Lithuania, 74
Londregan, John, 144–45, 148
Lopez, Alfonso, 259
Loyalists, North American, 296
Luebbert, Gregory, 155
Lula da Silva, Luis Inácio, 88, 89

McClintock, Cynthia, 363
MacFarlane, Alan, 284
Machine-dominated civil society, 394, 400–402
Madariaga, Salvador de, 288
Madison, James, 69
Magna Carta, 285
Mahoney, James, 374
Mainwaring, Scott, 75, 256
Mair, Peter, 75, 82
Making Democracy Work (Putnam), 94, 98
Malloy, James, 374
Management-worker cleavage, 76, 362, 369
Manufacturing, colonial, 331, 332
Manzetti, Luigi, 404
Market-sustaining federalism, 334
Market systems, 70–71, 161, 237, 329–43
Marx, Karl, 23, 157, 160
Massachusetts, property holding in, 323
Mass culture, 233; in Catholicism, 190–93
Mass society, 92, 93, 119–25, 201, 203, 216
Mauritius, 176
Maximilian, Emperor of Mexico, 266
Mayhew, David, 43
Mediation, civil society and, 95, 119–30, 236
Meloen, Jos, 167
Mendoza, Carlos, 264
Menem, Carlos, 251
Meritocracy, 294, 307
Mexico, 248, 265–68, 278, 296, 298, 299, 302, 313; capitalism in, 337; civil society in, 380, 381; democratic and authoritarian rule in, 279; economic development in, 315; family farm index, 325; income inequality in, 343; indigenous people of, 287, 288; labor force in agriculture, 326; land distribution in, 327, 328; participation in organizations, 414; political parties of, 6–7, 9, 73, 79, 266–68, 365; urbanization of, 385, 388; working class in, 342

Middlebrook, Kevin, 353, 365
Middle classes, 153–55, 158, 162, 164, 201, 340; in Argentina, 249, 250; in Bolivia, 252; in Costa Rica, 262, 263, 412; in Latin America, 349–50, 351; in North America, 309; and political parties, 364, 365; and populism, 374; in Uruguay, 274, 412
Middle East, 150, 232
Middle-income countries, 142
Military interventionism, 214, 287, 398; in Argentina, 249, 250, 251; in Bolivia, 253; in Brazil, 254, 255, 256; in Costa Rica, 261, 302–303; in Ecuador, 264; in Latin America, 246, 350; in Paraguay, 268, 269, 270; in Peru, 271, 272; in Uruguay, 273–75, 401
Miller, Arthur, 73
Milosevic, Slobodan, 7
Mineral wealth, in Latin America, 244
Minimum income, 162
Minorities, 63, 112–13, 154, 206
Mita system, 316, 317
Moderation, 202, 203, 204
Modernization theory, 90, 140–42, 143, 145, 149, 150, 164, 201
Moi, Daniel arap, 220
Monarchies, 215, 216, 217, 222, 234; English, 285–86; Spanish, 282–83, 298
Montesinos, Vladimiro, 273
Moore, Barrington, 155–56, 157, 160, 338, 375, 376
Moral considerations, in study of democracy, 24, 25
Morelos rebellion, Mexico, 298
Morrow, James D., 33
Morse, Richard M., 291–92, 317, 385
Movimiento Nacional Revolucionario (MNR) (Bolivia), 252, 253, 363
Mozambique, 178
Muller, Edward, 106, 107, 118
Multiparty systems, 28, 29, 48–49, 65–66, 355, 357
Murray, John Courtney, 190

Nationalism: in Latin America, 302; in United States, 295, 305
Nationalization: in Bolivia, 252, 253; in Chile, 258
Navia, Patricio, 229
Nazis, 46, 124–25, 394
Negotiation, social trust and, 116, 119

Neoliberalism, 92; in Costa Rica, 263; in Latin America, 366
Neo-Marxism, 201
Nepotism, 97
Netherlands, 66–67, 155, 315, 328, 342, 345, 369
Neumann, Sigmund, 93
New Democrats (Canada), 92
News media, 83, 87–90
Newspapers, 88, 392
New Zealand, 160, 173
Nie, Norman, 167
Nigeria, 7, 9, 173, 176, 177, 178, 236
Nobility, 155
Nongovernmental organizations (NGOs), 127–28, 405, 406
Nonviolent social conflict, 35
North, Douglass, 242, 285, 292, 300–301, 334
North America: civil society in, 379–82, 391, 392; colonization and colonial legacy in, 173, 242–46, 281, 286–89, 292–97; cultural values and development in, 305–309, 320; family farm index, 324, 325; indigenous populations of, 287, 288; land distribution in, 309, 314, 315, 319–28; market system in, 332, 333, 334; religion in, 389–90
Northern Ireland, 8
Norway, 180
Nyerere, Julius, 220–21

O'Dea, Thomas, 189, 192
O'Donnell, Guillermo, 78, 141–42
Oil-producing countries, 150, 151, 232
Oligarchy, 12, 23; of Chile, 256, 257; of Costa Rica, 261; in Latin America, 302, 372; of Peru, 271
Olson, Mancur, 33, 34
One-party states, 56, 64
Open community, 96
Open-list voting, 47, 423n.15
Opposition, political, 218; and capitalism, 159; and diverse economies, 151, 152; in new democracies, 81–82; trust and, 118
Oppression, 23
Organizations: democracy and, 55, 57, 58; factionalism in, 61. See also Civil society; Political parties; Social movements; Voluntary associations
Oviedo, Lino, 270

Pakistan, 7, 173, 175
Paraguay, 268–70, 313; capitalism in, 336, 337; democratic and authoritarian rule in, 279; economic development in, 315; family farm index, 325; income inequality in, 343; labor force in agriculture, 326; land distribution in, 328; participation in organizations, 414; poverty in, 345; urbanization of, 388
Parliamentary systems, 25–26, 40, 41, 44–48, 234; English, 285; experienced cabinet ministers in, 46–47; instability in, 46; no confidence vote in, 45; and political parties, 47, 66, 355; winner-take-all systems, 44
Parochial orientation, 199, 200, 201, 203, 204
Participants, in democratic culture, 199, 200, 201, 203, 204, 234, 352; in England, 285
Partido Acción Nacional (PAN) (Mexico), 9, 267
Partido Justicialista (PJ) (Argentina), 251, 367
Partido Revolucionario Institucional (Institutional Party of the Revolution; PRI) (Mexico), 7, 73, 266, 267, 268
Pateman, Carole, 201
Paternalism, 307, 318
Patron-client relations, 361, 368, 370, 400; in Bolivia, 252, 253; in Brazil, 255, 384; in Uruguay, 273
Patterson, Orlando, 107, 108, 112
Paz, Octavio, 287, 299
Paz Estenssoro, Victor, 253, 254
Peace, democracy and, 230
Peasantry, 155, 156, 160, 318, 330, 339, 341, 363, 364, 368, 384
Pedro I, Dom (Brazil), 303
Perez, Carlos Andres, 277
Periphery countries. See Developing countries
Perón, Isabel, 251
Perón, Juan, 156, 181, 250–51, 350, 364, 403
Peronist movement (Argentina), 250, 251, 363, 364, 404
Personalism, 307, 361, 382; in Argentina, 404; in Bolivia, 252, 254; in Brazil, 256; in Paraguay, 269; of Perón, 250, 251; in Venezuela, 399

Peru, 7, 9, 270–73, 313; capitalism in, 337; civil society in, 380, 399–400; democratic and authoritarian rule in, 279; economic development in, 315; family farm index, 325; income inequality in, 343; indigenous people of, 287, 305, 363; labor force in agriculture, 326; land distribution in, 328, 331; participation in organizations, 414; political parties of, 363, 365, 378, 382; poverty in, 345; urbanization of, 385, 388; violence in, 272

Peru-Bolivia Confederation, 295

"Pessoptimism," 11, 36, 187, 230

Philippines, 214

Pinochet, Augusto, 6, 257, 258, 396, 397

"Pinochet effect," 227

Pius XI, Pope, 189

PLN (National Liberation Party) (Costa Rica), 402

Pluralism, 44–45, 64, 245, 410; in India, 311

Poland, 61, 72, 73

Police, trust in, 132

Political culture, 202–204

Political development, democracy and, 228

Political Man (Lipset), 124, 140, 165

Political parties, 21, 28, 29, 45, 52–58, 64–82, 182, 347; anti-system parties, 46; and civil society, 64, 80, 91, 125–30, 234–37, 379, 382, 392–407; communication and, 64–65; European, in interwar period, 126–27; incentives for development of, 69–75; in International Typographical Union, 55, 56, 57; Latin American, 347, 351–79, 392–407, 412, 413; and legislature compromise, 48–49; modern, organizing challanges in, 80–82; organization, 75–82, 82–91; organized opposition of, 69; in parliamentary systems, 47; party discipline, 74; platforms of, 67–68; and proportional representation, 47; syncretic function of, 67, 68; in United States, 45, 64, 351, 353, 354, 355, 365, 367, 377, 391, 406–407

Politics of Mass Society (Kornhauser), 120

Polyarchy, 20, 30–31, 32

Poole, Keith, 145, 148

Poor democracies, 146–48

Populism, 92, 156, 307, 374; in Latin America, 356, 360, 365, 366, 377

Portugal, 184, 210, 211, 283, 285, 286, 303

Portuguese colonies, 174, 176, 178, 243, 286, 289, 299, 321, 331, 332; postindependence problems of, 301, 303. *See also* Brazil

Post-Communist states, 71–73, 75, 167, 222

Postmodern cultural studies, 196

Post-World War II era, 172–73, 177, 181, 222

Poujadism, 120

Poverty, 159–66, 229, 344–46; liberation theology and, 193; political parties and, 365; trust and, 108

Power, balance of, and democracy, 164, 165, 166

Praetorianism, 260, 394–95, 397, 398, 399, 401, 403, 404, 405

Preemption, 321

Presidential systems, 25–26, 39–44, 47, 48, 234; fixed terms in, 45–46; and gridlock, 41, 42, 43, 45; in Latin America, 348–49, 356; and political parties, 355; and proportional representation, 44; with strong presidents, 44; with weak presidents, 39, 42, 43, 45, 234; and winner-take-all election systems, 41, 42, 44, 422n.6

Prior democracy, and level of democracy, 143

Prisoners' dilemma, 211–14, 224–26, 448n.6

Private property, 139, 161–62, 330

Private sector, 163, 231

Prohibition party (U.S.), 67

Projection, and social capital, 100, 101, 115–16

Property distribution, 323; and political parties, 69–70

Property rights, United States, 321

Proportional representation (PR), 39, 44–45, 47, 234, 348–49, 355–57

Protestantism, 76, 184, 185, 188, 189, 194, 245, 286, 309, 389–91

Przeworski, Adam, 11, 19, 26, 29, 31, 34, 35, 41, 44, 140, 142, 143, 146, 149, 150, 181, 183, 196, 197, 204–205, 207, 313

Psychology, and social change, 170

Public goods, 33–34

Public opinion, 43; and mass society, 121

Public sector service, income and, 163

Putnam, Robert, 87–88, 93–94, 98, 105, 128

Quality of life, and democracy, 165–66

Quebec, 186

Race, 112–14, 367, 458n.6; in British colonies, 177; in Latin America, 363

Radicalism, 5, 24, 180; in Latin America, 362; of Spanish left, 156
Rama, Martín, 275, 401
Rangel, Carlos, 301–302, 318
Rational choice, 142, 204–207
Rationalism, 189
Rational-legal legitimacy, 215, 218, 219
Reactionary position, 23
Reagan, Ronald, 6
Reciprocity, 96, 97
Redistribution of wealth, 23–24, 161, 162
Refah (Islamic party), 67
Referenda, 25, 26–27
Regionalism: in Latin America, 362
Reinicke, Wolfgang, 30, 31
Religion, 76, 77, 90, 158, 184–96, 198, 232–33, 389–92, 414, 415; and cleavage in Chile, 375, 376. See also Catholicism; Confessional parties; Protestantism
Rent-seeking coalitions, 161
Repartimiento system, 316–17
Representation, 27, 297, 410, 411
Republicanism: in England, 285–86; in Latin America, 391; in North America, 304, 410; in United States, 348
Republican party (U.S.), 64, 367
Revolutionary dissent, 24
Richard, Patricia Bayer, 105, 117
Riggs, Fred, 45
Right-wing movements, 6, 80, 120, 127, 398–99; in Chile, 397–99; in Colombia, 397–99; in Latin America, 310, 401; in post–Communist states, 72; in Uruguay, 401; in Venezuela, 399
Roberts, Kenneth, 365–66, 368
Rochon, Thomas, 117
Rodriguez O., Jaime E., 296
Rokkan, Stein, 69, 70, 76, 77, 79, 81, 88, 180, 353, 357
Roldos Aguilera, Jaime, 264
Roosevelt, Franklin, 367
Rousseau, Jean-Jacques, 391
Rowen, Henry, 148–49, 166
Rueschemeyer, Dietrich, 154, 165, 247, 248, 278, 279, 338, 339, 370
Rummel, R. J., 34, 229
Rural population, political parties and, 363, 364, 368–69
Russia, 8, 24, 34, 71, 74, 118, 160, 173, 179, 227, 237
Rwanda, 178

Salinas de Gortari, Carlos, 268
Sao Paulo prison riots, Brazil, 89
Sarmiento, Domingo F., 306, 392
Sartori, Giovanni, 64, 83, 86, 89
Saskatchewan, agrarian socialism in, 51
Savelle, Max, 288–89, 332
Scandinavia, 180, 245
Schmitter, Philippe C., 78, 384, 392
Schumpeter, Joseph, 19, 120
Scobie, James, 319
Secondary associations. *See* Voluntary associations
Secularism, 90, 186–87, 193, 198, 202, 203, 257, 362, 375
Selectorates, 33–34
Self-determination, benefits of, 33
Self-interest, 53, 206
Seligson, Mitchell, 106, 107, 118, 314
Semifeudal societies, 369
Sen, Amartya, 3, 15, 60, 182, 187, 229
Sendero Luminoso (Shining Path) movement, 272
Senegal, 7, 178, 236
Separation of powers, 350
Serbia, 7, 9–10
Service sector employment: in Latin America, 369
Shaping the Political Arena (Collier and Collier), 362
Sharecropping, 317, 329–30
Shining Path movement, 272
Shipping, 332
Singapore, 184, 196
Single-commodity economies, 151, 152, 232
Single-issue movements, 67–68, 85
Single transferable vote (STV) systems, 47
Siverson, Randolph, 33
Skach, Cindy, 46
Skepticism, associations and, 124, 125
Skocpol, Theda, 14, 157, 158, 391, 392
Slavery, 286, 318
Smith, Adam, 321, 322, 332
Smith, Alastair, 33
Smith, David, 166–67
Snow, Peter, 404
Social alienation, 120
Social capital, 93–102, 105; and civil society, 116–19, 129, 235–36; and trust, 115–16, 131–36; voluntary associations and, 121
Social Capital Community Benchmark Survey, U.S., 108–11, 114, 131, 236, 414, 415

Social change, 170–71
Social cleavages, and political parties, 69–71, 74, 76–79, 81, 235, 352–63, 365–70, 373–78, 412, 413
Social closure, 96, 97; and trust, 115
Social conditions, democracy and, 50–51, 54
Social democratic movements, 245, 339; in Chile, 382; in Costa Rica, 262–63; in Denmark, 180; in Germany, 179, 382, 424n.4; in Sweden, 180; in Venezuela, 382
Socialism, 153, 162, 164, 180, 188, 189, 237, 335, 369; in Chile, 6, 257, 259
Social mobilization, 391
Social movements, 84–85, 406
Sojo, Carlos, 402
Solidarity (Poland), 61, 73
Soltow, Lee, 322, 323
Soto, Hernando de, 321
South Africa, 219, 234, 236
South America, 141, 142, 247. *See also* Latin America
South Korea, 184
Soviet-controlled countries, 174
Soviet Union, 6, 14
Spain, 62–63, 78, 155, 156, 184, 211, 221–22, 234, 281–86, 298, 310–11, 383
Spanish colonies, 174, 176, 242–45, 282, 286, 287, 289–93, 295–99, 409–12; economic development in, 319; economic regulation in, 331–34; land law and tenure in, 321; postindependence problems of, 299–305, 334; urban bias of, 331
Spanish Republic, 156
Squatters, North American, 320–21
Sri Lanka, 8
Stability, 198, 233; and civil society, 130; in industrializing states, 181; in Latin America, 246, 247, 278–80, 303, 378; and legitimacy, 216, 217; trust and, 106, 107, 108; and violence, 348
Standard of living, 143, 144, 150, 228
State-aristocracy alliances, 164
State-owned enterprises (SOEs), 336–40
Statism, 338, 339, 340, 360, 413
Statistical Package for the Social Sciences (SPSS), 131
Status: and democracy, 58–59, 61–62; land as symbol of, 330; Latin American emphasis on, 308, 356, 389

Stehlik-Barry, Kenneth, 167
Stepan, Alfred, 46, 210–11
Stepan-Norris, Judith, 59–61
Stephens, Evelyne Huber, 154, 165, 247, 248, 278, 279, 338, 339, 370
Stephens, John D., 154, 165, 247, 248, 278, 279, 338, 339, 370
Stolle, Dietland, 106, 117
Stone, Carl, 176
Stroessner, Alfredo, 269, 270
Suarez, Adolfo, 310–11
Suárez, Francisco, 282
Subject role, in democratic culture, 199, 201, 203, 204
Subsidiarity, principle of, 189
Suffrage. *See* Voting
Summerhill, William, 242, 292, 334
Sweden, 106, 117, 180, 325, 338, 340, 342, 380, 381
Switzerland, 25, 155
Syncretism, 67, 68, 85, 91, 116

Taiwan, 184, 236
Tajikistan, 8
Taliban, 444n.7
Tanzania, 220–21, 236
Taxation, 33, 296, 332, 449n.2
Technology, 82–84, 86–87, 89–90, 182, 235, 309
Television, 83, 84, 86–89, 429n.82; and trust, 112, 114–15
Templates, and collective action, 98–99
Thailand, 196
Third Wave, The (Huntington), 4, 188
Thomas, Robert, 285
Thomism, 282–83, 360
Tocqueville, Alexis de, 24, 51, 56, 61–62, 93, 94, 95, 120, 198, 235, 306, 347, 378, 387, 392
Toledo, Alejandro, 273
Tolerance, 167, 198, 202, 203, 204
Tordoff, William, 177
Totalitarianism, 55, 120, 121, 167, 189
Touraine, Alain, 228, 229
Trade, 245, 331, 332
Traditional legitimacy, 215, 216, 217
Trotsky, Leon, 179
Trow, Martin, 52–58, 92, 120, 121, 173
Trudeau, Pierre, 185, 190
Trust, 102–16, 118–19, 131–36, 200, 432n.20; and prisoners' dilemma, 212; social capital and, 93, 94, 96–103, 116

Truth and Reconciliation Commission (South Africa), 219
Tsebelis, George, 48, 49
Tupamoros, 275, 401
Turkey, 67
Two-party systems: in Costa Rica, 402; in International Typographical Union, 57–58; and political parties, 355; and presidential government, 49
Tyranny, 12

Uganda, 8, 177
Ukraine, 74, 173
Union Democracy (Lipset, Trow, and Coleman), 52–59, 92, 120, 121, 124
Unions, labor. *See* Labor movement
United Automobile Workers (UAW), 59–62
United Kingdom, 315, 328, 342, 343, 345. *See also* Great Britain
United States, 176, 179; agricultural labor force in, 326; capitalism in, 330, 335–38; civil rights abuses in, 237; civil society in, 117, 126, 382, 384, 392; Civil War, 295; Constitution of, 215, 218, 300; culture and development in, 306; democracy in, 280; economic development in, 312–15; election of 1992, 33; election of 2000, 426n.38, 463n.2; encouragement of democracies by, 6; family farm index, 325; Great Depression in, 206; independence and state consolidation in, 293; inequality in, 342–43, 413; land distribution in, 314, 319, 321, 322, 323, 325–29; Latin America compared with, 241–43; Latin America influenced and dominated by, 247; and Latin American conservatives, 378; legitimacy in, 218, 413; market system in, 329; policy compromises in legislature of, 48–49; political consciousness in, 200; political parties of, 45, 64, 351, 353, 354, 355, 365, 367, 377, 391, 406–407; poverty in, 344–46; presidential system of, 39, 42, 43, 45, 234; private sector opportunities in, 59; protocapitalist phase of, 160; public sector and private sector incomes in, 163; religion in, 189, 198, 389; republicanism in, 348; Revolution, 289, 292–97, 304, 305; urbanization of, 384–89; voluntary associations in, 379–82, 392, 414; working class in, 342

Urban business class, 154
Urbanization, 165, 181; of Chile, 257; and civil society, 384–89; and class consciousness, 368; in Latin America, 331, 340; and political parties, 369
Urbanski, Edmund, 320
Uruguay, 246, 273–75, 313, 412; agricultural labor force in, 326; capitalism in, 337; civil society in, 380, 381, 394, 400, 401, 405; democratic and authoritarian rule in, 279; economic development in, 312–15; family farm index, 325; income inequality in, 343; land distribution in, 328; participation in organizations, 414; political parties of, 351, 352, 354, 356, 377, 412; poverty in, 344, 345; urbanization of, 388; violence in, 275, 351, 401; working class in, 342
Uslaner, Eric, 88, 106, 108, 111, 118
Uzbekistan, 8

Valen, Henry, 180
Valenzuela, Arturo, 257, 397
Valenzuela, J. Samuel, 158, 362, 375, 376
Values, formation and differences, 206, 307–308
Vandor, Augusto, 250
Vanhanen, Tatu, 165, 324, 325, 388
Vargas, Getúlio, 156, 181, 255, 350, 364
Vatican II (Second Vatican Council), 190, 192, 391
Velasco Alvarado, Juan, 272
Véliz, Claudio, 333
Venezuela, 7–8, 43, 78, 80, 82–83, 236, 276–78; agricultural labor force in, 326; capitalism in, 336, 337; civil society in, 380, 381, 382, 394, 395–96, 399, 405; democratic and authoritarian rule in, 279, 280; economic development in, 312–15; family farm index, 325; income inequality in, 343; land distribution in, 328; participation in organizations, 414; political parties of, 352, 353, 363, 364, 365, 396; postindependence problems of, 300; poverty in, 345; urbanization of, 385, 388; working class in, 342
Verba, Sidney, 94, 117, 185, 198–204
Veto, minority, 63
Veto players, Tsebelis's notion of, 48–49
Veugelers, Jack, 79

Viceroyalties, Spanish, 290, 291, 298, 301, 410–11
"Video–Power" (Sartori), 83
Violence, 34–35, 229; in Argentina, 251; in Chile, 397; in Colombia, 30, 259, 260, 351, 401, 405; in Ecuador, 405; in Latin America, 348, 351, 352; in Mexico, 266, 268; in Peru, 272; in Spain's former colonies, 292; in Uruguay, 275, 351, 401
Voluntary associations, 51, 58, 92–95, 98, 99, 120, 121, 123–27, 379–82, 392, 406; European, in interwar period, 126–27; and interpersonal trust, 106, 109, 112; membership diversity in, 116–17; participation in, 414; of Saskatchewan farmers, 51; and social capital, 116–19. *See also* Political parties
Voting, 354, 355; full suffrage, 81; as proxy for violence, 34

Waisman, Carlos, 161
Walesa, Lech, 73
Wars, 229–30, 300–305, 409–10. *See also* American Revolution
Washington, George, 304, 348, 358–59
Wave of democratization, Huntington's notion of, 4–5
Wealth. *See* Economic development
Weber, Max, 117, 149, 194, 195, 215, 242, 389
Weigel, George, 188, 191
Weimar Germany, 124–25, 209, 217, 382, 394
Weiner, Meyer, 173, 174

Weingast, Barry, 206, 242, 292, 334
Welfare state, Costa Rica as, 263, 402, 403
Wentworth, Thomas, 286
Whitaker, Arthur P., 297–98
White Americans, trust and, 113, 114
Whitehead, Lawrence, 404
Wiarda, Howard J., 302, 317
Wieseltier, Leon, 9–10
Winner-take-all electoral systems, 41, 42, 44, 422n.6
Women, 154; primary schooling of, 143
Wood, Gordon, 285–86, 293, 294, 329, 394
Woodward, Ralph, Jr., 333
Woolcock, Michael, 97, 99
Worker-management cleavage, 76, 362, 369
Work ethic, in Latin America, 316, 318, 320
Working classes, 141, 153–58, 164, 179–81, 338–42; in Argentina, 250; in Brazil, 255; in Chile, 257, 377, 392; in Latin America, 349, 350, 351, 362, 369, 373; and political parties, 364, 373
World Trade Organization protests, Seattle, 89
World Values Survey, 223, 379–81
Wright, Robin, 195–96

Xenophobia, 122, 123–24

Yamagishi, Midori, 102
Yamagishi, Toshio, 102

Zapatistas, 268, 288
Zimbabwe, 7, 9, 66, 176, 221
Zweifel, Thomas D., 229